TRANSLATION UNDER STATE CONTROL

Children's Literature and Culture
Jack Zipes, *Series Editor*

The Case of Peter Rabbit
Changing Conditions of Literature for Children
by Margaret Mackey

The Feminine Subject in Children's Literature
by Christine Wilkie-Stibbs

Ideologies of Identity in Adolescent Fiction
by Robyn McCallum

Recycling Red Riding Hood
by Sandra Beckett

The Poetics of Childhood
by Roni Natov

Voices of the Other
Children's Literature and the Postcolonial Context
edited by Roderick McGillis

Narrating Africa
George Henty and the Fiction of Empire
by Mawuena Kossi Logan

Reimagining Shakespeare for Children and Young Adults
edited by Naomi J. Miller

Representing the Holocaust in Youth Literature
by Lydia Kokkola

Translating for Children
by Riitta Oittinen

Beatrix Potter
Writing in Code
by M. Daphne Kutzer

Children's Films
History, Ideology, Pedagogy, Theory
by Ian Wojcik-Andrews

Utopian and Dystopian Writing for Children and Young Adults
edited by Carrie Hintz and Elaine Ostry

Transcending Boundaries
Writing for a Dual Audience of Children and Adults
edited by Sandra L. Beckett

The Making of the Modern Child
Children's Literature and Childhood in the Late Eighteenth Century
by Andrew O'Malley

How Picturebooks Work
by Maria Nikolajeva and Carole Scott

Brown Gold
Milestones of African American Children's Picture Books, 1845-2002
by Michelle H. Martin

Russell Hoban/Forty Years
Essays on His Writing for Children
by Alida Allison

Apartheid and Racism in South African Children's Literature
by Donnarae MacCann and Amadu Maddy

Empire's Children
Empire and Imperialism in Classic British Children's Books
by M. Daphne Kutzer

Constructing the Canon of Children's Literature
Beyond Library Walls and Ivory Towers
by Anne Lundin

Youth of Darkest England
Working Class Children at the Heart of Victorian Empire
by Troy Boone

Ursula K. Leguin Beyond Genre
Literature for Children and Adults
by Mike Cadden

Twice-Told Children's Tales
edited by Betty Greenway

Diana Wynne Jones
The Fantastic Tradition and Children's Literature
by Farah Mendlesohn

Childhood and Children's Books in Early Modern Europe, 1550-1800
edited by Andrea Immel and Michael Witmore

Voracious Children
Who Eats Whom in Children's Literature
by Carolyn Daniel

National Character in South African Children's Literature
by Elwyn Jenkins

Myth, Symbol, and Meaning in Mary Poppins
The Governess as Provocateur
by Georgia Grilli

A Critical History of French Children's Literature, Vol. 1 & 2
by Penny Brown

Once Upon a Time in a Different World
Issues and Ideas in African American Children's Literature
By Neal A. Lester

The Gothic in Children's Literature
Haunting the Borders
Edited by Anna Jackson, Karen Coats, and Roderick McGillis

Reading Victorian Schoolrooms
Childhood and Education in Nineteenth-Century Fiction
by Elizabeth Gargano

Soon Come Home to This Island
West Indians in British Children's Literature
by Karen Sands-O'Connor

Boys in Children's Literature and Popular Culture
Masculinity, Abjection, and the Fictional Child
by Annette Wannamaker

Into the Closet
Cross-dressing and the Gendered Body in Children's Literature
by Victoria Flanagan

Russian Children's Literature and Culture
edited by Marina Balina and Larissa Rudova

The Outside Child In and Out of the Book
Christine Wilkie-Stibbs

Representing Africa in Children's Literature
Old and New Ways of Seeing
by Vivian Yenika-Agbaw

The Fantasy of Family
Nineteenth-Century Children's Literature and the Myth of the Domestic Ideal
by Liz Thiel

From Nursery Rhymes to Nationhood
Children's Literature and the Construction of Canadian Identity
By Elizabeth A. Galway

The Family in English Children's Literature
Ann Alston

Enterprising Youth
Social Values and Acculturation in Nineteenth-Century American Children's Literature
Monika Elbert

Constructing Adolescence in Fantastic Realism
Alison Waller

Crossover Fiction
Global and Historical Perspectives
Sandra L. Beckett

The Crossover Novel
Contemporary Children's Fiction and Its Adult Readership
Rachel Falconer

Shakespeare in Children's Literature
Gender and Cultural Capital
Erica Hateley

Critical Approaches to Food in Children's Literature
Edited by Kara K. Keeling and Scott T. Pollard

Neo-Imperialism in Children's Literature About Africa
A Study of Contemporary Fiction
by Yulisa Amadu Maddy and Donnarae MacCann

Death, Gender and Sexuality in Contemporary Adolescent Literature
Kathryn James

Fundamental Concepts of Children's Literature Research
Literary and Sociological Approaches
Hans-Heino Ewers

Translation under State Control
Books for Young People in the German Democratic Republic
Gaby Thomson-Wohlgemuth

TRANSLATION UNDER STATE CONTROL

Books for Young People in the German Democratic Republic

GABY THOMSON-WOHLGEMUTH

NEW YORK AND LONDON

First published 2009
by Routledge
711 Third Ave, New York, NY 10017

Simultaneously published in the UK
by Routledge
2 Park Square, Milton Park, Abingdon, Oxfordshire OX14 4RN

First issued in paperback 2014

Routledge is an imprint of the Taylor & Francis Group, an informa business

Typeset in by Minion by IBT Global.

Library of Congress Cataloging-in-Publication Data

Thomson-Wohlgemuth, Gaby.
Translation under state control : books for young people in the German Democratic Republic / by Gaby Thomson-Wohlgemuth.
p. cm. — (Children's literature and culture ; 63)
Includes bibliographical references and index.
1. Children's literature—Publishing—Germany (East) 2. Children's literature, English—Translations into German—History and criticism. 3. Translating and interpreting—Germany (East) 4. Publishers and publishing—Political aspects—Germany (East) 5. Literature and state—Germany (East) 6. Children—Books and reading—Germany (East) 7. Youth—Books and reading—Germany (East) 8. Paratext. 9. Socialism and youth—Germany, East. 10. Germany (East)—Cultural policy. I. Title.
Z321.4.T48 2009
070.509431—dc22
2008051107

ISBN 13: 978-0-415-99580-1 (hbk)
ISBN 13: 978-1-138-82839-1 (pbk)

Contents

Tables and Figures

Tables

Figures

Abbreviations

BfU	Büro für Urheberrechte (copyright office)
CDU	Christlich-Demokratische Union Deutschlands (Christian Democratic Union of Germany)
CSCE	Conference on Security and Co-operation in Europe
DBG	Deutsche Buch-Export und Import GmbH Leipzig (German book export and import Ltd Leipzig)
FDJ	Freie Deutsche Jugend (Free German Youth)
FRG	Federal Republic of Germany
GDR	German Democratic Republic
HV	Hauptverwaltung Verlage und Buchhandel (Central Office for Publishing and Book trade)
LDP	Liberal-Demokratische Partei Deutschlands (Liberal Democratic Party of Germany)
LKG	Leipziger Kommissions- und Großbuchhandel (Leipzig enterprise which distributed the printed books to the individual traders)
NÖS	Neues Ökonomisches System (New Economic System)
ÖSS	Ökonomisches System des Sozialismus (Economic System of Socialism)
SAG	Sowjetische Aktiengesellschaft (Soviet Joint Stock Company)
SED	Sozialistische Einheitspartei Deutschlands (Socialist Unity Party of Germany)

VEB	Volkseigener Betrieb (nationally owned factory)
VOB	Vereinigung organisationseigener Betriebe (merger of enterprise owned by a mass organisation)
Zentrag	Zentrale Druckerei-, Einkaufs- und Revisionsgesellschaft (i.e. the umbrella of all printing enterprises)
ZK	Zentralkomitee (Central committee)

Series Editor's Foreword

Dedicated to furthering original research in children's literature and culture, the Children's Literature and Culture series includes monographs on individual authors and illustrators, historical examinations of different periods, literary analyses of genres, and comparative studies on literature and the mass media. The series is international in scope and is intended to encourage innovative research in children's literature with a focus on interdisciplinary methodology.

Children's literature and culture are understood in the broadest sense of the term *children* to encompass the period of childhood up through adolescence. Owing to the fact that the notion of childhood has changed so much since the origination of children's literature, this Routledge series is particularly concerned with transformations in children's culture and how they have affected the representation and socialization of children. While the emphasis of the series is on children's literature, all types of studies that deal with children's radio, film, television, and art are included in an endeavor to grasp the aesthetics and values of children's culture. Not only have there been momentous changes in children's culture in the last fifty years, but there have been radical shifts in the scholarship that deals with these changes. In this regard, the goal of the Children's Literature and Culture series is to enhance research in this field and, at the same time, point to new directions that bring together the best scholarly work throughout the world.

Jack Zipes

Acknowledgments

This book is the revised version of my PhD thesis which I submitted at the University of Surrey, UK, in spring 2007 and which was supervised by Prof. Gunilla Anderman and Dr Gillian Lathey. I warmly thank them both for their guidance, their interest in my work and their undiminished belief in me.

This study would not have come to life without the invaluable help and experience and many fruitful discussions of the following: Hans Bentzien, Esmy Berlt, Reinhild Böhnke, Werner Creutziger, Elmar Faber, Edda Fensch, Hannelore Fischer, Silke Fokken, Patrick Graetz, Hans Joachim Grimm, Andreas Henselmann, Reinhard Hillich, Klaus Höpcke, Karl-Heinz Jähn, Karen Jesserer, Siggi Jörn, Irene Kalau, Ingeborg Kolinko, Heinz Kuhnert, Hannelore Lange, Siegfried Lokatis, Sabine Mähne, Steffen Peltsch, Heinz Püschel, Lieselotte Remané, Helgard Rost, Claudia Rouvel, Sandra Schaur, Martina Seifert, Karlheinz Selle, Walter Tölg and Ursula Winnington.

The staff at Bundesarchiv Berlin, who tirelessly delivered endless streams of files to my desk; the staff of Kinderbuchabteilung der Staatsbibliothek Berlin (Carola Pohlmann and her team) and of Deutsche Bücherei Leipzig, who all supported me in every way possible, who speedily provided me with stacks of children's books and with encouraging smiles, while I was working my way through them.

I am especially grateful to the Conference of University Teachers of German in Great Britain and Ireland and to the Horst Kliemann Stiftung für Geschichte des Buchwesens for their generous financial support which eased the economic burden of living in Berlin for my research stays of more than six months.

Many thanks go to Steve Wheeler for proofreading and commenting on first drafts of my chapters.

Above all, however, I would like to wholeheartedly thank my husband for all the discussions of thoughts and ideas, for his unbroken support of my academic work, for practical assistance with all matters linked to the use of the computer and his unlimited willingness to step over piles of photocopies and books scattered around on the living-room and dining-room floor. This book is specially dedicated to Ian.

Introduction

Attitudes to literature for young people tend to be somewhat ambivalent. On the one hand, it is recognised that children's books[1] form part of a child's education and, therefore, it is important what children read; on the other hand, there is a tendency to regard books for young readers as a 'lower' form of literature with a lesser value than literature for adults. One of the scholars defining children's literature as of lower status in a social system is Zohar Shavit. Drawing on the concept of Polysystems, Shavit locates children's literature on the periphery of the literary system, attributing it an inferior position in the literature of a society (see e.g. 1986:33–59). Similarly, Shavit claims that "the norms governing adult literature never simultaneously govern children's literature" and that "it has become impossible to attribute 'high literary quality' to books for children" (1994:6). As much as this framework may fit contemporary Western societies, it falls short in describing many of the former Eastern Bloc societies. This book explores the status of children's literature in one of these states, the German Democratic Republic (GDR), and analyses the reasons behind and the consequences of the different attitude to children's literature in that society. As will be elaborated in the following chapters, children's literature was ascribed an especially high value in the GDR. In fact, it is demonstrated in this study that, in the GDR, the systems of literature for adults and for children experienced the same development and that, indeed in some instances, children's literature even functioned as the trendsetter, leading the way for mainstream literature. This, however, is not an isolated phenomenon; the same was true in other Eastern Bloc states. For instance, Mazi-Leskovar (2003:250–265; 2006:155–169), Dimitru (2006:73–82) and Tarrend (2005:66–96) report similar stances with regard to the function and status of children's literature in their countries during the time of the Cold War, i.e. ex-Yugoslavia, Bulgaria and Estonia.

It appears that socialist countries, on the whole, not only acknowledged the importance of what children read, but took control of their national children's literature and attempted to lift it up to the level of adult literature. There are several reasons for this, not least of which is the recognition that the attitudes to society and the overall worldview of future citizens are formed by their education and what they read. In other words, there is a societal aspect to the handling of children's literature, and socialist countries acknowledged the position of children's books in the social context.

In a wider sense, it can be argued that every society applies its own rules when selecting literature for publication, and this holds true as much for children's literature as for adult literature. In contemporary societies, it is accepted that it is publishers who decide which books to publish, in order to run their businesses profitably. However, a case can be made that this is perhaps not the best way of deciding what children read and, in fact, in the GDR, it was not left to the discretion of the publishers. The decision over which books are published or not represents the primary filter in the literary development of a society. Patrons, that is, people equipped with ideological, economic and/or political powers (see e.g. Lefevere 1982a, 1985b or 1992), provide the primary influence behind the selection process and, consequently, will most likely be directly associated with the publishing industry itself. How these groups, i.e. patron groups, are formed and under what constraints they operate is determined by the societies to which they belong. Equally, the criterion by which they select the literature to be published will be determined by their individual ideologies or the ideologies prevailing in their societies. It is reasonable to assume that the selection of literature, particularly of foreign literature, brings into focus the attitudes of patrons. As a consequence, investigating how translated literature is dealt with by a society reveals much about the attitudes and ideology of the society.

The literature of the GDR is the literature of a monolithic society with only one ideological truth. In order to entirely understand the phenomenon of 'East German literature', one has to look back at the country's historical and social roots. The GDR was born as a reaction to both the capitalist/imperialist and the national socialist societal order when, after the Second World War, the East German government, under the protection of the USSR, seized the opportunity to break away from the West and build 'a new kind of nation'. This was to be a nation based on the Marxist-Leninist premise which propagated a Historical[2] Societal Evolution for all mankind. This premise entailed, in the final stages, a development leading from the capitalist/imperialist order to the socialist and, ultimately, communist state. From the moment that the regime had come to the decision to transform the country and its populace, every aspect of society was made to serve this goal. Political, economic and socio-cultural development became interdependent and all spheres were interlocked and made to merge. Literary policy formed a unity with political, economic and social policy, a situation that Wendt expressed as "objectively, all authors and publishers have to submit to the interests of the East German society"[3] (1961:169).

This brought a new dimension to the notion of literature in the GDR. Literature had become part of a social system encompassing not only authors, publishers and readers, but also the Party, its ideology and its state machinery. Books were taken into the service of the agenda to build the new society, regardless of whether they were books for adults, adolescents or children. Coupled with a uniform, ideologically convergent and state-controlled education system, books for young readers were reshaped into tools for the all-round formation of a new kind of socialist human being. Literature for children and young adults became a vehicle of ideological education with the purpose of "explaining to the young the social conditions and teaching them correct [ideological] interpretations" (Krupskaja, as quoted in Altner 1988:38, 39). Based on the motto "He, who has the youth, has the future" (Liebknecht 1958:445), utmost significance was placed on conveying the 'correct' truths to the next generation.

This authoritarian and highly didactic approach by the regime in conjunction with the already immanent educational character of children's books meant that, in the GDR, a children's literature emerged which was a focal point for social progress. Knowing that children are, by nature, impressionable, literary authorities invested great care in the contents of any text published for children. "Children's literature is no peripheral field within the literary society [of East Germany] which should . . . be left to any one person . . . The books that are given to children determine in which direction their taste, their political reasoning and their growth into human beings and humanist individuals develops" (Becher 1956, as quoted in Altner 1988:154). Becher's expression of the power of literature to affect a society is fundamental to the understanding of its importance to the GDR regime. It was an integral part of the state's control of information and, hence, the knowledge and learning available to the population.

As books were given the mission to educate the general populace rather than purely entertain, children's books had to educate the younger generation. It was the seriousness of this intention that put immense pressure on literary matters. As it had the same, if not greater, importance as a didactic tool as adult literature, children's literature was placed on a par with general literature. However, it was without a doubt not only their function as an educational tool, similar to adults' books, which helped embed children's books in mainstream literature. According to one of the basic principles of Marxism-Leninism, children are involved in constructing and maintaining society as much as the older generation. They are viewed as "partners of the adults in societal development, as allies in the class struggle, as active builders of socialism and as potential representatives of the future" (Altner 1972:8). Additionally, a socialist society is a classless one, from which it follows that there is only one single culture (as opposed to the bourgeois system of cultures and subcultures), thus a notion that leads to child and adult forming a unit (as opposed to the bourgeois generation conflict) (Meier 1987:577). Consequently, children are regarded by socialism as of equal value and deserving of equal rights to adults.

As a result, the intention was that young people were to be taken seriously and become very much a part of socialist everyday life. In terms of their literature this meant conveying to them a set of criteria similar to that of adults. For similar reasons, bourgeois concepts were banned from children's books because the notion of a childhood situated in a sheltered environment, remote from the threatening adult world, was rejected as unreal. It was maintained that over-protection of the child and the creation of a sham reality with an idyllic, illusionary child's paradise produced a worldview which was artificial, narrow-minded, deceptive and distorted; detached from the adult world, it served to foster apolitical behaviour and disregard for social learning and activity. In contrast, East German children's books, as "part of the overall educational programme for society as a whole" (Pieper 1979:46), had to demonstrate a "high degree of practical usability in shaping and reshaping reality" (Emmrich et al. 1971:74). The main objectives for children's books were to encourage the children's readiness for constructing socialism, for becoming steadfast, revolutionary and peace-loving personalities who were willing to act in solidarity with respect to the *Internationale* (Ebert 1976:14, 15). Therefore, it was not enough for the books to depict situations in the family or with peers, but they had to orientate towards a wider inclusion of social events; and it was, of course, the socialist order, as understood by the SED (*Sozialistische Einheitspartei Deutschlands*; Socialist Unity Party of Germany), that was to be shaped consciously.

Frequently it was claimed that, in the GDR as a socialist society, children's literature should be firmly integrated into national literature, representing a significant strand of East German writing. What this meant was that it, too, like literature in general, was accountable to the same principles of guiding, planning and control. Canonisation and censorship applied to children's literature as much as to adult literature. Having an eminent role to play in the country's literature meant not only prestige and attention but also responsibility to the society and the fulfilment of a mission. As a result, a children's literature emerged which, according to Wild, has been able to develop into a noteworthy, autonomous branch of German literature in the course of the 40-year-long history [of East Germany] (1990:372).

Bearing in mind what has been said so far, in order to appreciate fully the premise of this book, it is necessary to detach oneself from the traditional notion of children's literature as a marginalised system existing meagrely at the fringes of society. The East German understanding of children's literature very much differs from conventional ideas, primarily because of the state's ambition to stress personal development and societal evolution. Publishing houses for young readers made conscious efforts to publish books that became increasingly demanding of the children in the course of time. Authors and translators of adult literature were commissioned on a regular basis to work in the children's book sector. Further, the discourse in the afterwords to books for young people frequently referenced titles, authors and events from adult literature. In what appears to be a bizarre step, in 1974, the age up to which a person was regarded as an adolescent was extended to 25 (Youth Law of 1974, as quoted in Kay 2001:78), which had consequences for the publication lists of Neues Leben, the publisher for juvenile literature, in that books from then onwards were published for adolescents that would normally be classified as reading for adults. Another point is that, given the centralisation and hence the unification of procedures, publishing strategies and processes were exactly the same for adults' and children's books. As East German society did not treat children's literature differently from any other, the contents of this book may read differently to those who are used to reading and writing about children's literature, and it might appear to them that it neglects or omits aspects typical of the children's book sector. However, this is not the case, as this study is based on East German behaviour and methods and, as a consequence, aligns itself with processes and mechanisms found in East German children's book publishing.

As is the case with most cultures, Otherness presented a problem to the state bureaucracy. This becomes especially apparent with translated foreign literature, imported into the GDR from Western societies. Hence, literature from English-speaking countries caused difficulties—not unexpectedly, as East and West occupied diametrically opposed positions during the Cold War period. Expressions such as "this book is irredeemable" (Franke 1993:119) or "this book can be rescued" (Krenn, *Binsenkappe*, Kinderbuchverlag, 1975, DR1/2274), which stem from publishers' discourse, have to be seen in this light. Any notion different from recognised socialist values constituted a cultural gap between the two systems, and these gaps had to be closed.

In order to assess the degree of ideological influence on the literary output, this study aims at investigating various aspects in the GDR society and book production. It is, in fact, concerned with what German scholar Ewers has coined the *Handlungssystem* in the children's literary sector (2000:10, 41–45), by which he refers to the system of agents and players in children's literature (authors, publishers, reviewers, parents, censors etc.), as opposed to the—in Ewers' terminology—*Symbolsystem*, i.e. the system dealing with the actual texts. Although text comparison between source and target text brings to light knowledge about translational strategies which, in turn, leads to conclusions about the underlying ideological value system, I believe that the approach of assessing all areas associated with the publishing and book industry will yield more comprehensive and meaningful data about the society as a community or system. For this reason, this book seeks to provide a *Gesellschaftsbild* (picture or study of the society), by identifying and explaining socio-cultural phenomena such as censorship, publishers' tactics in coping with censorship and the role of the state.

This book consists of two parts. The first part (Chapters 1 and 2) provides the theoretical backdrop necessary to understand the organisation and ideology of the 'GDR system' with respect to the publication of translated children's books. This includes a brief historical overview and developments in indigenous literature for children and adults. In the ensuing section, trends in translated children's texts are juxtaposed to the developments in the home-grown sector. Also, light is shed on the role of the Party and state apparatus, and censorship and the various strictures on East German publishing houses are explored. The second part (Chapters 3, 4 and 5) is dedicated to paratextual analysis. Following Genette (1997), this part focuses on epitext, i.e. textual items not published in the actual book, in this context the print permit files; and secondly on peritext, i.e. texts published within the actual books following the main text, namely afterwords. Drawing on data from a compiled book database covering all publications of translated English-language children's books between 1961 and 1989, several areas are examined, such as language used by the publishers in the print permit procedure or justification methods of books intended for translation and publication, broadly speaking strategies of rewriting texts as put forward by André Lefevere in his theory of patronage and rewriting. A case studies section aims to offer insights into how publishers argued in favour of texts. Representative case studies are taken from a wide range of children's books, allowing a comparison between the various texts and revealing striking similarities between the publishers' approaches to the texts.

Although general cultural issues and historical events will be considered back to 1945 whenever relevant to the discussion, the main body of the book covers only translated English-language books published in the period from 1961 to 1989 for the following reasons. In 1961, East Germany built the Berlin Wall, raising a physical barrier and cutting itself off from the Western world. Whereas before 1961 literary traffic occurred between East and West (predominantly in the eastern direction), the cut-off date caused a halt to such movement and effectively excluded all Western influences. Also, while in the 1950s, Party and state apparatus were being constructed, this process had come to an end by 1961. In a similar fashion, censorship also underwent continuous development and refinement during the 1940s and 50s, culminating in the foundation of the *Hauptverwaltung Verlage und Buchhandel* at the end of 1962, which was to be the censorship authority until 1989. Thus, the years 1961/1962 constitute a turning point in the history of the country, as it marks the time when the state machinery was solidly in place and books could be produced for a market screened off and under the total control of the Party. The year 1989 is self-explanatory, since it was then that the GDR ceased to exist. In settling on this period for the investigation, data can be obtained that are directly related to the field of study, as all undesirable external influences were effectively removed by the closure of the border.

Chapter One
The Historical Context of Children's Literature in the GDR

Any topic dealing with matters of translation should give consideration to the general literary environment in which translation takes place. As different societies have different policies about the role and function of their translated texts, the literary and cultural politics of the GDR ought to be examined, in order to define and contextualise translated children's books and their position within that country's systems. Contrary to the conventional notion of literature being autonomous, GDR literature took on a different character and value. Underlying this other kind of value system was the belief that literature had immense power in affecting the individual's consciousness and therefore could be used to bring the people forward in History, i.e. towards communism. Indeed, the Party, convinced of literature's pedagogical potential, assigned it the task of aiding in constructing this new type of society. This is where East German literary politics differed greatly from its Western counterpart. "Whereas in the West anything was published that promised financial profit, the East guided, with its Party's literary politics, what was printed by the publishers" (Mathäs 1992:41). Just as the economy was run by the motto 'planning, guiding and controlling', so were cultural matters. What this meant for literature was that nothing was left to chance. On the one hand, GDR literature was severely monitored and controlled; on the other, it was enormously fostered and promoted through designing and drafting its direction and course. The result was a literature which had a very high profile, which was widely noticed and much debated, but also much manipulated.

Given the importance of books with respect to their effect on the readers, the prime aim of the SED was to make sure that only the right kind of books reached the market. As a consequence, the Party claimed for itself the sole right to guide and control cultural politics. Joh. R. Becher, first East German Culture Minister, expressed this very well when saying "a state would give up one of its most central pillars, if it behaved neutrally and indifferently in cultural issues and permitted anarchy and chaos. Those who deny the state the right to influence cultural developments, those who believe that the state should not interfere in matters of culture and art underestimate the enormous importance of culture and art in educating the people" (Becher 1953, as quoted in Schubbe 1972:317). Accordingly, two principles prevailed in cultural policy:

- The education of the masses should be of paramount importance. In order for the consciousness of the people to move in the correct, desired direction, every process—present and future—in every cultural development was planned and designed to achieve the goal of a socialist society most effectively. For literature this meant drawing up short-term and long-term plans to accompany and steer the forward-movement of society.
- The monopoly of this planning and designing was in the hands of the Party. Following on from the statement that "all cultural politics express the political will of a government" (Becher 1953, as quoted in Schubbe 1972:316), it was the Party that dictated concepts, perspectives and lines of approach. This postulate of the SED's monopoly was maintained from the very beginning; hence, for instance, Otto Gotsche, East German author and, from 1966, member of the Central Committee, declared in 1951 that only on the political level could the needs of the workers be interpreted correctly and fulfilled appropriately (Gotsche, as quoted in Jäger 1982:32). This maxim was still upheld in the final years close to the state's demise when, for example, chief ideologue Kurt Hager claimed in 1984 that the strategy of East German cultural politics was clear and unambiguous, that it was in accordance with the Party resolutions and that there was no room for any private or other policy on that matter (as quoted in Ackermann 2000:15).

Throughout the entire existence of the GDR, literary politics were subjected to numerous interventions and, according to the respective political and socio-economic phase, experienced alternating times of repression and liberalisation. It is safe to say that every change in political direction had an immediate effect on cultural politics, for example, the Constitution of the state in 1949, the erection of the Berlin Wall in 1961 or later the policy of détente.

Since East German state ideology was closely connected with literary politics, the following chapter seeks to provide an exploration of the effect of Party politics on indigenous and translated literature. For the purposes of this discussion, I will use the four historical periods defined by the SED in alignment with their proclaimed societal transformation process:

1. Antifascist-democratic transformation period (1945–1952)

2. Period of socialist construction (1952–1963)
3. Period of consolidation (or else called Period of comprehensive construction) of socialism (1963–1971)
4. Period of the developed socialist society (1971–1989)

In order to provide the overall context, a brief overview of each period is provided here with respect to political and economic events, relating them to the respective, parallel developments in general literature and children's literature during the same period. Against this background, translational processes and, in particular, the translation of English-language children's literature can be located which, it is hoped, allows a clearer picture of the principles and standards governing translation and to understand the reasons underlying certain decisions that the publishing houses made or, perhaps, had to make.

1.1 Antifascist-Democratic Transformation Period (1945–1952) and Period of Socialist Construction (1952–1963)

1.1.1 Political Developments

Immediately after 1945, East Germany embarked on a programme to erase any notions of capitalism, fascism and anti-humanism. Fascism with all its anti-human facets, the product of capitalism, as it was claimed, was to be prevented forever. This could only be guaranteed by a socialist system, since it was only socialism that had overcome the age of capitalism and had entered the next societal phase in History on the path of the liberation of mankind, which was the path to communism.

Social re-engineering got under way using several drastic measures. Key-posts were filled with officials loyal to the communist system, and the administrative machinery became increasingly centralised and was given more and more powers. Mass associations like trade unions, youth organisations and culture associations were manipulated in the same fashion to converge with the Russian model. By order, from 30 October 1945, enterprises belonging to active Nazis, war criminals and war-profiteers were confiscated. Under the guise of antifascism and denazification, the property-owning bourgeoisie and landowners were deprived progressively of economic and political power. They found themselves dispossessed and their enterprises and factories received new management. Further, large enterprises were converted into SAGs (Soviet joint stock companies). The *Bodenreform* (land reform) was introduced. This resulted in expropriation of all privately owned agricultural land over 100 hectares and its subsequent redistribution amongst landless farmers, agricultural workers and tenants. In keeping with the total eradication of fascist assets and fascist thinking, steps were taken for a change in ideology in the people. A law reform brought new lawyers to the system; Nazi cultural assets were removed; and more than half of all teachers were dismissed and replaced by new conformist ones who frequently did not even have pedagogical training (Schoeller 1981:12).

Undeniably, these measures were introduced to restore capability in the state, both politically and economically. However, the fact cannot be overlooked that underlying it all there was a distinct move towards a socialist society and that one party was increasingly seizing the reins and preparing the ground for hegemonial power. As Sontheimer notes, the entire process of restructuring and re-education had been decreed and imposed from above and was realised by force with the help of communist instruments of power, regardless of the desires and interests of its population (1990:176). Accordingly, Ulbricht's motto from 1945 read, "It must look democratic but we must be in total control" (Emmerich 1996:32).

When on 23 May 1949 West Germany proclaimed its 'Grundgesetz', East Germany responded by constituting itself only a few months later (7 October 1949). On 15 October 1949, the USSR officially recognised the GDR and, in due course, the other people's republics in the Eastern Bloc followed suit. This East German Constitution still drew upon the constitution of the old German Reich from 1919 and provided for a potential re-unification with West Germany (Article 1: Germany is an indivisible democratic republic, composed of German states). It bore the stamp of a compromise with the two other political parties (CDU, LDP) who were, at that time, still capable of exerting their own political influence. Despite this fact, it is an open secret that "this Constitution was realised only in parts and that the fundamental rights and the voting right laid down were never carried through, [also that the SED] often interpreted the Constitution against its wording and whole parts of the Constitution were made void by issuing new laws without a change in the constitutional text per se" (Müller-Römer 1968:11). This has to be understood in the context of the role the SED had attributed to itself. As the 'Party of the new type' and the vanguard of the working classes, it saw itself as the only rightly instituted body to know which logical steps to take in the societal transformation process. As a consequence, the Party felt entitled to reduce and eventually eliminate other parties' and organisations' influence step by step.

With the support of the Soviet Union, Walter Ulbricht (founder of the SED, First Deputy Premier from 1949, and later First Secretary of the Party until 1971) transformed the GDR into a major socialist power. By the beginning of the 1950s, the SED had secured its supremacy. One of the prime targets of the new East German state was to induce its citizens to accept, intellectually and emotionally, integration into the Eastern Bloc. A progressive and forward-looking USSR was conveyed, combined with the notion of the 'New Socialist Personality' who is part of the collective and always ready for battle. At the Party's Second Congress in 1952, the time was deemed ripe to declare the country ready for the construction of socialism. This construction was to take place systematically and in all areas of society. At the same time, the Party announced the general intensification of class struggle and, also, solidarity with international liberation struggles against exploitation and suppression. It appears, however, that this positive ideological portrayal was not well received. The local East German economy was in difficulties with no foreign loans in sight, yet with high reparation payments to the Soviet Union; hopes for a swift German unification had been shattered following the inclusion of only the Western zones in the Marshall Plan and separate currency reforms in the East and West. East German citizens were faced with a grim reality which, on the one hand, offered them a shortage in supply of consumer goods and, on the other, price rises, increased work quotas and demands to raise productivity. This, coupled with several other measures designed to disadvantage the self-employed, discrimination against the church along with other enforced political measures, evoked the population's feeling of discontent against autocratic rule. Thousands of people reacted by leaving the country and emigrating to the West.

Resentment grew even further, after the announcement of the first five-year plan with harsh economic directives and a bigger emphasis on heavy industry instead of consumer goods. So much so that, on 11 June, orders were given by the Soviet Union to take a more lenient course (*Neuer Kurs*); however, this came too late and on 17 June 1953, workers revolted. Proclaimed by the state as the future power-holding class, they now turned against it, demanding a withdrawal of the government, free elections and a change in economic policy. However, the revolt was suppressed violently by Soviet tanks, which had come to the East German government's rescue. In an official statement, the uprising was declared a fascist coup d'etat, deriving from the West, and no self-assessment or self-criticism was considered.

Despite more political moderation for a short period in the middle of the 1950s, Ulbricht continued to steer a hard course. By 1960, the *Bodenreform* had been enacted and farming land was collectivised, a policy which caused a vast number of farmers to leave the country. It was, however, not only the farmers who fled. Generally, people in the East felt attracted to the West, as life there seemed to be offering affluence, better job opportunities, better purchasing power and, most of all, absence of constraint and oppression. A large number of the refugees belonged to the younger generation, the very people in whom the SED had put high hopes to create the future utopia. Between 1949 and 1961 more than 2.5 million people had chosen to turn their back on the GDR.

With an apparently endless stream of people leaving the country, the Party had to act decisively. To ensure an undisrupted economy and further on-target socio-political development, there was no other choice than to make it impossible for people to cross the border. The solution was to raise the Iron Curtain. This meant physically closing the border and erecting a barrier through Berlin, separating its capitalist part from its socialist one—at first only through a barbed wire fence on 13 August 1961, and later by means of a concrete wall. Elizabeth Shaw, writer and illustrator of GDR children's books, described that day in her book *Irish Berlin*, "The GDR could no longer afford a further loss of the work force. At that time, we lived in Niederschönhausen and went to Wollankstraße, in order to convince ourselves. We watched how the Wall grew slowly, stone after stone. People stood crying on either side and waved their handkerchiefs, until they could not see each other any more" (1990:167).

1.1.2 Literature: General

In 1945, literary debate was generated with the foundation of the *Kulturbund zur demokratischen Erneuerung Deutschlands* (Culture Association for a Democratic Renewal of Germany). In keeping with the spirit of the time, this institution exhibited a non-partisan, pluralist and antifascist-democratic character. Its programme not only maintained the elimination of Nazi ideology in all spheres of life, but also co-operation with all democratic and religious movements and groups. Equally, drawing on Goethe and other writers of the Classical epoch, it declared itself against war and for a humanist approach.

After this relatively short period of conciliation following the end of the war, in which literature on progressive subjects and depicting class struggle was still put aside, debates about the role of literature emerged in 1947. Initial signs became noticeable at the First German Writers' Congress in October of that year where some authors advocated a revolutionary socialist approach. There were calls for "the development of a Socialist Realist contemporary literature, a literature which could be integrated actively into the struggles of everyday life and of the Historical epoch" (Jarmatz 1970:39). In the face of the catastrophic economic background the first Two-Year Plan was announced in 1948. A rebuilding of the economy, although urgently required, appeared possible only by a considerable increase in productivity which, subsequently, was achievable only through a mass initiative by the workers. In this situation, the SED harked back to the 'consciousness-forming' attributes of literature and art. The Party was convinced of the correlation between literature and material circumstances to a degree that literature could be utilised to raise economic output. If the economy could be planned, so could literature, and this then would effect productivity and the economy as a whole. Indeed, the Two-Year Plan evinces telling facts. It is the first officially released document directed at long-term central planning and at measures to consolidate and expand the state apparatus, in order to open up opportunities for a future socialist development. Another fact, however, becomes evident in this Two-Year Plan, namely the high position already held by literature in these early stages of the system. For the first time, major criteria underlying East Germany's cultural politics for the years to come were formulated and the powerful role attributed to literature is striking.

Because of its significance, the key points of this Two-Year Plan, as they relate to literary matters, will be looked at briefly (see Dietrich 1983:330–353):

- One of the major concepts of socialist art was mentioned already on the first page of the Plan, namely to postulate, with this Two-Year Plan, co-operation between workers and creative artists. The Plan stated that "creative artists have the opportunity to apply their scientific and professional and artistic knowledge for the humanist task of lifting the material and cultural basic principles of the life of our people" (Dietrich 1983:330). This fact is noteworthy because it was the endeavour throughout to narrow the gap between the country's working classes and its intellectuals. It was argued that the ruling classes had always exploited workers by withholding access to education and culture. Now the moment had come for workers to "regain status as human beings" (Hager 1972:31) and to be lifted to the level of the intelligentsia, using the slogan "art and life have to be connected" (Hager 1972:31).

Other measures in this direction were to break the education privilege and, through several laws and decrees, to provide everybody with the same educational opportunities (e.g. Youth Law 1950; or Education Law 1946 in order to introduce uniform schooling).

The separation between physical and intellectual work, between town and country was to be overcome. The overall objective was to make culture and education the possession of all (Dietrich 1983:330, 332).

- Commensurate with the previous point was the vision of a new kind of personality within the socialist community, highly conscious and filled by progressive spirit and ethos, attending to matters of cultural life and developing lively participation and interest in all forms of art and culture. The education of a new, young generation was particularly highlighted in the Two-Year Plan, a generation that was to learn to act responsibly and be utterly committed to peace and to the construction of democratic socialism (Dietrich 1983:345).
- This cultural construction, revolving around human beings and their professional and intellectual higher development, was to be attained with the aid of creative artists and people from the intelligentsia. Hence, authors were made "activists of the Two-Year Plan" (Dietrich 1983:332) who were to "give propagandistic support for the good cause of the Two-Year Plan" (Dietrich 1983:332). Their participation was required in the task of raising people's consciousness and consolidating their morality under the conditions of the construction of socialism. In order to equip them for their mission, artists had to be educated to enable them to depict life 'truthfully', which in other words meant not to portray it 'as a detached observer' but to portray it 'in the light of its revolutionary development'. Authors were to take on the role as "signposts, educators or prophets" (Münz-Koenen 1979:212) who showed the readers the way ahead.
- A further notable aspect of this Two-Year Plan was the fact that artists were given exact guidelines about how to best express and mould their works in order for society to gain the best results. All of these guidelines deal with aspects which in 1950, together with some further factors, were to be included in the East German main cultural concept of Socialist

Realism, the task of which was to portray, artistically, reality in its revolutionary development up to the final stage of communism.

a. The first of the premises was for depictions to be *realistic*; they were to show “our new social reality” (Dietrich 1983:332). Works of art were to be linked closely to everyday life in factories and in villages and farms, involving all the questions, problems, hopes and difficulties which moved people in their daily routine of socialist production and to which they therefore could relate well.
b. Linked with the dogma of the workers being able to relate to a known reality was the idea of *Volksverbundenheit* (also called *Volkstümlichkeit*, which was to say that a work was written ‘in the spirit of people’ and that it was accessible and comprehensible), by which literary works were meant to serve the interest of the people and to be easily comprehensible; artists were to aim their work at all the people in the country equally and write ‘in the language of life *per se*’.
c. All literature had to express the notion of *Humanism*. Especially after the Second World War, it had been the aim to re-educate people in an antifascist and humanist mode. Since fascism was regarded as a development of capitalism and, therefore, World War II presented an example of what capitalism was capable of, it had to be ensured that capitalism and fascism were overcome entirely, never to enter the country again. To this end, socialist humanism was incorporated into socialist art, which subsumed notions such as humanity, respect for people’s dignity and personality, freedom, and support for the liberation of people from exploitation and suppression.
d. The fourth precept was to radiate *Optimism*, to encourage people and generate willingness to work and be more active. Through optimistic portrayals people should be motivated to higher achievements in their work and in life generally. After all, it did not seem to make sense to depict socialist life in a pessimistic way, as a socialist future could only be bright and positive, because it meant social progress after having thrown off the chains of capitalist exploitation.

It is significant that the Two-Year Plan was, according to Ulbricht (speech at the Working Meeting of Party Writers and Artists, Sept. 1948, as quoted in Thomaneck and Mellis 1989:302, 303), “not a purely economic matter but a matter of implementing far-reaching changes in society and acquiring a new progressive culture . . .”; what was most important was “to change people”. Politics took a distinct direction towards building the new order, which required transformation of people’s consciousness. For literary politics this meant first and foremost putting more emphasis on *Gegenwartsliteratur* (contemporary progressive literature, dealing with issues of the present day) and, at the same time, overcoming the ubiquitous petty bourgeois and pulp literature. A new kind of literature, a *Nationalliteratur*, was to be created. This was to be a literature which should be accessible to all people and all social strata in the country and which would lead to the "final victory of socialist conditions of production" (Münz-Koenen 1979:52). In this, the Soviet Union as the leading light, ideologically, provided the answer by their literary doctrine of Socialist Realism. From the early 1930s, Soviet cultural politics had declared that art should illustrate realistic situations from socialist life and show ordinary people performing their day-to-day business. This type of art was to be optimistic and filled with heroism as it was the art of the progressive, upcoming class. Through such 'truthful' portrayals taken from everyday life, the readers were to be influenced ideologically in the spirit of socialism. Drawing on this Soviet precept, East Germany, in 1950, adopted Socialist Realism as their binding method for the creation of any work of art (Decree for the Development of a Progressive, Democratic Culture of the East German People, 16 March 1950). Socialist Realism remained the prevailing discourse until the early 1970s when, with the appointment of Honecker, ideological winds shifted toward a more open-minded approach.

Given the necessity of instilling into the people a particular kind of perception, of reforming the working people in the spirit of socialism, clear parameters for literature had to be specified and relatively little leeway was granted for creativity, human diversity and individuality. The criteria of Optimism, Realism, Humanism and 'writing conducted in the spirit of the people' have already been mentioned earlier. Additional tenets formulated and based on Socialist Realism were those of the '*Positive hero*', of *das Typische* (*the Typical, the Representative*) and of *Partisanship*, i.e. commitment to the Party and its directives. As has been pointed out, reality in socialist literature had to be created for the departure into the new world and making the readers keen to participate in this development (Jarmatz 1970:81). Therefore, so-called 'Positive heroes'[1] were called for, in other words, role models for the readers showing ideals of socialist culture and ideal human beings, who had to manifest the new attitudes so that the audience was able to discern the new direction in History. Writers were to portray all the richness of human possibilities and characteristics; above all, however, they had to demonstrate that difficulties were there not to leave people discouraged but to make them active; people were to be active members of their class and to live according to the slogan "this is difficult, therefore we'll tackle this" (Brecht 1956/1970:385).

Connected with the portrayal of the 'Positive hero' was the notion of what was 'representative' of the new order. 'Typicalities' manifested desired attributes which were deemed important for bringing mankind forward in History. In describing Socialist Realist art at the Fifth Meeting of the Central Committee of the SED, Lauter used the term 'Typicality' to express this forward-movement towards socialism when stating "by the portrayal of our best people, we wish for the typical traits of a progressive personality to be depicted; and we have a right to demand this, not only because such people really exist . . . but mainly because they personify the new that is going to lead to a future bright and more beautiful" (1951:30). One characteristic of 'typicality' was the idea that the development of socialist personalities was only possible in the collective and that they found fulfilment only in the community of equals and by becoming integrated with society. In Nadeshda Ludwig's words, "revolutionaries fighting as lone wolves are doomed, [rather revolutionaries are] members of an ever-strengthening collective, the collective of the socialist camp, and represent . . . the socialist ideal of mankind" (1958:10).

Having defined the criteria which make up the paradigm of Socialist Realism, the last maxim, Partisanship, pulls them all together. Whichever text, book or piece of art was produced, it had to support the Party spirit and, under all circumstances, side with societal progress. This meant it had to adopt the standpoint of the Party and to remain loyal to its policies, however much these policies were adjusted. Nor was it sufficient for a book to show that problems existed, or that these problems were solvable through society; texts had to show loyalty to the Party's ideals. "Partisan creation means coming to decisions on socialist terms . . . , it means to use the instrument of art to reach decisions in the spirit of our politics and ethics" (Hager 1972:41). Since socialist literature had to reflect reality,[2] this led to the belief that "reality as portrayed in fiction was only possible when linked closely to the Party, because this link ensured the 'correct' notion of reality. What followed was that the reality prescribed could not be equated with true objectivity but constituted rather an ideological reality, a 'more real' reality according to Party tactics" (Clauss 1978:15, 16; my emphasis). For the author this meant producing a literature that was to be of benefit for the public and that demonstrated socially essential and useful characteristics instead of being 'merely beautiful'. There was no room to accommodate subjective views. As a result, readers were left with a literature suggestive of a particular kind of reality.

It was not only the paradigm of Socialist Realism that was propagated in striving for a *Nationalliteratur*. In order to 'functionalise' literature fully, a canon was formulated, determining the kind of literature which was supportive of generating the new order and of transforming the population. For this, cultural traditions were rediscovered, since the GDR claimed to be the true home of the great German cultural heritage. This was based on the belief that German history had been a history of continual progress to which indeed the bourgeois class had contributed. However, at the point when the bourgeoisie had settled for becoming a class of exploiters themselves, exploiting farmers and workers, Germany had left the path of revolutionary evolution. In restoring this continuity through the East German revolution, progressive ideals and deeds were rekindled. Therefore, the GDR saw itself as the sole rightful executor of the estate, carrying on the immortal humanist heritage of German national culture and continuing all progressive, liberal traditions.

It was contended that all the great Classical writers had been humanists and realists; their opus had told of societal development and had also formed the consciousness of past generations. In the same sense, it would now contribute to solving the current Historical task of the East German people. Therefore, for political and cultural reasons, it was considered necessary to draw on the Classical cultural heritage. Particular tribute was paid to the humanist Goethe, who "in his belief in the invincible power of human reason" (Orlow, as quoted in Schubbe 1972:167) was exemplary of an individual continually striving for knowledge and improvement. Consequently, the SED was of the opinion that the acquisition of Classical bourgeois ideals was capable of stimulating consciousness and, subsequently, work enthusiasm, which they then linked to an increase in productivity. Further genres which were canonised were those of Soviet literature and exile literature from antifascist German authors. Amalgamating the humanist realistic heritage and the revolutionary traditions with Socialist Realist aesthetics, it was hoped to pave the way for a *gebildete Nation* (educated and well-read nation) and to a *Literaturgesellschaft* (society of literature).

From this it follows that, under all circumstances, literature was to be upheld and protected from any kind of distortion, perversion, falsification, adulteration, mutilation or destruction. "From the very beginning, the SED regarded itself as the Party of renewal of German culture, furthering the nation's true greatness by fighting all damaging and reactionary traditions" (Schlenker 1977:66), which were, it was claimed, stemming from the West. Extensive campaigns sought to highlight the anti-humanist and anti-democratic character of Western culture, describing it as modernist, decadent, cosmopolitan or formalistic. Anchored in the maxim of art as a medium to help recognise reality and real life which contained high value contents, it was argued that Western art forms placed more importance on the form of the artefact *per se* as compared to the importance of its content. This was then necessarily leading to a type of art which was becoming more abstract and surrealist, which distorted reality and, therefore, was going to destroy every culture in which it appeared. In East German terminology this meant that, under the guise of developing something new, formalistic[3] art broke with the Classical cultural heritage. The result was an uprooting of national culture and destruction of national consciousness. Formalism was also perceived as turning away from the principle of *Volksverbundenheit* and, hence, denied the principle that art be at the people's service. Such art, it was contended, was an expression of late-bourgeois hopelessness as well as of disintegration and decline of capitalist culture, in particular that of the United States. It was also concluded that this was an imperialist abuse of art as a weapon in the daily competition between socialism and capitalism (Abusch 1950b:145). "Ideological subversion and attempts at influence have become a form of battle of West German imperialism in the struggle between the two systems in Germany" (Haid 1963:390). Formalism was said to be directed at destroying national culture and, thus, national consciousness of peoples, in order to prepare them for subjugation through imperialistic forces. This policy required, as a counter-attack, a battle against the growing "American cultural barbarism" (Lauter 1951:17) by fostering the national cultural heritage and by encouraging and developing a kind of art which revolved around tasks that would help the people to solve the issues of their lives. "Battling for world peace" (Abusch 1950a:142) entailed propaganda and campaigns against all types of Western kitsch, of crime stories, Wild West stories, pornography, comics, in short all art indicative of the American "Boogie-Woogie-cult" (Poiger 1997:122). Speaking of the "American colonisation of our culture" and "mental Marshallisation", Alexander Abusch (1950a:141) discerned, as the only solution, an irreconcilable battle against the undermining influences of imperialistic decline and a revolution in favour of a new German culture which educated the people to fight against all forms of cultural barbarism.

It is evident that, from its constitution as a state in 1949, one of the main goals of the GDR was a dissociation from the class enemy and a strengthening of its own national position. Steps were announced to structure politics and cultural policy through to the end of the decade in order to combat this situation. *Aufbauromane* (novels of construction) were to describe and to celebrate the economic and social construction and to accompany and make palatable political measures like the collectivisation of agriculture and nationalisation of the economy.

Political events throughout the decade, for instance the workers' revolt in 1953, the thaw between 1953 and 1956 or the 1956 revolution in Hungary, determined the extent of rigidity with which literary politics were carried out. However, by the mid-1950s, it had become discernible that East German literary politics with its prescribed political-aesthetic programme had failed. Imports of Western books had increased to such a degree that for every two titles from the West only one title was imported from the USSR (Barck et al. 1998:62). Moreover, people were still reluctant to read progressive socialist literature; and even worse, petty bourgeois middle and low-brow genres such as women's novels, love and crime stories abounded. Authors had also failed to show sufficient interest in producing works on socialist topics that complied with the declared socio-political policy. Official statements claimed that authors had problems in seizing and recording reality analytically and in comprehending that they were not merely chroniclers of the new social order, but were also to take sides and declare themselves in favour of progressive ideas. At this point, it had become more than evident to politicians that it would still take a long time to overcome the alienation between intellectuals and the ordinary people.

In 1957 at the 30th Plenary Session of the Central Committee and, subsequently, at the Fifth Party Congress in 1958, a hard line was decided on, in order to further socialist *Gegenwartsliteratur.* With the slogan "Workers, conquer the heights of culture!", the foundation was laid to one of the most extensive movements in literary history. The 'Bitterfeld Path', named after the town of Bitterfeld, where a ground-breaking conference was staged in 1959, constituted an attempt at creating a new socialist classical literature. The aim was to organise a broad movement of local cultural activities for all the people and to awaken their creative energies, a project which, in Reid's words, was "possibly the most ambitious attempt of the ruling Party to 'administer' literature and to overcome the division between culture and society" (1990:35). The Bitterfeld motto "Grab your Pen, Comrade, the Socialist German National Literature needs You!" was to be understood as the ultimate link between art and life, between artists and people.

In an effort to realise the leading role of the working classes, the Party used its dominant influence to introduce measures to raise the workers' cultural levels. Not only should the campaign for *lesende Arbeiter* (reading workers) be developed further, workers were now to assume the role of creative artists themselves. They were encouraged to begin to write, to document their daily struggles and successes in their jobs and, in so doing, advance themselves mentally and culturally. Authors were required to give support to workers in their endeavours and, as mentors of writing circles or literary groups, teach workers how to produce pieces of art. Equally, writers were to overcome their lack of immersion in the processes of the working classes and to embrace the newly formed association between artists and workers. They were to swarm out to production sites, factories or agricultural combines, form alliances with the workers there, get to know production processes from the bottom up and portray these conditions in their texts. Authors who took as their theme the literary treatment of problems arising from socialist transformation were to be given priority; also, publishers were commanded to redirect their publishing activities in this direction.

Notwithstanding the significance of the 'Bitterfeld Path' and its effects on East German literature, it is possible to interpret this movement differently. As has been mentioned, socialist *Gegenwartsliteratur* had suffered a considerable setback during the entire decade. Since consumers had refused to buy this 'new' literature with its political ideological content, bookshops had rather stocked easy-to-sell books from the West, for which, however, more foreign currency had to be paid. Additionally, print-runs of GDR authors were on average lower by comparison, which meant a further outflow of currency. Here, Barck et al. detect the growing lack in foreign currency as the undeclared driving force behind the Bitterfeld Movement, because the Party may have seen it as a way to prevent final financial disaster, by attempting to propagandise and promote indigenous and, thus, currency-saving literature on a wider basis (1998:64).

In the beginning, many of the renowned authors followed the call of the Party. A new genre, *Ankunftsromane* (novels of arrival,[4] named after Brigitte Reimann's novel *Ankunft im Alltag*, see p 28) emerged and, in order to continue the programme, a Second Bitterfeld Conference was organised in 1964.

However, long-term success in uniting manual workers and intellectuals failed to materialise because of passive resistance from the intellectuals. Authors refused to collaborate with the masses and to be restricted to forms of propaganda production. One of them, Werner Bräunig, criticised the generally held opinion that literature written by the intelligentsia would automatically achieve new qualities, once authors knew what a lathe looked like up close (as quoted in Münz-Koenen 1979:236). Another, Franz Fühmann, adults' and children's author, wrote a letter to the Cultural Minister in 1964, stating that he did not intend to write the *Betriebsroman* (novel of production) he was expected to write. On the one hand he felt that he did not have the aptitude for such a genre; on the other he sensed he would never be capable of portraying the present-day workers well enough to live up to a truthful picture of their thoughts, dreams, desires and feelings. Going into production sites would add insufficient experience to make the long time spent there worth it. Further, Fühmann contended that for authors to deliver quality work they ought to know ten times more about the subject than they actually put into a book and, indeed, he did not have this depth of knowledge with the Bitterfeld genres and, what was more, he could not see himself ever acquiring it (1983:9–12).

1.1.3 Children's Literature

After World War II, the situation in children's literature, as in adult literature, was "relatively open and undecided" (Doderer 1993:191). Although the publishing industry had been hit hard by war destruction, there was great enthusiasm to stimulate an environment favourable to cultural and literary development in the children's book sector. In children's literature, as in adult literature, conscious efforts were undertaken to root out all vestiges of Nazi ideology in reading matter and to generate new ideals and a new, more humane perspective. Similar to adult literature, the types of books which were to be published were chosen with care and a vast majority of works were dismissed as inappropriate for youngsters growing up in a progressive society. For children's literature, five main sources were defined:

1. Classic heritage (German heritage, e.g. the Brothers Grimm, Wilhelm Hauff, Ludwig Bechstein, J.H. Campe, but also foreign books, in particular by authors who were regarded as belonging to the bourgeois progressive camp, such as Charles Dickens, Walter Scott, J.F. Cooper, Mark Twain, Jack London, R.L. Stevenson, Daniel Defoe, Jules Verne)
2. Bourgeois humanist heritage (notably Erich Kästner)
3. Proletarian children's literature of the Weimar Republic (e.g. Alex Wedding, Max Zimmering, Lisa Tetzner, Auguste Lazar)
4. Literature written in exile during the Third Reich (e.g. Kurt Held, Willi Bredel)
5. Soviet children's literature (e.g. N. Ostrovskij, A. Gajdar[5])

Soviet children's literature, in particular, had a huge impact on the evolution of East German children's literature, as it followed the same objectives and was based on the same ideological outlook as those of the emerging East Germany; for example, Böhm maintained that Soviet books encouraged the belief in the good in people, in the Historical power of the people, in love of work and in the workers and their strength (1980:25). "Man in Soviet art was portrayed as a fighter, as a re-organiser of the world" (Küchenmeister 1967:6); "Soviet children's literature conveyed humanist socialist ideas while taking children completely seriously, both as readers and as acting subjects" (Meinck 1967:5); "for the first time, children's literature was counted with the serious, 'big' literature and all authors, who wrote for children, saw themselves as equal literati and therefore worked with a sense of responsibility and a mutual goal" (Feustel 1967:16).

Not unexpectedly, East Germans also turned to the USSR when, in 1950, the construction of socialism in children's literature was decided. The principles of Socialist Realism were also declared binding for young people's books, and the necessary educational and literary background theory was derived from Soviet experts, among others, A.S. Makarenko, educationalist; Lenin's partner Nadeshda Krupskaja, theorist; and first and foremost Maxim Gorki, playwright, theorist and reviewer of children's books, who had formulated numerous thoughts on a socialist children's literature. By 1948, Soviet children's writing was sufficiently highly rated in East Germany that, at the First Authors' Conference, Honecker (who at that time was involved in youth matters) demanded the goal of "finding an Ostrovskij for German youth" (as quoted in Havekost 1993:25), referring to the reputable Soviet writer of *Wie der Stahl gehärtet wurde* (*How the Steel was Tempered*), a bestselling author in his country and viewed as a trendsetter in East Germany.

Internally, the GDR had prepared the ground for a viable East German children's literature by putting in place all necessary legislation and setting up the two big leading state publishing houses for children's and juvenile literature, respectively (Kinderbuchverlag, established 1 June 1949; Verlag Neues Leben, established 9 December 1946), in which all the state power was centralised. After passing the Youth Law (1950), which called for the creation and development of a socialist children's literature, further measures were installed for a systematic promotion of this sector by the state, for instance, organising regular writing competitions or incorporating discussions about literature into the school curriculum.

Gone was the time of "searching, trying out and feeling one's way carefully" (Kuhnert 1991:35). The aim was, as in adult literature, to create a *Gegenwartsliteratur* which advertised to children the advantages of socialism. It was a literature targeted at integrating, not emancipating children, in accordance with Gorki's postulate "the socialist state cannot come true, unless children become socialists" (Kuhnert 1991:35, 36). Commensurate with the 'deficit model', East German children, as the foundation of the future, were classified according to their usefulness for society and had to be trained and prepared for this new utopia.

For children to be taught to subordinate themselves to society, their literature had to subject itself to Socialist Realism and to the state's ideology. Construction literature for children was as narrowly defined ideologically as its counterpart for adults. In a partisan way, it presented the vision of the new being. Moralistic model stories were constructed to make children identify themselves with the Historical changes and processes. For Altner, East German professor at the Pedagogical University in Zwickau, children's books were mere *Gebrauchsliteratur* (functional literature), which "had to educate and train the young generation, to stimulate their social activities and to prepare them to master day-to-day life" (1988:8). The aim was to turn them into individuals who were against any form of exploitation or oppression, and for humanism, freedom and respect for each other; who understood that a gracious fate did not exist but that people had to become active and fight, in order to change themselves and, ultimately, society; who were encouraged to act politically and to take a stand against capitalism, imperialism, fascism and war, and in favour of proletarian Internationalism, a revolutionary brotherhood and a patriotic attitude displaying an optimistic outlook to a socialist future.

Again, as in adult literature, the 'Positive hero' as the model figure had to bring home to young readers preserved values and traits and show them their place in society and their tasks. Richter differentiates between two types of protagonists in children's books of that period. The first one has no longer to be convinced of the new ideals; he acts in the interest of the collective and is clearly an example to the reader. The second one, on the other hand, is still hesitant or an outsider who eventually finds his way into the collective. Both heroes, however, are part of their wider social milieu, linked to vital issues of adult life (Richter 1995a:84; 1996:198, 199). Moreover, although fictitious children were allowed adventure and play, these did not take place isolated from social procedures but were related to the community on which it had a beneficial effect. The village was the preferred location for the plots of children's novels of that time. The reason for this choice is found in the Party's wish to propagandise their reforms to nationalise agriculture (*Bodenreform*) to a child as well as an adult audience. A second aim was to integrate the child's world with the adult world and with society, by having the protagonists encounter the struggles with respect to building a new type of social order. Thirdly, it was easier to convey social progress and the notion of collective work in a village environment than in any other workplace. In general, *Gegenwartsliteratur* depicted children within a wider social context, i.e. village collective or Pioneer group, in order to create a link from the child's world to the current burning issues of social life. At the same time, "child protagonists are not educated by adults but appear to carry the ideals of the new society already in them" (Richter 1995b:292, 293).

From a multitude of examples, two books will suffice to exemplify the black-and-white portrayal of children's construction literature. In the book *Mit 17 ist man noch kein Held* by Werner Schmoll (1962, Mitteldeutscher Verlag), the protagonist Hannes is caught between the two antagonistic social systems. His father, as the representative of the class-bound society, believes in the old system: private property, money, greed and hegemony of the church. Hannes, on the other hand, feels drawn to the new times and, as his father disapproves of his preference, begins to fight the old structures and his father. Nadeshda Ludwig called Hannes' conflict truly socialist, because it demonstrated that it arose from an ideological difference and not from a generation problem. Furthermore, she claimed, it illustrated the principal problem of the nation, namely the decision for or against socialism, for a Germany of peace and humanism as opposed to war and fascism (1964:875, 876).

A second example, *Tinko* by Erwin Strittmatter, was regarded as one of the most significant East German children's books of its day and was, therefore, included in the official literary canon and put on school reading lists. The significance attached to it is also demonstrated by the fact that it was not only published by Kinderbuchverlag, but also by Aufbau-Verlag, the largest publisher of socialist and communist literature for adults in the GDR. In *Tinko*, too, the decision of the protagonist for or against a socialist order stands out as the key theme. However, *Tinko* has a second theme, dealing with 'the Typical' and the reality of a socialist life. The book was published by both publishing houses in 1954, which was the decade in which the restructuring and nationalising of the country's agriculture and the creation of big agricultural combines took place, and the novel is set against this background. Tinko, the 'Positive hero', has to make a decision between his grandfather, a private landowning farmer, and his father, who has returned from being a prisoner of war and now involves himself actively in building a socialist village. Needless to say, the boy eventually goes with his father and thus socialist re-organisation. This book, together with *Trini* by Ludwig Renn, also published in 1954, was attacked by reviewers as 'too adult' in its technique to the extent that it became incomprehensible to children and was hence not appropriate as a children's book. Nonetheless, children's literature experts and Kinderbuchverlag (publishing house of both *Tinko* and *Trini*) celebrated them as a breakthrough in the field of children's literature. Kinderbuchverlag contended that both were books "which broke the cliché of children's writing as being simplistic, unambiguous and without any reflection of the protagonists" (Neubert 1995:179). In society's ambition to narrow and eventually close the gap with adult literature, these two books proved that children's literature was indeed on the way to ending its status as a marginal phenomenon in society.

From the beginning, the endeavour was to plan and design systematically fiction for children (*Literaturentwicklung*), in order to promote children's development towards becoming socialists. However, *Literaturentwicklung* had a second objective, namely to create a socialist children's literature which was to lift children's books out of the "Spielecke des Lebens" (playpen of life) (Tiede 1971:32) and give them an equal place with the adult domain. From the outset, the publishers Kinderbuchverlag and Neues Leben had begun to seek contacts with renowned adult books' authors, in order to interest them in producing works for children. This wish for co-operation between adult and children's literature had been indicated already in the first book to be published by Kinderbuchverlag in 1949, *Der verwundete Sokrates* written by Bertolt Brecht. This book signalled the wish by the publisher to create "a new literature for children which would lead away from the idyll and plainness of the past centuries", as was maintained by long-term Kinderbuchverlag chief editor Katrin Pieper (1988a:14). Strittmatter's and Renn's (two authors of books for adults) contribution to children's books certainly constituted a powerful influence and was to spark off further collaboration, moving children's literature into realms so far unreached.

Similar to the scenario in mainstream literature in the early and mid-1950s, the influx of Western pulp and mass literature (comics, cheap detective and adventure stories, girls' stories) gave rise to concern also in the field of children's writing. Lively debates about the damaging effect on the younger generation took place and the class enemies, especially West Germany and America, were accused of attempting to win over the young generation to their end. Strategies to fend off inimical propaganda became imperative. Legislation was passed to keep literature of this kind out of the country (e.g. Decree for the Protection of Youth of 4 October 1955). Moreover, the state decided to produce its own, indigenous comics and adventure stories, tinted, however, by socialist ideology, and to sell them cheaply so that young people could afford to buy them. These East German versions would then, it was hoped, dissuade the young people from obtaining Western ones. Since comics and adventure literature were classified as low-brow literature and East Germany was attempting to raise literary standards in general, purists opposing these genres had to be convinced that many readers were still not conscious enough for high art and, hence, preferred these kinds of novels, and that in order to discourage them from wandering off to light fiction from the West, it would be better to welcome these genres on the home market but produce them in a way which served socialist purposes. Adventure stories in particular, it was argued, lent themselves to satisfying the natural need of the young readers for suspense and action and, simultaneously, to teach them ideologically valued traits like courage, determination, fortitude and honesty. The additional bonus was that this education was "not only a humane one, not 'an education per se', but a political one; an education to the ideals of our new (non-bourgeois) morale" (Richter 1954:162). The storylines and actions of heroes in adventure stories could illustrate the cruel behaviour of rulers and exploiters far better than any propagandistic motto, it was argued. Such books could "make young people realise the hostile forces which were operating in 'civilised' Western countries and make them understand the necessity of a struggle against these forces by workers and the suppressed 'natives' living in capitalist countries" (Richter 1954:163).

Another purpose for this light reading was to gradually provide a bridge for the reader to a more sophisticated literature in the long run. This is why care was taken to produce adventure literature which fulfilled the demand for quality, by which was meant a Historically objective portrayal, authenticity and non-racist depiction. *Die Söhne der großen Bärin* by Liselotte Welskopf-Henrich (1951, Altberliner Verlag Lucie Groszer) was ranked as an outstanding example which provided a truthful picture of the battle of North American Indians and, in defeat, their newly found position within American society. Among the publishers for children and adolescents it was Neues Leben, on the whole, which produced adventure paperback series. Series like *Das Neue Abenteuer*, *Spannend erzählt* or *Neue Edition für junge Leute* focused attention not only on adventure stories written by East German authors but also promoted a great number of translated works for the GDR market.

With the intention of keeping bourgeois influence out of the country, another children's literature genre was debated fervently in the 1950s. Eager to remove bourgeois viewpoints, all girls' books had, from 1949, been eliminated from publication and the term 'girls' book' had even been omitted from specialist dictionaries (Oy 1993:580). It had been argued that these books were aimed at preparing girls for their second-class role in society and at creating uncritical and apolitical behaviour in girls, in order to make them passively accept their fate as dependent and exploited housewives and mothers. Moreover, it was held that socialist education did not differentiate between the sexes, a fact which could by definition not support different reading interests in boys and girls. Hence, books written particularly for girls would be superfluous. What was needed instead were books which were interesting and educational for boys and girls equally.

In the mid-1950s, however, diverging opinions were voiced, among them that of writer Alex Wedding, who, in her article *Der Schrei nach dem Mädchenbuch* in 1954, stated that there was indeed a difference between boys and girls and that it was intolerable to hinder girls' need for reading and social development through a lack of appropriate literature. Moreover, she argued, girls would only fall back on Western girls' novels easily obtainable on the market, which not only constituted pulp literature but also carried Western, and thus hostile, ideology. As a consequence, Wedding called for socialist girls' books which were of high aesthetic quality and of ideologically correct content (1954:164–166). In subsequent years, the need for special books for girls was acknowledged, but fictitious heroines had to demonstrate particular traits; the "socialist Eve" was no longer "willing to wait for the knight of her dreams at the cooking pot" (Könner 1957:102). She had to strive for independence and success, look for her place in society, be active either because of economic necessity or because of a developed consciousness, be emotional but not sentimental, be an achiever in the workplace and not afraid of getting involved. Despite certain progress in the acceptance of girls' books, this genre remained controversial; Inge Borde, for instance, gave a report from a meeting by the work-team for children's literature within the Writers' Association in 1967, where half the participants were arguing in favour of girls' books, the other half against (1967:173). Similarly, in 1987, Emmrich, East German children's literature theorist (and Professor at the Pedagogical University of Dresden), urged experts and reviewers to take up the phenomenon 'girls' book' and, after years of delay, to begin scientific work on this matter (1987:60).

The genre of fairytales was debated with a similar vehemence. Already in the 1940s shortly after the War, sceptical voices pointed to a connection between the cruelties depicted in fairytales and those committed by National Socialism. In particular, Grimm's fairytales were attacked as one of the main cultural assets of the Third Reich. Arnold Zweig contended that Grimm's tale *Der Jude im Dorn* (The Jew in the Thornbush[6]) created anti-semitic attitudes which were seen as a danger after the experiences of the War; equally, the tale *Hänsel und Gretel* was linked to Nazi incinerators because of the oven into which the witch is pushed in the tale. Another objection against fairytales drew on the socialist arguments of the 1920s in which fairytales were regarded as showing the backwardness and dependence of the lower classes caused by their servitude. Similarly, it was questioned "whether it was at all justifiable to tell fairytales, in which kings, princes and princesses were the main actors, to our children in our times, particularly since children were educated at school about the true conditions of feudalism" (Wardetzky 1991:8). In addition, fairytales were rejected, because miracles and fantasy were in conflict with the dogma of Socialist Realism; it was feared that children's perceptions of realism would become distorted. Therefore, fantastic elements seemed incompatible with the training of a rational and realistic behaviour (Emmrich 1987:64). All of these notions helped to create uncertainty about the value of fairytales for a socialist society.

For these reasons, only particular tales which matched the conception of the world were selected. Also in the 1950s and 1960s, adapted versions only were published in which critical passages were left out or changed. Göritz mentions radio programmes of that time which aimed at equipping fairytales with a progressive touch, by having the hero refuse the crown because he would rather be a head forester than a king or by making him use his newly attained power to introduce social reforms (1986:155, 156). In addition, didactic commentaries were added to justify attitudes concerned with the socialist ideal of manhood. One of these commentaries, for instance, describes the tale *Frau Holle* (Mother Holle) as being "highly valuable pedagogically because it awakens love for work . . .; in *König Drosselbart* (King Thrushbeard) the moral is quite evident, as the arrogant and lazy princess has to be taught honest work by Drosselbart, having disguised himself as a beggar" (Wardetzky 1991:8). These comments, according to Wardetzky, pedantic though they might seem, were nothing other than attempts to legitimise fairytales, in order to preserve them for children. In such processes, Richter too detects the overly dogmatic behaviour of the earlier years, in which the narrow-minded discourse of realism prevailed and did not allow for a more multi-faceted outlook on life (1987:16).

Gradually, fairytales were repositioned as products of class-conscious proletarians. In 1954, Kahlo, for instance, objected to the belief that they had originally been the possession of the ruling classes and, in the course of time, had moved down through the strata of society to end up with the working classes. Pointing out that fairytales were "siding with the poor" and that "social conditions were told merely from a proletarian viewpoint", Kahlo declared them to be the true heritage of the proletariat (1954:16, 17). Korn took a similar stand when maintaining that fairytales were truly realistic, as they reflected the predecessors' material conditions and thinking. "The main characters in our fairytales are always ordinary people: hunters, farmers, shepherds, fishermen, soldiers, servants. In all fairytales, the revolutionary power of the ordinary people is portrayed much more strongly than that of kings and princesses" (1952:440).

In later years when the concept of cultural heritage was widened to embrace magical and fantastic elements, the fantasy in fairytales received a new understanding. It was interpreted as deriving not so much from relying on magic but from the desire for change; a desire that, in Ebert's opinion, doubtlessly revealed revolutionary traits and a healthy criticism of society (1976:43). Fairytales therefore were regarded as of great educational value to the child. They demonstrated that the struggle of the heroes to succeed was rewarded by the aid of good forces and that, unless they give up, happiness and fulfilment of hopes could be achieved. Moreover, the child, equipped naturally with a distinct sense of justice and siding with the weak and oppressed, would learn about the bitter fate of workers in the olden days, and that the poor often had to resort to tricks, in order to ensure the most essential necessities of life (Hänsel 1969:92). Finding a worldview repeatedly confirmed in fairytales which was optimistic and active-oriented, children would adopt a system of ethical beliefs and a sound grounding for being able to cope with potential difficulties in life.

This repositioned approach opened not only the door for easier publication of German fairytales, but also those of many other countries or continents. With an emphasis on internationalism, the fairytale was discovered as a tool to convey the idea of uniting nations. By pinpointing similarities and differences between peoples it was hoped to dismantle past prejudices and to build international understanding. Of course, emphasis was placed on publication of stories from the Soviet Union and other socialist countries, but many tales originating from Africa, Asia, Latin America and the English-speaking world were translated or retold and published in large print-runs.

Other genres were introduced in the 1950s, such as literature dealing with antifascist topics and East Germany's relationship to West Germany, historical and contemporary biographies, all of which, however, remained within the confines of the officially accepted cultural political paradigm. Children's literary planning and development was, after all, a prescribed social task. Hence, children's authors wrote books, the majority of which followed a clichéd, schematic black-and-white pattern, with purely didactic intent and in which the 'real' reality was not discernible.

The reverberations from the Bitterfeld conference manifested themselves also in literature for young people. Although the number of children's production novels was nowhere near as high as in adult literature, attention was paid to making children aware of this part of socialist reality. One of the projects embarked on by Kinderbuchverlag and the author Edith Anderson in the aftermath of Bitterfeld was the picture book *Der verlorene Schuh*; a story about Sepp, a little boy who has lost one of his shoes and, in order to obtain a new one, visits a shoe factory where he gets to know all the stages in the production of shoes. It was the intention of the publisher to convey with this book to the young readers "knowledge about an area of our socialist production and to teach them the value of work and of a good relationship to people working in factories“ (print permit file DR1/3940). The publisher's assessment also mentions the excellent advice and co-operation of the workers of [the factory] *VEB*[7] *Goldpunkt* with the author and the editor. Not unlike authors of adult literature, Edith Anderson seemed to have difficulties combining the production of her manuscript with collaborating with *VEB Goldpunkt*, because the publisher's assessment states (DR1/3940),

> It was not easy to develop this title with Mrs Anderson. She had to gain experience first by inspecting the factory and consulting the workers. Her first manuscript does not reflect the impression of the factory as positively as the final version, because she was still overcome by the perceptions one receives when first entering such a production site, e.g. ear-splitting noise or smells of leather. This was reflected in the first version of her manuscript. Also, the first manuscript did not contain the contact between the workers and Sepp. Therefore, much work needed to be done with the author.

Another example of a juvenile Bitterfeld story shows the close connection of East German children's literature to national literature. *Ankunft im Alltag* (Brigitte Reimann, 1961, Neues Leben) resulted from the author's direct study of adolescent socialist everyday life, by performing shift work herself in one of the country's combines *Schwarze Pumpe*. Working together with young people, Reimann endeavoured to make a contribution to bridging the gap between art and day-to-day business. Based on her encounters, she wrote the novel, describing a year in the lives of three youths who had volunteered to join a work brigade in *Schwarze Pumpe*. Although published in Neues Leben, the publishing house for books for adolescents, *Ankunft im Alltag* attracted nationwide attention because of its novel and significant content, so much so that the title lent its name to the new, national genre of *Ankunftsliteratur*. After the 1954 publications *Tinko* and

Trini, this book was hailed as a new and necessary step in the development of a national literature.

Despite such self-congratulatory remarks, the general conviction was that not enough had yet been achieved. This stance became evident at the Writers' Conference in 1962, held on current issues in children's literature. Referring to the majority of the books of the past decade, their "simplistic unambiguous portrayal of [fictitious] child activists who do not possess inner conflicts and who understand intuitively, even at the beginning of the story, that their happiness lies in their work within the collective" was identified (Richter 1995b:293). It was pointed out that (real) children had reached a higher level of consciousness and that children's fiction had not kept pace with their development and intellectual growth. It was further claimed that children's books were still packaged pedagogy and were, therefore, measured against a different standard from adult literature. Hence, bearing in mind the desired goal of children's books being received into national literature, many commentators complained of a failure. An explanation was found in the fact that a limit had been reached in children's literary development which, for the time being, could not be surpassed by authors without lending them some kind of assistance. What was not mentioned, however, was that it was actually the restrictions of cultural politics which were playing a big role in this. While it may indeed have been true that the books showed a limited, biased world, this had to be put down to the fact that Party politics did not allow the authors to portray a more open, multi-faceted world.

Improvements were considered necessary and, from 1963, a journal dealing with children's literary matters was launched (*Beiträge zur Kinder- und Jugendliteratur*). Moreover, the *Tage der Kinderliteratur* (Days of Children's Literature) were introduced, an annual event which took place in a different location every year, gathering hundreds of authors, illustrators, translators, people from publishing, teachers, librarians, parents and, last but not least, young readers. Accompanying these events, theoretical conferences were organised (*Theoretische Konferenzen anläßlich der Tage der Kinderliteratur*), bringing together experts and professionals from the field. The speeches held there revolved around issues related to artistic techniques and various individual topics of interest for society. Gradually, experience was gained about what children liked and did not like, and the difference between theory and practice became apparent. Nevertheless, children's authors remained loyal to societal development and continued to subject themselves to the narrow stipulations of Socialist Realism.

1.2 Period of Consolidation of Socialism (1963–1971)

1.2.1 Political Developments

The year 1963 represented a turning point as it marked the beginning of a new direction in politics. Institutions and policies were now established (see Chapter 2) and the GDR was in the position to consolidate its political-economic structure with minimal interference from Western society. At the Sixth Party Congress in this year, two new principles were proclaimed. In economic terms, a new system was propounded which was to revolutionise the previous economic policy, aiming at modernisation and rationalisation.[8] Socially, a new phase was initiated which heralded the dawn of 'consolidation of socialism' (or also called 'period of comprehensive construction of socialism').

It would appear that the 1960s were a decade in which specific emphasis was laid on the concept of socialism and its importance for all spheres of East German life. Alongside the Economic System of Socialism (ÖSS) and the 'comprehensive construction of socialism', Ulbricht coined the notion of the *sozialistische Menschengemeinschaft* (community or collective of socialist human beings), which was meant to symbolise harmony, togetherness and stability and was to be widely quoted thereafter. Correspondingly, the year 1968 saw the proclamation of a new East German Constitution. It differed sharply from the first Constitution of 1949 in that it stressed a conscious move towards socialism. Its introduction was argued on the basis that this new period in the development of society required a new constitution. Hence, Ulbricht argued, "the socialist German Democratic Republic is no provisional arrangement" and "the Constitution comprises the fundamental regulations for shaping the developed societal system of socialism and it focuses strategically on the victory of socialism" (Müller-Römer 1968:9, 19). Therefore, the new Article 1 of 1968 read "The German Democratic Republic is a socialist state of the German nation". Whereas the old Article 1 had named "Germany as an indivisible Democratic Republic", the new approach clearly stated that the GDR should be a separate state in its own right, which manifested a distinct move away from the West and towards the Eastern Bloc.

After an economic upturn at the beginning of the 1960s, the East German economy soon reported a drop again, mainly due to an inflexible attitude to economic innovations, arising from a biased preference for particular industries and a failure in appropriate planning of the supply of goods and services. In spite of instituting certain elements of a market economy, the government did not want to do away with a centralised, planned economy, which resulted in suppressing the production of consumer goods compared to the relatively high investment in heavy industry, a scenario which came hard to East German citizens. In the light of growing discontent amongst the population and of Ulbricht's inability to deliver results, it was considered necessary to make a new man Party leader.

1.2.2 Literature: General

In literature, the Bitterfeld precepts remained in force and, as in the 1950s, periods of restriction took turns with periods of relaxation, depending on economic and political conditions. In the wake of Bitterfeld, the main literary topics involved events in the working environment and, in the case of *Ankunftsliteratur*, the arrival of the protagonist in a state of real existing socialism. Other themes dealt with the past, in particular with Nazism and antifascism. Although the early 1960s represented a relatively liberal phase, the literary canon was still narrowly defined and, with it, the notion of cultural heritage and realism.

As long as the majority of writers subjected themselves to the officially prescribed discourse, antagonistic opinions did not interfere in the literary production process. Tensions arose, however, when authors no longer wanted to restrict themselves to the discursive paradigms and when voice was given, increasingly, to a widening of the concept of heritage and to inclusion of themes which were not compatible with the accepted concept of realism. After the Second Bitterfeld Conference in 1964, where a renewed campaign was undertaken in favour of a socialist literature (mottos coined in connection with the New Economic System (NÖS) in 1963: 'authors as pacemakers, planners and managers', and 'demand for managerial literature'), the debate reached its peak in 1965 at the Eleventh Plenary Session of the Central Committee, which went down in history as the *Kahlschlagplenum* (Axing Plenary Session). Awkward artists and disloyal (as it was seen) executive cadres were rebuked or sacked. Writers and artists were accused of still failing to comprehend fully the new and characteristic aspects of the epoch and of still possessing insufficient knowledge of Marxist ideology and, therefore, of not being able to cope with the "problems and requirements of our socialist construction" (Verner at the Eleventh Plenary Session of the Central Committee of the SED, in Schubbe 1972:1112). Art of bourgeois content was sharply criticised as being of insufficient socialist substance and, on the whole, imperialist ideology was heavily condemned. The attempts to liberalise literature were interpreted as manoeuvres or plots of the class enemy who now not only attacked from the outside, but operated with the help of allies from inside the country. Doubt, scepticism and all decadent literary forms deriving from the West were viewed as "agreeing with the policies of the enemy, directed at the intelligentsia and youth" which were "weakening and watering down the GDR from the inside" (Honecker in 1965 in a report of the Politburo to the Eleventh Plenary of the Central Committee of the SED, in Schubbe 1972:1080). As a result, there were rigid literary interventions, which were later reinforced after the Czech Revolution in 1968. What is more, the state security increased their operative activities in literature and the arts. In 1969, a separate department was set up within the Stasi (HA XX/7), in order to monitor cultural and media issues more effectively. It does not come as a surprise that it was in these times that authors began to reject the regime's lack of willingness to compromise.

Because of the narrow confines of literary politics, new forms and ways of expression were sought. Writers looked for new methods of fulfilling the conventional forms, and new ways of writing could no longer be suppressed, although, however, they were not yet recognised within the concept of Socialist Realism. The focus on historical topics was widened and, at the same time, myths, folk tradition and fairytales were re-appropriated. As a means of legitimately expressing motifs and topics which were out of bounds in the official discourse, these genres became highly popular as adult genres. With this development, a change in the structure of literary politics becomes discernible, showing a shift away from the sole emphasis on the Classics and a re-evaluation of the Romantic heritage. "Within the framework of widening the notion of national tradition and cultural heritage, works were appropriated whose authors or styles (for example Romantics) had previously been frowned upon; hence, many methods of narration and topics gained acceptance, whose appropriation had, up to that time, been hindered" (Hanke 1987:157).

This development accounts for the integration into literature of two notions which previously had been found unacceptable, i.e. fantastic elements and individuality. In a discussion centred around socialist reality and truthfulness to real patterns of life, elements of the surreal and fantastic had been disapproved of as incompatible, as escapist and alienating. In the late 1960s, albeit in its initial stages, the 'fantastic' began to be incorporated into the narrative; a technique which later, during the following two decades, came to the fore fully as a means of expression. By incorporating such fantastic elements into the texts, the portrayal of reality received a new quality. Deviating from the unequivocal, black-and-white interpretation of reality, instances taken from everyday life under socialism were now conveyed in a metaphorical way, showing the 'familiar' open to individual interpretation and avoiding 'realistic' discourse.

Similar to the 'fantastic', notions of subjectivity and individuality found their way into discussions in the 1960s and, to a certain degree, into works of literature. Opening the field to subjectivity, it became possible to speak about hopes, fears, dreams and wishes, making a gradual movement away from the collectivist stance to the individual. Author and long-term president of the Writers' Association, Anna Seghers, had already pointed out during the mid-1960s that the moulding of socialist personalities needed the focus on not only the collective but also very much on the individual. Paradoxically, it would seem that Ulbricht's coinage of the 'socialist personality' might be seen as one of the triggers for this development, because here, for the first time, stress was placed on the personal characteristics of the individual within the *sozialistische Menschengemeinschaft*. Another cause of this development might have been the introduction of the NÖS, the economic programme which proclaimed managerial abilities and individuality in the planning of production processes. Simultaneously, sciences like sociology and psychology were given more attention and the role of the socialist individual began to come to the forefront of discussion.

Opening literature to the fantastic and to individuality in the 1960s was only the beginning and their use did not become widespread until after 1971. This is evidenced by the "Axing Plenary Session" of 1965, where these early attempts were criticised by the official reviews as being untypical of socialist society, as outside of the community, the collective and society and even as anarchist. Hence, they were assessed as being counter to the socialist cause and were censored.

1.2.3 Children's Literature

Up to the mid-1960s, East German children's literature continued to be a literature with a strong political bias, a literature of conformity and subordination. Authors who were not willing to subscribe to the Party line turned to historical or biographical subjects, in order to escape the rigidly regimented genre of *Gegenwartsliteratur*; however, frustration and unease were growing also in the field of children's literature.

The cultural and political turbulences in the wake of the 1965 Axing Plenary Session did not, on the whole, manifest themselves in children's literature, except that some authors, who had written books for adults which were criticised by the regime, found that their children's books were also criticised. However, an indirect effect was felt in the sphere of children's books; from 1965, authors of adult literature increasingly turned to producing work for children, a fact welcomed by the publishers of books for young people because, striving for an increase in quality, they were always looking for innovative input.

Innovation and new directions were also the aim of three conferences on children's literature (held in 1965, 1967 and 1968). The 1965 conference revolved around the topic of 'fantasy and reality in children's literature'; in 1967, such questions were on the agenda as whether the entire richness of life was being brought into children's novels, whether the whole abundance of artistic possibilities was utilised and how the image of a human being could be improved to portray a complete, well-rounded personality; in 1968, various problems about the creation of a *Menschenbild* in children's books were discussed, following a noticeable trend nationwide to attend to the issue of individuals and their personal, subjective make-up.

These three conferences picked up on phenomena which had already commenced in children's' literature (and indeed in national literature); on the other hand, they were to set in motion further developments. The path which children's literature was going to take was the same as that of adult literature. Subsequent to the publication of Peter Hacks' *Der Frieden*, 1962 (adapting Aristophanes for adult readers) and Franz Fühmann's *Reineke Fuchs* (1964) for children, both works concerned with legend and mythology, mythical subjects began to find their way into children's books. During the late 1960s, a number of mythical narrations, retellings and adaptations came to the fore, eventually blossoming in the 1970s. For books for smaller children, it was

Kinderbuchverlag initiating a long-term project dealing with myths and epics, with the intention of publishing "a collection of the big legends and myths, each one narrated by a writer of our country" (Schulz 1993:140). Neues Leben followed suit shortly afterwards with productions for adolescents.

Several motives were behind the switch to this genre. After the successful implementation of fairytales into the canon of children's literature, it was claimed that children should be made familiar with another cultural asset, namely myths, legends and epics. Unquestionably, they were seen as belonging to the cultural heritage, the appropriation and preservation of which had been declared to be a children's literary maxim of the state. Thus, the appropriation of myths was widely regarded as "a class mission for socialism and as part of the ideological battle" (Spiewok 1974:89). With respect to children in the capitalist class society, it was maintained that only children of the higher classes were given access to this cultural asset in their education (Emmrich 1979:65), in an attempt by the bourgeoisie to use this part of the cultural heritage to their end, aiming at strengthening their class rule. Reviving mythological stories in the GDR, therefore, supported the shaping of consciousness and appeared the next logical step in the literary development of children and young people.

Furthermore, as opposed to fairytales, myths were considered to be a better reflection of reality than fairytales. Fühmann, one of the ardent advocates of the incorporation of myths into children's literature, expressed this notion well when commenting that the fairy-tale pattern of black-and-white and good-and-evil did not express the nature of real life. Real life encompassed internal *Widersprüche*, he claimed, i.e. insoluble conflicts, psychological contradictions and constellations in a person, none of which were inherent in fairytales, albeit very much extant in myths. Hence, Fühmann viewed myths as more representative of reality and, in turn, of higher educational value for children, in terms of teaching them about circumstances in life (as quoted in Richter 1988:30).

Peltsch, pedagogue and editor of the GDR children's literary journal *Beiträge zur Kinder- und Jugendliteratur*, also had the explanation that Kinderbuchverlag, with this myth project, sought to register protest on behalf of the children. In introducing polytechnic schooling into the education system (Law on the socialist development of schooling in the German Democratic Republic of 1959), the state had eliminated Classical humanist knowledge from the curriculum, which Rodrian, director of Kinderbuchverlag, considered an essential part of education. Peltsch proceeded to say that prior knowledge of mythological themes enabled readers to understand parables and metaphors in advanced literature, which helped them to decode another layer of interpretation of a text, and without which the book would be a mere description of superficial external physical events (1990a:13).

There is, however, another, quite remarkable reason why authors increasingly turned to the subject matter of myths. Given that from 1965 censorship had become more severe and, also, that a number of authors had become discontented with their position of solely acting as a mouthpiece of the regime, mythology provided an outlet by its nature of allowing a variety of readings. This openness to interpretation was of indispensable help in finding a way to circumvent the censors, who were looking for justification for the socialist cause in every book they had to assess. This ambiguity permitted the censors to find an interpretation which satisfied their need for a socialist theme. Thus, the socialist critic Emmrich, who ideologically opposed religious concepts, praised the Greek Gods' "de-mythification by having them portrayed as ruthless aristocrats living at the expense of the people who depend on them"[9]—interestingly, Emmrich failed to see the other possibility, namely that of interpreting the Greek Gods as mirroring the functionaries of the socialist regime. His view on Prometheus[10] is similar; he admired Prometheus as the untiring learner and maturing protagonist fighting for the rights and dignity of the individual. Yet in mythology, Prometheus became Zeus' opponent because he disapproved of the lust for power exhibited by the Father of the Gods. As to another mythical subject, Emmrich discussed the *Nibelungenlied*,[11] condemning the nature of the feudal system. The reader supposedly learned here about Burgundian power politics and encountered the fall of the Burgundian dynasty, evoked by purely inflexible and uncompromising attitudes which, as a logical consequence, had to lead to their demise (all examples: Emmrich 1979:66–73). However, is this not also notably reminiscent of the subsequent historical events in the GDR; and could a realisation of this other interpretation perhaps have prevented the regime's failure?

The number of authors dedicating themselves to this project was considerable and several of them joined from adult literature. All of them had begun to perceive contradictions within the system and realised the discrepancy between the ideology in which they believed and its questionable practice in reality (Steffen Peltsch, personal communication, 28 April 2002). And all of them, as is evident from the literature, had the same objectives about ideas and beliefs which became increasingly pressing and noticeable and could therefore not be suppressed in society. Their aim was to define the term 'human being' for children; to teach them the values of being human and staying human; to show them the patterns of basic human situations; to explain to them that life is not only black-and-white but full of shades, complexities, inconsistencies and options, and to make them aware of the inner conflicts in human behaviour. In order to achieve this, mythological heroes were individualised and their own subjective struggles were illustrated. In particular, the rewriting of myths provided plenty of opportunities to accommodate certain insights, since the originals were written and read from the present East German point of view. The fact that the myths were narrated from new perspectives allowed for critical comments and links to the present. They avoided the happy-end of the fairytale and drifted into a far-off idyll, because they were not intended to "function as comforting elucidations of life or to fabricate agreement with the prevailing ethos but to break up decrepit social structures" (Lange 1993:149). Without doubt, a species of texts evolved which, to a certain degree, required an adult mediator, in order for the child to realise the complexity of the characters, to be able to understand the allegories and to become aware of the socio-political criticism (Richter 1990:117). What is more, it set the scene for a kind of children's literature marked by two new characteristics, namely placing emphasis on the individual personality and, secondly, embracing non-realistic, fantastic narration. Both meant a new direction for the writing for children (just as it did for that of adults) and were going to shape the following two decades until 1989, interestingly coinciding with the shift in power politically from Ulbricht to Honecker.

1.3 Period of the Developed Socialist Society (1971–1989)

1.3.1 Political Developments

The 1970s began on a promising note with a new direction created at the Eighth Party Congress in 1971, which resulted in the implementation of significant changes in Party politics. After officially declaring that socialism was not only a transitional state, but that it was going to be a longer-lasting phase (in fact longer than originally anticipated), the new concept of the 'developed socialist society' was proclaimed as the next objective of the state. Subsequent to the past years of inflexibility, rigidity and lack of scope for initiative, a general re-orientation took place on the political stage. Reforms with respect to more economic and social welfare were undertaken focusing on the citizens' well-being, particularly considering the satisfaction of consumers' needs. Similarly, in the light of the country's international political recognition at the beginning of the 1970s, the Party grew more self-confident and liberal and allowed itself to act in a more conciliatory manner.

A new man had replaced Ulbricht as head of the Party in 1971, Erich Honecker,[12] who was to stay in power until the collapse of the GDR in 1989. Because of Honecker's policy, for the first time East Germans benefited directly from the subsequent economic upswing. The decision to go for more consumerism might have come as good news to the citizens inwardly but the actual economic framework was weak. The East German economy had been in serious difficulties for many years and it may be debated whether the state could afford financially, at that stage, to allow more consumption. Nevertheless, it was a tightrope they had to walk: to decide between the mounting discontent of the population and the actual constraints of the economy.

As a country whose currency was not convertible on the world market, the GDR had to deal with various disadvantages, with provisos and special conditions to its contracts when trading internationally. Inflation on international markets did additional damage to the East German economy. Additionally, East German products showed inferior quality compared with Western ones, and the country's productivity was low.[13] On the other hand, with respect to its foreign policies, East Germany was able to make respectable achievements. In 1972, it concluded the *Grundlagenvertrag* (Treaty on the Basis of Relations between the Federal Republic of Germany and the German Democratic Republic), which changed the nature of its trade relations with West Germany. In 1973, it became a member of the United Nations and, with the ratification of the final agreement of the Conference on Security and Cooperation in Europe (CSCE) in Helsinki in 1975, the GDR's international reputation appeared to have reached new heights.

Domestically, another change to the Constitution was thought necessary. The 1974 Constitution entirely abandoned the concept of German nationhood and defined the GDR as a socialist state of workers and farmers (Article 1), tying in the country even more closely to the Eastern Bloc. This obviously implied constitutionally granting the leadership to the working classes and its vanguard, the SED. Article 6 stressed, as a new amendment, the alliance with the Soviet Union forever and irrevocably, thus defining East Germany as being indivisibly a part of the community of socialist states. Equally, the new Constitution promised support to all states and peoples in their struggle for social progress and for national freedom and independence. In the light of East Germany's simultaneous opening towards the West, the need for this new constitution may be interpreted as an attempt at re-assuring the Soviet Union of the GDR's loyalty.

In signing the CSCE Treaty in Helsinki, the GDR had committed itself to the recognition of human rights as well as to freedom of thought, opinion and religion. This was a step which encouraged those people in opposition to the Party to protest against the regime. They openly expressed their resentment about the prevailing conditions and demanded a 'democratic' socialism. Not only did the SED have to face a gradually strengthening opposition; it also could not prevent the formation of alternative subcultures, such as peace groups, ecological groups or minority groups. For years, the regime had hushed up the existence of groups such as homosexuals or punks, with the argument that these were an appearance of imperialism only and that through its socialist revolution, the GDR had overcome these manifestations. Children's literature reflected and took up this general development—in the 1980s, books appeared which concerned themselves with, for instance, ecological issues in the GDR or social outcasts; one example of which was the release of several productions by Kinderbuchverlag, the state publishing house for children, dealing with environmental problems in the GDR; another example is *Umberto* by Günter Saalmann (1987, Kinderbuchverlag), a book which has antisocial behaviour as its subject and portrays on its front cover a boy with a punk hairstyle and an earring in his left ear (not surprisingly, *Umberto* caused problems with the censor).

In 1985, Mikhail Gorbachev entered the political stage and, with him as the leader of the Eastern Bloc, changes in the political climate took place. He envisaged a policy of transparency, Glasnost and Perestroika and encouraged the leaders of the other Eastern Bloc states to follow suit. "The times are over when a country or a group of powerful countries were able to force their opinions and their policy on the rest of the world, and this sometimes in a quite violent way" (as quoted in Alcandre 1991:17).

While some of the other people's republics embarked on the new political course, Honecker remained unmoved despite a few attempts to soften the course and attach a 'new feel' to it. Colin Good (1991:12), among others, reports on attempts, only one year before the fall of the Wall, to change linguistic structures, give socialist-toned words a less harsh meaning, rid them of their negative associations and re-establish them as positive concepts. Good interprets these as attempts to create new ideological structures, from which new motivation should have flowed. However, at that stage, ideology had ceased to be a motivating factor in East German society and these attempts seemed nothing more than half-hearted appeasement and rescue measures on a completely inadequate level. This lack of commitment to the current political trend of liberalisation and to the actual needs of the population is evident in a metaphor coined by Politburo member Kurt Hager, "if your neighbour newly decorates his flat, would you feel obliged to also decorate your flat?" (as quoted in Pätzold 1992:103). Instead, the Party press entered into campaigns against Soviet press organs and even the word 'Glasnost' became taboo. Open discourse was not tolerated and, in 1988, several Soviet films and magazines were banned (Pätzold 1992:104).

This new freedom could not be concealed from the East German population who, already enraged, launched into a growing mass movement. It was, in particular, the younger generation who were carrying this mass protest. Staritz (1985:227) suggests two reasons for this: first, born after the years of radical change and the rebuilding of the new socialist society, their views had not been formed by repression to such an extent and, second, they had become accustomed to a higher level of prosperity. Therefore they, more than the older generation, were inclined to challenge convention and to search for alternatives and for a sense in life. To their questions, the Party could give no acceptable answer. The institution, however, which could give them an answer, and in fact did, was the church. It was receptive to people's worries; it allowed open discussion and controversial debates and showed tolerance. The protest movement, which arose from a small group of intellectuals, had grown and, with the increasing dissatisfaction with the political environment, had mushroomed. If only a few in the beginning were not afraid to speak out, now it seemed that the whole country was in uproar. Demonstrations and mass protests took place on a regular basis. The government acted vigorously with arrests and intervention by police and state security, but in the long run it turned out to be impossible to cover up the disarray and unrest among the population and to gain control over the escalating conditions. On 18 October

1989, Honecker was deposed and three weeks later, on 9 November, the Wall came down.

1.3.2 Literature: General

Culturally, the liberalisation manifested itself in allowing literature and the arts greater autonomy. Without doubt, Honecker, the new man at the top, gave cause for hope of more freedom in cultural circles when, in 1971, stating that "if one comes from the firm position of socialism, there is, in my opinion, no reason for taboos in the spheres of art and literature. This relates to questions of content as much as to style—in short: to questions of artistic proficiency" (Jäger 1982:136). On a similar note, chief ideologue Hager characterised socialist art as allowing for a wide variety of themes and topics, for a richness in form, style and technique (1972:46, 47). Continuing, he called for literature to take up artistic description of difficulties and problems of the socialist society since these, in his words, did not constitute a flaw in the socialist evolution but rather a driving force for forward-movement. Writers responded with texts revolving around contemporary topics, not so much dealing with the ideal, shallow and pat images of socialism used in the majority of the books so far, but embracing the 'real' reality as they saw it. Special emphasis was put on the depiction of individuals and their relationship to the society by which, frequently, positions critical of the East German socialist order were voiced. It had become possible to discuss subjective needs of people, without dictating from above what the needs of the people were and, based on this, commissioning literature discussing these very needs.

The principle of the uniform *sozialistische Menschengemeinschaft* was abandoned, a concept which had been defined by Ulbricht as aiming at homogeneity of the interests of all. Inasmuch as authors were granted more individuality, literary forms and techniques were augmented. Traditional, omniscient narrators, whose task was to present model experiences to learn from, lost their dominant status; exemplary 'Positive heroes' were increasingly replaced by protagonists displaying a range of shortcomings and problems and who were frequently unsuccessful in their actions; conflicts tended to be individual and often remained unsolved; open endings left the door open to different interpretations; the through-going story-line was dissolved, and conventional literary language gave way to dialect and slang. Associated with this was the assumed maturity of the readers, as literature moved away from being unambiguous and prescriptive. It was accepted that readers would use their own personal interpretation of reality, since now a variety of reading possibilities were allowed. Overall, Socialist Realism received a broader definition, going beyond the traditional interpretation, with a widening of its boundaries to be multi-faceted and diverse in its conception, which represented a renunciation of its interpretation in the 1950s/60s. All of this has led many to believe that the notion of Socialist Realism had, in essence, come to an end in the 1970s.

Regardless of all the modifications and relaxations since 1971, it must be understood that these steps towards liberalisation remained within the confines of a socialist order, the universal structures of which were still not to be questioned. "Changes [in the approach] came from the top and remained embedded in the dogma of correct politics, which was pursued consistently and was only altered according to necessities demanded by a new evolutionary phase" (Jäger 1982:135). Despite the seeming relaxation in the relationship between SED and intellectuals, the Party remained vigilant and introduced several legislative changes which could be used, should there have been a need to discipline unruly authors. So, for instance, changes were introduced in Criminal Law (1974, 1977, 1979) with respect to propaganda hostile to the state, derogatory descriptions of public order, institutions and authorities, and making contact with any opposition organisation or passing unauthorised material to any foreign organisation; similarly, the Foreign Currency Law was tightened (1973), in order to deter authors from publishing antagonistic material in the West. Further evidence of the Party's covert distrust is evinced by the increase in control of the cultural sphere by state security since the beginning of the policy of détente in the 1970s. However, particularly after 1976, the date of singer-songwriter Wolf Biermann's expatriation,[14] artists were kept under observation more assiduously than previously (Emmerich 1996:64). In 1976, yet another subdivision was put in place within the HA XX in the Stasi, in order to concentrate more effectively on monitoring authors and artists. According to a memorandum by the state security organisation, it had become vital to receive timely information about the planning and the publication of literary works with any indication of being critical of or endangering society (Stasi-exhibition, Berlin 2002). Even the changes to the Constitution in 1974 emphasised the desire of the SED leadership to remain in a place of absolute power.

All of this goes to show that literature still played a large part in society in that it had a function to fulfil; a fact that is also manifest in chief ideologue Hager's speech from 1972. Although placing emphasis on more variety in literary expression, Hager insisted that East German society required art because of its personality-forming quality, which as a consequence excluded every notion of 'l'art pour l'art' (1972:32). Equally, as encouraging as Honecker's remark on the absence of taboos might have been, he did in fact refer to a position firmly rooted in socialism. This would indicate an ongoing strong inclination towards a Marxist-Leninist set-up which it was deemed safe to temporarily relax but which could be restored at any time, if the need was felt.

In spite of all the enthusiasm, these were early warning signs. When conditions worsened within the country (due to the 1970s' oil crisis, currency problems and the growing human rights campaigns in the West), the SED sensed that the country's developing economy and, in fact, the whole system was endangered. As a result, the ideological concessions of the past years were revoked and, in 1976 eventually, the situation escalated with Biermann's expatriation and the subsequent storm of protest among authors. It had become clear that the earlier hopes for more long-term freedom had been an illusion. Sanctions and restrictions followed, censorship increased and, because of this intolerable situation, a great many writers left for the West, a scenario which was to last into the early 1980s. However, it ought to be pointed out that, despite restrictions, literary conditions never again deteriorated to the levels of the 1950s and 1960s because, to a certain degree, critical texts were still published and were not totally suppressed. Hence, there is reason to disagree with Clauss, who, like many others, contended that "the developments of the years before were shattered overnight and cultural politics had reverted to its pointless practices which had already been viewed as past" (1978:38).

"Subsequent to the Biermann incident, the [East German] cultural scene was impoverished. Yet . . . the authors who stayed in the country, did not shirk their responsibility of portraying people and conditions in the way they saw them. Rather, criticism of mistakes and defects grew sharper and more differentiated" (Helwig 1986:14). Subjects taken up in the 1970s remained an issue and were extensively used in the 1980s, such as environmental pollution, the army, social outcasts, drugs or suicide; subjects about which society and the media kept quiet, as their appearance would have compromised the clean socialist image. Together with the growing pressure from alternative groups and subcultures, writers were less and less prepared to cover up defects in society. However, in a similar fashion to other groups in society, they were not against socialism in general; they only rejected the shape it had taken in East Germany. Since mass media were regimented, literature was assigned extra-literary values, assuming a surrogate role through documenting and informing the people about problems and opinions. Notwithstanding harsh censorship, many books reached their readers and contributed to stirring up emotions. An indication of the growing alienation between Party and people was an emergent sub-cultural scene (the most famous manifestation of which were the authors of *Prenzlauer Berg Szene* in Berlin). These young writers no longer wanted to belong to the establishment. Refusing to join the Writers' Association, they arranged readings in private circles and published their texts in unofficial journals in small print-runs. This decision was based on the legal regulation which stated that works with a circulation of more than 100 copies needed a print permit, which led them to the logical conclusion that circulations of 99 were exempt from censorship (Mix 1995:53). The SED's reluctant attitude in following the relaxations in other socialist countries after Gorbachev's presidency gave rise to widespread disapproval in cultural circles and, in 1987 at the Tenth Writers' Congress, writers were outspoken in their declaration against censorship. "The authorisation procedure, state supervision, or to put it more succinctly and no less clearly, the censorship of publishers and books, of publishers and authors, is outdated, pointless, paradoxical, inhumane, against the interests of the people, illegal and a punishable offence", as Christoph Hein famously stated in 1987 (as quoted in Wichner and Wiesner 1991:34). Similarly, Günter de Bruyn spoke about the restriction of the enlightening effects of literature under the conditions of censorship. If only problems which had already been resolved in society were permitted to pass the censor, then in his opinion literature had lost one of its main functions, namely that of a stimulating debate (1988:129). This time, such words, expressing the bottled-up anger of a professional group that had been suppressed for a long time, did not miss their target. Although debated several times in the development of the GDR, but never put into practice, in January 1989 censorship was abolished.[15] Albeit celebrated as a victory, it did nothing to help the country survive.

1.3.3 Children's Literature

Given the striking correspondence in developments between children's literature and adult literature during the earlier periods of the 1950s and 1960s, one may also expect to find similarities in the 1970s and 1980s. The beginning of the 1970s was viewed as a turning point in children's literature. Changes were considered to be so radical that experts even spoke about the rise of a new image of the child. However, this image was anything but the officially prescribed *Menschenbild*; rather, it was an image quite contrary to the official conviction, which was postulated, for instance, in the *Bildungsgesetz* (Education Law). "Outstanding books of the past 20 years [the 1970s and 1980s] show a new child image, namely that of sceptical, questioning, searching, vulnerable young people, who discover themselves and, in doing so, are often insecure and helpless, who experience limits in East German society and find themselves left alone to pressures of norms and doubt whether they are accepted for being themselves or not" (Kuhnert 1991:41). Heroes came to life whose deeds were merely their quest for their own personality, for acknowledgement and for a meaning in life. They were no superheroes but people whose mistakes and shortcomings the readers could analyse and learn from. As Peltsch has it, "The non-winners, the un-best [heroes] became attractive. . . . The dreamers, the sensitive ones. Characters moved to the centre of interest who so far had had the function of providing a contrast" (1990a:18). In addition, protagonists also increasingly developed an awareness for restrictions imposed on them by society. Kuhnert indicates that more and more children's characters formulated individual objections to paths of development and patterns of behaviour enforced by the authorities. However, children's literature, he claims, offered a possibility to tone down these social antagonisms by portraying them as generation conflict (1991:42). Particularly in later years, "adults are blamed individually and criticised for their behaviour, however, their behaviour is also linked—albeit hidden in irony—to conditions in society" (Rouvel 1995:185). So, for example, Christa Kožik, committed children's book author of the last two decades, has Moritz, her nine-year-old boy character, say, "I'd much rather want to live my life myself instead of having it explained to me" (1980:37). In an interview, Kožik expressed her view on childhood in East Germany, which had prompted her to write her books in the way they were written,

> Several encounters with young people of our society made me painfully aware that some of our children are diligent, well behaved, educated, but also quite 'tamed'. They subordinate too easily to every norm; their intellectual flexibility, their own thinking falls by the wayside. If we continue to press them into a net of dependence, they will become passive and unable to cope with life. But responsibility must be passed on to the next generation.... (Siegel 1985:48)

In unison with the arrival of these new child protagonists and their 'psychologisation', an augmentation in a variety of topics and new narrative techniques emerged for children's literature, a process corresponding to developments in mainstream literature. In a fashion similar to that in mainstream literature, the fantastic element was included in children's narration. Having evolved from a stage in which the fairytale found reception into the canon and when fairy-tale-like and fantastic elements were "rather tolerated than accepted" (Richter 1995c:34) to its eventual recognition in the form of myths and mythical story telling, fantasy found its way into stories for young readers in the 1970s by virtue of pseudo-fantastic features. Positions had changed sufficiently for fantasy to be now "interpreted as an enrichment of notions of realism" (Richter 1987:115), and it was understood that fantasy provided a stimulus for the intellectual growth in children. Also, "leaning on anti-authoritarian and fantasy literature from the West and borrowing from international trends (namely Scandinavian and Soviet books critical of society), an innovative type of children's writing was spurred in the GDR" (Rouvel 1993:12) which made its presence felt in the country and put itself forward as a part of East German culture that had to be taken seriously.

By interweaving fantastic devices with day-to-day events, an artificial world was constructed which at first sight appeared simple but actually received a remarkable new dimension. With the texts becoming more open to interpretation, young readers were challenged to deal actively with these different layers of interpretation through applying imagination and, in so doing, think about and comprehend certain social processes. In this way, it was hoped that the 'fantastic' helped them to see and examine ordinary life afresh and that the present became more transparent and contributed to finding the readers' own position in society (Pieper 1987:31).

On the whole, fantastic novels had two aims: firstly, they were to help children understand and cope with the difficulties and problems in life and activate their inner strength in asserting themselves (*Lebenshilfe*); secondly, they sought to provide reflections on life and society in the GDR. The second goal, in particular, was to have a wider impact on further developments. Following the Biermann incident, after which critical allusions in literature generally increased, critical tendencies also began to show in children's writing. It had always been the case for East German children's literature that it had as its aim (or rather up to then it was required) to initiate social change; this was, however, particularly true for this period. Authors increasingly became advocates for children and urged parents, adults and, in fact, the whole of society to allow children their right to individuality and to take them *really* seriously as the future of society. This was to be understood as an appeal for a less uniform and regimented life at school or in the Pioneer group and for treating children and adolescents with respect by paying attention to their personalities. One of many examples is *Meta Morfoß*, a story written by Peter Hacks for eight-year-olds (1975). Meta, a little girl, has the habit of changing her physical appearance, very much to the surprise and also to the anger of other people who do not recognise her any more. No matter how much trouble or how many complaints Meta's aunt must put up with, she is of the firm belief that, regardless of the opinion of other people, "I don't think that one can change her [Meta] much. And if . . . I could, I don't think I would have the right to do so" (1975:38)—similar words were articulated with growing frequency. A responsible attitude was demanded of society with respect to many topics, first covertly but, in the course of the 1980s, increasingly overtly. "In the 1980s, children's books formulated questions more and more clearly, openly and with more urgency" (Peltsch 1990a:17). These were questions about issues which the public East German discourse attempted to conceal, which therefore did not find any mention or only biased mention in the media and, subsequently, were treated as non-existent in the GDR. The rigid education system was one of them; ecological damage another; disability; antisocial behaviour, in later years suicide among youth; alcoholism—all of these were social problems which, according to the official East German statements, certainly occurred in capitalist countries but which socialism had overcome. Further subjects heavily tabooed but gradually taken up by children's stories were religion, hooliganism, crime, the Wall between East and West and the longing for access to Western countries.[16]

In delivering such a stark warning with the help of children's texts, it becomes apparent that these books were not only directed at their main audience, the children, but at a second, adult readership (one may even argue that they were addressed at a third and fourth reader, i.e. Party functionaries and future grown-ups). As mentioned previously, East German literature, and indeed children's literature as well, had to make up for conformist media reporting. It is for this reason that the picture conveyed in books for a young audience about matters and subjects concerning youth differed greatly from that conveyed in youth magazines and journals. Whereas the latter radiated all-round optimism and happiness, the former portrayed life more truthfully. For authors of books, this meant a continuous battle as to how much truth they were able to pack into a text and how to wrap up the message, in order for it still to be identifiable by the public. As much as adults, children sought contact with authors. In letters, reading sessions, school talks and at conferences, they asked for advice and moral help. Hence, authors saw it as their mission to write about problematic issues. Generally, it was an open secret which books were blocked from publication by censorship and, inevitably, everybody was watching out eagerly for precisely these books to appear on the market eventually, as they carried an important message for the country. Although these books would then be slightly modified and some sensitive passages would be toned down, the public was sensitised enough to pick up signs and read between the lines—Aesopian language[17] was not only a technique employed in the production of texts for adults but also in those for children. It did not happen as frequently in children's as in adult literature that books were refused a print permit, but those few that were denied a permit caused a rush for the bookshops when they were finally published. *Umberto* by Günter Saalmann (1987) was one of them. Written several years before its final publishing date, the book was denied publication for a long time and the author was required to rewrite passages for years, because of its sensitive subject concerning antisocial behaviour in socialist childhood and family life. When it appeared eventually, the public was already highly aware of it and had been waiting impatiently for its arrival.

Bearing in mind that books carrying socio-political criticism through direct realistic narration were more difficult to steer through the censorship procedure, fantastic devices aided in disguising particular facts. Kožik, for instance, states about her book *Der Engel mit dem goldenen Schnurrbart* (published in 1983), "I took advantage consciously of fantasy, in order to give voice to bitter truths . . . Had such statements about our education system been made in a purely realistic way, they would not have been possible" (Kožik 1992:1). The story deals with the arrival of the angel Ambrosius in a girl's home, where he decides to stay. He and the girl become friends and the angel is adopted by the family. However, he has to turn into a 'proper' human being, which includes being sent to school. At first, the principal refuses to have him in his school, because Ambrosius looks different and behaves in a different way. "No angel enters my school. Well, unless . . . he abstains from flying and abides by our school regulations" (1989, 4th ed: 47). Ambrosius agrees only in order to make the little girl happy, but not for himself. One lesson, in which the pupils learn about 'primitive societies as early forms of communist communities', bores him so much that he simply flies out of the window (1989:68–70). Other truths that the book voices are, for example, that lifting oneself off the ground and flying is liberating (and it is telling that the Head teacher has forbidden Ambrosius to fly), although it is pointed out that one better ought not fly too much to the left, since this was forbidden because of the border (1989:31, 32); or that "there are things between heaven and earth that we do not learn at school" (1989:66). Again and again, the story stresses the necessity of Ambrosius "having to adapt to our way of life" (1989:61) and having to make more efforts to fit in; what is more, the procedures to make him fit in turn increasingly severe. So, for instance, he has to wear a pullover instead of his long white nightshirt, in order to hide his wings and to make him unable to fly. With time, his hair turns grey, feathers fall off his wings, his feet hurt (as angels fly and do not usually walk) and he becomes increasingly sad. As expected, the story does not end happily—when the girl begins to clip his wings to force him into conformity, Ambrosius flies out of the window, leaving her behind.

Certainly, social criticism manifested itself particularly in texts which linked a day-to-day story with fantastic elements. Tying in with this phenomenon, Schulz regards the emergence of fantastic literature in children's and adolescent books in the GDR as a warning sign, highlighting the overwhelming level of frustration in the population at being hindered from expressing their own individuality (1993:148). Irrefutably, ambiguity and allegory helped in articulating the most explosive facts. One undoubtedly extraordinary example is the children's novel *Kicki und der König*, which received its print permit in 1989 and was published in 1990, after having been written in 1986/1987 and after a long struggle between the author and the publishing house Kinderbuchverlag, because the publisher deemed the book too rebellious (Kožik 1992:2). In the style of a fairytale, its main plot describes the adventures of a speaking cat who travels round the country with its king, pointing out to him defects and mismanagement which he had failed to see and which, eventually, he puts right. It came as a surprise to many that this book was able to pass the censors at all, because of the blatantly obvious similarities to the GDR. However, it was thought that benevolent censors had turned a blind eye, arguing that the story played in a fairy-tale land, far away, and thus had no connection to any present-day condition. This process, on the whole, seemed to recur many times and the label 'children's literature' appears to have aided many a book carrying controversial subjects to reach readers. It might have been the case that with books addressed 'only at children', which were therefore thought to be innocuous, censors did not look closely enough to notice the underlying connotations of a text. Alternatively, they might have pretended not to notice the nature of the content, for the simple reason that they did not believe children capable of comprehending the allusions and analogies. There is, however, a third, quite audacious explanation, namely that some censors wanted a book to be printed and they thought the easiest way was to justify this position to themselves and in the eyes of watchful Party functionaries by dismissing these as 'only children's books'.

In fact, practices within book reviewing lead to the conclusion that there were forces at work in the country favouring the publication of literature with a critical potential. Assessments of children's books tended to trivialise the message of sensitive texts and avoided the social context—"deliberately", as Richter would have it (1995c:37). This evasion of outspoken criticism by reviewers was, quite frequently, taken as neglectful marginalisation of children's literature in public theoretical discourse. However, it has to be put into political perspective to comprehend fully why reviewers kept clear of salient issues, as in the words of children's book author Peter Abraham, "book reviewers, for sure, knew precisely what a book was about but they were also in alliance with the authors. It was regarded as dishonourable for a reviewer to give the Party an opportunity to reprimand" (1990:7).

Another, quite striking phenomenon in East German children's texts of this period can only be ascribed to this 'exile' status of children's books. It was children's, and not adult literature, that began to depict certain spheres of life, such as damage to the environment and concern for nature, handicapped children and the themes of education and tolerance. The GDR had banned, for instance, ecological issues from public debate far into the 1980s. Ecological disasters were reported only in connection with capitalist countries or "since Perestroika, not without deeper meaning, with the USSR" (Peltsch 1990b:17), if they were reported at all. More than a decade earlier than in adult literature, one of the first children's stories dealing with ecological issues appeared in 1970 (*Der Baum*, Horst Beseler), dealing with the rescue of a tree. It was followed by a range of other, similarly dedicated books, among which an illustrated book for younger readers deserves mention: *Der Klappwald*, Edith Anderson, 1978. In this book, the author portrays a nightmare scenario, in which ecological disasters have struck the country and people choke in fumes, rubbish, traffic and concrete. Because there are no trees and no green around any more, an old man—reminiscing on bygone days—cuts out paper trees in the desire to build a forest, an enterprise that in the end fails deplorably when rain soaks all the paper. In the East German environment of heavy industry which did not shy away from destroying entire villages and displacing their population into concrete blocks of flats in satellite towns, this book illustrates to young children the significance of an intact nature and the importance of protecting it. Equally, trusting in children's natural need to bond and befriend and in their desire for harmony, literature took up the subject of outcasts from society and handicapped people. The aim was not so much to create feelings of pity in the children but to teach them consideration for people's individuality and respect for one another. Again, dozens of children's books had dealt with these subjects long before adult literature began to take up the theme.

In children's literature, no sub-scene similar to the *PrenzlauerBerg Szene* took place for the obvious reason that children's authors dealt with a different audience which needed to be addressed through the official channels of publishing. Also, children's authors did not wish to lodge their protest by withdrawing from the official literary stage because they endeavoured to deliver their message to as wide a readership as possible; and as in adult literature, their aim was not so much to abolish socialism as a political system but to introduce reforms within the country. To this end, they realised increasingly that children's texts could be a viable vehicle for the dissemination of their protests. When Sibylle Durian manifested her opposition in her children's novel *Der Tag, an dem die Schule verschwand* (1985) by calling the everlasting 'Positive hero' Timur a fearful boy, she not only scratched the East German hero image but undermined the ideology of the GDR nation (Rouvel 1995:182). When Wolf Spillner (*Wasseramsel*, 1984) has a company director erect a private weekend house in a nature reserve, he shook the very foundations of the East German bureaucracy with its practice of according privileges to Party functionaries and Party members. When Spillner, in 1987 (*Taube Klara*), told about the killing of a pigeon, the pet and last refuge from total isolation for an old woman, by her daughter-in-law, he—like many others—made an appeal for more tolerance for individual freedom and freedom from prescriptive and authoritarian attitudes. How serious children's authors were in their intention is indicated by the 'Theoretical conferences on the occasion of the Children's Literature Days' in 1988 and 1989. After the vociferous demands of 1987 for more freedom by abolishing the censorship ritual, these two children's literary conferences followed suit, emphasising the social value of tolerance and calling for open confrontation. Werner Heiduczek encouraged his fellow-writers to "wanton thoughts according to which that which is forbidden is often that which is actually required. . . . Christa Kožik expressed her opinion about literature . . . by adding, it [literature] acted as a diagnosis and an indicator and it should warn against unhealthy developments in good time" (Kuhnert 1991:50). There is no doubt that Kožik put into words this belief when writing her book *Kicki und der König*, which was heralded as the "first Perestroika book in the GDR" (Peltsch 1990a:23) by those working with the manuscript and those knowing it. Thus, had socialist rule not ended before the actual publication of this book, children's literature would again have acted as a trendsetter by pointing out defects in the country and calling outspokenly for a comprehensive programme of reforms.

A concluding point may need to be made for clarification. The dogmatic type of children's writing remained on the market throughout. This was literature written, for instance, on the occasion of anniversaries or chronicling the life of politicians or ideologues, dutifully hailing the superiority of socialism. It was, however, the other type of children's literature that challenged outdated taboos and encouraged young people towards self-exploration and a closer examination of real life. It is arguable whether to call this literature subversive or not. Some would happily agree with this stance as they link, with it, the connotation of dissidence and undermining the system. Peltsch is one of those who tend to disagree. In his opinion, the term 'subversion' is too drastic, because it targets a complete dismantling of the system which the intelligentsia did not want; "they wanted another GDR and not no GDR" (personal communication, 14 April 2002). Whichever of these two views one subscribes to, in every respect, East German children's literature had become an engaged literature in its reflections of social and political conditions and was prepared to take an active stand in the pursuit of its intents and ideals.

From what has been shown, the regime's need of directing all literary output becomes very apparent. It was not only literature written for adults that followed a certain trend reacting to events on the political stage; children's literature did so too. This would suggest that books for young readers were definitely not marginalised. What is more, another fact becomes more than evident: both systems clearly followed the same patterns. Whereas the early years saw the production of orthodox books, children's as well as adults', rigidly following the cultural political directives of the state, both systems commenced to open themselves at the same time, incorporating the same techniques and, thereafter, increasingly allowing the inclusion of aspects critical of the state and its politics. With a parallel development as striking as this, there are two conclusions one may arrive at. The first is that the literary scene was fully interconnected, linking each action to another; consequently, what affected one had a follow-on effect on the others. The second is the observation that there was a power somewhere who, similar to the director of a stage production, pulled the strings behind the scenes and was very much in charge of the entire production.

Throughout this discussion there is the ever-present issue of translated literature. Although East German cultural politics concentrated on producing home-grown literature appropriate to the education of the masses, there was always the concept of translating literature from other languages, especially from the USSR. What then was the position of translations from the English-speaking canon of world literature? Originating from the class enemies, the translation of books from the English-speaking world would be expected to undergo special scrutiny. This study aims to show that the special circumstances (i.e. the documentation of censorship) that existed in the GDR allow an insight into the process by which ideology affects the translation of literature both directly and indirectly. The following section provides an overview of the production of translated works from English, in order to set the context in which the discourse in the 'print permit files' and 'afterwords' for these translations took place (Chapters 3, 4 and 5).

1.4 Translated Books for Young People

As can be seen from the general discussion earlier, the objective of re-engineering society was taken seriously, so much so that the country was even locked away and nothing but socialist influences were permitted to enter. It is demonstrated in later chapters that this desire also led to a closure of the literary border and that censorship determined what kind of literature was given permission to cross this border. Foreign children's literature was viewed with extraordinary suspicion because of the alien concepts it carried, especially that from non-socialist societies. Given this rigid control, the questions now to be asked are: which were the foreign books that were deemed acceptable, what were their characteristics, and were there any trends similar to the development of indigenous writing for young people? These are questions for which this section attempts to provide some answers.

Before turning to the issue of genres of books, it may be of interest to determine the scale of translated literature within the total book production. Given that Kinderbuchverlag and Neues Leben were the two state publishing houses responsible for the majority of the output in books for young readers, only their production will be considered in the following investigation. The figures underlying the analysis derive from the *Verlagsverzeichnis* (publishing programme) published by each publisher, covering the period between 1949 and 1989 (Kinderbuchverlag) and 1946 and 1989 (Neues Leben), respectively.

Table 1.1 illustrates the proportions of published books (1946/1949–1989) according to the following regional categories:

- GDR indigenous
- Socialist countries (translations from books originating in the Soviet Union and former Eastern Bloc countries)
- Europe (excluding Great Britain and Ireland)
- English (British, Irish, American, Canadian, Australian and from Asian or African states but written in English)
- Other (for instance, African or Asian countries, yet translated from texts written in their national language)

The figures in Table 1.1 appear to indicate that both publishers were producing approximately the same proportions of national and foreign literature. This is in accordance with the East German tenet of publishers aligning their production with particular *Proportionen* (ratios in book production according to the country of origin of the book, see p 81), as stipulated by the government. Judging from the figures, this ratio seems to have been, for children's books, approximately 20% from other Eastern Bloc countries (*sozialistisches Ausland*) and between 60% and 75% for home-grown production.

Table 1.1 Production Percentages

Region	*Neues Leben Production Percentage*	*Kinderbuchverlag Production Percentage*
GDR	65.3	77.1
Socialist	19.4	17.4
Europe	7.7	2.7
English	7.1	2.6
Other	0.5	0.3

The remainder was reserved for publications from the non-socialist world (*kapitalistisches Ausland*). The two diagrams reveal that the average proportion from the non-socialist world was higher for Neues Leben, a fact that may be explained by the older age group of the target audience. Kinderbuchverlag had a large number of books addressed at very small children, many of them only a few pages long and containing little tales or nursery rhymes, hence leaving less room for the publication of foreign books for slightly older children. The higher figure representing the indigenous output by Kinderbuchverlag substantiates this assumption. Also, the dramatic decrease of translations of English-language picture books further reveals the main emphasis on East German production for the little ones (see discussion on picture book genre following).

The proportion of books translated from English, at approximately 5% over the entire period, appears to be quite a low overall figure. However, if the political situation and the difficulties in producing foreign literature are taken into consideration, it may be argued that it is higher than expected. The fact that nowadays translations from abroad make up only 1–4% of the entire production of children's books in Great Britain and the USA (Thomson-Wohlgemuth 2005:88) also puts the proportion of 5% in East Germany in a different light—especially when taking into consideration the political circumstances. Whereas nowadays Great Britain and the USA are free to choose their production out of the entire global production available, the East German 5% refer only to the English-language market with the additional obstacle of severe censorship, which even further reduced the number of books accessible for a translation project.

It has been demonstrated in the previous section that GDR literature for young people, especially in the period before 1970, was intended to bring art and life closer together and that it was considered by some as *Gebrauchsliteratur* (functional literature). Contemporary East German books, like novels of production, portrayed a socialist reality with the aim of reinforcing an East German national identity. English literature could not be utilised to such an end because, on the whole, it was not written to advertise socialism. How then was Western literature made to fit in? Probing the individual titles that were selected for translation, it is found that, generally, there were two kinds of books chosen to be translated. Firstly, there were those books describing Western, i.e. capitalist, societies in a negative light, with the covert motive of making socialism appear superior; secondly, there were texts which did not emphasise negative aspects but provided some education of a general kind and were, therefore, regarded as appropriate and useful for children. Books of the second category were books that did not oppose the fundamental political ideological line and that could be subsumed into the acknowledged canon. With the help of skilful interpretation and rewriting (see Chapters 3, 4 and 5), they could be declared as 'bourgeois humanist heritage' and, as such, were no longer deemed harmful, because they could be appropriated to the requirements of Socialist Realism.

It was equally as important for translated books to conform to the paradigm of Socialist Realism as it was for texts written in the GDR. This becomes clear when studying the discourse with which publishers described and advertised the books to the censor. In particular, books which did not supply a socio-critical portrayal of the West necessitated validation by using Marxist-Leninist concepts. The two main principles employed in almost all descriptions were those of Realism and Humanism. Realism was an acceptable narrative mode, regardless of whether the book dealt with depicting life in Dickensian times or in the America of the 1970s (e.g. the anthology *Unser weißer Hirsch*, Petersen, 1978, Kinderbuchverlag); Humanism was defined as a notion, comprising many facets, for instance, support for the oppressed (e.g. *Im Augenblick der Stille*, Benson, 1974, Neues Leben), or active fighting for equality or freedom (e.g. *Johnny geht zur Schule*, Hellstrom-Kennedy, 1961, Neues Leben), or simply showing respect for other people or creatures (e.g. the picture book *Jannis Deckchen*, Miller, 1969, Kinderbuchverlag). Books defined as 'meaningful to children' were fulfilling their requirement of being *volksverbunden*; be it, for example, children helping a soldier who does not want to stay in Ireland and be responsible for the death of innocent people (*Der Deserteur*, Gray, 1978, Kinderbuchverlag) or a boy being reassured of his grandmother's love for him, even though a witch had turned him into a mouse (*Hexen hexen*, Dahl, 1988, Kinderbuchverlag). Optimism in translated English-speaking books was not so much linked with radiating a bright positive future for the socialist/communist society, but it was sufficient to express optimism about actions that promised a successful outcome and proved to the reader that it was worthwhile becoming involved (e.g. *Schnappschüsse*, Gray, 1982, Kinderbuchverlag). The 'Typicality' of a situation could be shown in any books depicting historical or cultural settings in a context considered representative of that time or location (such as a Jewish Shtetl in *Die Purim Ziege*, Suhl, 1983, Kinderbuchverlag; or the feudalist society in *Ivanhoe*, Scott, 1965, Neues Leben).

Translated literature could, just like indigenous literature, prove to be Partisan by subordinating its ideological stance to the Party's cultural political stipulations or by giving evidence that the foreign author was in support of the socialist cause. The only concept that English-language texts were not able to exhibit was that of the socialist 'Positive hero', understandably, since brigade workers in factories or co-operative farmers did not feature in Western books. However, in earlier years, foreign books could make up for this shortcoming by showing determined, energetic, steadfast, yet sympathetic, caring and honest protagonists (like Jane Eyre in *Die Waise von Lowood*, Brontë, 1963, Kinderbuchverlag) or the picture book character Indian Two Feet in *Der kleine Zweifuß und sein Pferd*, Friskey, 1961, Altberliner Lucie Groszer) and, as it transpired, from the 1970s, the notion of the 'Positive hero' had eventually lost its importance. What all the books translated had in common was a real-life situation with which children were confronted, explaining to them that life did not take place in a secluded, secure surrounding but that, sometimes, it presented one with problems that needed to be faced. Books with a beautified, sentimentalised depiction of life or in which events and adventures took place in a sheltered environment were never considered for translation.

With respect to the various events in East German cultural politics and the developmental stages of East German indigenous literature, a correlation between these and translated English books is visible. However, it was dependent on the respective genre as to how closely it followed the overall trend. This opens the question of the reasons behind changes in the production for specific genres and, in general, what affected each genre.

Table 1.2 provides a breakdown of the various types of literature (constituting the output of all East German children's book publishers and also all other books classified as 'children's' by the National Bibliography), which were translated from English and brought out for children and adolescents in the period between 1961 and 1989. On the whole, the groupings are self-explanatory; three, however, might need further clarification. 'Adventure'[18] has been defined as comprising classic stories out of copyright (e.g. stories by Defoe, Dickens, London, Stevenson, Swift, etc.) dealing with quests, missions or conflicts, involving action and courage of the (mainly) male protagonist. General fiction entails stories of romance and historical content, modern adventure stories featuring children as protagonists (e.g. books by Eilis Dillon) but also the few books with a fantastic plot, such as *The Hobbit*, *Doctor Dolittle* or *Winnie-the-Pooh*, which cannot be ascribed to the fairy-tales genre and which were published at irregular intervals in the period under investigation. The very small figure of 'other' is made up by poetry productions (thin booklets produced intermittently by Neues Leben) and two books by church publishers, one a children's bible, the other a factual book about the construction of a cathedral.

As Table 1.2 demonstrates, adventure stories represent by far the highest proportion; and this for several reasons. Although adventure stories had been frowned upon in the very beginning, it was soon found that children enjoyed and needed literature with suspense and action, which resulted in a rise in

Table 1.2 Percentage of Production (1961–1989) by Genre

Adventure	*General Fiction*	*Contemporary Socio-critical*	*Fairy and Folk tales*	*Wild West*	*Racism*	*Crime and Detective Stories*	*Picture Books*	*Animal Stories*	*Science Fiction*	*Girls' Books*	*Other*
40.8	14.8	8.7	7.4	7.2	5.4	4.4	3.5	2.2	1.2	0.2	4.2

status for this genre. Even more importantly, this was literature of which in the earlier years there was not much home-grown East German writing available, thus allowing foreign adventure books to fill the gap. Moreover, these were novels not only deemed suitable for boys but also for girls, since there was a directive to educate girls in the same fashion as boys. Further, the adventure genre did not pose too many difficulties for incorporation into the GDR canon, because of its tendency to favour descriptions that could be classified as realistic and humanist. Tied in with this, it was classed as high-quality literature, adding extra weight to the books in the midst of concerns and warnings to keep pulp literature out of the country, in particular that stemming from the West. This, in turn, supported the argument of a literature that provided useful education apart from being enjoyable and exciting reading. Another factor may have been that, in the 1950s and 60s, a large number of Western children's books still conveyed a typically bourgeois picture, which made their translation to the GDR impossible. This meant, further, that there were not many books for publishers to choose from, should they consider the production of foreign books; and of course, the indisputable advantage was that these texts, due to their age, had fallen out of copyright and, thus, were cheaper to produce, an argument weighing heavily in the literary scenario of the post-war years where money was scarce.

The graph of adventure publications shown in Figure 1.1 is higher compared to the graphs of the other genres, making classic adventure stories the most published genre. Overall, however, the linear trend shows a slight decline, which may be a direct result of the corresponding rise of other genres due to the country's more lenient approach towards arts and literature from the 1970s.

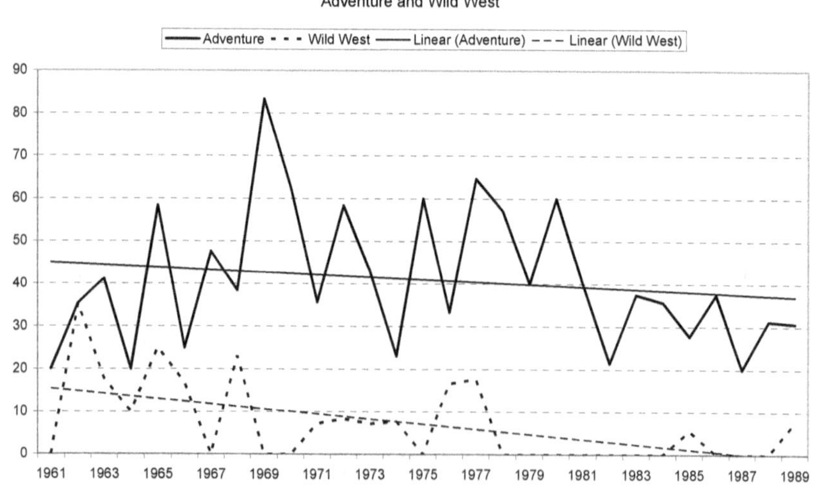

Figure 1.1 Adventure and Wild West publications.

Another genre displaying a decrease in production was that of Wild West literature (also Figure 1.1). It may be assumed that this decline occurred for reasons similar to the classic adventure story. The high numbers produced in the earlier years are due, in the main, to several editions of James Fenimore Cooper, by Kinderbuchverlag and Neues Leben, respectively. This, again, may be explained by the texts' ideological purposefulness (against the oppression and extinction of native Americans), by their inherent didactic usefulness and by the circumstance that their production was affordable, because there was no longer copyright on the books. Similar to adventure books, Wild West literature may have found itself replaced by other genres in later years. What is more, in the 1980s, Neues Leben began their publication of Karl May books, which had been banned, but which young readers had craved for decades, because of their image, as they were sold and widely read by children in West Germany.

Two genres that gained an increased share of the market were crime and detective literature and contemporary socio-critical literature with topics from non-socialist societies. The root of this upsurge may be attributed to the widening of the canon because, from the 1970s, novels written in East Germany became increasingly critical while, simultaneously, integrating fantastic elements and centering around heroes that had more depth of character; a development which also had an impact on the kind of books permitted to enter the country from a Western society. For three decades, crime literature had been in disfavour (albeit that indigenous crime stories were present and published), because it was regarded as low-brow and not suitable for children; and only in the 1980s did it become possible for translated children's literature to embrace stories by A.C. Doyle, Edgar Wallace and G.K. Chesterton (see Section 4.5, Case Study 5, Crime and detective literature). The increase in the output of crime stories coincided, once more, with the fact that the copyright for all three authors had expired, which made a production in the GDR considerably easier. In contrast, socio-critical novels dealing with problems in non-socialist (especially capitalist) societies had not posed much of an ideological problem in the earlier years; however, East Germany's opening to the West politically and economically (from the 1970s) was not unimportant for co-productions and, to a certain degree, for the acquisition of rights to the books. Perhaps one may also argue that, in the 1970s and 1980s, literature for young people produced in the West had also become more critical, dealing more outspokenly with shortcomings and social problems, which therefore made for just the kind of literature suitable for publication in East Germany.

As to Science Fiction, it is very evident that, before 1972, this genre had been rejected since times were not ripe for fantasy and unrealistic depictions. The production of Science Fiction commenced with the official recognition of fantastic descriptions in literature and with the institution of a department for *wissenschaftlich-phantastische Literatur* (i.e. Science Fiction) in the Writers' Association in 1972. Children's literature did not take long to react and published a Science Fiction anthology of translated stories in 1972.

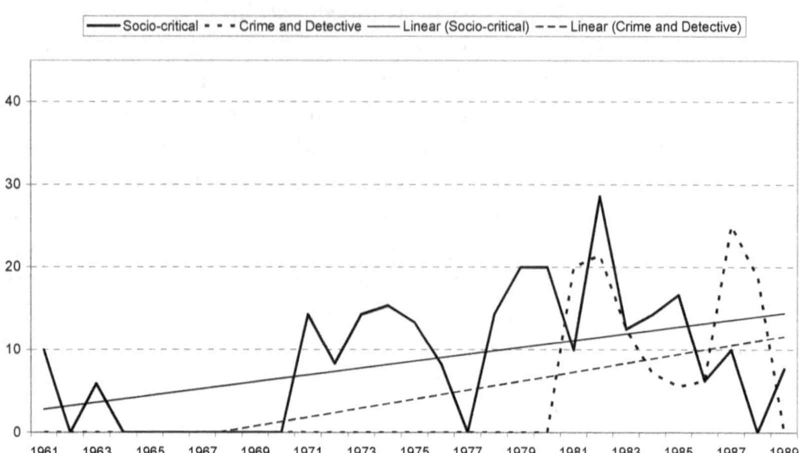

Figure 1.2 Contemporary socio-critical and Crime and detective publications.

The fact that the linear trend does not demonstrate a noticeable upward trend may be attributed to the genre being relatively new in literary terms and that, therefore, royalties would have been due if a publisher wanted to bring out a Science Fiction story. In contrast, home-grown Science Fiction writing experienced an augmentation and thrived (as did the home-grown crime and detective story—not only for financial reasons, it may be added, but also because both genres lent themselves to concealed criticism directed at politics and politicians, as Hillich describes in his article, 2005:105–116).

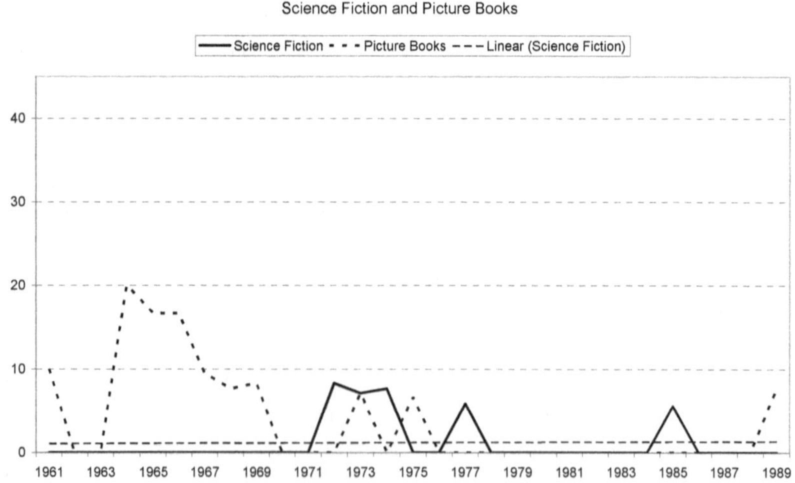

Figure 1.3 Science Fiction and picture book publications.

It may come as a surprise that the production of picture books reduced to such a degree that, after 1975, only one picture book was translated from English. This decline, however, may be ascribed exclusively to reasons of finance. The production of picture books is relatively expensive and the country was permanently struggling to find sufficient foreign currency for even urgent projects. Thus, the decision may have been to drop the production of foreign picture books altogether and to focus on home publications, employing artists resident in the country and with the additional benefit of topics that were specifically tailored to East German requirements. This assumption is substantiated by the two picture book productions in 1975 and 1989 by Kinderbuchverlag. The author, Elizabeth Shaw, an Irish national who had taken residence in the GDR, published in each year a picture book both originally written in English and subsequently translated into German.

The genres of animal stories, fairy and folk tales, general fiction and fiction dealing with racism, slavery and the issue of Afro-Americans in the America of the present day demonstrate a fairly steady, if not unexciting, production, suggestive of a recurrent and unchanging demand. This may also be the explanation underlying the somewhat erratic curve related to animal stories. The fact that books from this genre were again produced in the 1980s, despite a zero production over a period of several years, may not indicate a loss in interest but rather may be, once more, motivated by money matters, especially when considering that the books brought out in 1984 and 1985 were re-editions, which meant that they were cheaper to produce and had already been granted a print permit in earlier years. It would seem that Kinderbuchverlag had opted, during these years of absence, to spend their quota of foreign currency on literature that could be of more immediate interest to East German children. Again, it may be conceivable

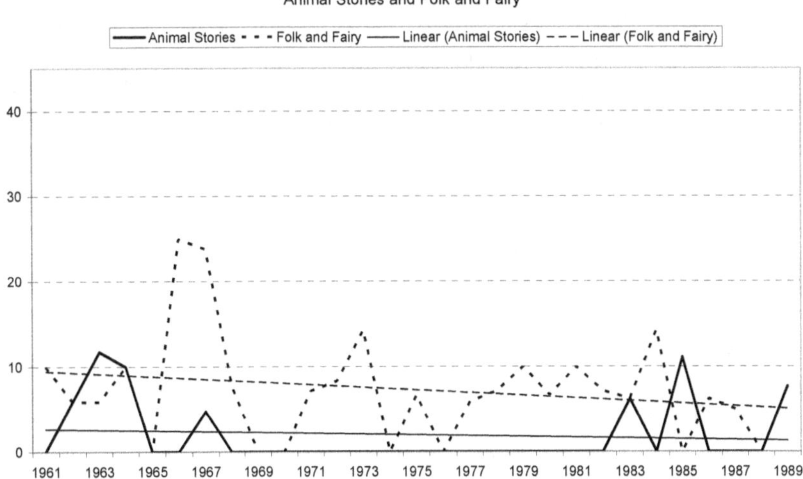

Figure 1.4 Animal story and fairy and folk tale publications.

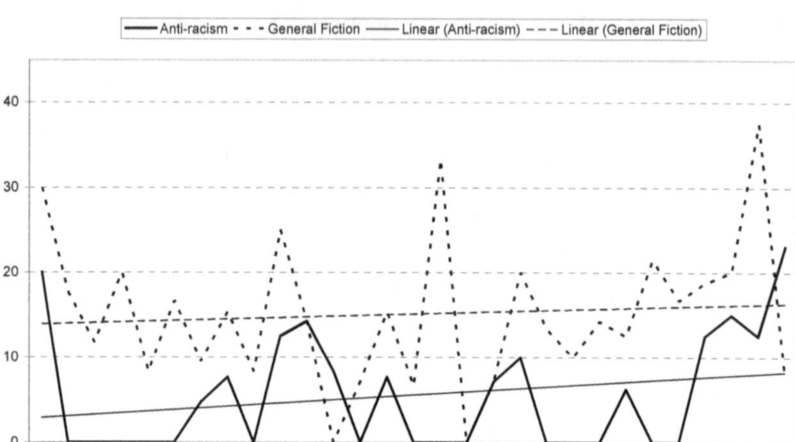

Figure 1.5 Anti-racism and general fiction publications.

that no books were available in the West appropriate to the GDR's criterion of authenticity and depiction of animals in their genuine habitat.

Girls' books is the last genre to be examined. It is striking to find the production of merely one book in 1963, particularly given that this genre has for long been highly popular in Germany. Already in the Germany of the nineteenth century, the so-called *Backfischroman* was addressed at the young female audience, attempting to persuade girls to give up personal ambitions of self-realisation and find happiness in married life looking after children and household. Although topics have been adapted to the respective conditions of a changing German society, German publishers to this day address girls specifically, producing books that portray a more or less stereotypical life (e.g. *Schneiderbücher* by publisher Franz Schneider in Munich).

As stated earlier, girls' books did not represent a genre much in favour. Although, with time, the genre gained in reputation and East German authors indeed wrote fiction for girls, Western novels portrayed values incompatible with the East German worldview. Not unexpectedly, the only girls' book produced in the GDR, in 1963, was not what one could call characteristic of a girls' book: it was the first part of Charlotte Brontë's *Jane Eyre*, a production, for which—again—financial considerations may have been the decisive factor for publication.

Being embedded in the East German cultural landscape and integrated in publishing policies, there is little doubt that translated literature was affected by national politics. Up to the mid-1960s, while East German writing was motivated by the need to conform and stories were populated by fictional characters who were predominantly happy and thought positively about socialism, translated books were restricted to the realm of classic stories. Although both types of literature were officially declared as being representative of reality by the cultural establishment, neither of them were; the first, East German novels, depicted a fake idealised 'socialist' reality and the second, translated ones depicted romanticised stories from another time and age. With the later integration of mythological elements into literature, both systems experienced a change. It is not coincidental that, in 1968, Franz Fühmann retold Shakespeare tales for East German children (Kinderbuchverlag) and, in 1972, Shakespeare's *Midsummer Night's Dream* (also Kinderbuchverlag), as this corresponds exactly with the phase where mythological stories from the classics were being retold in indigenous GDR literature. This was the first stage in opening the gates to the wider literary world.

From then onward, East German contemporary novels underwent, step by step, a gradual adjustment towards the portrayal of reality in the chosen texts; an array of human emotions was permitted and stories were no longer limited strictly to a realistic narration. Also, light fiction was no longer frowned upon, as long as it fitted in with the still prevalent didactic purposes. As to books imported from the West, they also underwent a transformation. If in previous decades the publication output was predominantly dedicated to classics; now increasingly contemporary stories (particularly from the USA) appeared on the bookshelves. These were novels presenting protagonists who had become conscious of and were critical of an adverse situation; many of whom had become self-aware, were depicted as thinking about their role in society and whose self-reflection went together with deep emotional turmoil. This development of opening the canon to more contemporary Western novels commenced, in 1970, with James Ngugi's book *The River Between*, in which the author described the reactions of Africans towards their colonialising oppressors and their achievement of self-determination; this book was followed by Anne Moody's *Coming of Age in Mississippi* (1971, Neues Leben) and Reba Lewis' *The Brahman and the Belle* (1971, Neues Leben) representing the pioneers of the new attitude in the GDR. The acceptance of a fantastic element made possible the publication of *The Hobbit* (Tolkien, 1971, Kinderbuchverlag), several Science Fiction volumes, later crime and detective stories and culminated, in 1988, with Dahl's *The Witches* (Kinderbuchverlag), the production of which would have been beyond the bounds of possibility only a few years earlier (see Section 4.3, Case Study 3, Roal Dahl *Hexen hexen*).

Despite the indisputable parallels between indigenous and translated literature, there is one difference. The East German contemporary novels of the 1970s and 80s more and more turned into a tool with which authors voiced their protest about East German social and political conditions; East German fantastic literature was a means to express criticism that could not be expressed openly otherwise. For obvious reasons, translations from the West were not written as a specific allegory of conditions in the GDR. If Western contemporary novels exhibited a critical dimension, they found fault with

America, Britain or perhaps some group of people who were holding or seeking power over others.

From what has been said about English-language (and perhaps other Western) books for a young audience which were selected for translation, it has become apparent that their role was largely to complement what publishers had planned as their primary production. Of course, the shortage of foreign currency constituted a restriction to begin with; however, it was first and foremost ideology that posed a severe obstacle, giving precedence to a literature that was distinctly separated from that of non-socialist societies and, therefore, did not leave English literature much room, other than filling out gaps in the home production. Given the state's mission to re-educate its citizens and re-shape society, it is more than evident that indigenous writing could best fulfil what was officially required from texts 'useful' to children. Indigenous writing could also react with immediacy to particular home situations and circumstances, which authors felt needed to be addressed, as was the case especially in later years. In this, the majority of English source texts did not have much to contribute and, thus, necessarily could only assume a marginal place. Moreover, those translated books that were accepted into the native canon were selected with a particular concern for their suitability to support domestic affairs.

Chapter Two
Publishers and the Lion's Den

In the majority of cases, it is the task of publishing houses to select, edit and publish texts. However, all these activities take place within a social context and are affected by political policies, administrative structures and other social interactions of the society in which they take place. Therefore, in order to gain a better insight into translation processes in East Germany, it is helpful to take a look at publishing policies and strategies as they developed under the socialist regime. It is the objective of this chapter to explore the processes put in place within the publishing machinery and to investigate where key decisions about the publication of books were made and, further, how they were reached. Hence, this chapter examines the hierarchical structures in the planning and monitoring processes and, also, the instruments with which this control was exercised.

Bearing in mind the findings of the previous chapter, which unearthed close parallels between adult and children's literature, this chapter again demonstrates similarities between these two literary systems—not unexpectedly, since the GDR constituted a centralised society, where all power was concentrated in a single party. With respect to the book industry, therefore, all publishers were treated the same, regardless of whether they produced books for a younger or an adult audience. With the same cultural paradigms prevailing, the criteria for the choice of books were the same throughout the industry and so were the strictures placed on publishers during their selection process. It is for this reason that processes and publishers' strategies are discussed in general terms and mention of specific children's literary matters is made only in those cases where aspects or incidents particular to the children's literature sector need to be pointed out, or in order to supply useful background information. This once more provides evidence of a children's literary system that was held in high esteem and was valued by society as highly as mainstream literature.

Formulating this chapter was complicated by the interdependence of structures within East German society. The main dependency network was found to be between the state and the Party apparatus and the often unfathomable structures and relations between these two authorities. Although outwardly it was the state and its bureaucracies that directed the actions of the country, it was the Party that sat in the background watching, controlling and correcting the course of events, when it saw the need. The nature of this interdependency makes it difficult to determine the extent of influence each had in reality. Another cause of difficulty lay with the practice of withholding information, particularly near the top of the hierarchy, and of only including certain people at certain times for certain tasks. Even high Party functionaries were included in this culture of secrecy. Possessing information meant possessing power. Thus, secretiveness and keeping facts to oneself was a characteristic of those in power, a behaviour which exacerbated—if not impeded—any communication between the different spheres of society and which had the side-effect of provoking rumours and doubt; at the same time this is a behaviour which, years later, generates considerable problems for the researcher who tries to look through, and make sense of, the dense jungle of relations and structures. A typical feature of this opaqueness was the possibility of arbitrary decisions made by powerful players within the system. Cultural politics kept changing in cycles, alternating between more and less lenient times. Even within the censorship authority there appear to have been two, if not more, cultural political lines competing with each other and, in spite of the prescribed Party-line, there seems to have been some room for manoeuvre and some leeway to interpret or even circumvent Party resolutions. What is more, it appears that under certain conditions official decisions could be circumvented by informal, orally agreed arrangements. Knowing the right person, at a level higher than one's own position, could effect miracles and in sensitive and urgent cases it may have been more useful to address the higher functionaries directly. Mixing all of these ingredients together creates a cocktail of ambiguity and impenetrability, most unwelcome for any researcher.

Censorship in the GDR was a concept which involved far more than mere text manipulation. It also entailed, for instance, all the editorial pre-work, the handling of resources, such as paper and ink, or the influencing of foreign trade in books. It manifested itself as a complicated network of institutions and bodies which, on one hand, worked in isolation from each other but which, on the other hand, were connected through hidden, intertwined paths. Although it can be seen that clear sets of rules had been laid out, nevertheless, book production became an uncertain venture. Already strenuous for the publishers, such a set-up becomes even more demanding to the researcher. It appears at first sight that an utterly indecipherable system of guiding and monitoring had been in operation, with units weaving horizontally and vertically, in which regulations were written down but, at times, could be avoided. Moreover, censorship, and everything connected to it, is an area of the East German society about which, nowadays, some would rather remain silent. After all, censorship itself was taboo and, according to Ulbricht in 1968, there was no such thing as censorship in the GDR (Jäger 1993:18). As a result, much is hushed up; there are gaps in information, contradictions and misinformation, as different people have different viewpoints on one and the same issue from the past. Further, much information was destroyed in the short period just after the GDR regime collapsed; as Joachim Walther explained to me, after the collapse of the GDR government in November 1989 until the German re-unification in March 1990, the Modrow government[1] allowed comrades to cleanse their own files; "for weeks, the files of the HV Verlage und Buchhandel[2] had been cleansed by the SED members of these institutions, similarly the files of the Writers' Association, Copyright Office, etc. . . . Since I occupied myself politically with the transformation processes during this time, I was able to see this cleansing in person, for instance, in the Writers' Association or in the HV Verlage und Buchhandel" (Joachim Walther, 7 January 2005). There appears indeed to be truth in Walther's words, since there are gaps in the print permit files in the Bundesarchiv Berlin, i.e. the paperwork stemming from the Ministry of Culture, where the censorship authority was located, and not all publishers' applications for print permits for children's books can be found in the files.

The preceding scenario makes it a mammoth task for the researcher to see through these complex and complicated structures of interwoven sub-systems and to present a complete picture. It is for this reason that, despite tireless effort and endeavour to uncover the details, descriptions in this chapter cannot be exhaustive and no claim for comprehensiveness can be made. The following is based not only on source material found in books and articles but also on personal interviews and e-mails with people who knew the system, because they either worked in it during GDR times or because they have researched and published on this topic themselves.

2.1 Party and State Apparatus

The following provides a brief description of the Party and state hierarchies, illustrating the main nuclei of power. Authoritative structures and area of competence are described only insofar as they serve the purpose of understanding the scope of this study.

2.1.1 Party Sector

Similar to cultural politics (as laid down in the Party Programme of the SED and in the resolutions of the Central Committee and being defined there as the only valid political orientation), in publishing too there was to be "no private policy of any person; equally, there exist[ed] no right of any individuals or institutions to advocate any other line than that decided by the Party" (Hager 1984, as quoted in Ackermann 2000:15). Being the representative of the working classes, the Party claimed political as well as ideological leadership in all spheres of life, rigorously enforcing this right, and this was no different in all matters relating to book production. It is firstly for this reason and, secondly, for the particular role that culture and literature played in socialism that the SED felt itself entitled to monitor each phase of book production and dissemination. It was argued that, because of the high status and great significance of culture, a system of 'planning and guiding' [variously referred to as *Planung und Lenkung, Planung und Leitung, Planung und Anleitung, Planung und Steuerung*] had to be introduced for all cultural institutions (Autorenkollektiv unter Leitung von Heinz Püschel 1969:12). The fact that the Party considered itself as the representatives of the populace seemed to give them sufficient licence to influence all cultural developments. Party functionaries operated (sometimes more, sometimes less) in the background and key decisions originated from the highest Party hierarchies, as will become evident. There was a determination not to let the written word stand in the way of Party interests and of the officially declared dogma of societal progress. When maintaining that it was "up to the society to plan and guide and to decide when a work deserved to be produced and disseminated" (Autorenkollektiv unter Leitung von Heinz Püschel 1969:56), it was in actual fact the Party who gave orders and wielded control. "As regards the literary system—the most important decisions, such as filling director's posts, distribution of resources, co-ordination of plans etc., the Party reserved for itself" (Löffler 2002:2).

The East German state and government did not, however, truly represent the citizens nor work in their interest. Although ministries, a council of ministers and the *Volkskammer* were installed, these were widely considered to be marionettes under the control of the SED. This means, the state was used as an instrument of power by the SED, "a tool in the hands of the working class . . . in order to build socialism" (Glücksmann 1962:4). In other words, state institutions were installed by the SED for the purpose of creating and bringing into force the kind of control necessary for transforming society towards a communist ideal. All institutions linked with children's literary production were subsumed into this framework, precisely as was the case with adult literature.

The hierarchy of Party control is described in the following sections and is illustrated in Figure 2.1:

1. **Secretary General** As the supreme decision-maker, he had the power to intervene in processes in the last instance. He also held the position of chairman of the Politburo, i.e. the most important control centre of political power.
2. **The Politburo** This acted as the "head of the bureaucratic hierarchy of power and supreme body for decision-making with binding resolutions" (Walther 1999:43). At the time of East Germany's demise, the Politburo consisted of 21 members and 5 candidates. It was responsible for all planning, decision-making and control in all key areas and it dealt with all political issues of general importance but especially of contentious content; "members of the Politburo tended to seize decisions which, in their opinion, were of political significance. This was made possible through a lack

of legal provision about the competence of the supreme authority levels for state matters" (Löffler 2002:2, 3). Regarding production and dissemination of books, the Politburo's members' main competences were: granting publishing licences and, through these licences, defining delimited areas of working; decisions about ownership of publishing houses and enterprises of the book trade; the fundamental political ideological direction of cultural politics; this went as far as becoming involved in individual literary procedures and decisions. The Politburo's resolutions were binding for all authorities, be it state or Party.

3. **Sekretariat des ZK** (Secretariat of the Central Committee) This was the supreme executive authority in the state. It formulated the draft-resolutions for the Politburo's regular meetings, executed the Politburo resolutions and directed the state apparatus; under Honecker, the *Sekretariat des ZK* consisted of four *ZK Sekretäre* (directors of *Sekretariat des ZK*); a *ZK-Sekretär* was automatically also a member of the Politburo, which, in practice, meant that the same people prepared topics and resolutions, later discussed them in their capacity as members of the Politburo and, subsequently, executed what they had planned and decided. Thus, all power was concentrated in this office, making it part of the "inner circle of power" (Walther 1999:43). The *Sekretariat* also appointed the so-called Commissions, i.e. committees for particular areas of society. Two Commissions were of interest for publishing:
    1. Ideological Commission (president: chief ideologue Kurt Hager, 1960–1989), which was called into existence in 1960 and which was concerned with all cultural political issues.
    2. Paper Commission, which was responsible for the distribution of paper, used in the production of books and journals.

   This is to say that, for cultural matters, Kurt Hager acted as the supreme authority, being *ZK-Sekretär* of art and cultural matters of the SED, as well as leader of the Ideological Commission and member of the Politburo.

Both the Politburo and *Sekretariat des ZK* concentrated the highest powers within their members. Both sat once a week under the chairmanship of the Secretary General and, needless to say, their meetings were closed to the public and there was no control over these committees, not through the Party, the state authorities or the parliament (*Volkskammer*).

4. **Zentralkomitee (ZK) der SED** (Central Committee of the SED) This was the assembly of the most important functionaries of state and Party and, thus, the embodiment of the political elite, but also the leading and controlling committee between Party conferences. In the 1980s, more than 200 members and candidates belonged to this body, amongst others, members and candidates of the Politburo, ministers, leading functionaries from economy and science and from the artists' associations (amongst

them, Gerhard Holtz-Baumert, author for adults and children and in charge of the scientific journal "*Beiträge zur Kinder- und Jugendliteratur*", which was published by Kinderbuchverlag). The ZK's functions included the administration of the SED's possessions, i.e. the so-called *parteieigene Betriebe* (Party-owned enterprises), to which belonged the children's and the youth publishing houses Kinderbuchverlag and Neues Leben (Walther 1999:45) (see also p 73, Zentrag).

5. **Abteilungen** (Divisions) Divisions were subordinate to a *ZK-Sekretär* and superior to the Council of Ministers, which, in reality, meant that they carried more power than the individual ministers. A Division occupied a prime position in implementing the directives deriving

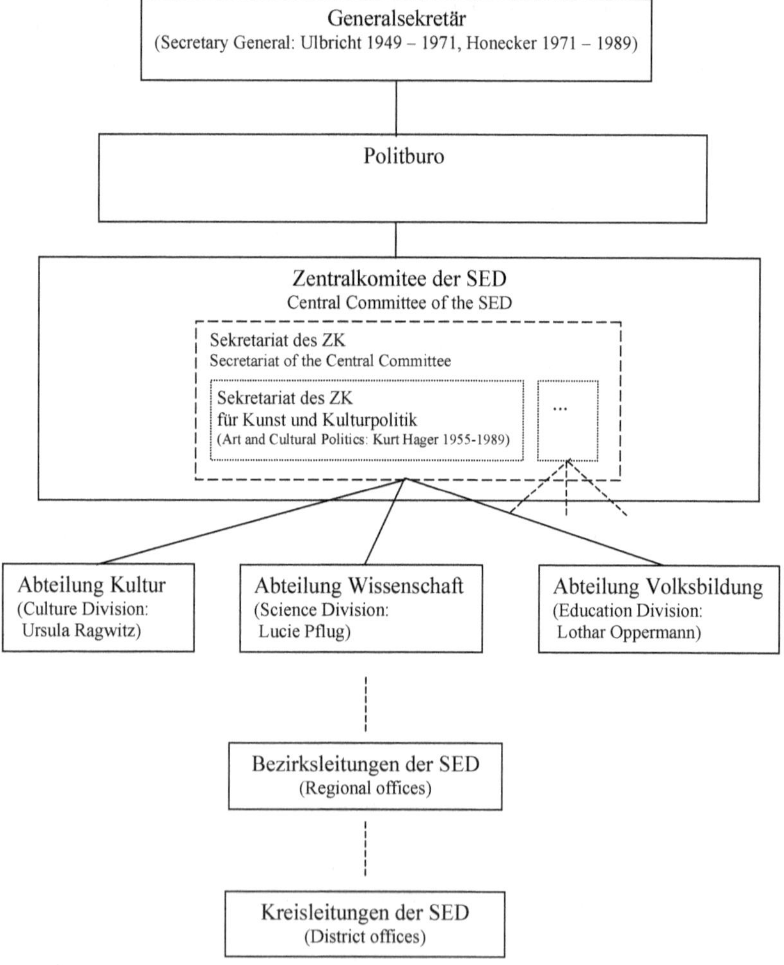

Figure 2.1 Party hierarchy.

> from supreme Party functionaries; "there were ... approximately 30 Divisions, subdivided in accordance with the departments in the state apparatus" (Harik 1999:30); their task was to prepare all important decisions and to check that all resolutions were enacted by all Party institutions as well as all state institutions, such as the Ministry of Culture and all artists' associations.

For issues of book publishing, two Divisions were responsible, i.e. *Abteilung Kultur* (Culture Division, responsible for art and literature) and *Abteilung Wissenschaft* (Science Division, responsible for publishing houses), both of which had Kurt Hager as their direct superior.

2.1.2 State Sector

The aspect of state control is also described only to the extent to which it relates to areas of publishing and censorship; the hierarchy of the state apparatus is outlined in Figure 2.2.

1. **Ministerium für Kultur** (Ministry of Culture) In general, ministries had the supreme authority for their particular sphere within the Council of Ministers; in the case of cultural political issues, all authority lay with the Cultural Ministry. In its statute, the Ministry of Culture was defined as the "central organ of state administration, being responsible to the Council of Ministers of the GDR" (Münzer 1963:49) and, being the foremost state organ, it had the function of ensuring that the cultural politics decreed by the Party were enacted.
2. **Hauptverwaltungen** (Central Offices) These were directly in charge of their respective industries. The directors of a *Hauptverwaltung* were in charge of political, economic and administrative tasks commensurate with the politics of the government and the directives of the minister. Within the scope of their competence, the directors had the right to give directives to the enterprises subordinate to them. In the field of book production, it was the *Hauptverwaltung Verlage und Buchhandel* (*HV*; *HV Verlage und Buchhandel*) which was responsible for all questions of publishing and book trade, with Klaus Höpcke presiding (it is worth noting that Höpcke also acted as deputy Minister of Culture). As Figure 2.2 reveals, all cultural domains (e.g. theatre, concerts, literature, even circus performances) were under supervision by individual Central Offices. Figure 2.2 further reveals the substantial degree of centralisation in the area of book production. With the division into sub-departments within the HV, every individual aspect was planned, directed and monitored centrally. With respect to literature, different sections were in place, each dealing with all questions of its own branch (thus also children's and juvenile literature), maintaining a close grip on them. The HV was the main government authority dealing with all

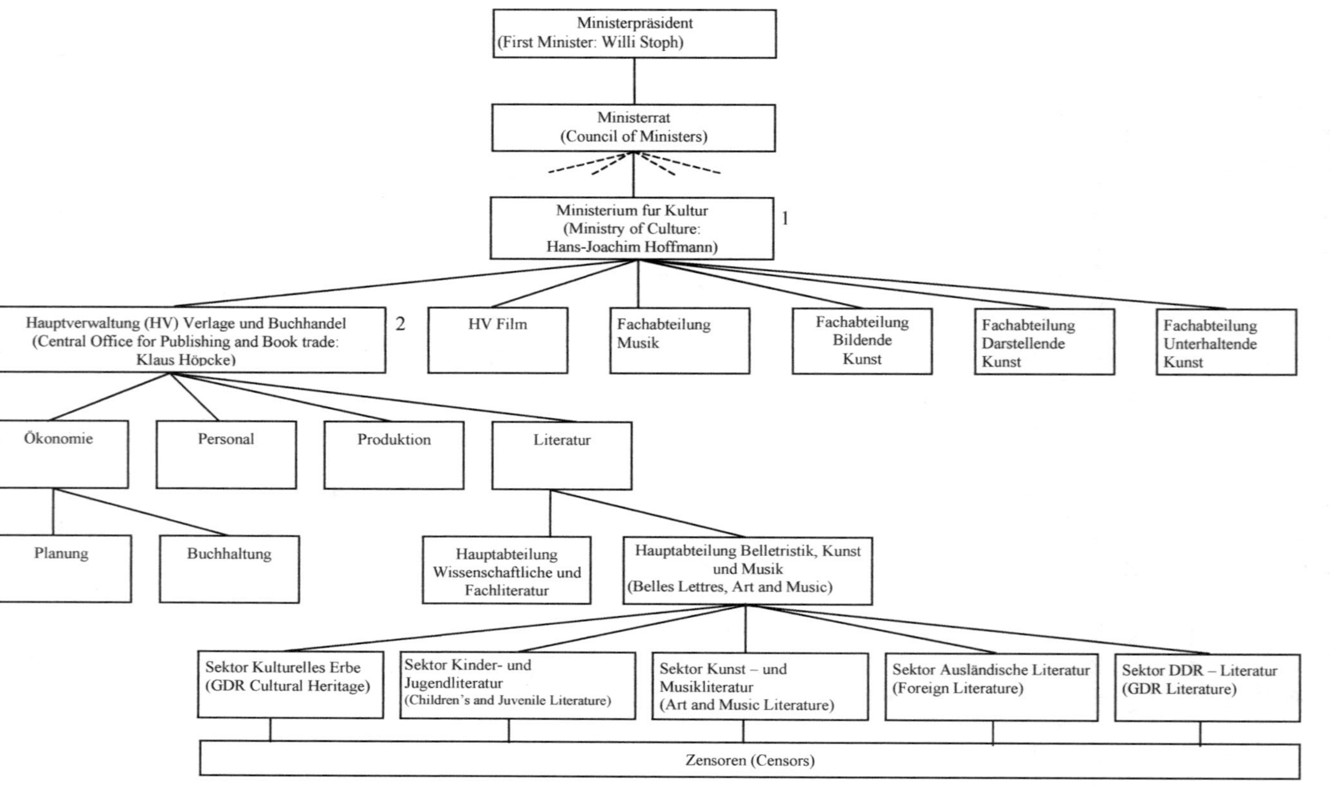

Figure 2.2 State apparatus.
(Source: Karlheinz Selle (deputy director of HV))

aspects of book publication in the GDR. It had full responsibility for all areas of finance, planning and the entire literary output of the country. Part of this included its function as the main censorship authority for every book published in the country.

2.1.3 *Interrelation of State and Party*

From what has been said so far, one can envisage the East German political system as a dual system, comprising parallel structures in the state and the Party. This is to say that each institution in the state apparatus was overlain and instructed by a corresponding Party institution.

The hierarchies of the state apparatus, although seemingly located at the same level as that of the Party, were in fact lower-ranked and were accountable to the Party system; what this meant was that state authorities were not able to make autonomous decisions but were instructed and monitored by the Party and its functionaries; in other words, in their decision-making, ministers

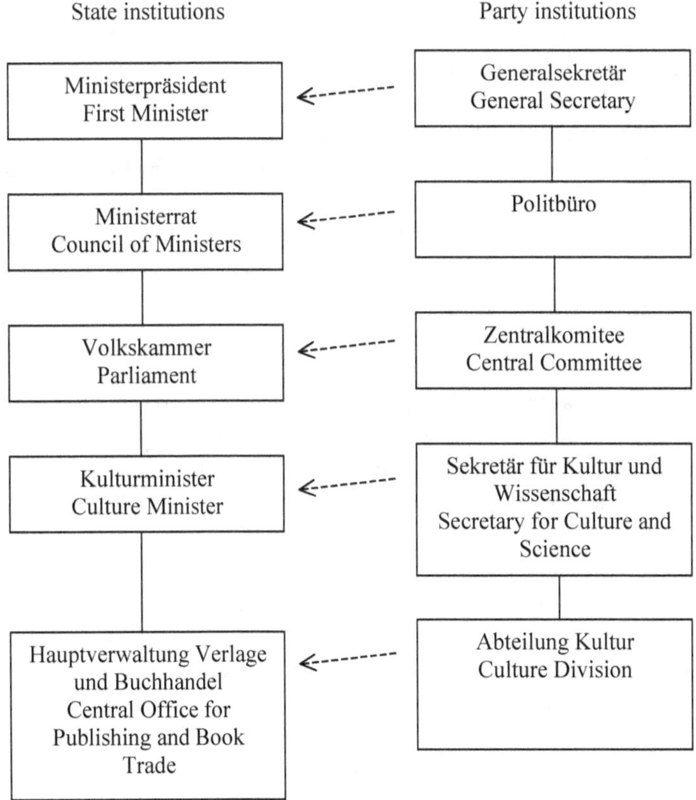

Figure 2.3 Relationship between state and Party sectors.

would turn not to the Council of Ministers but to the Politburo (Ackermann 2000:19). So, for example, "ministers sought the reassurance of the Party for certain issues. For instance, Culture Minister Hoffmann asked Hager for confirmation of a draft speech for an international conference of culture ministers of socialist countries" (Ackermann 2000:45), an act which attributed to Hager all the power to steer the Culture Minister's entrance. Equally, the *Hauptverwaltung Verlage und Buchhandel* (aka censorship authority), incorporated within the Ministry of Culture and, thus, nominally subjected to resolutions by the Culture Minister, "received their directives from the Culture Division in the Central Committee" (Walther 1999:42). In the same fashion, Harik reports that there was only narrow scope for decisions within the Council of Ministers; often resolutions made by the ZK of the SED were passed in identical wording by the *Ministerpräsident* (First Minister) (1999:19).

Similarly, in the case of key decisions or key events taking place in the Culture Ministry, members of the Party's *Abteilung Kultur* would often participate, in order to listen in and be ready to influence procedures. Höpcke, director of the HV, reports that frequently he "was asked to report to the Division about preparations for important events" (Ackermann 2000:48, 50), which then were discussed with him being present. When asked about the authority of the SED, Höpcke readily admitted to the Division's instructing and monitoring function over the Ministry of Culture (Ackermann 2000:50).

This substantiates that "the state system was always subordinate to the corresponding Party institution . . .; in important cases, it had become routine for the Party to interfere in state problems without the legal provision in place to do so" (Löffler 2002:1). Erika Hinkel, close colleague in Hager's office from 1975 and as such very influential as a contact person, lends weight to the fact that the Party was not authorised to issue directives. She is reported to have said that

> naturally it was the case that, when Kurt Hager had said something, this was done. But it was not the case that there existed an official authority to issue directives [with the Party functionaries]; such a thing did not exist. Such an authority lay [only] with the Council of Ministers or the First Minister; however, when Kurt Hager or another of the Secretaries of the Central Commission held an opinion, then there was hardly anyone who would have said: no, this is not how I will do it. (as quoted in Ackermann 2000:51)

All of the preceding seems to indicate strongly that all power was united within the SED. Whereas in pluralist democracies the principle of separation of powers prevails (i.e. the three powers of execution, legislation and judiciary), all control was centralised under East German 'democracy'. The Council of Ministers, as the East German government, albeit nominally in charge of the executive power, was answerable to the Politburo and *ZK Sekretariat*. The *Volkskammer*, as the East German parliament, was also reduced to puppet status, since all members of parliament had to be members of the SED in one form or another and, officially, had to acknowledge SED leadership; thus, legislature functioned by acclamation of draft law drawn up by Politburo and Divisions of the Central Committee. In the same way, all jurisdiction was in the firm hands of the SED. This situation was exacerbated by the frequent changes in office by the cultural political elite between state and Party apparatus or between state apparatus and organisations. Two such striking examples for the area of children's literature are the changes in office by Gerhard Dahne and Hans Bentzien. In 1979, when private children's book publisher Altberliner was bought by the SED, Gerhard Dahne, formerly director of the Department of Belles Lettres in the HV, was appointed director of Altberliner Verlag, after having fallen out of favour with the regime due to an ideological conflict; similarly, Hans Bentzien, who had acted as a Culture Minister of the GDR 1961–1966, was appointed director of the state publisher for young adults Neues Leben. In Walther's words, "a good, multifunctional comrade from the state apparatus could have worked, any time, in the Party apparatus (and vice versa) and indeed did, should the Party so wish". He concludes, "ultimately it was all one—the Party had the first word and succeeded in the final word" (1999:42, 43). Without doubt, this position of monopoly and centralisation found its continuation in publishing policies, with every phase of book production being guided and monitored.

2.2 Publishing Sector

Publishers in the GDR were attributed a role quite different from that of their Western counterparts—firstly, as a result of being the mediator between authors, readers, state institutions (aka the Party) and their own ideas and predilections and, secondly, from operating in a market governed by a planned and centralised economy. This is not to say that their areas of responsibility and their internal structure differed considerably from Western enterprises. As in the West, they comprised individual spheres, including editorial office, planning department, personnel department, costing and accounting, production, marketing and overall management of the business. The difference lay rather with the characteristics of a socialist market and the restrictions placed upon the publishers by the ruling authorities.

It was not difficult for publishers in the GDR to sell their products. The East German market was a sellers', not a buyers' market, in which the booksellers courted the publishers instead of the publishers having to sell themselves and their products. The number of copies of a book printed could be treated as equivalent to the sales concluded—in short, people bought what was produced (with the exception of orthodox Party-line literature, which tended to be left on the shelves). However, although in a place of high social importance, East German publishing houses had far less room for manoeuvre in their daily routine than publishing houses in the West. The underlying reason for this can be seen in one of the main precepts of socialism, namely in the principle of—what East Germans called—'democratic centralism'. According to this, "all key tasks are to be planned centrally and are binding on everybody" (Köhler 1962:11). It was believed that only decision-making from one central body would ensure that the different areas of the economy were going to develop in the right proportions to each other, which was regarded as essential for societal progress. Hence, participating in a centrally planned economy meant that enterprises subordinated themselves to economic as well as ideological precepts and that they gave up any ambition of self-determination.

2.2.1 *Centralisation*

Financially, central planning meant that there was an annual budget available, made up from all the past year's earnings accrued by the total East German national economy. It represented the entire finance available for the whole of the national economy. Annually, it was split and shared out amongst each existing industry according to a distribution ratio. Depending on the sector, on the economic results of the previous year and on the particular Party politics announced in their plans for a given period, this resulted in certain stronger industries propping up the financing of other, weaker ones or, vice versa, receiving financial help in the form of large state subsidies, which had originated from a well-performing market sector. Determining whether an industry belonged to the first category or the second posed questions such as "is the product or service provided of value to our economy? Is there a demand in our Republic? Will the populace benefit?" As a rule, publishing enterprises belonged to the viable market sector.[3] Thus, the state authority responsible for publishing, i.e. *HV Verlage und Buchhandel*, was in a position to announce profits every year (Karlheinz Selle, deputy director of the HV, personal communication, 25 July 2002).

Without doubt, this approach of collection and redistribution of wealth had repercussions also on publishing, in that publishers were autonomous only to a certain degree. When balancing their accounts annually, all their earnings were submitted to the state. As a consequence, they had to begin afresh each financial year, using their annually allotted quota from the overall national budget. Whatever the state deemed economically and ideologically justifiable was the amount of capital publishers had to work with as their budget. This put them into a position where no long-term planning was possible; it stopped any form of capital reserves and savings and made investments impossible. There was, of course, also an ideological reason behind this restriction. Long-term planning means greater freedom and more opportunity to realise independent projects, and organisations could not be relied upon to make 'socially responsible' decisions. Another reason was to prevent publishers from accumulating capital and becoming prosperous by turning into 'inhuman exploiters of mankind'. It was held that profit orientation and accruing of company capital took the business a step closer into privatisation, a development which had to be avoided at all costs.

As "ideologische Fremdkörper" (ideologically alien elements) (Haendcke-Hoppe 1982:12), private businesses were said to orient their activities solely according to market rules which implied producing merely what promised sales, neglecting their social task of producing what was 'of actual benefit to the country' and disregarding their cultural political mission to educate the people in the right spirit, in favour of capitalist greed for profit and the exploitation of the workforce.

Nevertheless, private children's book publishers did exist in the GDR (e.g. Alfred Holz Verlag, Altberliner Verlag Lucie Groszer, VEB Postreiter Verlag), albeit woefully few in number. In the main, they had managed to survive because of their good reputation abroad and for their high-quality publications which sold well and earned a great deal of foreign currency for the state. As editions produced by private publishers, these books were free of any features reminiscent of socialist propaganda—an additional reason for their saleability in the West. Ironically, it was such 'un-socialist' literature that helped boost the socialist East German market. However, as private organisations, they were taxed so highly that, at the end of a financial year, there were hardly any profits left for investment. This, paired with other impediments such as allocation of less paper, fewer printing and binding capacities or refusal of loans, put much strain on their otherwise healthy businesses. Cutbacks in resources, especially paper, led to a decrease in turnover, which resulted in falling revenue. One by one, they had to surrender and change their status to either become nationalised (*VEB*, *Volkseigener Betrieb*, i.e. put under state control, as with Postreiter Verlag in 1972) or integrated into one of the state-owned or Party-owned publishing houses (Holz, e.g., was partially taken over by Kinderbuchverlag in 1963 and fully in 1974) or to be bought by the Party directly (Altberliner Verlag Lucie Groszer, 1979).

Centralisation was inextricably connected with monopolisation. Only sole rights could guarantee unified policy and protection from undesired influences. So, for example, Kruschwitz and Gnad explain the requirement for the monopoly on foreign trade, claiming it as a necessity essential to fend off any unwanted influences and, in particular, to destroy any attempt at disturbing the construction of socialism (1962:11). Hence, it was regarded as imperative to reserve the exclusive right of the state to exercise functions and provide commodities and services. Undoubtedly, such exclusivity also had effects on publishing. All areas essential to the publication of books were in the hands of one institution, areas like printing, transport, imports, exports and access to foreign currency. By eliminating competition, all variety and diversification were removed. Publishers, children's and adults' alike, had to accept, on the whole, what was on offer and the conditions under which it was on offer.

The following institutions important to a publication business were held under central control. The most obvious, in the case of publishing, is printing, which was under direct control of the Party; the VOB[4] Zentrag[5] (*Zentrale Druckerei-, Einkaufs- und Revisionsgesellschaft*), i.e. the umbrella of all printing enterprises, was founded already back in 1945 and was instructed and monitored by the *Abteilung Finanzverwaltung und Parteibetriebe* (SED Finance and Party enterprises Division) of the Central Committee of the SED (this Division was also responsible for all financial control). "No GDR citizen was allowed to buy or import a duplicating or printing machine . . .; all such machines required a licence and were to be kept locked up. Only particularly selected people were given permission to use them and to keep account over content and number of reproductions" (Jegensdorf 1980:26, 27). Not only did this mean that the Party had the control over all that was printed in the country; it also meant that profits accrued from printing were not delivered to the Finance Ministry but directly to the Party. One influential function of the Zentrag was to negotiate with the HV the quota of paper for each publisher (Karlheinz Selle, personal communication, 1 November 2004).

Equally, storage and delivery of books were centralised. All business of that kind was monitored by the HV and was, thus, under direct Party control. In 1946, the *Leipziger Kommissions- und Großbuchhandel* (LKG) had been founded as the central storage and delivery organisation on behalf of all publishing houses, with the purpose of ensuring the broadest possible distribution of books amongst the population. Particularly, the people working in remote rural regions and in factories were to benefit from this move. Thereby, all printers delivered their production directly to the LKG, which then on commission administered their distribution to the individual national and international bookshops. By the same token, the LKG bought all imported literature for further onward domestic delivery.

A major business area in publishing is the trade with foreign publishing houses, to be more specific, dealing in buying and selling of licences and with the import and export of books. This, to the GDR, represented a potential risk, since undesired ideas may have entered the country through these international connections. As a result, the state was constantly on guard against foreign contacts in the publishing industry. Although East German publishers were to initiate foreign business, they were not free to finalise and have ultimate control over their business dealings with foreign partners. Two institutions were put in place to control the incoming and outgoing streams of literature and foreign currency. These were *Deutsche Buch-Export und Import GmbH Leipzig* (DBG; German Book Export and Import Ltd Leipzig) and *Büro für Urheberrechte* (BfU; Copyright Office).

The DBG was established in 1953, in order to support the systematic construction of the foreign book trade. In terms of earning foreign currency, it acted on behalf of the Ministry of Foreign and Intra-German Trade (*Ministerium für Außenhandel und Innerdeutschen Handel*), which was the central authority for the entire foreign trade. Its second master in terms of monitoring and directing its business actions was the HV in the Cultural Ministry. As the foreign trade enterprise equipped with the monopoly, it administered and handled all export of books (all imports became the responsibility of the

LKG after 1955). The DBG concluded the contracts with the foreign buyers, albeit in consultation with the publishers; i.e. all foreign contracts were registered and authorised by this institution. It also decided on the proportion of exports of each title, by determining the overall need for exports by the national economy and, accordingly, arbitrated this proportion in the annual discussions of the publishers' production plans (see following). The need for East German enterprises to export was so great that a 'target of action' (*Kampfziel*) was declared which required publishers to export a certain fixed percentage of their production or rights.

The BfU (set up in 1956) was subordinate to the Culture Ministry. It authorised all licence deals and administered the *Valutaplan* (foreign currency plan) drawn up annually by the Culture Ministry. Hence, it worked closely with the Culture Ministry but also with the Finance Ministry, whose regulations over circulation of foreign currency it had to follow, and the *Deutsche Notenbank* ([East] German bank of issue; i.e. the only place in the GDR entitled to hold foreign currency), as all incoming payments were put into an account there. It was incumbent on the BfU to authorise all contracts with foreign business partners. All authorisations were only permitted in accordance with the cultural political guidelines announced by the Culture Ministry, and also only within the limits of the amount of foreign currency granted to each publisher in their individual foreign currency plan. The BfU was empowered to administer foreign currency (inclusive of the West German Mark) commensurate with the *Valutaplan* of the Culture Ministry. Further to its authorisation function, the BfU could carry out all actual incoming and outgoing payments for royalties and licence fees. Lastly, its task was to provide legal advice in the field of copyright law.

What this indicates for foreign literature, imported and translated, is an accumulation of bureaucracy. To exemplify this, in the case of a licence sale abroad, the BfU and the DBG would be involved as a rule; if on top of this, the books were printed in the GDR for export, Zentrag and LKG were added to this list. It is evident that a huge weight of machinery needed to be in operation for foreign business, which made procedures cumbersome and which was prone to cause delays. The original thought behind centralisation had been that, by taking matters out of publishers' hands and centralising them, the industry would run more economically, as all procedures were carried out once by the same organisation. While this was achieved to a certain degree, at the same time, this central apparatus was large and inefficient. This inefficiency arose, in part, from the state creating tools to exert influence on publishing matters, taking individual decisions out of the hands of publishers.

It is safe to say, however, that centralisation was not only to be understood in financial terms in the form of handing out and taking in sums of money. It also applied to ideological matters, i.e. cultural political tasks and bringing them in line with technical and economic issues (Köhler 1962:12). The significance of a social mission was emphasised repeatedly, and it took priority over commercial interests. Publishers were to regard themselves as "servants" to the state (Institut für Bibliothekswissenschaft und wissenschaftliche Information 1974:41, 42). In a similar vein, Wendt states, "Only if the publisher . . . is not entirely motivated by profit . . . can he fulfil his mission to initiate literary creation, to be an advisor, assistant and promoter to the author and not only a passive mediator between author and reader, striving for profit" (1967:32). Comments like this demonstrate the high value placed upon the political ideological role publishing houses played. Firmly incorporated into official cultural politics, they were an institution used by the state, in order to produce and disseminate culturally important writing. After all, literature was seen as "a weapon in the class battle" (see e.g. Becker 1962:4, Streul 1988:5, Wendt 1967:21) and publishing houses were exactly the places where these weapons were forged. This notion of publishers as active and fully conscious builders of the new socialist society is, for instance, reflected in the publishing plan for 1958 by young adult book publisher Neues Leben, which deemed it indispensable

> to educate all GDR youth to be enthusiastic fighters for socialism and to mould them into the young avant-garde in the battle for a socialist Germany. Literature contributes considerably to fulfilling this task. Therefore, particularly the publishing house Neues Leben has to open up new paths to the hearts and minds of the young people, even more successfully than it has done so far. (Kay 2001:6)

All of this goes to show that, similar to their finance, publishing houses were not self-regulatory in their decisions about publishing lists and contents of their books, but had to align themselves with the cultural politics stipulated by the Party.

2.2.2 Planning

In 1958, the regular official communication within the Culture Ministry announced to all employees, "The knowledge of the close interdependence between economy and culture enables the state to strengthen and cement our workers-and-farmers-state by planning its cultural development; this means that planning of cultural developments through appropriate measures . . . can help these developments to break through faster. It is for this reason that we not only have the possibility but the urgent necessity to plan cultural activities" (Verfügungen und Mitteilungen des Ministeriums für Kultur 1958:1). This provides evidence of the significance of the process of planning in a socialist society. In the GDR, planning was a process not only referring to the definition of targets (i.e. planning ahead) but it also included the subsequent guidance of the processes, in order to achieve these targets (Löffler 2002:1). Based on the assumption that planning was a key tool to keep the influence of market mechanisms and of commercialism out of the country and to prevent capitalism from re-entering society, every aspect of society was subject to planning. It was incumbent on the Politburo, as the most authoritative institution, to determine the production objectives, to formulate the plans, then to transmit these in the form of directives to the state institutions which, in turn, passed them on to each individual enterprise whose task it was to put these directives into practice.

In a similar fashion to economic processes, it was believed that literary politics could be and needed to be planned. If means of production could be planned and guided, so could the *geistige Produktivkraft der Urheber* (intellectual production of authors) (Autorenkollektiv unter Leitung von Heinz Püschel 1969:58). Underlying this notion was the new role of the state in socialism. As opposed to "older state systems" who "do not care so much about poetics and belles lettres" and therefore "underestimate them" (Köhler 1988:2443), the socialist state had introduced the function of planning and regulation to its literature. In terms of production of books, planning entailed deciding which genres were to be produced in which quantities. Such fixed quotas were believed to eliminate the notion of books as mere commodities, a characteristic of bourgeois society, and enhance them to become true cultural assets. Another effect of planning was, of course, to eliminate adverse influences and to produce only literature which was beneficial to society. Thus, in awareness of their social mission, publishers were to develop the right kind of literature. In doing so, they were to "overcome any spontaneity and subjectivism as much as possible" (Autorenkollektiv unter Leitung von Heinz Püschel 1969:57) and to recognise in good time which works were necessary for furthering the progress of society. What is more, not only were they to recognise upcoming developments and problems within the society; they also had the task of awakening needs amongst the populace, and not just any needs, but the right kind of needs (Köhler 1962:12). Nevertheless, whatever they proposed, it was done in accordance with the decisions, announcements and guidance of the Party.

A central tool to the planning of literature was the so-called *Literaturentwicklung* (development of literature), which was said to turn publishing houses into "political ideological centres directly affecting the development of productive forces" (DR1/1234). It was not that a kind of publisher was sought who "waits for what an author will write and will offer to the publisher, but one who actively stimulates the creation of new [i.e. progressive] works" (Glücksmann 1960:832). In other words, a publisher who engaged in developing literature was to recognise the necessity of a particular work for society, approach one or more authors with concrete ideas, discuss the content and length of the book with the author(s) and, in so doing, exert influence on a work's creation. Thus, literary development specified tasks for all writing well into the future, "covering cultural political, ideological and thematic elements which had to be taken note of and which set out the direction of future work" (Institut für Bibliothekswissenschaft und wissenschaftliche Information 1974:62, 63). Again, it was the Party that undertook the task of extracting those needs which were emerging through societal development nationally and internationally, and formulating them through their resolutions; and it was the publishers who were required to demonstrate creativity, originality and initiative in transforming these resolutions into a programme which was both liked by their audience and accepted by the Party.

In order to develop literature effectively, various kinds of plans were put in place. Much importance was attached to these plans for three reasons; firstly, they were seen as an instrument to prevent overlaps in publishers' lists and, thus, avoid waste of time and resources; secondly, they were to stop undesired literature entering the market; thirdly, they were to strengthen the role of literature on the path of East Germany becoming a *gebildete Nation* (cultivated and educated nation). Overall, planning was considered to be a prerequisite for accomplishing cultural politics; these plans were "first and foremost of an ideological nature", determining the "direction, goal, content and extent of publishing activities" (Köhler 1962:12, 13). On the whole, planning was classified into long-term and short-term, and a range of different kinds of plans was put in place, the following of which were the most central and thus merit discussion.

The *Perspektivplan* (wider plan for future developments) reflected the long-term fundamental direction of works by a publishing house in terms of programme and resources. It discussed all future developments, topical areas and titles of main emphasis. Before drawing it up and submitting it to the HV, editors-in-chief and directors of publishing houses called a conference (*Verlagskonferenz*) to debate which books were feasible, 'safe' and could therefore be put forward. Regarding titles, those were listed which had been confirmed either by agreement with the author or by some other contract, independent of the actual date of publishing. *Perspektivpläne* oriented themselves alongside the five-year plans (in some cases also three- or two-year plans) and to the cultural political resolutions of the Central Committee, which were transmitted to the *HV Verlage und Buchhandel* in the Culture Ministry and, from there, to the individual publishers. By the same token, being controlled by a higher authority, a *Perspektivplan* acted also as an instrument of supervision. Once a year, these plans were submitted by the publishers to the Culture Ministry, where they were evaluated and validated by specially nominated panels, i.e. so-called *Beiräte* (advisory committees) and *Literaturarbeitsgemeinschaften* (literary work panels).

A *Perspektivplan* was made concrete through the *Themenplan*,[6] also called *Jahresthemenplan* or *Jahresplan* (thematic plan, i.e. annual plan of titles in production for one year), which put into reality the publisher's cultural political mission. Its major part was made up by titles from the validated perspective plan. According to Köhler, the value of a well-planned and well-prepared *Perspektivplan* found expression in the thematic plans; in-depth and long-term planning was seen to constitute a profound basis for well-defined annual thematic plans, which were more than simply a loosely linked list of titles which, by chance, had become ready for production (1962:18). The *Themenplan* listed and assessed all titles the publishers were hoping to produce in the following year, specifying, for instance, numbers of copies, whether they were a first print or reprint, their role within the future literary development, etc. However, a certain amount of places in the plan was left open (*Vakattitel*, blank titles), in order to squeeze in late proposals; this room for improvisation was necessary, because of the cumbersome bureaucratic machinery, within which publishing was operating and in which there was little room for manoeuvre.

In the middle of the year, the HV sorted all items of the thematic plans according to various literary groups (children's literature being one of them) and passed these lists on for discussion in that particular panel of the *Literaturarbeitsgemeinschaften* that concerned itself with this genre. Subsequently, a draft thematic plan was drawn up (*Gesamtthemenplan*), capturing the entire book production for the GDR for that particular year; this overall thematic plan required authorisation by the Minister for Culture. Alongside this *Gesamtthemenplan*, another document was produced, i.e. *Themenplaneinschätzung* (assessment of the thematic plan), "which provided a general account of the planned year's fiction for consideration and approval by the Central Committee" (Darnton 1990:7). In a meeting with the highest Party functionaries from the Culture Division of the Central Committee, the director of the HV (from 1973 until 1989 Klaus Höpcke) explained and justified individual items in this overall plan. This meeting was "where the ultimate decisive cultural examination occurred which meant scrutinising the selection of topics, book content and protagonists for the entire annual production of the state" (Löffler 2002:31). Characteristically, the result of this deliberation was not made officially public; rather, "Höpcke would return with decisions, always verbal and never with any accompanying explanation" (Darnton 1990:7).

However, another step followed before the publishers were informed of the outcome. Economic figures were evaluated, such as allocation of paper and foreign currency,[7] a procedure which involved cross-matching with other types of plans, namely those specifying the allocation of resources granted by the Party to the HV (it must not be forgotten that the HV itself was allocated only a certain amount of the entire available resources by layers of authority above them in the hierarchy).

Once the approved and validated *Themenplan* had been sent back to the publishers, it became binding as a target for the ensuing year's production (i.e. production plan). Every *Produktionsplan* had a number assigned to each title in a running order; also it specified number of copies for every book, paper requirement, printing capacity or foreign currency required, if necessary. As production plans were binding, every change had to be applied for by the publisher through the HV and required special permission.

Consequently, as other industries (e.g. printing and binding enterprises, the book trade) were connected through their plans with this bureaucratic set-up, these then had to be informed about respective changes or delays (Löffler 2002:31).

As mentioned previously, plans were deliberated in the HV by specially nominated panels. The *Literaturarbeitsgemeinschaften* (DR1/1234; DR1/1337) were established in 1958[8] and were to assist in putting publishing on a broad basis and aid in recognising upcoming needs in good time and in ensuring their satisfaction. These panels were subdivided into sub-groups, each dealing with special literary areas, such as cultural heritage, German contemporary literature, literary studies, or indeed children's literature. These panels, it was stipulated, were to provide an interface between politics, science and publishing. They were instituted to formulate programmes for literary development, to debate and elaborate on them. It was their task to discuss perspective and thematic plans and co-ordinate them, to investigate the proportions of literary genres (see following), match them with the Party-political precepts and, as a follow-up, to suggest necessary changes to items such as number of copies printed, foreign currency allocated or publication date. Their function was solely advisory; nevertheless, they were a forum, discussing ideological political problems in literature and, as such, served as a body for decision-making, apt to be used as an instrument for putting orthodox literary politics into practice. Evidence for this is given by Barck et al. (1998:98, 99), who describe such a planning meeting in which the two state publishers, Kinderbuchverlag and Neues Leben, behaved as distinct guardians of socialist children's literature, having their thematic plans assessed favourably, while the plans of the (absent) private children's book publishers were treated disparagingly, assessing them as listing a varied, yet decisively un-socialist programme. As a result, Kinderbuchverlag's and Neues Leben's applications for more paper were granted, whereas Alfred Holz Verlag, Altberliner Lucie Groszer and Ernst Wunderlich Verlag had to accept cuts, because their thematic plans did not satisfy the demands of a truly socialist education.

The results of the deliberation arrived at by the *Literaturarbeitsgemeinschaften* were further debated in one of the three advisory boards, located within the HV, dealing with either social sciences, natural and technical sciences or belles lettres. These committees (founded by resolution of the Politburo in 1962) consisted of directors of publishing houses, editors-in-chief, representatives of the Writers' Association and of the Academy of Arts. It is worth noting that the results of the deliberations of these three advisory commissions formed a major part in drawing up the HV's *Gesamtthemenplan* and its assessment (*Themenplaneinschätzung*), which were put forward to the Culture Division of the Central Committee. It is further worth noting that Kinderbuchverlag and Neues Leben were present in these committees, whereas none of the other children's book publishers were.

Like everything else in the GDR, accounts and financial records of publishing activities were closed at the end of the planning year, with the publishers producing an annual report which covered, amongst other issues, the fulfilment of economic parameters and, perhaps even more importantly, the fulfilment of cultural political tasks (i.e. volume of publications, assessment by the publisher of the literature produced, reasons for deviations from the original plan, assessment of the manuscripts in preparation for the following production year). Every January, these reports were submitted to the HV, to the Science Division of the Central Committee and, if applicable, to the organisation responsible for the respective publishing house and its matters (Löffler 2002:31), which, for instance, in the case of Neues Leben was the organisation entitled Free German Youth.

One criterion taken very seriously in all planning activities in the various spheres of a socialist state was the quantitative relationship between different kinds of literature, in East German jargon called *Proportionen* (proportions). Drawing on Lenin, working to plan comprised conscious adherence to proportions, by which was meant taking care that all individual industries of a national economy were developing in the right relation to each other (hence also the necessity of a centralised administration, in order to make all processes in the country visible and to make them line up). Culture and literature could not be excluded from this process because of their important role in instructing and enlightening the populace (children as much as adults) and, ultimately, achieving social and economic progress (according to Marxism-Leninism). As a corollary, the Cultural Ministry agreed upon the necessity to watch over proportions in order to "be in line with general economic and cultural political targets" (Verfügungen und Mitteilungen des Ministeriums für Kultur 1958:3). Fundamental to the calculation of proportions were questions of the political and economic necessity of literature, or literature's role in the wider perspective. It is therefore evident that literary proportions were not a fixed parameter but shifted in keeping with Party politics. Taking into consideration the right proportions was a task to be performed in the publishing houses but also, and even more so, one level up in the Culture Ministry, where all submitted plans were co-ordinated. It was here especially that the 'correct' proportions were determined and the plans aligned accordingly. This final co-ordination was deemed of particular necessity for society because "the thematic plans submitted by the individual publishers may be correct within themselves; however, in the ensemble of the entire publishing industry wrong proportions may arise" (DR1/1073).

Proportions had to be achieved in various areas of literary politics. So, for instance, authorities were to ensure the correct composition of literary groups (e.g. political, scientific, agricultural, children's literature, belles lettres), the criterion for which was evaluated on the basis of important central decisions, such as resolutions of the Central Committee or culture conferences. Similarly, the correct composition between all national literatures had to be considered, i.e. the relationship between GDR original writing, literature from the USSR, from other socialist countries (*Sozialistisches Ausland*), from West Germany and other capitalist countries (*Kapitalistisches Ausland*). Indigenous East German literature was regarded as of highest priority, followed by Russian and other socialist literatures; capitalist literatures, on the whole, were of least concern. Another criterion was the proportion between contemporary socialist literature and cultural heritage; in the main, contemporary socialist writing was rated of higher value. However, texts from the cultural heritage had the advantage of having run out of copyright, which made them cheaper to produce. Similarly, money played a role with the proportions between first prints and reprints. Reprints meant less investment by publishers; however, first prints were of higher priority in the publishers' thematic plan, because they represented an actual production achievement and, with this, the concrete putting into practice of the cultural political mission. Additionally, from an economic point of view, first prints, exhibited at the Leipzig book fair, could possibly lead to sales in the West, resulting in foreign currency income. Proportions equally played a role at the level of publishing houses, where it was negotiated as to the amount of resources allocated to each editorial office.

As should have become clear, the concept of planning, like centralisation, can not simply be reduced to an ideological rationale. It is not possible to budget for more than is available and, despite the most diligent economic planning, resources were never enough. Therefore, while it is true that the reasoning behind planning and proportions was highly ideologically motivated, the general economic situation must not be overlooked in any reflections. With culture being firmly incorporated into the national economy, publishing was linked to all other areas of society, a fact which entitled publishers to only a limited share of the available resources. Allocation of paper etc. had been decided upon centrally at a higher level in the hierarchy and, thus, represented a given in the accounts of the HV. There was little or no room for overrun and, because of this, discontent on the part of the publishers was regularly expressed year by year.

2.2.3 The Call to Economise

Planning automatically implied economising workforce, material and finance. Most means of production were 'socialist property' belonging to everybody, and everybody was called upon to handle resources wisely. Moreover, the ambition was to boost the national economy, in order to reach—and possibly exceed—Western levels, as the country considered itself to be in a "peaceful economic competition with capitalism" (Kruschwitz and Gnad 1962:1). For these reasons, waste could not be afforded. For the arts this meant "spending with care and purpose, making full use of the existing capacities, building new capacities not grandiosely and only if needed and saving material whenever possible" (Verfügungen und Mitteilungen des Ministeriums für Kultur 1958:2). Clarifying the significance for a socialist state, Glücksmann maintains that only after the most careful and personal examination may publishers commission a work; consequently, they may only commission works of which they have become convinced of their positive fulfilment and objective success (1964:208). Through their literary plans and their organisational business activities, publishers were incorporated into the overall national economic plan, a fact which had consequences for the running of their businesses. Items and entries of all plans had to correspond, match up and balance out, and underachievement in one area led to disruptions of other areas. Changes to plans resulting from poor planning caused the same disruptions. *Doppelarbeit* (duplication) as well cost dear, as the work was performed in two or more places, wasting money on labour and resources. A major point of concern was the fact that the wider business activities were, the less overseeable the economy became. Therefore, the objective was throughout to make publishing more transparent with simpler procedures and simpler internal structures and, thus, simpler to run.

One of the earliest measures introduced to create more clarity in the publishing sector was for each publishing house to create a profile (*Profilierung*), a development introduced in the 1950s and followed single-mindedly into the 1970s. The intention was for publishing houses to align themselves with the endeavours of the overall national economy, to increase productivity and also to become more efficient in publishing. It was hoped that this could be achieved through far-reaching specialisation and centralisation, by way of restricting publishing houses to specific areas of publication. The aim was rationalisation; removing overlap between publishers, slimming down the manufacturing process by removing duplication and making the industry less cumbersome and more cost effective. By the same token, internally in the publishing houses, overstaffing and unnecessary augmentation of the workforce in editorial, organisational and technical areas had to be avoided. The long-term objective of *Profilierung* was the establishment of a small number of specialised publishers with high production and high productivity (DR1/1234). As a matter of fact, this trend of slimming down the publishing sector is very noticeable during the era of the GDR, and publishers of books for children and adolescents were not excluded from this development. So, for example, Walter Tölg, from the marketing and export department of Neues Leben, reported that the publisher "had been active in many areas, something that changed in the beginning of the 1960s, when an extensive phase of specialisation of publishing houses took place, instigated from the top. For instance, the publisher Urania was to take on the entire national production of popular scientific literature, of which Neues Leben also had a good share in its programme . . . , with the effect that all editors and authors, working in this sphere, left the publishing house" (as quoted in Kay 2001:115, 116).

Specialisation went so far that children's book publishers were restricted to very limited production areas. For instance, VEB Postreiter was the main publisher in the country who produced *Leporellos* (folding picture books for toddlers), Altberliner mainly produced picture books for pre-school children, or Alfred Holz's main production was based on animal stories. However, despite such specialisation, repeatedly publishers were merged and/or gave up that particular line of their production with time. Although the two big state publishers were split into production for children (up to 14 years) and for youth (14–25 years), their range was not restricted to such a degree. They had all genres in their programme, covering the whole market.

Undoubtedly, *Profilierung* may have had its economic benefit; however, it should not be overlooked that, with it, publishing also became more transparent ideologically, and literary processes became more easily steered. Evidence for this lies in the fact that the two state publishers of children's literature, Kinderbuchverlag and Neues Leben, were promoted considerably, whereas non-state (private or church-related) publishers were not allowed to grow. "Striving for the right size of publishing house" (DR1/1234) certainly meant monitoring which publisher was allowed what type and quantity of output in the national economy; hence, the production of publishers like Altberliner or Alfred Holz was regarded as sufficiently large, or even in need of being reduced, because the production of private publishers did nothing to contribute to socialist enhancement. Similarly, fewer publishers with limited areas of work meant creating a better focus on their tasks. Monitoring of texts, decisions on thematic plans and determining the future of children's literature became more amenable to oversight, and control over publishers and their programmes was easier to manage.

Being economical and spending money wisely was all-encompassing for the economy and the whole of society. As a part of the national economy, publishers felt the full force of this integration in three notable areas, namely regarding access to paper, printing facilities and foreign currency. Not only did these three commodities have limited availability; they were also linked, in one way or another, with export of books, which, in the GDR, was given highest priority. Therefore, if any of these resources at any time was required for selling books abroad, it was withdrawn from the internal market with immediate effect. Another observation is that, because of their scarceness, they had to be used domestically with the utmost care, which had the consequence of biasing provision towards projects with cultural political usefulness to the nation. This was a situation sufficiently difficult for state enterprise; however, it was much more difficult for private publishers or for publishing projects dealing with non-socialist literature. As a rule, they took second place to ideologically or economically more 'necessary' ones. Since paper, printing and foreign currency affected publishing substantially, they will be given consideration in the following section.

2.2.3.1 Starved of Resources

The internal economy of the GDR operated as a single organisation and all financial transactions within this organisation took place on paper only, i.e.

using a system of accounting that required no actual cash transactions. Further, the value of all commodities within the system was determined by the policies of those in power and not by market forces. The corollary to this is that all internal transactions were cash-free because all the commodities were owned by the state but all external transactions with foreign entities involved 'real' money, hence perhaps the increased emphasis on external transactions and the value of 'foreign currency'.

Paper and Printing:

Paper was the planning item that caused most problems for publishers. The paper industry and paper trade had been nationalised, with the result that paper could no longer be bought from the free market but was distributed by the HV commensurate with the *Gesamtthemenplan* (overall national thematic plan), i.e. according to the requirements for the authorised titles for each publisher. Therefore, based on the *Proportionen* in a given year, an exact paper consignment was calculated in the HV for every publication of each publisher. However, publishers did not have the paper delivered to their premises; it was sent directly to the printers, where it was stored until utilised. This meant that publishers had to plan their following year's projects in accordance with a quota of paper that would—hopefully—be allotted to them. In other words, they were not given the exact amount at the time of drawing up their plans for the following year, but only a rough guide. If, in the end, publishers were not allocated the amount of paper they had hoped for, it could have a considerable effect on their plans and production, with onward effects for other industries. One instrument used by publishers to handle this risk more smoothly was the usage of *Vakattitel* (blank titles, see p 79) in their plan, as discussed earlier, which allowed for a few emergency short-term adjustments.

What, however, needs to be taken into account is that the HV itself was not in charge of the ultimate decision over paper resources but only had an administration and distribution function. The ultimate decision lay with the Paper Commission within the Central Committee; remarkably, from 1970 onward, there was no longer a member of the state present in this commission (Löffler 2002:27) but the decision over paper distribution was the exclusive responsibility of the Party, similar to printing. Corresponding with the prevailing economic situation, there was more or less paper to be distributed; but as a rule, it was never sufficient. An area, however, for which paper was always available was book export, owing to the foreign currency it brought into the economy.

The allocation of paper had a very noticeable and direct effect in that it determined the number of copies to be printed and distributed. In fact, reduction, or indeed increase, of paper allocation for certain productions, topics or certain publishers was used as an instrument for steering literary production, in effect creating a form of indirect censorship. Löffler confirms, "the allocation of paper constituted an instrument for steering the publishing programmes, by using paper quotas as a factor in deciding publishing lists, even down to individual titles" (2002:29). So-called *Auflagenpolitik* (policies for deciding the number of copies to be printed) was employed to direct a 'useful' book at a bigger audience and a book regarded as of less value at a smaller audience. "The more copies reach the public, the bigger the potential number of readers to whom the author speaks through his work" (Autorenkollektiv unter Leitung von Heinz Püschel 1969:290). This approach is reflected in the situation of children's books translated from Western countries; they were normally given a lower print-run than indigenous contemporary fiction or translations from the USSR, a fact that held true for both the big state publishers Kinderbuchverlag and Neues Leben and most certainly for the private ones.

It was not only the amount but also the quality of paper that led to constant complaints by publishers. In particular, the production of children's books suffered in this respect, because of the many illustrations which need a higher quality of paper, coloured books even more so than black and white. It required some thought on the part of the illustrator to achieve best possible results with the given quality of paper; thus, for instance, illustrator Klaus Ensikat is reported to have said that bad paper makes one inventive (Katrin Pieper, personal communication, 11 July 2001).

A further obstacle publishers encountered was hold-ups due to limitations in the printing capacity. Even with fixed agreements between publisher and printer, these arrangements did not necessarily turn out to be binding because of the printer's own dependency on events outside their control. It could happen that the paper delivery would not arrive at the printer's, if for instance the delivery lorry was stranded due to a shortage of petrol. Two frequent sources for delay were related to the fact that all printing was in the hands of the Party; firstly, there was a sense of urgency attached to all ideological material; thus, all printing would be stopped to give precedence to an urgent, unplanned print job for state propaganda material; secondly, all jobs promising to generate an income of foreign currency were a matter of the greatest importance; hence, jobs heading for the West were always treated with high priority, since they resulted in that urgently needed foreign currency. East German publishers felt the times before Christmas particularly painfully. Then, their projects were moved back to make room for the more pressing Christmas business, since all print-runs destined for the West had to be completed before Christmas, while in the GDR books sold well anyway throughout the whole year. All of these scheduling difficulties were frequently the cause for *Überhangtitel* (carried over titles), i.e. editions planned for a particular year but, for various reasons, not completed and carried over into the following year of production.

Foreign Currency:

In terms of finance, and notably with foreign currency, the dual principle of *Sparsamkeit und gesellschaftlicher Nutzeffekt* (economising and usefulness for society) weighed particularly heavy. When it came to foreign, in particular

Western, currency, East German publishers found themselves in a double dilemma. On the one hand, publishers wanted imports in order to make foreign literature available to their readers but foreign currency was scarce and, also, the East German Mark was devalued next to Western currencies, both of which made Western foreign books fairly expensive. On the other hand, publishers had an export target to fulfil, which meant that they needed to identify early in their long-term plans projects with high export potential. First and foremost, these had to be integrated into their perspective and thematic plans, calculating parameters such as number of titles, number of copies and selling price, in order to earn a fixed amount of foreign currency per year. Evidence of this can be seen in the publishers' assessments about titles when applying for a print permit. If a title was estimated as having sales potential in the West, the addition '*für Export ins kapitalistische Ausland geeignet*' (suitable for export into capitalist countries) would say so. It should be pointed out, however, that the possibility of earning foreign currency was sometimes used as a publisher's device to make a book attractive to the censors and to obtain a print permit.

Literature export was taken seriously to such a degree that, on frequent occasions, publishers were urged to intensify sales for export. Furthermore, the DBG (as the central state foreign trade enterprise) was tasked with assisting publishers in market analyses and in opening unexplored routes for exports. In meetings to discuss thematic plans, both publishers and DBG were to assess export opportunities for each title, "setting themselves action targets" (Bähring 1962:54), which is to say that they were to co-operate in determining optimal export demands to maximise the benefit to the country in foreign currency. Thus, for economic reasons, the state was more interested in exports than imports of literature from the West in particular, an antagonistic situation which generated a vicious cycle for publishers: they were pressured to export; however, in order to keep exports going, businesses in the long run had to import, because their partners also needed sales; yet again, import represented a problem because the East German state was reluctant to spend foreign currency. A further obstacle to imports of Western literature was the fact that publishers were not in a position to re-invest their earned foreign currency but had to hand it over to the state in support of the national economy. At no time did they receive the amount in earnings back from the state, which they would have wished to use in pursuit of foreign business. What is more, book imports were made even more difficult due to the fact that not just any book was a candidate for import and publication in East Germany, especially not books from a capitalist country. These books brought with them the potential danger of thoughts unfavourable to the state ideology and had to be vetted carefully for their suitability for home readers.

It is for these reasons that one of the main activities of a publishing business, namely exchange of literature by way of buying and selling rights to books, constituted a marathon task for GDR (children's) book publishers. While the exchange with other Eastern Bloc publishers did not pose too many problems, in their business with Western partners, publishers were faced with major difficulties. The two central questions with which they were confronted were: which books from the West are ideologically justifiable and therefore will pass the censors; and secondly, in Pieper's words, "are we going to produce for our own children or in order to earn foreign currency for the state?" (personal communication, 11 July 2001). Another way of illustrating this point is to consider four categories of books, which meant that, internally, publishers had to create their own proportions as to what was achievable in terms of *weltanschauung* and finances:

1. indigenous titles which, owing to their content, were highly suitable for the home market but, for exactly this reason, were not exportable to the West;
2. indigenous titles which could be sold locally and also in the West;
3. books originating from abroad, which were suitable for the local market and were financially viable;
4. finally, books either too expensive or with the wrong kind of content.

Yet another question needed to be addressed in this equation, i.e. that of the selling price for a book. The importance of making profits by export and of earning as much foreign currency as possible has already been mentioned, but also the price to be attained on the domestic market could not be neglected, as it was also a tool for accruing earnings. On the whole, books, as precious cultural assets, were subsidised by the state and were sold rather cheaply. This was particularly true for what was called 'ideologically valuable', i.e. orthodox books. This literature was produced in high numbers with high subsidies, yet generated less profit, sometimes even selling below production costs. In order to adjust for such losses or lower earnings, certain editions had to be sold at a higher price; these were books which sold easily, including all literature from the West. However, the selling price for this kind of fiction had to be adjusted even higher, since these books normally had a lower print-run, owing to their lesser ideological importance, and because they therefore received little or no state subsidy. Profits for foreign texts could be increased further, if titles had fallen out of copyright (which was the case with many classic texts translated for children). From 1 April 1964, book prices were frozen; this meant that all reprints had to be sold at the same price as their first prints, regardless of their publishing year. Since price levels and thus production costs had risen in the meanwhile, publishers had to resort to different strategies, in order to be able to raise book prices. Any change in presentation of the books (e.g. different kind of edition, different illustrations) justified a correction of price upwards, helping the profit margin and increasing earnings. It is very noticeable that children's book publishers used this strategy with translated English books. Many reprinted texts had not been changed, but the edition was listed as a first print because of a change in presentation, subsequently enabling the publisher to raise the price.

Publishing lists of children's book publishers (mainly Kinderbuchverlag and Neues Leben) reveal that the trading of rights was a practice widely used within the Eastern Bloc as well as with Western countries. As to trade with other socialist countries, business was facilitated through bilateral arrangements to exchange quotas of suitable national literature, agreed upon between the Copyright Offices (BfU) of the Culture Ministries in individual socialist states, grounded in the belief that culture was a matter of the state, planned and regulated centrally. For this reason it was possible, and even desired, within the Eastern Bloc to plan and negotiate literary issues; a procedure opposite to that in the West, where literature is a matter of private enterprise and, hence, does not lend itself to planning. Notwithstanding these bilateral agreements, the question of copyright was imperative for the GDR, both in the trade within the Eastern Bloc as much as worldwide. The GDR was a signatory to four multilateral copyright agreements, i.e. World Convention for the Protection of Copyright[9] (founded in 1952 in Geneva; entrance of GDR in 1973); World Intellectual Property Organisation[10] (founded in 1967 in Stockholm; entrance of GDR in 1970); Montevideo Agreement (founded in 1889; entrance of GDR in 1927/1959[11]); but most importantly the Convention of Berne (founded in 1886 in Berne and revised several times afterwards; entrance of GDR in 1928/1959). Acknowledging the importance of the Berne Convention, East Germany became a further signatory in 1968 to its revised Stockholm version[12] and, in 1980, to its revised Paris version (Püschel 1975:145; Püschel 1982:36–40).

Being a member of these multilateral agreements meant that the GDR was able to protect its own literary and artistic works but it also meant that it was required to buy rights from other signatories. In 1973, when the USSR joined the World Convention for the Protection of Copyright, the protection was effectively worldwide.[13] This worldwide protection, albeit crucial, was expensive for deals with Western partners for which the copyright fees had to be settled in dollars, Swiss francs or West German marks in part, if not in full. Therefore, what was a source of income, on the one hand, turned into a stumbling block, on the other. To successfully import a work, it was critical where the rights to it lay. In many cases, a West German publishing house had secured itself the all-German rights, since the economic superiority of West Germany allowed the publishers more money to purchase rights. For the GDR, this meant buying the rights from West Germany, which was the situation in the case of many children's and juvenile texts. Another reason given by one of the interviewees was the fact that West German editors were free to travel anywhere, in order to attend meetings and conclude contracts, if a copyright had become available; such an activity was impossible for East German editors, because they were hindered by lack of money and by the slow-moving bureaucratic machinery to issue a travel permit in good time.

Also, some rights lay with West German publishers simply due to the fact that Germany had become divided after the war and these rights happened to be on the Western side. If, however, a copyright did not lie in West Germany, it was with another foreign publisher and again required negotiation in terms of cost and conditions. In short, any copyright resting in the West demanded payment in hard cash and, thus, turned into a costly affair for the East. In this scenario, private publishers were normally put at a disadvantage, simply because private enterprise was frowned upon by socialist culture. So, for example, Gerhard Dahne, director of Altberliner Verlag, commented after Germany's reunification that the programme of his publishing house had consisted, almost without any exception, of books written by East German authors, "because we were never allowed any foreign currency, in order to take on a licence" (Dahne 1991:1593).

Since foreign currency was not readily available, East German publishers had to resort to special arrangements, in order to arrive at a licensing deal with Western publishers. The one used most frequently was to agree to a kind of tie-in deal. Such a deal had the advantage to bring a foreign text into the country, while helping to save foreign currency; therefore, these deals were viewed more favourably by the state and the authorities were not overly reluctant to spend foreign currency. The most common deal between West and East Germany was a co-production, made possible on the basis of the common language German. In the case of a project involving foreign rights, a co-edition was arranged with a West German partner; thereafter, East Germany printed both German editions in the same run and delivered the pre-arranged copy number to the West (*Mitdrucklizenz*). This had the advantage for the East German publisher of access to the rights for a book free of charge or at reduced cost and, for the West German partner, of saving production costs, which would have been higher in the West. The only condition West German partners frequently set was that the West German edition was printed on better quality paper which was available in the GDR and was set aside especially for such international deals; or in many cases the West German partners themselves supplied the kind of paper they wanted. Hence, editions were produced which were identical to the East German ones apart from the cover, title page and bibliographical details at the beginning of the book in the colophon (*Impressum*). Another, similar form of deal was the *Exportauflage*, which was also frequently used in East Germany. This concerned texts written originally in the GDR, or without a foreign copyright. Again, a pre-arranged number of copies was printed in the GDR for the partner in the West.

Every *Exportanteil* (part edition for export) or, better, an entire edition was highly sought after by the East German state, as they resulted in direct foreign currency payment. A look through the print permit files confirms that *Mitdrucklizenz* and *Exportauflage* were common agreements between East and West German publishers and were generally given print permission (e.g. all three books by Bernard Ashley in the 1980s were a co-production with the

West German publisher Klopp). This goes to show that, for purely financial reasons, publication of foreign literature was positively influenced by such arrangements.

Anthologies were another way to avoid overly high payment of royalties, offering several advantages. Firstly, as collections of short stories, rights to these stories were cheaper and it was not necessary to purchase all the rights, normally linked to an entire book. Secondly, they often concerned stories written by less well known authors (renowned authors were already employed by West German publishing houses), who had not been discovered and translated in the West, with the additional benefit that either no or at least smaller royalties were due. Also, since they offered a broad spectrum of stories about a country or particular theme frequently linked to the West, they sold very well. They had the further advantage that more than one translator could be commissioned, giving work and income to several people. Another reason has to be seen against the backdrop of censorship; authors who, for ideological reasons, had not yet found their way on to the East German market were introduced through one or more short stories, inconspicuous to the censor; however, once on the market, one could refer back to them as evidence of publication when requesting new books by the same author, since it had been demonstrated that they no longer presented a danger to society.

A licensing agreement, linked to a foreign text, often included consideration regarding the rights to the translation and in what manner this translation was to be dealt with. In the case of texts where the author's copyright had expired, the translation might still have been under protection, which meant that money had to be paid for the translation. Therefore, it was the case sometimes, if a translation was too expensive, that East German publishers decided to buy only the copyright to the original and to translate themselves. This practice carried the additional benefit that the new translation had the potential to be sold to West Germany. Since translations produced in the GDR had a high reputation in the industry, they were indeed very saleable, frequently constituting another source of foreign income.

Publishers were not entitled to buy and sell copyrights themselves. It was the state which possessed the monopoly of foreign trade and foreign currency, exercising sole control over exports and imports. Whereas they were encouraged to initiate business, they were only permitted to go as far as unbinding negotiations. Under no circumstances were they "to commit themselves in a way that resulted in any transfer of foreign currency" (Autorenkollektiv unter Leitung von Heinz Püschel 1969:383). In a similar fashion, publishers were neither entrusted to formulate final versions of copyright agreements nor to evaluate the right amount of foreign currency required to finalise a deal. Instead, they were to apply to the BfU for registration and authorisation of their contracts with foreign partners and for the subsequent allocation of foreign currency; simultaneously, they were required to apply to the HV, justifying why they wished to acquire the rights to the book (this, it ought to be mentioned, was an application separate from the print permit, which then only occurred at a later stage in the procedure). Agreement between HV and BfU[14] was essential for furthering the deal.

The correct proportions between imports and exports formed a substantive part of the discussions; imports "unnecessary to the national economy" (Kruschwitz and Gnad 1962:2, 9) had to be prevented at all costs. In terms of books from Western countries, imports should "take place only in so far, as this literature serves our interests, particularly taking into account the contents" (Kruschwitz and Gnad 1962:22). Foreign currency was provided only for texts, useful to society, thus "serving societal progress, dissemination of humanitarian ideas and ensuring peace and friendship between peoples" (Glücksmann 1975:14). This notion of usefulness led to an approach in publishing which did not even consider books with petty-bourgeois content, books like *Trotzkopf* by Emmy von Rhoden, a highly successful girls' book in the West, or all books by Enid Blyton; also books with a harmless, playful character providing a kind of sanctuary for children had problems within the socialist framework and, therefore, often no attempt was made to publish them. So, for instance, when Alfred Holz wished to make available *Winnie-the-Pooh* for the East German market, this book caused problems with the censors, who found its message to be too neutral, not sufficiently progressive and, hence, not representative of East German society, as the following extract from the print permit files from the year 1959 demonstrates,

> Winnie the Pooh is exclusively about fantasy, happiness and child's play. Certainly our children are not less imaginative in their play, but it cannot be denied that the fantasy of our children moves in another direction. Our time is not so much about a single child with his toys on his own—and if this does prevail in a child, it is not desired and does not match our didactic ideals. Thus, the value for the education of our children is minimal and it is not worthwhile spending foreign currency on it. Yet, should it be taken on in exchange for publishing one of our valuable children's books in West Germany, a publication should not be refused.[15] (DR1/5039a)

Sauerstein held the view that "for the major part, licence agreements demonstrated the liberal-minded and cosmopolitan attitude in the literary programme of the GDR" (1981:54). From the modern vantage point, one would, however, tend to disagree with him. While it is true that foreign books were on sale and that they showed to their readers parts of the world inaccessible to them, these were only those books which were carefully selected to show certain parts of the world and chosen foreign cultures. Ideological compliance, paired with a multitude of problems linked to resources and facilities, with restricted possibilities in publishing, restricted titles and copy numbers show the GDR as a country crippled by limitations. Also, another fact becomes apparent, in that all the aforementioned institutions, practices and, in fact, the whole set-up had originally been put in place and motivated by the wish to generate an orderly, efficient system, to simplify processes and, hence, make them more transparent and, finally, to avoid waste. However, all of them could be used, and indeed were on certain occasions, as a tool of ideological steering and as a means of control. To give an example, thematic plans had been introduced, in order to compare publishers' programmes to avoid duplication of titles, waste of paper and printing facilities. Once these plans had been established, publishing had become transparent and it had also become easier to influence programmes and to gain control over publishers' lists. Similarly, the BfU was an institution dealing with all matters concerning copyright law and, on the whole, was doubtlessly beneficial for publishers; at the same time, it had the key role of issuing foreign currency which made it a powerful authority with control over foreign literature. One of the core instruments of East German literary control was the procedure to obtain a print permit, without which no manuscript reached a printer. Because of its eminent significance in book production, the following section is dedicated to a closer investigation of censorship, its development and practice in East Germany.

2.3 The Rise of Censorship

The ideological re-organisation of Eastern Germany after the Second World War involved considerable changes in the publishing sector. However, the reconstruction of publishing took place under the strict control of the Soviet occupying power, to a large extent imposing themselves and their ideology and having a significant say in the emerging composition of literature in the GDR. The scrutiny of book production was regarded as essential for two reasons; firstly, as already discussed, paper, printing and other supplies were short. Given the important task of re-educating the population, it was not acceptable to handle resources carelessly. Secondly, not all literature was considered suitable, and having an eye on the right kind of literary output was essential. However, emphasis was not only on eradication of texts portraying a fascist worldview; "we must not forget that many works, which have absolutely no connection with National Socialism, are still far from being appropriate to create a new personality who is immune to falling back into the mistakes of the past" (Kielmeyer 1947:335). By using the expression "mistakes of the past", the author not only pointed to the Third Reich but to the desired Historical development of leaving capitalism behind and entering a period of socialism. Therefore, publishing houses had to examine in detail "whether a work is really relevant to the present day or merely a matter of the past" (Kielmeyer 1947:335). In order to avoid a relapse, publishers and their products had to be controlled. To this end, on 2 August 1945, the Soviet Military Administration passed a decree requiring the monitoring of all printing and publishing activities. Existing publishing houses that had been responsible for disseminating literature with national socialist content did not have their licence renewed. Several new publishing houses were established; for children's book production, the main ones were: Alfred Holz Verlag 1945; Neues Leben 1946; Altberliner Verlag Lucie Groszer 1947; Kinderbuchverlag 1949. Also, Volk und Wissen, the central publisher for school books in the Soviet zone, began to operate. Finally, the publishing house SWA, owned by the Soviets, took up business and, from 1946, also produced Soviet literature for children and adolescents. All publishing licences were issued with a restriction on the publication area to which publishers had to keep. Failure to comply with these restrictions could result in the licence being withdrawn.

A second measure to gain the upper hand over literary output was to scrutinise the actual books and manuscripts themselves. In 1946, a blacklist was published indicating all the literature (i.e. books and magazines) which was to be rejected.[16] In June of the same year, the *Kulturelle Beirat für das Verlagswesen* (Cultural Advisory Council for Publishing) was put in place, a committee which embodied the beginnings of East German censorship. Important powers were transferred to it from the Soviet authority. It was in charge of resource allocation, of working with authors and examining re-applications by publishing houses. Most importantly, it was given the power to examine and approve of manuscripts (which so far had lain decentralised with several local authorities) before they were sent on to the Soviet authorities for final consent. With the *Kulturelle Beirat* set up, the first step to centralisation of censorship was taken. From that time, the development progressed inexorably.

After constituting East Germany in 1949, matters of censorship were transferred into the exclusive domain of the East German authority. In 1951, the *Amt für Literatur und Verlagswesen* (Office of Literature and Publishing) was instituted, taking on the tasks of the *Kulturelle Beirat* (which was dissolved at the same time). All existing publishing licences were re-examined and it was decided whether or not to renew them. In accordance with Article 2 of *Verordnung über die Entwicklung fortschrittlicher Literatur* (Decree about the Development of Progressive Literature, 16 August 1951) (as quoted in Kaemmel 1956:65), only those publishers who were found to be in line with Party political doctrine had their licences renewed. The newly issued licence, however, carried the caveat of entitlement of such publications only as was claimed by the publisher's programme and as confirmed by the state authority *Amt für Literatur und Verlagswesen*. Numerous publishers lost their licences because "their existence was no longer socially justifiable" (Selle 1972:37). In parallel with the Party's declaration of 1952 for the construction of socialism (see Section 1.1), publishers were placed under the obligation to cover SED resolutions in their publications.

During the subsequent ten years, and corresponding to nationalisation endeavours in industry and agriculture, state and Party bureaucracies were constructed and, in parallel with it, changes in the publishing sector took place.

The early 1950s saw an alignment of publishing law with socialist maxims. It was also at that time that the first standard contract for authors and translators was formulated (see p 111). In 1956, the BfU was instituted, focusing on issues of copyright and licence deals between publishers. Publishing itself experienced re-organisation as, with time, more and more publishers lost their licences or merged. After two rounds of centralisation, the first in 1963, the second in 1971, the list of licenced publishers had dropped to 78, among which were 22 publishers of belles lettres and children's literature (Börsenverein der Deutschen Buchhändler 1985:4). Given that, in 1949, 160 licenced publishers had been operating (Rumland 1993:7), this figure had dropped by half, signalling a substantial change in the publishing landscape.

With respect to the number of East German children's book publishers, sources are not in accordance with each other. Whereas for instance Köhler speaks of six publishers altogether (1988:2138), Rumland identifies seven in total (1993:11). Doderer again mentions six[17] publishers of books for young people plus another seven[18] producing picture books and *Beschäftigungsbücher* (booklets with instructions for children to create items of handicraft) (1975:298, 299). In part, an explanation for this divergence lies in the different publication dates of these sources, between which publishers had merged or closed their businesses. Additionally, this discrepancy is engendered by a confusion of publishers' profiles and of a clear definition of children's literature. While some count, for instance, *Leporellos* and picture books for toddlers as part of children's literary production, others do not. In a similar fashion, the question needs to be asked whether publishers who produce children's books at irregular intervals between their other, main productions can be classed as publishers of children's literature, as is the case with the church-related publishing houses. In its 1985 publication *Die Verlage der Deutschen Demokratischen Republik*, the Eastern section of *Börsenverein* lists the publishers given in Table 2.1 as producing material or books for children.

To this list, one might add Evangelische Verlagsanstalt Berlin and St. Benno-Verlag GmbH, who specialised in publications of church and religious fiction and, from time to time, also published children's fiction of a religious nature. It might also be mentioned that, by the publication date of 1985, all production of the former private publisher Holz took place within the production of Kinderbuchverlag, since Alfred Holz Verlag had been fully taken over by this state publisher in 1974. Also, from this list, it emerges that the publishing houses Gebrüder Knabe Verlag and Verlag Ernst Wunderlich are missing, an indication that they had gone out of business; regrettably, no additional information is available. Under these conditions it can be determined that the state publishers Kinderbuchverlag and Neues Leben were indeed the prominent publishers, setting the example for the others on how to follow the Party line, while at the same time being directly affected by changes in the political course of the GDR and having to react to the current political situation.

Table 2.1 Children's Book Publishers in 1985

Publisher	*Publishing Profile*
Altberliner[1]	children's and juvenile books
Der Kinderbuchverlag Berlin [including the 'Edition Holz']	children's books for children between the ages of two and fourteen
VEB Postreiter-Verlag[2]	Leporellos, picture books for children from two to five, youth books for eight to fourteen year-olds, but also calendars
Verlag Junge Welt	publications for children, mainly Bastelbücher, Beschäftigungsbücher and magazines
Verlag Neues Leben Berlin	juvenile literature, factual books for adolescents, but also novels, fiction, poetry by contemporary and foreign authors
Volk und Wissen	school books, books in the area of pedagogy and psychology
Verlag Karl Nitzsche	colouring books, Bastelbücher, picture books for children between the ages of two and five

1. After being bought by the Party, the publisher's name was changed and the previous owner's name 'Lucie Groszer' was erased.

2. The addition VEB in the publisher's name indicates that it had already lost its private status and had been made state-owned.

(Source: Börsenverein der Deutschen Buchhändler zu Leipzig, 1985)

Despite the move towards more centralisation, several forms of ownership were in use for publishers. Publishing houses could be state-controlled (*VEB, i.e. volkseigener Betrieb*), or partially state-controlled; there were those controlled by a mass-organisation (*VOB*), those owned by the Party and private ones. This may sometimes cause problems for the present-day researcher in terms of lack of clarity of accountability to the specific presiding authority because, in those restructuring procedures during the 1950s, areas of competence in economic administration and ideological political guidance kept shifting between different bodies or within the various departments of one body itself; similarly new institutions were put in place and responsibilities transferred. It would, however, go beyond the scope of this work to give an in-depth description of the processes during the 1950s. This development had come to an end by December 1962, when the resolution was passed to establish a new kind of authority within the Ministry of Culture. This authority, the *HV Verlage und Buchhandel*, commenced work on 1 January 1963. With this date, centralisation in publishing had entered a new phase, a phase of tighter centralisation, and a phase that would last until the collapse of the GDR in 1989. With the set-up of the HV, unified economic, cultural political and political ideological control of the publishing industry and the nationalised sector of book trade in the GDR had been achieved. All power of determination over all possible aspects of publishing was united in this one body. It was of course also the time when the Wall had been erected and, from now on, all publication was produced for a market screened off from alien influences under permanent control of the SED regime.

The responsibilities of the HV were decided upon by the Politburo and regulated through decrees by the Council of Ministers (Löffler 2002:4). In the main, they comprised planning of production and distribution of books (nationally and internationally), inclusive of the authority over BfU, LKG and DBG; planning and distributing of resources; financial planning and accounting of all matters related to publishing and the book trade; control over the library sector; organisation of all perspective, thematic and other plans, all within the framework of cultural politics officially propagated; and evaluation and authorisation of manuscripts. The HV was, however, not responsible for printing (which continued to rest with the Party) and for magazines and newspapers (an area moved to the press office of the chairman of the Council of Ministers, at the time the HV was created).

Although the HV was the highest state authority deciding over matters of publishing, it was not the uppermost institution in the hierarchy. As Figures 2.1, 2.2 and 2.3 show, the Party was the supreme power in all key decisions which the HV had to follow in their everyday business. This becomes apparent when considering the following facts; all planning by the HV happened within the framework issued by the Party resolutions; secondly, all HV plans (literary and economic) were validated annually by Party authorities and, without such a validation, all processes would come to a halt; thirdly, censors themselves found it necessary to safeguard their decisions during the process of assessing manuscripts by obtaining second opinions on controversial texts. As evaluation of manuscripts and granting a print permit was one of the main tasks of the HV, a brief description of this process follows.

2.3.1 *Censorship*

Censorship, that is, the system of monitoring and adjusting opinions, was a taboo concept itself in East Germany. Euphemistic terms in use were *Begutachtung* (assessment) and *Druckgenehmigungsverfahren* (procedure to obtain a print permit), in order to identify the procedure of authorisation of all manuscripts for their suitability for society. Other preferred expressions in the official discourse were *Anleitung und Hilfe* (directing and assisting; Barck et al. 1998:199) or *Planung und Lenkung zum Zweck der Literaturförderung* (planning and guiding for the purpose of promoting literature; Wichner 1993:208; Jäger 1993:21). According to the *Richtlinien für die Begutachtung* (Guidelines for the Assessment), "promoting and preventing [the production of] literature constitute a unity", which meant nothing other than "publications in line with the principles and laws of our state deserve[d] to be promoted [while] harmful publications need[ed] to be blocked" (DR1/1827; DR1/1287). This notion led to softened expressions speaking of decisions to promote a work or simply not to promote a work, or similarly "the office

[HV] does not prohibit, it only refrains from a publication" (Jäger 1993:30, 31). In keeping with such neutral tones, a number of censors viewed themselves as promoters of literature, as demonstrated by Darnton in his interview (1990:6–9) with two censors of the *Abteilung Belletristik* (sub-department of Belles Lettres); one of them described her activity as promoting literature, on the basis that, had she not erased several problematic expressions, a fair number of texts would have caused outrage within the Central Committee and would have never appeared in print (Darnton 1990:6).

Not being anchored in the Constitution, the *Druckgenehmigungsverfahren* was only written down in the 'Decree about the Procedure to obtain a permit for products of publication' (*Anordnung über das Genehmigungsverfahren für die Herstellung von Druck- und Vervielfältigungserzeugnissen*, issued by Culture Minister Abusch on 20 July 1959) and in the aforementioned 'Guidelines for the Assessment', a document communicated within the Ministry of Culture (dated 25 July 1960), and of such a secret nature it was not to be quoted or given out (Franke 1993:105; Barck et al. 1998:191). Censorship may have been a taboo in general, but these two documents certainly reveal that it was not a taboo subject within the discourse of the Ministry of Culture. The 'Decree about the Print Permit Procedure' clearly states the necessity of a state print permit and lists exhaustively which type of publications needed to be authorised[19] (Articles 1 and 2). Article 3 identifies the two instances in which a print permit was granted, firstly, in the case of the text document being commensurate with the legal regulations, with the principles of socialist construction and cultural requirements; secondly, in the case of the resources being at the disposal of the authorisation institution within the framework of the national economy plan. However, the 'Guidelines for the Assessment' address the matter in an even more candid way, by declaring, "literature against the construction of socialism in the GDR, against maintenance of peace, against the principles of proletarian Internationalism and the unity of the socialist camp, literature which is anti-humanitarian, revisionist and distorting Marxist-Leninism, such literature must not appear in the GDR"; continuing, "the assessment enables us to contribute to the improvement of the quality of each individual book permanently. Help to the publisher is to be given at the earliest possible point in time of the work on the manuscript, because an alteration of the book's content at the print permit stage constitutes a delay in time and involves economic waste" (DR1/1827; DR1/1287). This appears to substantiate that censorship had already been put in place during the early stages in the book production, i.e. with the choice of text, the drawing up of publishing plans and the allocation of resources. Censorship was certainly not only manipulation of text documents but it was shifted to the forefront of the production procedures. This, however, could only be achieved with the co-operation of the employees of publishing houses. Indeed, it was the intention of the HV to transfer acts of censorship increasingly to publishing houses.

Editors were to take more and more responsibility for their actions in cultural political and economic terms. In order to do so, it was stipulated that, in addition to their university degrees, they should be further trained to the same level in political ideology. Thus, "to shape their political consciousness and to qualify them in technical and social terms was considered central for them to work on the political ideological front of socialist society" (Leitung der Sektion Lektoren 1960:92, 93). As "political functionaries" (DR1/1234), they were seen to participate in the cultural political education of all citizens, being accountable for the texts they were working on and being watchful that no wrong influence flowed into a manuscript (DR1/1234); editors had to "be capable of helping [an author] politically when he was erring on a subjectively wrong track" (Wendt 1963:387). An editor working with foreign literature had to strive for the closest possible co-operation and agreement with the translator, although it was acknowledged that "the translator has copyright to his translation and modifications to his work can only be effected with his consent" (DR1/1234). All of the translators interviewed by me recognised this practice; nonetheless, they claimed that some of the editors had been more forceful in their approach than others. However, the ultimate goal was to produce a text which was permitted for print and would reach its audience. Therefore, in all negotiations, formulations were attained that satisfied both parties to a certain degree. After all, it was in the interest of everybody that the manuscript was acceptable to the censor, as all interviewees asserted.

In a similar fashion, editors-in-chief were made "responsible for ideological and artistic contents of the publications, while the directors [were] regarded as fully responsible to the Party and to the state for the entire activities of their publishing house" (DR1/1234). Cadre politics[20] in the publishing houses, and in fact in all cultural institutions, ensured that all senior and executive positions were filled with people loyal to the Party. By means of this step, it was intended to achieve more ideological awareness on the side of the publishers, resulting in manuscripts that were in line with the 'needs of society' (as officially propagated) and, hence, did not require too much work at the end by the censor. "Publishing houses carry the obligation to submit manuscripts that are valuable culturally and politically and that are ready for printing [which] means: with his signature, the editor-in-chief confirms that the production of the book is necessary politically and socially" (DR1/1287). "Behaviour [of an editor or publisher] that rejects this responsibility will no longer be tolerated. If a harmful book reaches us, we will claim that, without us, it would have appeared on the market and we will call you to account for this behaviour, just as if it had appeared" (Wendt 1963:389).

This role of editors and publishers was recognised by Barck et al. (1998:232), who, in their research, found that the major part of censorship took place in the publishing house. Other evidence of how this policy functioned is provided in the print permit files with translated children's and juvenile texts.

As is revealed there, it was a rare occurrence that translated children's books were refused a print permit; in fact, according to the files, the only book was *Doktor Dolittle*, which, in 1966, ran into problems with the censor (see Section 4.1, Case Study 1, Hugh Lofting, *Doktor Dolittle und seine Tiere*). Most books passed through the system without any problems, thus demonstrating that publishers were aware of what would and would not be acceptable and made suitable decisions to that end. In spite of the conscious participation of editors and publishers in the censorship procedure through selection of texts and, if deemed necessary, adjustments, they were still not trusted to perform their tasks to the full satisfaction of the state. This was the reason why the *Druckgenehmigungsverfahren* was never abolished by the state (aka the Party), despite several attempts to do so (notably in 1956, 1965 and 1972), the impetus for which came mainly from authors, publishers and even from within the HV itself. The fear that "publishers might evaluate a work incorrectly with respect to its social effect and its necessity for society" was insurmountable and, under all circumstances, called for the services of "the HV . . . exercising its function of directing and controlling" (Wendt 1967:29).

2.3.2 Application for a Print Permit

This section explains in brief the procedure publishers underwent during the final stages of book production, before the text was finally ready to be sent to the printer, namely the application procedure for a print permit, representing the actual censoring process. The process will be illustrated, using two example applications for a print permit, firstly, for a children's book and, secondly, a book for young adults; the first one, *Molly Baumwollschwänzchen* (Molly Cottontail, Erskine Caldwell, Kinderbuchverlag), dates from 1968 (DR1/2257), the second, *Das Haus an der Küste* (The House on the Shore, Eilis Dillon, Neues Leben), from 1977 (DR1/3552).

The form for the application for a print permit was an A3 sheet, folded in half. Figure 2.4 illustrates what the outside front page of this sheet looked like. Points (1) to (5) specify the main technical information about the book, which are the publishing house (1), the author of the book (2), the title of the book (3), the language from which it was translated (4) and the translator (5). Point (6) mentioned the date of contract between the publisher and the translator (this was not filled out in most of the cases). If the title was to appear in a *Schriftenreihe* (i.e. serialised edition), it had to be stated in line (7). Indications of previous editions and previous copy numbers were made in (8).

With respect to the time frame, the beginning of the setting, printing and delivery of the book should have been entered (9), which, however, was not always the case. The kind and amount of paper required for book and blurb and the book format were filled in (10). Fields (11) and (12) show the retail price of the book and whether the publisher applied for any subsidy.

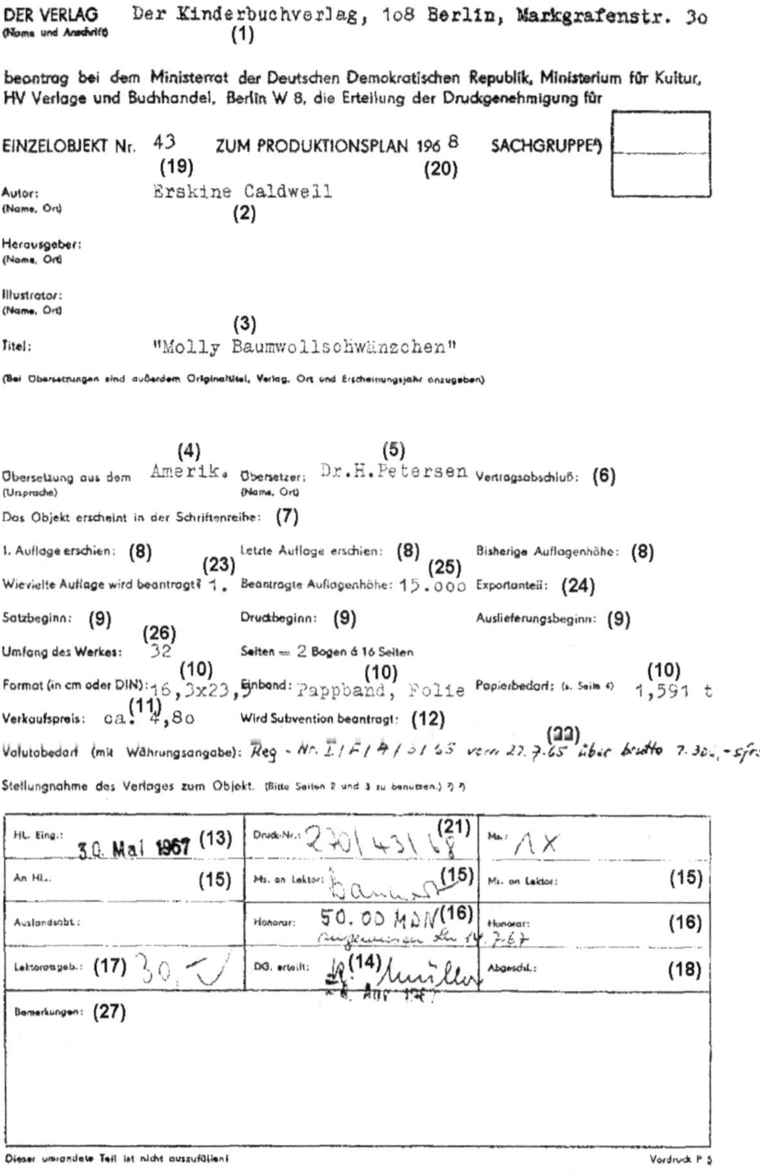

DER VERLAG (Name und Anschrift) Der Kinderbuchverlag, 1o8 Berlin, Markgrafenstr. 3o (1)

beantrag bei dem Ministerrat der Deutschen Demokratischen Republik, Ministerium für Kultur, HV Verlage und Buchhandel, Berlin W 8, die Erteilung der Druckgenehmigung für

EINZELOBJEKT Nr. 43 (19) ZUM PRODUKTIONSPLAN 196 8 (20) SACHGRUPPE*)

Autor: (Name, Ort) Erskine Caldwell (2)

Herausgeber: (Name, Ort)

Illustrator: (Name, Ort)

Titel: (3) "Molly Baumwollschwänzchen"

(Bei Übersetzungen sind außerdem Originaltitel, Verlag, Ort und Erscheinungsjahr anzugeben)

Übersetzung aus dem (Ursprache) (4) Amerik. Übersetzer: (Name, Ort) (5) Dr.H.Petersen Vertragsabschluß: (6)

Das Objekt erscheint in der Schriftenreihe: (7)

1. Auflage erschien: (8) Letzte Auflage erschien: (8) Bisherige Auflagenhöhe: (8)

Wievielte Auflage wird beantragt? (23) 1. Beantragte Auflagenhöhe: (25) 15.000 Exportanteil: (24)

Satzbeginn: (9) Druckbeginn: (9) Auslieferungsbeginn: (9)

Umfang des Werkes: (26) 32 Seiten = 2 Bogen á 16 Seiten

Format (in cm oder DIN): (10) 16,3x23,5 Einband: (10) Pappband, Folie Papierbedarf: (s. Seite 4) (10) 1,591 t

Verkaufspreis: (11) ca. 4,80 Wird Subvention beantragt: (12)

Valutabedarf (mit Währungsangabe): Reg. - Nr. I/F/4/31 65 vom 27.7.65 über brutto 7.30-,- sfrs. (22)

Stellungnahme des Verlages zum Objekt. (Bitte Seiten 2 und 3 zu benutzen.) *) *)

HL. Eing.: 30. Mai 1967 (13)	Druck-Nr.: 270/431/68 (21)	Ms.: AX
An HL.: (15)	Ms. an Lektor: (15)	Ms. an Lektor: (15)
Auslandsabt.:	Honorar: 50.00 MDN (16) angewiesen am 14.7.67	Honorar: (16)
Lektoratsgeb.: (17) 30.-	DG. erteilt: (14) Müller 8. Aug 1967	Abgeschl.: (18)
Bemerkungen: (27)		

Dieser umrandete Teil ist nicht auszufüllen! Vordruck P 5

KOPIE AUS DEM BUNDESARCHIV

Figure 2.4 Print permit: *Molly Baumwollschwänzchen.*

Matters of censorship become apparent in box (13), which indicates when the manuscript reached the HV. Box (14) was reserved for the censor's signature and the date (in the case of a positive decision for a print permit). Thus, the difference between box (13) and box (14) indicates the inspection period of the manuscript within the censorship authority. As a rule, the longer the period between these two dates, the more likely difficulties would have occurred in the inspection process.

The second line (15) was reserved for second/external reviewers, the third line (16) to enter the fees for the reviewers, mentioned in (15). As this file shows, *Molly Baumwollschwänzchen* was reviewed by a person in the children's literary scene with one of the highest loyalty standings possible, i.e. Holtz-Baumert; this may be due to the fact that it was a work imported from America which, by its nature, was regarded as a suspicious matter. Box (17) in the fourth line indicated the fee to be paid by the publisher for processing the application within the HV. Box (18) was to be used to enter the final date of processing the manuscript in the HV; in most of the cases, however, this date was entered in (14), together with the censor's name.

Fields (19) and (20) describe the year of the production (production plan, i.e. list of the books for publication after the authorisation of the thematic plan) and the project number that a particular book had been attributed within this annual production plan (e.g. the book *Molly Baumwollschwänzchen* was attributed the object number 43 within the production plan for the year 1968). Once a book had passed the censor's assessment positively, its object number and the production year were integrated in the print permit number and entered in the print number field (21). An East German print permit number consisted of three parts, the first the identification number of the respective publisher, the middle the object number of the book and the last part specifying the production year.

The manuscript would then be passed on to the printer, who was required to incorporate the number into the bibliographical details in the front of the book. Printers were only allowed to print books which had been given a print permit number by the censorship authority. Item (22) deals with the question of obtaining a copyright. On this line, the registration number was written (which the publisher had been given by the BfU as a sign of approval for the deal) and, next to it, the amount and the currency required (e.g. in order to produce *Molly Baumwollschwänzchen*, the publisher needed 2,300 Swiss francs). Item (23) indicates the number of the print-run. Translations from the West frequently only got one print-run, as further runs were deemed too expensive and unnecessary. Classic titles, which could have many more print-runs, formed an exception for two reasons; firstly, because they were viewed as 'Classical heritage' and 'world literature' and therefore played an important role in educating the masses. Hence, the most important standard works of the German and foreign cultural heritage had to be available on the market at all times (Barck et al. 1998:167). Secondly, financial considerations played an important role, as there were no royalties to be paid on them.

Item (24) represents the part-edition for export, specifying the quantity of books to be exported out of the whole print-run (25). For *Molly Baumwollschwänzchen* there is no entry in this field, as it was destined for the home market only. This is different in the second example (see (28) in Figure 2.5).

DER VERLAG (Name und Anschrift) Neues Leben, 108 Berlin, Behrenstr. 40/41

beantragt beim Ministerrat der Deutschen Demokratischen Republik, Ministerium für Kultur, HV Verlage und Buchhandel, 108 Berlin, die Erteilung der Druckgenehmigung für

EINZELOBJEKT Nr. 54 ZUM PRODUKTIONSPLAN 1977 SACHGRUPPE¹) 7721

Autor: (Name, Ort) Eilis Dillon, England

Herausgeber: (Name, Ort)

Illustrator: (Name, Ort)

Titel: Das Haus an der Küste

(Bei Übersetzungen sind außerdem Originaltitel, Verlag, Ort und Erscheinungsjahr anzugeben)

Übersetzung aus dem (Ursprache) Engl. Übersetzer (Name, Ort) Gisela Peterson Vertragsabschluß:

Das Objekt erscheint in der Schriftenreihe: Neue Edition

1. Auflage erschien: – Letzte Auflage erschien: – Bisherige Auflagenhöhe: –

Wievielte Auflage wird beantragt? 1. Beantragte Auflagenhöhe? 25.100 Exportanteil: 5.100 **(28)**

Satzbeginn: – Druckbeginn: – Auslieferungsbeginn: I/77

Umfang des Werkes 272 Seiten = 17 Bogen à 16 Seiten

Format (in cm oder TGL): 12,5x20 Einband: Pappband Papierbedarf: 6,6 t

Verkaufspreis: ca. 5,60 M Wird Subvention beantragt:

Valutabedarf (mit Währungsangabe): Reg.Nr. E/N/1/308/75 – 2964,– netto in DM

Stellungnahme des Verlages zum Objekt. (Bitte Seiten 2 und 3 zu benutzen.) ²) ³)

HL. Eing.: 31. 05. 76	Druck-Nr.: 305/54/77	Ms.: 1X /
An HL.:	Ms. an Lektor:	Ms. an Lektor:
Auslandsabt.:	Honorar:	Honorar:
Lektoratsgeb.: 50,– /	DG. erteilt: 1.6.76 [signature]	Abgeschl.:
Bemerkungen:		

Dieser umrandete Teil ist nicht auszufüllen! Vordruck PS

KOPIE AUS DEM BUNDESARCHIV

Figure 2.5 Print permit: *Das Haus an der Küste.*

The application form for Eilis Dillon's book *Das Haus an der Küste* shows that, out of the 15,100 copies constituting the entire print-run, 5,100 copies went for export to West Germany.

Given that the average numbers for indigenous GDR children's literature were 25,000–30,000 per print-run, *Molly Baumwollschwänzchen*'s 15,000 copies (25) are a significant proportion, particularly when taking into consideration that translations from the West did not have that high a priority. However, this might be attributed to the fact that it was a picture book and one copy consisted of only 32 pages (26). Further, the author Caldwell was seen as critical of capitalist ideology and, also, had a previous history of his work approved and published in the GDR. Eilis Dillon's book amounted to 25,100 copies, which represent a significant number, as well. However, Neues Leben, as opposed to Kinderbuchverlag, had higher print-runs on the whole. One reason for this may be that, according to its *Profil*, Neues Leben produced for an audience comprising a mixture between adolescents and adults, which increased the number of readers and necessitated higher copy numbers. Another reason may have been that, being the FDJ publisher (*Freie Deutsche Jugend*, Free German Youth, i.e. the state youth organisation of the SED), Neues Leben was slightly more prestigious and, with the support of the state youth organisation, would have had access to more resources and, therefore, could afford to conduct higher print-runs. Finally, item (27) shows the box in which the censors could make any remarks or demands for additions or changes, should they wish to do so.

So far, the main technical and economic parameters associated with the production of a book have been described. Details about ideological issues and the significance of the manuscript for the East German market were enclosed on the inside of the folded application form. Key documents stored there were the publisher's evaluation of the book and reviews of one or more evaluators. In his statement to the HV, the publisher had to give reasons for the selection of the book. The main requirements were to state what educational effect the book had, in what way the reader benefited from it and how it contributed to the construction of a socialist society. Frequently, the authors' origins, their biographies and stance toward the socialist cause were mentioned. Another observation is that publishers gave much thought to the way they were presenting a book to the authorities, promoting the book to the censor by incorporating supportive messages that highlighted certain characteristics of the book. For anti-Western books, the publishers' evaluations of the books found in the censorship files are keen to emphasise factors such as the inhumanity of the Western systems with their high unemployment rate, their racism and class-thinking, exploitation and suppression or colonialism and to prove that such a society was doomed to fail, very much in contrast to the worthiness of socialism. The significant role of publishers in this selection process was evident. Not only did they have to consider the general quality of a book (like any other publisher in the world); they also constantly had to take into account how a particular book would be judged "higher up" (Charbon 1998:175), i.e. in the censorship authority.

One such consideration concerned the choice of external evaluators for each publication (as further elaborated in Chapters 3 and 4). The selection of these evaluators was generally crucial, but could be vital for more problematic books. First and foremost, evaluators were chosen for their reputation and for the likelihood that they would provide a favourable assessment of the book. The content of these evaluators' commentaries, although important, should not be misunderstood as literary scientific discussions but as a political move by the publisher. It was up to the evaluators to apply tactical strategy and to play down or accentuate certain features of the text. If the book did not carry sufficient socio-critical content and was, therefore, likely to experience problems with the censor, the evaluator's approach was to admit this particular shortcoming and to stress other constructive elements, in order to present the book in a more positive light. Similar tactics were used by the publishers in their evaluation, pointing to those instances "where the books clashed with the official ideology. If they did not do so . . . , they could be purported to have hushed up critical issues deliberately or they could be reproached for lacking in competence or for being foolish" (Mix 1993:299).

Closely related to the subject of interpretation of the text is the topic of fore- and afterwords to books (discussed in detail in Chapter 5). Their content was intended as a reading aid for the audience and was, as a result, very sensitive, since they told the reader how to interpret certain passages or ideas. Consequently, they also needed to be assessed by external evaluators, either together with the book or in a separate assessment by another evaluator. Like the assessment of the actual manuscript to the book, afterwords laid emphasis on the mediation of the 'correct' ideological concepts. Paradoxically, the majority of these ideological explanations appeared at the end of the book after the reader had finished reading the book, a fact that is indicative of a second, other function of afterwords, as Chapter 5 will show.

Many texts did not experience any difficulty when inspected in the HV. If, however, a text turned out to be controversial or if the assessments submitted by the publishers were not in agreement, it would be passed on to colleagues in the HV and to an external reviewer (*Außengutachten*) for second opinions (see boxes (15) (16)). Other kinds of manuscripts requiring a second viewpoint were those proposed by publishers whose "inadequate work does not guarantee a good quality content" (DR1/1287), which referred to private or church-related publishers; and further, all literature which was of high importance politically, socially and artistically and was to have wide effects. *Außengutachten* served to stress ideological questions of the texts and, in the majority of cases, remained anonymous to the publishers. By releasing a text document for print, the censors were responsible for each manuscript, confirming with their signature that "a publication is necessary, correct and possible" (DR1/1827; DR1/1287). After print, two copies of the book had to be sent to the Culture Ministry to be stored there for reference purposes, together with a *Produktionsmeldungskarte* (notification card that the book had been produced) for billing and accounting; further copies of the book were submitted to Deutsche Bücherei Leipzig, Staatsbibliothek Berlin, regional public libraries and to Deutsche Bibliothek Frankfurt (the latter did not always take place, however). In the case of a rejection of a manuscript, there was no legal right of objection available to the publisher; rather, necessary changes had to be achieved for future re-application with the HV.

Bringing in the service of external evaluators and reviewers worked to the benefit of both the publishers and the HV, as it was not only a strategy utilised to sell a book to the establishment; it also constituted a mechanism for safeguarding one's position, "as a matter of protecting one's own skin", in Darnton's words (1991:213). Since publisher and censor, with their signatures, were made responsible in person for the 'quality' of a text, they felt it necessary to obtain a second opinion to fall back on, should the higher authority find the book not suitable or even harmful.

In the course of time, and particularly in the 1980s, the files reveal another picture to the researcher. Although still having to prove the evils of capitalism, the publisher's assessments of books become shorter and less detailed. Also, very often, the print applications were submitted without external evaluation and, interestingly, the length of the censor's inspection of a manuscript became shorter. This process of liberalisation appears surprising, as there is no formal document sanctioning such a modification. Nonetheless, the following discussion may provide an explanation. The construction of socialism had, by official declaration, ended at the beginning of the 1970s. This might have been considered a reason for literature to abandon its rigid educational role and to become more open and liberal (Franke 1985, as quoted in Köhler 1988:2415). Also, from the 1970s, the GDR had begun to open itself in terms of foreign politics and perhaps sought to appear more liberal to other countries.

Alternatively, Darnton (1990:6) has the following suggestion. In the interview mentioned previously, the two former East German censors claimed that, increasingly, colleagues in the censorship authority joined the liberal wing of the SED, when they came to realise that East German socialism was moving slowly but steadily closer to Soviet Stalinism. This explanation seems probable, given that, in the 1970s and more so in the 1980s, frustration was mounting within the populace about the *status quo* of real socialism, and increasingly reforms were demanded. Equally, in this time period, more and more socio-critical books appeared—several of them children's books (to hark back to the examples from Chapter 1, these are e.g. the books by Christa Kožik, Wolf Spillner's *Wasseramsel* or Sibylle Durian's *Der Tag, an dem die Schule verschwand*)—with more or less open/hidden criticism, a fact which would indicate that some censors had turned a blind eye to the underlying messages in the text and had let them pass. Barck et al. (1998:431) also seem to support this notion, arguing that numerous powers had an effect on the

Culture Ministry "and also within the HV a factional dispute prevailed with the various cultural lines competing with each other". They continue to claim that, from within the HV itself, an impetus emerged to overcome cultural political narrow-mindedness, advocating a more modern and critical kind of literature in the GDR (1998:431).

Censorship in the GDR was not a fixed process; it changed, as might be expected, with the political environment. It appears that in the early days, when cultural political postulates were clearly defined, censors willingly toed the Party-line, as is also supported by Darnton (1990:6). From the beginnings of the 1960s, however, circumstances became more relaxed. The scope for interpretation had widened and it occurred increasingly that "two evaluators did not arrive at the same conclusion over a manuscript. Each manuscript provided explosive material for hefty debates and, depending on whether it was accepted or rejected, created a precedence and, in turn, set a new benchmark" (Barck et al. 1998:195, 196). Strategies of argumentation were many; there was a lack of well-defined criteria in publishing politics and everyday conflicts and events influenced the print permit procedures (Mix 1993:227). It was left to individuals to apply their own assessment of a given situation. Moreover, culture on the whole was a system that itself was permanently changing owing to constantly alternating cultural politics. This state of affairs generated considerable uncertainty for all players. From the viewpoint of publishing, the judgements as to whether or not to apply for a project may have been affected; problems may also have been caused due to the length of time that a book took from its planning stages to the actual application; what was acceptable at one point may no longer have been so two years on. However, censors themselves were in a similar state of uncertainty and were constantly weighing and reviewing situations; instinct and sensitivity were needed, in order to sense which were emotive words or problematic topics with their superiors (Darnton 1990:8). Additionally, each censor had their private tastes and beliefs which would flow into their decision-making over a manuscript. Therefore, according to changes in political course and depending on the particular censor, censorship was handled more rigidly at times, and more loosely at other times. This may have had the effect that publishers were even more cautious in their proposals and in their descriptions of the books to the HV, perhaps not taking a risk at all with certain books. Censors, less adventurous, on the other hand, may have acted more heavy-handedly than was actually necessary from anxiety to protect their own skins.

2.4 A Niche in the Den—Literary Translators

After determining publishers, censors and Party functionaries as the main players in literary politics, the role of translators should not be overlooked under the weight of this bureaucracy. As has been shown, it was the task of publishers to select a book and to advertise it to the censorship authority, by alluding to the officially recognised paradigms. It was the editors in the various publishing houses who constituted the link to the people producing the texts, i.e. the translators, to maintain communication with them but also to monitor and, if necessary, guide the text production with the aim of achieving socially appropriate contents and wording. Eventually, it was the translators who performed the actual work with the texts; they were responsible for transferring the foreign text into the East German cultural setting. This *status quo* therefore indicates that translators were placed at the bottom of the hierarchy, only being involved in the actual work of translation. On the other hand, since all matters associated with literature played a key role in society, one would, at the same time, expect the GDR to put emphasis on creating a favourable climate for translation, in which translators would find positive work conditions and in which they were in a position to pursue their work to good effect, following the socialist paradigm. It is the aim of this section to outline conditions and the social position of those players so far not mentioned in book production, namely the literary translators. The information underlying this section derives, in the main, from interviews personally performed with East German literary translators and from the study of the files of the East German Writers' Association.

2.4.1 The Path to a Translator's Contract and Further

Translation in East Germany was not seen as a technique or a craft but as a "cultural activity" (Autorenkollektiv unter Leitung von Heinz Püschel 1969:339) and as a contribution towards strengthening the East German *Nationalliteratur* and to support the identification of the East German identity. Accordingly, there were discussions early on about translation being partisan and the translator being a propagandist. Ambitious plans had the objective of defining a Marxist-Leninist translation theory. However, it turned out that this ambition was not to be accomplished, owing to a lack of precise instructions and directives. Nonetheless, back in March 1947, the *Schutzverband der Deutschen Schriftsteller Großberlin* (Association for the Protection of German Authors in Greater Berlin) had put in place a department uniting all translators (literary and technical) under its umbrella. The main motivation for this move was concerns about how to achieve high-quality translations. Before candidates were admitted to the Association, the quality of their work was assessed carefully and, only if found satisfactory, the new member was entered into a card index which served as evidence for their skills and as a recommendation of their services.

It was not until 10 April 1953 that literary translators were fully acknowledged by society through the establishment of their own separate institution, dedicated solely to literary translational issues and problems. It was set up within the East German Writers' Association and there were three main reasons given to underpin the translators' integration into this organisation. Firstly, it was claimed that translators were, as a matter of fact, creators of literary works and, therefore, ought to be classified as 'recreating authors', a notion which appeared to justify the move of translators into a body set up for authors. The second objective was to establish an official representational body for the profession, which was to be the *Sektion Übersetzer* (Department for Translators) in the East German Writers' Association. Hence, the minutes which reported on the foundation meeting claimed,

> until 1953, literary translators have neither been organised in the Union nor in the Writers' Association nor have they in any way been supported by the Association. Moreover, it is impossible for literary translators to become a member of the Union, as only colleagues being in an employee-employer relationship are permitted to join. Thus, freelance translators are hanging in the air. Therefore, the Writers' Association will assume the role of the Union for our translators. (Protokoll der Initiativsitzung der Sektion Übersetzer, 10 April 1953, VS 257 neu)

Thirdly, it was decided to put in place a central body where all issues related to translation could be managed centrally; thus, the intention was, for instance, to spread the workload evenly amongst translators; or to organise seminars or create other services to improve the quality of the work.

The Writers' Association as the official state representative of authors, translators and publishers was an institution which was completely loyal to the state and which, indeed on several occasions, used its disciplinary powers. For instance, the Association's influence emerged in the Biermann incident in 1976 when it became heavily involved and which led to the exclusion of several 'unruly' authors. As Werner Creutziger, himself translator and active in the *Sektion Übersetzer* in the Association, stated, "a professional organisation in a totalitarian state can be considered an instrument of this state. The state provides the money and has a say in practically everything" (1998:30). Thus, the Association was infiltrated with Party functionaries and members of the Stasi who either held powerful positions or worked covertly. A telling example of this fact is provided in the Association's statute (although it was amended in later years, on the whole, it kept its ideological content),

> The East German Writers' Association recognises the leading role of the working class and its Party in art and literature. The members of the Association recognise Socialist Realism, which is rooted in Marxist-Leninist ideology, as the only method to grasp reality correctly and to reflect it artistically. They oppose with determination all theories of ideological co-existence and the penetration of bourgeois beliefs into

> literary spheres. They are active builders of a socialist present. Their art aims at shaping socialist thinking, feeling and action in the people. In doing so, they contribute to the all-round construction of socialism in the GDR and live up to their responsibilities and patriotic duties towards the whole German people, whose future is embodied in the first German nation of peace of workers and farmers. (SV609 neu)

Despite these ideological constraints, it was considered desirable for literary translators to be members of the Writers' Association. As has been pointed out earlier, they were not organised in the Union and, hence, the Association represented their professional organisation. The *Sektion Übersetzer* was an active branch. Its members met regularly, debating their members' concerns or problems as well as looking after translation matters and giving intellectual support. Further, they looked after public relations work and represented the translators' interests in the Association's committee. As the translators held the same position as the authors within the Association, the same rights were granted and the same facilities were open to them, such as courses or recreational facilities. One facility that was particularly popular were the two *Autorenheime*, i.e. old mansion houses, owned by the Association and used as 'authors' retreats', where the members could withdraw for a week or two, free of charge, and could focus on their work in a peaceful environment and undisturbed from the hustle and bustle of the rest of the world. Attendance at translators' conferences or study trips, provided they were taking place in a socialist country, were also readily paid for. Exceptionally, there were rare cases in which a translator was allowed an exit permit into the West (after intervention of the Association).

East German literary translators, although freelance, were socially protected, enjoying the benefits of social security, which meant that they could afford to fall ill without worrying about loss of income and, also, that they were entitled to a pension after retiring—luxuries of which Western literary translators could only dream. Since East German translators were freelance, they had to pay not only the employees' contribution towards their social security but also that of the employers. As members of the *Schriftstellerverband*, however, the employer's contribution was paid for them, another precious advantage of being a member. From 1971, the social security for members was further improved, as they became insured with the *FDGB, Freier Deutscher Gewerkschaftsbund* (Free German Trade Union Organisation) and, as a consequence, were entitled to the same benefits as workers and employees. The three major improvements were:

1. For all members: sick pay from the first day of medically attested work incapacity (so far this had been granted only from the 29th day of illness in Berlin; out of Berlin nothing at all had been granted).

2. For female members: maternity pay and child care payments at a rate of 100% of their taxed income (so far they had been granted only 50–65% of the contributory income).
3. For unmarried or single mothers: sick pay, in order to nurse an ill child.

A further benefit was the *Normalverlagsvertrag* (standard contract for literary translators). Drawn up in co-operation between the Writers' Association, the Union and the Ministry of Culture and published on 31 May 1955 (SV 1118 alt), it aimed to re-shape working conditions with respect to general conditions and payment, in order to enable the translators to perform thorough work. Once established, the contract was amended and improved approximately once every decade (also, in 1965 it was included into the newly formulated East German Copyright Law).

The contract guaranteed the translators a basic fee paid for every page of the manuscript. A third of this fee was payable to the translator on agreement of the contract, another third on submission of the manuscript, and the last third on the publisher's acceptance of the translated manuscript.[21] This means that the translator was paid a major part of his/her fee even before beginning actual work on the translation. It is worth pointing out that the fee paid to literary translators was higher than that paid to technical translators, which expresses how much literary translators were respected by society. This economic advantage over technical translators was still true shortly before the fall of the Wall, as Schmitz confirms, "the most recent increase of fees, giving them [the literary translators], for the time being, a fair economic advantage over sci-tech translators, took effect from January 1988" (1989:129).

A further incentive in the contract was a clause stipulating profit-sharing for reprints to be paid to the translator. This was:

If a licence to a book was sold to another publisher, the translator received royalties from the profits of the rights to the book (initially 5%, the contract was later amended to allow any percentage between 5 and 50%).

Further, translator's rights and duties as specified in the 1955 version of the contract were:

- The translator was required to discuss all remarks and corrections made by the editor and to accept well-founded corrections and improvements;

Table 2.2 Royalty Rates for Reprints (1971–1977)

Volume Published	*Profit Sharing*
10,001 – 20,000	3 % of the basic fee per 1,000 copies
20,001 – 30,000	2 % of the basic fee per 1,000 copies

(Source: Stiftung Archiv der Akademie der Künste, file SV(neu) 758)

s/he also had to exercise the final editing of the translation and to proof read the galleys. As soon as the translation was submitted, all rights to it passed on to the publisher.

- The publisher, on the other hand, was required to cite the translator's full name on the title page (however, when compiling the corpus of children's books, it has been found that that was not always the case). Also, the publisher had to provide the translator with 10 free copies of the book (from the first print-run) and with 5 free copies of every following edition. Should the translator wish to buy additional copies for personal use, the publisher was obliged to supply the translator with them at a reduced price. This last clause was especially useful as books made nice gifts in a country where not much else was available to give as presents, even more so for relatives in the West.

As mentioned earlier, the *Normalverlagsvertrag* was revised a few times and always to the benefit of the translators; so, for instance, in the mid-1970s, the fee per page was raised by nearly 50% and, in the 1980s, the benchmark of 2,000 characters per page was lowered to 1,800.

By and large, it would appear that East German translators led relatively secure financial lives. They were able to make a living from literary translations without having to resort to moonlighting. Partly, this may be attributed to the educational system, which was planned to be in alignment with the job market and trained the right number of students for the right jobs. Therefore, there was no unemployment in the GDR and translators did not have to be sidetracked into odd jobs to improve their income. Equally, as a rule, women went out to work, which prevented the formation of an amateur sector of housewife translators. Admittedly, translators of literature from Russian and languages from socialist countries had an advantage. More titles and bigger print-runs were produced from these countries, for ideological and economic reasons. This meant more jobs were available and the chances for profits on reprints were higher. However, translators of Western languages fared comparatively well, particularly in the latter period of the GDR. Western authors, as opposed to 'progressive' ones, were regarded as 'safe' by publishers, because their works sold, i.e. despite the governmental propaganda about capitalism, these books were in great demand. Being locked in by the Iron Curtain, East Germans could only experience the world on the other side of the Wall through the written word; therefore, they eagerly observed the official advance notices of books in the *Börsenblatt für den Deutschen Buchhandel, Leipzig* and, within hours of the books' delivery to the bookshops, Western books were sold out.[22]

These were the books on which *Überzeichnungen* by the booksellers were performed; in other words, the bookshops ordered copies many times over the actual demand, because they knew that there would be delivery problems and they would only receive a fraction of their order. By inflating their order, they hoped to increase the percentage of books delivered and, in doing so, ensure a sale for at least their regular customers. This in turn led to the development of *Bückware*,[23] a term describing goods which were desperately sought after and which were held back by the shop owners for special customers, not infrequently in exchange for other goods or services, for example, a pallet of bricks or a dental appointment. However, one interviewee mentioned that taking a bunch of flowers to the shop assistant every now and then also helped to make oneself a privileged customer and candidate for *Bückware*. Equally, several interviewees mentioned that they were happy to have connections in publishing houses because, through these, they were able to obtain first print editions which were published under a licence agreement with a Western publisher. These books were especially sought after, because everyone knew that this licence had a limited duration and might never be renewed, which meant that the book might never be published again.

Translators knew not only from the sales of their books that their work was appreciated. On a personal level, they were aware of their value. Many of them stated in their interviews that it was unusual for the East Germans to know a foreign language well, let alone study it at university level—a fact which made them feel respected and an authority in their field. Occasions when translators experienced the immediate respect, regard and affection of their audiences were those moments when they, as was the practice for authors, travelled the country and read from their works. Similar readings for children took place regularly at schools or in libraries or during the Children's Literature Days, which were staged in a different part of the country each year (see p 48). One translator reported in his interview about one of his first reading assignments, in which he was sent to a tiny village far away from any town in order to read and speak about his latest translation. At first, he had not taken this job too seriously, as he did not expect 'those farmers' to be too interested in literature. He was, however, surprised when he found the whole village, men and women, children and adults, gathered and very informed about the latest trend in literature. This farming community was full of expectation of what new information this Berlin person would bring to them and ready to enter eager discussions (Karl-Heinz Jähn, personal communication, 19 July 2001).

Another reason for the choice of being a literary translator lay in the opportunity to escape the many constraints of socialist life; and indeed, this was an aspect that should not be underestimated, as it was mentioned by several interviewees. Being a literary translator meant working in a niche and evading the general political climate. In spite of the guidance, control and censorship exerted by the government, publishing houses were still enclaves from socialist reality, undisturbed by the usual propaganda. Literature meant freedom. It meant dealing with a world that did not know physical or time constraints. Besides, most translators—unlike authors—did not have too close a contact with the censorship authorities because, in the majority of cases, it was up to the publishing house to choose the right books and then approach the translator. This stands in contrast to authors who had to defend ideologically every line they had written and who, at times, went through long debates over words and meanings. Usually the translators' contact with their publisher was limited to meetings with their editor in which the correctness and quality of the translation was discussed, which—according to the interviewees—occurred most frequently in a friendly and constructive atmosphere. The few times that translators did have to fight for their work, as Lieselotte Remané pointed out in her interview (20 August 2001), was with more fussy editors who were over-correct and became set on a particular formulation. Certainly, there were editors who had a fixed view on a narrow orthodox interpretation of certain concepts in a book, but they were in the minority, as was contended unanimously.

Therefore, on the whole, East German translators seem to have felt quite happy about their choice of profession, especially since they knew about the fate of their West German colleagues, that their situation was not very favourable, and they certainly did not envy them. Compared with their Western counterparts, it would indeed appear that the GDR translators led a relatively secure financial life. It might be true that their lifestyle was much simpler and without luxuries, but that must be put in context of the overall lifestyle in East Germany and with the fact that luxuries were hardly ever available. What the state did was to take care that people had enough of the necessities which, moreover, were cheap, as these were subsidised by the state. People had come to accept not to expect too many additional things. Everybody had the same and there was nothing from which to create envy or competition. This explains the attitude of some of the interviewees who claimed that they were happy with their work contract and did not even care to read through it, when being commissioned, or to check the figures, because they felt they had all they needed—work and sufficient income to buy food and pay the rent. As long as their work paid for such a lifestyle, there was no need to be worried about better pay. In this light, job satisfaction was high; it also speaks for the mind-set of the GDR, because many translators were of the opinion that they would certainly not have opted to be a literary translator, if they had lived in the West (Creutziger 1998:14). Reality proved them right because, after reunification in 1990, nearly all interviewees chose to stop translating, because of the low income, lack of time which meant having to rush through jobs, and the regular humiliating treatment from editors in publishing houses.

Chapter Three
What the Files Say

The socio-political and cultural environment that existed during the period of the GDR has been described in the previous chapters, as it is believed that setting the context is a necessary step in understanding any investigation of literature. The analysis in this chapter draws on Lefevere's theory (see e.g. 1982a, 1982b, 1985a, 1985b or 1992) of patronage in cultural systems, a concept which defines one or more preferred poetics[1] in alignment with the prevalent values and beliefs of a given society. Lefevere points to a broader notion of the 'rewriting' of literature,[2] which encompasses not only the rewriting of the text by, for example, translators, but also the way in which a (national) literature becomes rewritten in a more fundamental way by the mechanisms which select and attribute 'meaning' to the literature that is to be made available in that society. What is then required, according to Lefevere, in order to understand the literature produced by a society, is an investigation of "how the interaction of writing and rewriting is ultimately responsible not just for the canonization of specific authors or specific works and the rejection of others but also for the evolution of a given literature, since rewritings are often designed precisely to push a given literature in a certain direction" (Lefevere 1985b:219).

The factors at work in the selection process of literature depend to some degree on the society under discussion; however, Lefevere suggests two main elements. These are, firstly, the insiders, i.e. those who work within the literary system, namely writers, translators, critics, teachers and others who, in their rewriting, are tied to those parameters set by the agents from outside; secondly, the patrons, who for the most part operate outside the literary system, i.e. the "powers (persons, institutions) which help or hinder the writing, reading and rewriting of literature" (1985b:227). The last chapter has revealed that, in the context of the GDR, there was a high correlation between the concept of patron and the Party, so much so that publishers found themselves in a place where they had to comply with the directives of the Party at all times. Bearing in mind that publishers were able to realise their book projects only within this given framework and, thus, with considerable limitations, it is felt that they ought to be subsumed into the *insiders* of the East German literary system, rather than staying outside the system along with those powers who determine literary developments in the first instance, as Lefevere suggests.

This chapter and Chapters 4 and 5 will focus on and analyse two visible aspects of rewriting as performed by those elements inside the literary system of the GDR, in their endeavour to adhere to the norms set by the patron, the SED on the outside. A considerable part of East German rewriting took the form of paratexts written to accompany the production. In general, paratexts may aid in shedding light on the norms and conventions of a literary system and illuminate the context under which translations took place, pointing to issues which would not be brought to the fore by an analysis of the translated texts alone. The two paratextual text types under examination here belong, firstly, to the category of epitext (i.e. texts commenting on books or translations but located outside the actual books), secondly to the category of peritext (i.e. immediately surrounding the translation and thus located within the books themselves) (see e.g. Genette 1997:xviii, 1, 2, 5). Hence, this chapter will address the discourse in the print permit files, followed by case studies in the next chapter, while Chapter 5 will centre on afterwords produced and printed directly after the translated children's or juvenile texts. Exploring the contents of the print permit files (in other words, assessing the phrases used by publishers and assessors when addressing the censors) will bring to light the various ideological components and will illustrate how they manifest themselves in the files. In so doing, it is hoped to identify the core criteria which publishers employed in their discourse and on which the censors based their ultimate decisions, each of which ultimately had an impact on the production and reception of translations.

3.1 Why the Files?

In many societies, the procedures of text selection and text handling are not made transparent; judgements may vary from instance to instance, and from person to person, commensurate with personal taste; not much is written down and thus becomes unavailable for historical research. Consequently, translation scholars frequently have to resort to a comparison of source and target texts and, from their findings, work backwards in order to establish a limited picture of a society and its values. On the other hand, the East German bureaucracy with its requirement of traceability produced solid written evidence in the form of documentation required to obtain a print permit. These files were archived after the collapse of the GDR and became known as 'print permit files' or 'censorship files'. The availability of these paratexts provides an invaluable resource for the study of the effects of social beliefs on literature, since all the relevant concepts are made visible in the written word. Hence, it is believed that the data dormant in the files will provide conclusive evidence of the key concepts used in the GDR literary discourse and book industry, notably so for the selection of Western texts and the fashion in which they were handled by translators and publishers.

Although the discourse in the files provides, first and foremost, information about the books themselves, it also permits conclusions about the cultural and ideological environment and its influence on the publishing industry and, as a consequence, about editorial control and editorial decisions.[3] These texts have to be seen within the entire context of the censorship procedure, rather than as isolated assessments about publication projects. They were the publisher's one and only chance to advertise a book to the censor before final judgement was passed. Hence, the justification for the selection of a book had to be well-placed and the description of the content had to assure the censors that the books did not pose any threat to socialist principles. Since it was a one-way discussion, a monologue as it were, publishers had to make their best effort, because they were not given a second opportunity for further clarification and more exhaustive comment. The argument had to be succinct, to the point and in a fashion that the censors expected and could understand, in the respective given cultural political climate. It is precisely for this reason that the files deliver irrefutable documentary evidence of the acknowledged and sanctioned literary paradigms.

3.2 What is Visible in the Files?

In order to understand what is visible in the files, it is necessary to return briefly to the role of the patron and elaborate on the mechanisms involved in the production of literature. Again, Lefevere's theory with its notions of rewriting, power and patronage has been found useful for the following explanations and, thus, they form the foundation of the discussion. As might be deduced, the concept of *patronage* represents the overarching concept which determines all that lies below. In East Germany, patronage was undifferentiated (see e.g. Lefevere 1985b and 1992); this is to say, there were not multiple patrons but all power was united in a single institution, the SED. As a result, there was only one dominant ideology, as opposed to the multiple ideologies that exist in pluralist, differentiated societies. The patron, i.e. the Party, exerted both power and influence over all aspects of literary production, including how it was ordered and administered, for instance, aspects such as granting literature (and thus writers and translators) a high status in society, or putting in place an administrative apparatus (in the main, all issues dealt with in the previous chapters).

Lefevere identifies three main branches under the patron, namely: ideology, economics and status. Whereas the elements of economics and status have been discussed (see Section 2.2), the element of ideology will constitute the focus of investigation here. Following Lefevere, ideology and the concepts derived from it by the patron determine the rules which are applied to the production of literature. It is these rules that define which criteria are desirable and which are undesirable for literary output. As a consequence, it is ideology that controls both the selection process of literature and also the actual content of the literary output—which Lefevere defines as poetics. All rewriting, according to Lefevere, is an "interpretation undertaken on the basis of a certain concept of what the world should be like (ideology) as well as a certain concept of what literature should be like (poetics)" (1985b:217). This poetics, or codification of an ideology in terms of literary production, is the action that leaves a visible mark both in the literary vocabulary of a society and in the functional production of its literature. It is these visible markers that this research aims to reveal.

A correlation may be drawn between the branching of ideas from an ideology and the institutions which support it (see Figure 3.1).

The left-hand tree represents the branching of ideas from the 'ideology', where each level refines and adds substance to the layer above. Hence, 'ideology' is defined by a number of (socialist) concepts which, in turn, define the policies for selecting the (literary) product of the society, ultimately defining what is a good product and what is a bad product. Corresponding to this refinement is the hierarchy of the ruling power promoting the ideology. This means that, in the GDR, the Party represented the embodiment of the 'ideology'. The state apparatus, which was an extension of the Party (see Section 2.1), implemented the ideological concepts insofar as it enacted and controlled the rules of the society. The publishers, under the control of the state and the Party, as the producers of the literature, selected or commissioned the appropriate literature and, subsequently, decided on (according to

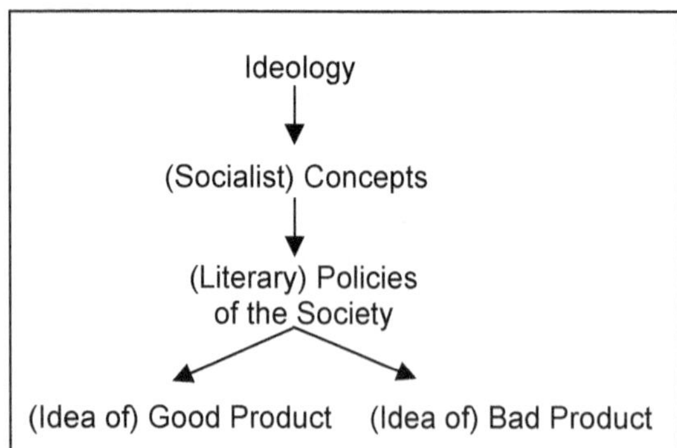

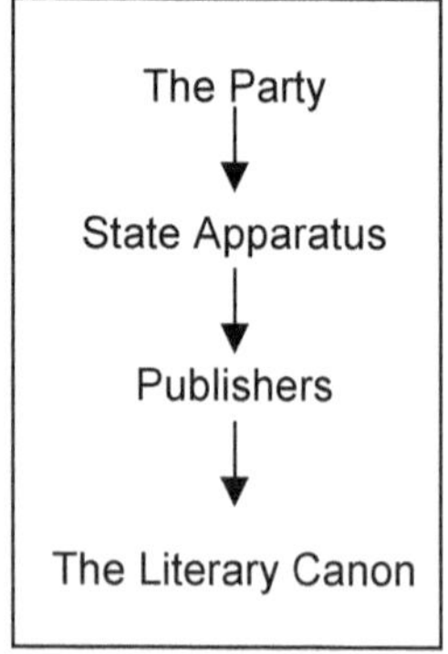

Figure 3.1 Poetological and institutional trees in the GDR.

the policies) the content of the literature, thereby creating the literary canon of the society.

The final codification of the rules, derived from the prevailing ideology, is ultimately made visible in the products of the system. In the case of the GDR, these were not only the primary texts, i.e. the books, but also paratexts as, for instance, the discourse in the censorship files and the afterwords accompanying the books. In many respects, these texts associated with the surrounding literary production provide a deeper insight into the codification mechanism than the children's books themselves, because the books represent only the final stage of a complex (and normally invisible) sequence of steps leading to a 'good' product.

3.3 Codification in the GDR

Before progressing, it is considered helpful to recap briefly the main ideas of Socialist Realism (as described in Section 1.1.2), in other words, the main codification concept used in the GDR, which was adopted as the central cultural political and ideological paradigm from the early years but which experienced a transformation caused by political changes at the beginning of the 1970s. While some regard this as a relaxation of the rigid orthodox interpretation of the concept, others claim to have detected a complete abandonment of the idea. Regardless of the school of thought, the files demonstrate that the key concepts of Socialist Realism were employed in the argumentation across all the years up until the collapse of the regime.

As the embodiment of the politicisation of art, Socialist Realist principles were to form a part of every oeuvre, in order to reflect agendas linked with the construction of the East German socialist society and to contribute to societal change. Hinging on six postulates, all writing was to shape the reader's consciousness, a process which was envisaged to function through identification of the readers with the reading material. Because of the requirement that readers learn from the material they read, the books had to be easily accessible and understandable (Postulate of *Volksverbundenheit* or *Volkstümlichkeit*). In order to represent useful teaching, literature had to be determined by its content; it had to be anchored in real-life situations; it was to have a clear association with contemporary ideas and, arising from this contemporariness, was to point to the future and demonstrate the emergent social, Historical perspective, which was expected to be real because it was bound to develop at some future stage (Postulate of *Realism*). Tied in with reality and a glorious future, all literature was to be of an optimistic nature, giving readers a feeling of being victorious over old traits and beliefs and making them eager to fight for the new world (Postulate of *Optimism*). It was paramount for people to possess special attributes; hence, protagonists of East German fiction had to be exemplary characters, worth emulating, in order to awaken the good in readers.

These values encompassed certain traits of the individual and the emphasis on human dignity, but also all features supportive of peace, social progress, solidarity and understanding among peoples (Postulate of *Humanism*). Pulling these threads together, literature had the aim of portraying typical people, situations and conditions—not isolated cases—by referring not only to the qualities most prevalent in (any) society, but to those most complete, correct, wholesome and impressible, in one word, prototypes which would ensure progress (Postulate of *Das Typische*, the Typical being representative of a particular situation or circumstance). Lastly, Party and Marxist-Leninist doctrine represented the ideology that everyone and every book was expected to support (Postulate of *Parteilichkeit*, Being partisan).

These postulates were nevertheless open to interpretation; consequently, there is no single definition. They were understood differently from person to person, from instance to instance and from period to period, a situation compounded by the continuous changes in the ideological climate within the literary system itself, commensurate with the political climate in the country. In the print permit files, this shows as a covert power struggle between publishers and state officials, as to the 'correct' interpretation of works of literature. The name of the game was to apply the officially recognised concepts and paradigms and bend and stretch them, in order to give outwardly the impression of bowing to the rules, yet shifting the meaning with the ultimate goal of edging the books towards acceptability.

According to Lefevere, rewriting happens under the strictures of poetics (which itself hinges on ideology, as Figure 3.1 has demonstrated) and its codification. From what has been said in the previous chapters, it is evident that this also holds true for the GDR. Indeed, the files give clear evidence of "creat[ing] images of a writer, a work, a period [and] a genre" (Lefevere 1992:5). Through the concept of Socialist Realism, the purpose of literature and the preference for certain authors were defined, certain genres were prioritised and so were "literary devices, genres, motifs, symbols, prototypical characters and situations" (Lefevere 1985b:229). Although the Socialist Realist framework was not a rigid and inflexible model, it did prescribe to society which kind of literature was, at any given time, permitted to be selected and which function it played in society. It also provided a certain set of concepts and terms, against which all literary production was measured and which codified all texts and marked them as being convergent with or opposed to the system. This development, again, is in alignment with Lefevere, who contends, "a codification of poetics leads to canonization of the output of certain writers whose work is seen as conforming most closely to the codified poetics" and "is then used as an example for future writers to follow" (1985b:230, 231). As will be illustrated below, there is abundant evidence in the files for the fact that only certain writers were considered appropriate for the socialist environment, many of whom had a socialist bias and whose ideas fitted well into the Marxist-Leninist belief system. As will also be shown, there was a strong leaning towards certain themes in the books and one will search in vain for books with other subjects, since they were completely excluded from the native canon and not allowed into the country. There is yet another observation evinced by the files; to a certain degree, Western books with ideological shortcomings or potential sensitivities could be made palatable to the censors by shrewd argumentation that made use of the ideologically accepted concepts and terminology, representing what Lefevere defines 'the codification of literary language'.

3.4 Who Does the Rewriting?

As Lefevere states, all rewriting "reflects a certain ideology and a poetics and as such manipulates literature to function in a given society in a given way. Rewriting is manipulation, undertaken in the service of power" (1992:1). Rewriting is closely linked to the interpretation of texts and results in acceptance or rejection of literary works, and in their canonisation or non-canonisation. According to Lefevere, inherent in every culture is the existence of one or more patrons whose "efforts will primarily be directed at preserving the stability of the social system as a whole, and the literary production ... will have to further that aim" (1992:17). Under such a system of patronage, Lefevere maintains, the rewriter chooses either "to 'go with the system', so to speak, to stay within the parameters delimited by the constraints ... or, alternatively, he or she may choose to go against the system, to try to operate outside the constraints of his or her time, by reading works of literature in other than the received ways" (1985b:225).

Lefevere names translation as the most obvious instance of rewriting (1985b:234). Translators, amongst others, rewrite and adapt works of literature until they can be claimed to correspond to the poetics and the ideology of their age. As has been mentioned earlier, while translators operate from inside the literary system, the instances of power, i.e. the patrons, exert control from outside. Lefevere subsumes publishers in the latter, outside group. Applying this assumption to the GDR does not, however, fit with the reality of their position within the system. It is indeed true that East German publishers "help[ed] or hinder[ed] the writing, reading and rewriting of literature" (Lefevere 1985b:227). However, unlike in Lefevere's model, in the GDR, publishers clearly acted from inside the literary system and, what is more, they acted not on their own account but on behalf of a higher instance of power, namely the Party and its functionaries. Both aspects indicate that, in East Germany, publishers did not belong to the patronage situated outside the literary system, but that the patron was situated above publishers, and it was this higher authority in the overall hierarchy that patronised literature and ultimately decided, in Lefevere's words, "what [would] 'make it' and what [would] not" (1985b:236). This is clearly visible in chief ideologue Hager's comment, which is indicative of the SED's pivotal position, "It is now the hundred-thousandth time I am saying this: when asked whether we have a cultural political strategy, one can only answer that the cultural politics of our Party have been laid down in the Party programme of the SED, in the resolutions of the Tenth Party Meeting and in the resolutions of the Central Committee. There is no other political orientation" (as quoted in Ackermann 2000:15).

This points to the ambivalent role given to the East German publishers. As explained in Chapter 2, they were declared by the state to be the promoters of socialist culture and the educators of the readers; it was their task to disseminate suitable, pedagogical literature. In this facilitating function, publishers were not only regarded as protectors of achieved cultural political values, but they were also assimilated by the regime and acted as state officials. Or so it would seem. The fact that, in unison with such honour, they were made personally accountable and could be penalised for any error by those censoring, in effect, locates them on a lower level in the hierarchy. This conflict in the publishers' status also becomes noticeable in the discourse in the files. The following are examples of instances in the files, signalling solidarity and team spirit, and seemingly placing publishers alongside the regime. "We are happy that our children are deliberately kept away from bad wild-western-style novels, because the ideological concept of these books does not correspond with the humanist ideas of a socialist education" (Harte, *Allein in der Prärie*, DR1/3993); or "this ensures that we end up with an edition which better conforms to educational and artistic requirements" (Reeves, *Märchen aus England*, DR1/3706); equally, "the readers will arrive at the conviction that our social order without doubt has the greater advantages" (Hamilton, *Der Planet des Patrick Brown*, DR1/2287). However, the very fact that publishers had to apply for permission to publish books bears witness to their inferior position, a position in which they were ranked as recipients of an order, dependent and under control.

Therefore, for East German society, a re-assignment may be suggested, placing publishers on a level closer to translators inside the literary system. Both were admittedly in a position to decide what to alter and how to alter texts (with publishers as the controlling instance over translators); nonetheless, at the same time both were restricted by the parameters of their system, dictating to them the terms and conditions and thereby downgrading them in the hierarchy. However, as publishers were indeed the controlling instance over translators, a classification may be proposed, calling the individual translators 'rewriters of texts', but making publishers the 'rewriters of literature'. In other words, the concept of rewriting also encompasses publishers in that they had an immediate influence on the canon by selecting and rejecting certain books and by controlling the work of the translators; these, in turn, performed the manual rewriting of the actual manuscripts; all of which denotes a scenario in which rewriting took place in two phases, both, however, in accord with the regime's officially propagated line. The first phase entailed scouring the entire global book production and making a choice as to which works of literature constituted appropriate fare for East German readers, the second phase with the actual work on the texts, translating and—if necessary—altering them. Given this set-up, it may be safely assumed that pre-censorship in the publishing houses took place long before a manuscript landed on the desk of a censor. In their role as 'rewriters of literature', publishers produced text about texts, in other words, paratexts about the translations they planned to bring out, processing and reaching verdicts about the source texts. This means, in fact, that all translated texts that were granted a print permit had at least two (re)writers, namely the writer of the original text and one or more writers of paratext. Whereas the author of the original spoke to his future readership, children and adolescents, the writers of the paratext in the print permit files addressed the censor as their reader. Similarly, inasmuch as the source text author had to make the child readers interested enough for them to buy the book, the paratext writer had to arouse the censor's interest with the emphasis on obtaining a print permit. As a consequence, the paratext had to show certain properties, in order to appeal to its censor-reader, which simply meant describing the foreign text in a way that it became acceptable to the censoring authority. In this procedure, the rewriter (publisher, assessor) produced critical analyses attempting to acculturate the Foreign and adapting it to the parameters of native GDR ideology and poetics.

3.5 The Codes: Key Motifs and Socialist Realist Paradigms

It has been stated that the East German cultural political discourse adopted Socialist Realism as its primary codification of literary criteria for the evaluation of all literary and artistic production. Accordingly, it also dictated these norms on rewriting, prescribing the nature of texts which were allowed to cross the border. "Once a poetics is codified, it exerts a tremendous system-conforming influence on the further development of a literary system" and additionally, "each dominant poetics freezes or certainly controls the dynamics of the system. It achieves this goal more easily in systems with undifferentiated patronage" (Lefevere 1992:26, 35). In their endeavour to introduce foreign, Western literature to East Germany—and the discourse in the files underpins this ambition conclusively—publishers not only carefully selected texts for publication, but also attempted to make the texts compatible with native ideological and poetological norms. Investigation of the files shows that there was an almost ritualistic approach towards defending each work of literature, an approach which is marked by a regular emphasis on particular criteria and concepts, assisting in matching the foreign work with the codified East German standard. This becomes evident in common motifs, aiding in expressing the ideological position and in appropriating the Other by showing similarities. Broadly speaking, Otherness was regarded adversely and, therefore, had to be remodelled into sameness, a procedure that was achieved by applying defined standards. Non-socialist texts were explained in socialist terms and concepts, in order to make the texts fit the ideology. To put it bluntly: publishers had a social agenda, to which they bent their texts. In this process, notions that were in accord with the official cultural political rationale were emphasised, and notions that could potentially be taken as challenging and confrontational and act as an obstacle to a publication were underplayed in such a manner that commonly accepted symbols and norms (motifs) anchored authors and stories firmly in the socialist landscape.

Rewriters tend to "invent an appropriate critical vocabulary" (Lefevere 1985b:229). Predictably, there is a close agreement between the principal key concepts employed in the critical discourse in the print permit files, and those criteria propagated by the official poetics. All motifs had their roots in Marxist-Leninist doctrine and were chosen to support concepts and stereotypes of socialism, such as taking an active and political stance or exhibiting a love for work. Overall, there were two types of motifs used for argumentation and explanation; firstly, those that identified ideologically positive meaning in the texts and thereby tied the book to the orthodox political discourse; generally, these motifs served to legitimise a publication. Texts that exhibited a plethora of such positive concepts were upfront ideal candidates to incorporate into the approved canon. Hence, all critical evaluations in the files utilise several positive motifs to support the text, which was especially true for more 'problematic' books. On the other hand, there were those concepts with ideologically negative implications. As these could put a publication at risk, they had to be circumvented. Certainly, texts with too many negative concepts would have been rejected straightaway and would never have reached the stage of a critical evaluation. Nevertheless, it was found in the files that attention was also drawn to negative motifs, if only to be mitigated by concepts with a positive connotation.

The following diagrams are an attempt to place the motifs into logically motivated groupings. Nonetheless, a word of caution is necessary. With many motifs, the boundaries are blurred and, for this reason, this list represents a subjective interpretation. However, this approach appears justifiable, since there is no single, clearly accepted interpretation in literary science, precisely because of the ambivalent nature of the motifs. As mentioned earlier, concepts were stretched according to the political climate and the necessity of the moment. So, for example, while Individualism was frowned upon in the early days as having overtones of unwanted isolation and subjective personality, in later decades the concept was accepted if it appeared in unison with a supportive argumentation, for example, together with a strong, active and positive protagonist manifesting the ideal socialist personality (emphasising the Socialist Realist paradigms of Humanism and Realism). The special emphasis on Humanism and Realism in the files becomes more than evident. Given that "the literature of the German Democratic Republic is based on the best traditions of all humanist and realistic literature" (Autorenkolletiv unter Leitung von Horst Haase und Hans Jürgen Geerdts 1976:24), nearly all assessments employ both motifs as their key argument in an attempt to make books appear a true literary heritage and, hence, make them fit in and render them publishable.

Also, it is noticeable that for each positive motif there exists a corresponding negative one and vice versa. For instance, capitalism, constituting a concept with a negative meaning, gained a positive connotation when turned into its opposite, anti-capitalism. Thus, translated children's books from English-speaking countries, notably the USA and the UK, frequently depicted the egotistic and ruthless behaviour of people in an influential social position, depictions unacceptable for descriptions of any kind of a socialist society; however, in connection with capitalism they were interpreted positively, since they effectively told children about the evil qualities of such societies.

Following is a list of all motifs I have identified in the course of investigating and analysing the print permit files. These motifs in unison with the Socialist Realist concepts, once more listed below, represented a framework with which texts were declared as compatible with the political system and, certainly, they supplied the reasoning behind the decision of whether or not a text could be salvaged for incorporation into the system. The lists taken together epitomise the East German vision of the 'ideal socialist world'.[4]

Socialist Realist Paradigms

A. Partisanship
B. Realism
C. Humanism
D. Optimism
E. The Typical, Authenticity
F. Accessibility, Comprehensibility

Positive motifs

1. Contemporariness, having relevance to present-day life
2. Work ethos, Readiness to learn
3. Collective spirit, Solidarity
4. Active involvement, Initiative, Self-belief
5. Loyalty to the Party, the USSR and to Socialism
6. Peace
7. 'Positive hero' of translated literature
8. Educational usefulness
9. Social criticism

Negative motifs

1. Capitalism, Imperialism, Profiteering
2. Bourgeois values

3. Social difference, Class system, Drop-outs
4. Fascism, Semitism/Zionism
5. Religion, Fatalism, Superstition
6. Violence, Crime, Sex
7. Hooliganism, Criminal behaviour
8. Escapism, Drugs, Alienation
9. Fantasy
10. Racism, Exploitation, Colonialism, Oppression of any kind
11. Sentimental, romantic and kitschy expressions
12. Apolitical or Anti-political or Neutral thinking
13. Indifference, Resignation, Hesitation, Passivity
14. Individualism
15. Formalist elements, L'Art pour l'art-attitude

These negative motifs were regarded as traits outside the socialist worldview and, hence, undesired in a socialist personality. As a result, they did not correspond to the criteria of Socialist Realism, the aim of which was only to promote good and positive features. However, they were viewed as useful in describing states of affairs in non-socialist societies, providing a clear picture of how not to be or think. Furthermore, it ought to be added that the two motifs Individuality and Fantasy have been incorporated into this list of negative characteristics despite the fact that a different, more positive attitude was adopted towards them in the course of time. While solely regarded as negative in the earlier years, in later years books whose plots demonstrated one of these two characteristics became acceptable with the help of a skilful line of argument and together with other, supportive motifs. Equally, any of the motifs with negative connotations could turn into positive ones if in connection with Western scenarios or plots, where the aim was to point to shortcomings in these social systems and, hence, any negative description made the text desirable for the East German market.

From the lists of these concepts, it should have become apparent what content was looked for in a book. It also becomes apparent that themes were selected according to their social relevance and, further, that particular themes dominated. It is to be understood that these criteria have been identified only for texts translated from English sources for the purposes of this study and, additionally, that motifs may differ from translations from other languages, particularly, perhaps from Eastern Bloc languages.

3.6 Making the Right Choice

In selecting books for translation, motifs and Socialist Realist paradigms represented the principal criteria for judging what made a book permissible and socially adequate. However, they were not the only point of reference. When rewriting English-language text, all aspects of its provenance were accounted for, such as its status in the country of origin but also internationally, or the reputation of the author. Focusing attention on these aspects had the function of providing further explanation to the censor of why a text was deemed suitable for publication and supplying evidence that the text was well within the limits sanctioned. The main defence strategies used by publishers, according to the files, will be dealt with in the following two sections.

3.6.1 *Justifying the Author*

When a culture rewrites its literature, it constructs a certain image of its own literature and of foreign literatures. In the self-image it constructs, there will be no room for certain elements; on the other hand, the culture will make room for other, particularly desirable concepts. It has been shown that ideology, poetics and their codification determine acceptability or rejection of a work of literature. However, in the same fashion as works of literature have to fit in, so, too, have their creators. The East German files clearly demonstrate that not only the worldview of authors but also their achievements and reputation (in their native country and in the East German culture) had an impact on the decision as to whether or not an author's book was considered suitable. Authors were broadly separated into two camps, those with clear connections to the socialist ideal and those who needed favourable biographies to justify their position as suitable authors. The following two sections will describe how each group was handled in the files.

3.6.1.1 *Authors with a Stance Supportive of the Socialist Cause*

It was eminently advantageous when an author expressed sympathy with socialism and with its political and ideological values and goals. Such authors corresponded to the official attitude and provided a huge guarantee for texts in the right mind-set. These texts revolved around themes relevant to and of interest to East German society and, more importantly, did not generally require (much) adaptation.

The discourse in the files attached particular importance to the fact that an author was linked to the political left. Thus, for instance, Satyanarayan Sinha, author of *Munna und Munni* (1966, Holz), had been a pupil of Maxim Gorki. Also, he was sentenced to death by the English colonial power. He then received military training in the USSR and fought in the Red army against troops of Chiang Kai-Shek. He was a member of the Congress Party and a member of the Indian Parliament (DR1/2253a). Equally, Beverley Naidoo was "the daughter of H.A. Naidoo, South African communist and member of the Union" (DR1/2308). In another example, David Craig was described as a "famous author and editor of literary critical articles with a clear Marxist viewpoint . . . which guaranteed that he had selected a representative sample of British prose of the last decade, which will provide a realistic and comprehensive picture of present-day life in Great Britain" (DR1/5438).

Visits to East Germany were interpreted positively (e.g. Mulk Raj Anand, Alan Marshall), as were recommendations by a loyal author or a renowned East German personality (e.g. Rabindranath Tagore, David Craig).

Since many of these authors were still alive, the publisher could also—if required—have an influence on the writing process and on the final version of the text. An illustration is Gray's *Der Deserteur* (1978, Kinderbuchverlag; DR1/2282a) about whom the publisher Kinderbuchverlag wrote,

> the author has sent us the original manuscript of this short novel; it has not been published anywhere. In view of a publication with us, the author has again gone through the text critically and has changed it on our terms. Our editors now fully agree with this reworked version.

A second example is *Mora*, a picture book by Mulk Raj Anand (1960, Holz), for which a refusal of a print permit was pending in 1959, and the book was given a second chance, an astonishing concession for which the following explanations seem feasible. The final, rigid censorship apparatus had not yet been implanted in the state machinery by 1959. It was also a time when there was an acute shortage of foreign currency, which made the country resort to an increased production of indigenous literature (*Bitterfelder Weg*, see p 19); hence, anything foreign that had some potential might have been given special consideration rather than rejecting it outright—even more so, when it had been written by an author sympathetic to the socialist cause, as was the case. According to the file (DR1/3940), *Mora*'s history began in 1958. Anand had promised a story to publisher Holz. It was to be about elephants and their enemy, the humans, who chased and shot them. The underlying idea was a symbolic representation of the peoples of India by the elephants, and the colonial power by the humans; the story had the overall aim of depicting how the Indian peoples rid themselves of foreign rule. This version was rejected on the grounds that "the child reader may get the impression that mankind, in general, was cruel and was the enemy of all animals." When Anand revisited Berlin the following year, these reservations were put to him and, somehow, "he could not but agree with the argument"—it may have helped that, according to the file, an Indologist and another East German author had participated in the meeting. The final version, as produced by Anand, was described by Holz to the censor in the following way,

> Hunters have replaced the notion of general humanity. Still, hunters also have to be differentiated: only those hunters who kill them, either for the adventure or to become rich are the real enemy of the elephants. On the other hand, the other kind of hunters have to be viewed more benevolently; those who catch elephants so that they can help them with their work or so that people can enjoy them in zoos. It is these tamed elephants who have become the friends of the people; however, the wild elephants are still striving to be free. (DR1/3940)

This second, improved version obtained its print permit and was published in 1960.

As seen in the last example, the strategy of writing books particularly for an East German publisher was possible also for translated children's literature, albeit not too frequently (examples of other books which had a similar origin are: Franck, *Die Geschichte vom musikalischen Kater Tobias*, 1966, Holz; Anand, *Der Brahmane, der Tiger und der Schakal: Indische Märchen*, 1967, Holz; Winnington, *Silberhuf zieht in den Krieg*, 1972, Kinderbuchverlag; and Anand, *Der König und der Papagei: Märchen und Volkserzählungen aus dem Pandschab*, 1981, Kinderbuchverlag).

There was yet another grouping of authors who were looked upon favourably, namely those who were foreign but had decided to take up residence in the GDR (e.g. Elizabeth Shaw and Alan Winnington). Their texts did not cause too many ideological problems, as the files show. Moreover, these authors were actively approached by publishers to write books (according to the policy of literary development within which authors were commissioned to write works for children and adolescents). Thus, Alan Winnington was approached by Kinderbuchverlag to produce a sequel to his book *Silberhuf* (personal communication by his wife and translator Ursula Winnington, 30 August 2001).

Lastly, there was a small group comprising those English-speaking writers who were introduced to the East German system via translations done for the USSR market. For the area of children's literature, two such examples are found: Mayne Reid, *Die Quarteronin*, and Lev Chwostenko, *Geschichten vom Bruder Rabbit*, a variant of the Uncle Remus stories.

3.6.1.2 Authors not Supportive of the Socialist Cause

Numerous authors wrote in a form that was not entirely in accordance with the maxim of educational usefulness of literature, because of a lack of socialist elements or apolitical subjects; some of them so much so that it might even have made them appear obstructive to Historical progress. These authors could only be accepted when they possessed or displayed some trait that made them appear special and worthy of a publication alongside canonised writers. Therefore, publishers had to employ certain strategies, in order to gain them a place in the canon of the GDR. One, for instance, was to emphasise the author's national and international status. Thus, J.R.R. Tolkien was portrayed as an author of world reputation and a respectable professor emeritus of the prestigious University of Oxford (DR1/2264a). Eilis Dillon was shown as an author "who publishes with renowned English publishing houses such as Faber & Faber or Macmillan" (DR1/3539) and, similarly, Mildred Taylor had been awarded national and international prizes, such as the Newbery Medal and the Buxtehude Bulle (DR1/2312). In unison with examples from the book, using the Socialist Realist concepts of Humanism and Realism, in particular, these comments were to add enough weight to justify a publication of the book.

Often authors were characterised as 'pseudo-progressive', "progressive liberal" (Virginia Hamilton, DR1/2287) or designated as "a belligerent humanist" (Glendon Swarthout, DR1/3547a). Alexander Crosby was viewed as a "progressive bourgeois intellectual who has a sensitivity for burning issues in the USA but appears to have little contact with the organised working classes". This last remark was added by the publisher in their evaluation to weaken the assessor's complaint about a passage in the book in which Crosby had depicted builders in a very un-socialist fashion, namely as opposing a protest demonstration for peace in Vietnam (DR1/2268). Mary Benson's true-to-life description of the social conditions in South Africa was discussed in the evaluation on her book *Im Augenblick der Stille* (1974, Neues Leben). Despite being congratulated for her realistic plot, Benson was criticised by the assessor for displaying only the thinking of a "bourgeois-democratic humanism" as opposed to that of a socialist revolutionary. Apart from some sweeping statements and 'incorrect' comments about the African communists and the entire communist movement worldwide, the assessor found conclusive evidence for his opinion on the author in the following sentence, taken from the book, which read, "the sole object of revolution is the abolition of senseless suffering", with which the author had clearly not brought her thought to an end because "the bourgeois-democratic revolution can only be the beginning; the ultimate goal has to be the socialist revolution and the construction of a socialist society." He continued that, after a deletion of these controversial passages, the book would then reveal Benson's basic progressive attitude and show the readers solidarity, hatred of imperialism and respect for antifascist resistance (DR1/3547).

For authors who did not have any personal achievements worth referring to and who could not be described as more or less avant-garde (many of them from the classic canon), special emphasis was put on socio-critical elements and on the Socialist Realist concepts of Humanism and Realism. Hence, Walter Scott was claimed to write from the vantage point of a Romantic, rather than from a Marxist-Leninist worldview. Although, according to the file, his socio-critical analyses did not show the progressive enlightenment of people belonging to the socialist age, he exhibited a clear distance to the royal court; he condemned scheming, lies, cowardice, social climbing and thoughtlessness. He was viewed as a friend and connoisseur of life: "his ideals are not idealistic, he is in favour of steadfastness, truth and moral purity"; and an extra bonus: "he belongs to the big names in world literature" (DR1/5437). By the same token, Stevenson, in the evaluation of the publication *In der Südsee* (a report about his journeys to the South Sea islands), was portrayed as an author with much love for the native tribes, with a humanist attitude that urged for reforms, being convinced of the victory of the good in people, and detesting motifs of profiteering and avarice for gold. "Of course, he does not explain the reasons for the demise of the peoples in the South Sea from a Marxist standpoint" but "the book reveals to us the loveable and upright persona of this humanist author" (1972, Neues Leben; DR1/3545a). Similarly, Marryat's recognition of the social problems of his day remained, as was maintained, "only on the surface", because he lacked the forward-thinking of a Marxist author; but such a shortcoming was conceded as understandable and excusable, as it had to be explained from the period in which Marryat was born, and continuing, "he never loses sight of social injustice, he criticises the social order of his time, the corruption in the Navy, the hypocrisy of the aristocrats and the false piety of the clergy" (DR1/2260). There are innumerable, similar cases, all of which calling in the assistance of Realism, Humanism and social criticism and aiding in bringing the author fully in alignment with the prevalent ideology.

To give an illustration of a contemporary author, Bernard Ashley was considered to be an author who "does not have any socio-critical intentions and, for sure, is not linked to the political left . . . but his choice of themes and plots display a certain social consciousness, especially the stories set in the East End of London" (DR1/2298). As Ashley could not be described as progressive nor could he be praised for an emphasis on harsh criticism of British society, the evaluator hinged his motivation on instances of realistic portrayals in his book, attempting to pinpoint plenty of social criticism from there and, as a consequence, "the thinking reader may arrive at the question as to what chances such people as the ones depicted actually have in life" (DR1/2298).

Explanations of this more lenient approach towards this and other authors may be that many of them were published in later years at a time when censorship was no longer as harsh as in the earlier years. What is more, because of a less emphatic stress on socialist values and socialist themes in these books, several of them were suitable for co-productions and special editions destined for export to the West which would generate income in the shape of hard Western currency. The significance of economic prospects is substantiated by the fact that writers who did not fully side with socialism or whose worldview could not be called 'political' were accepted more easily, if the publication promised income. What was important in these cases, however, was to construct a solid argument as to why the books were of benefit to the readers.

As has been demonstrated, the image construction of an author allowed only for writers whose view of the world was compatible, or at worst not incompatible, with that of the East German system. If authors displayed slight shortcomings, they needed to be adapted in some shape or form congruent with the worldview desired. The files reveal that a large group of authors were canonised purely on grounds of sharing the same ideology and expressing this in their work. From this, however, one ought not to deduce that, automatically, all their oeuvre had a passport to enter the system. Publishers repeatedly claimed that, if an author had published other books than the one selected for translation, these were examined in as much detail as the first one and some of them were, indeed, found unsuitable (the principal reasons given were lack of quality, inappropriate themes, or they were too expensive).

The discourse in the files provides evidence that there were authors who were clearly unacceptable to the system.[5] To illustrate this point, in describing the process of putting together the contributions for his anthology, editor Petersen stated (without providing names, however) that "I had to remove a few authors again from the final compilation, because my research has brought to light certain stains in the biographies of these authors." A few passages later he explained, "in this anthology, only two authors sympathetic to the political left were considered: Philip Bonosky and Albert Maltz. The renegade Howard Fast cannot, with a clear conscience, be suggested for a contribution and, also, a few years will have to pass until the Nobel Prize Winner John Steinbeck can be taken into consideration again for literary projects, since he has thrown overboard his previous upright conviction with his recent attitude towards the war in Vietnam" (DR1/2282a).

3.6.2 Other Methods of Justification

What follows is a brief elaboration of other justification strategies found in the files.

- Publication of the book in the USSR or one of the People's Republics: Pointing to a publication of the text in one of these like-minded states served to legitimise an East German publication. In the main, it was only one sentence putting emphasis on another publication, as was, for instance, the case with Charlotte Brontë's *Die Waise von Lowood* (1963, Kinderbuchverlag); or Jerome's *Drei Mann in einem Boot* (1967, Neues Leben). On rarer occasions, a publication of a text similar to the one planned was mentioned for one of these countries, for example Singer's *Zlateh die Geiß* (1971, Altberliner), for which the publisher let the censor know, "I would like to stress that the Soviet children's book publisher has already put out Yiddish folk literature . . ., and therefore there is a failing on our side [for not having done the same as yet]" (DR1/3707).
- Reference to a film: Making a film out of the text which had been shown in the GDR, the USSR or another Eastern Bloc state was another method to validate a book project, e.g. Aldridge's *Der letzte Zoll* (1975, Neues Leben) had been turned into a film in the USSR; or the film version of Corman's *Kramer gegen Kramer* (1982, Neues Leben) had been a great success in the GDR, as the files claim.
- Mention of other books published by the author: Nearly every author of whom a second (or more) books had been published in the GDR was mentioned in the files together with his/her previous publications. If authors appeared with several different titles, as was especially the case with classic authors, the publishers resorted to a more general wording instead of listing every individual publication with its respective title. Reference was made not only to the publisher's own projects, but also to books brought out by other East German publishers.

- Selecting the 'best' work by an author: Communicating to the censor that another book, or several others, had been inspected and that the particular one selected for publication stood out owing to its quality was another way of making it known that the book had special value and was worth putting it out on the market.
- Pointing out analogies to other canonised texts or authors: This was a common and favoured method of legitimising a book. The objective was to compare some component, or all, of the target text with a canonised and accepted work, emphasising that the selected and the comparable text complemented each other. Thus, Smollett's *Die Abenteuer des Roderich Randoms* was put on a level with Fielding's *Tom Jones* (DR1/3554a); Smith's *Porto Bello Gold* with Stevenson's *Die Schatzinsel* (DR1/2262a); or Hamilton's *Der Planet des Patrick Brown* with Salinger's *Der Fänger im Roggen* (DR1/2287).

Regarding authors, Jeff Fields was said to show characteristics of Mark Twain with respect to colourfulness, originality and ribaldry (DR1/5435); Mary Benson's style was "reminiscent of Graham Greene who has already been published in the GDR" (e.g. *The Quiet American* or *The Comedians*) (DR1/3547). As to Dillon's *Die Irrfahrt der Santa Maria*,

> the contents and the way in which the story is told, the never-ending surprises, the irony and critical distance prevalent and the portrayal, with deep love, of the [Irish] country, the islands and the 'crazy' people, the ginger-haired energetic Maggie, etc.—yes, indeed, everything reminds us of Sean O'Casey and his plays, which are staged in our theatres. And without any doubt, this is world literature at its best! (DR1/3544)

In most cases, the comparison was kept brief, but in some evaluations, the similarities were described at great length. So, for instance, the comparison (DR1/2269) between Marshall's *Windgeflüster* (1973, Kinderbuchverlag) and Lindgren's *Mio, mein Mio* used up more than a page. Despite all similarities, the assessor attempted to underline the higher value of Marshall's book. Her key arguments touched on the following: although in both books a boy goes out into the world on a white horse, in order to fight evil and to liberate the good, Lindgren's boy is not conscious of this fact. As a consequence, he often uses words like "sadness, fear, anxiousness and regret of his decision." Also, Lindgren portrays an orphaned boy who desperately would like to have a father, something that contributes to the romantic melancholy and wistfulness. Moreover, the hero's father lets his boy go into battle without any assistance. All in all, Lindgren's book depicts a broken optimism running through the plot. On the other hand, Marshall's hero decides consciously to go out into the world; he has no father but this does not sadden him, because he has a good friend in a simple, ordinary man who is father and mother to him in one and, what is more, who is there for him whenever he is needed. Marshall's boy is happy, carefree and full of confidence and trust in his own strength and power. In spite of the many fantastic elements, *Windgeflüster* therefore was more realistic and truthful, the assessor concluded.

- Support by a Marxist personality or by other renowned people linked with socialism: As a person who had not only produced novels and drama but who had also concerned himself with children and their education, Maxim Gorki was given a number of quotations in the files, such as in the description of Bob, protagonist of the book *Der Planet des Patrick Brown* (Hamilton, 1980, Kinderbuchverlag), who acts courageously and fights all adverse circumstances in his life, hence a situation in which the assessor claimed that a Gorkian approach was clearly discernible. Another Marxist called into service was Karl Marx himself; thus, Schneider's anthology *Englische Erzähler* (1962, Neues Leben) was claimed to have the merit of "being compiled in such a fashion that it becomes understandable why Marx had said that the brilliant school of novelists in England uncovered more political and social truths than all professional politicians, journalists and moralists together" (DR1/5117). Another Marx citation mentioned Eleanor Marx, his daughter, who was said to have written about Marryat's *Peter Simpel* in her memoirs that "it was the first novel she had been given as a present and that her father had read this book and others with her and discussed the contents with her very seriously" (DR1/2260).

  In this respect, it should also be mentioned that, frequently, the services of East German literary scholars were secured to produce an entire assessment of a book, for which difficulties were anticipated; examples of which are: (children's) author and high-profile literary figure Gerhard Holtz-Baumert for Arthur Miller's *Jannis Deckchen* (apolitical and non-socialist stance, triviality and lack of social relevance; 1969, Kinderbuchverlag); literary reviewer Günter Ebert for Dahl's *Hexen hexen* (inhumanity, violence, swearing, overemphasis on fantasy; 1988, Kinderbuchverlag) or, as will be shown in one of the case studies, Günter Ebert for Lofting's *Doktor Dolittle* (1980, Kinderbuchverlag), which had failed to obtain a print permit in 1966 and, therefore, needed solid backing to be acceptable for a second attempt.
- Anticipation of potential problematic concepts or passages and presenting them in a favourable light: Inasmuch as positive support was required, publishers and assessors also had to be aware of issues that might have caused difficulties with the censor. Hushing them up might have turned out to be counterproductive. Since not everything could be eliminated by a mere deletion in the translation process, publishers had to attempt to smooth out these difficulties in their discourse by

finding the right line of argument. Thus, for the publication of *Zerrspiegel* (Stone, Neues Leben, DR1/3554), the assessor detected "a terrible hopelessness which makes one depressed", thus a clearly negative motif. However, he continued,

> our readers will, mainly, judge this book from quite a different Historical perspective and they will be capable of contextualising this hopelessness and come to the conclusion that the Historical alternative [of socialism] will, in the long run, also become apparent to the Americans who are burdened by the drudgery of such a hopeless everyday life. Further, it is my opinion that [this hopelessness] is necessary, in order to demonstrate, how this reality is reflected in American literature, which is dominated by a bourgeois standpoint appearing in many shapes and forms.

Not all observations give a counter-argument to the negative concept; for some books, it appeared to have been sufficient merely to show to the censor that the problem had been recognised but was, on the whole, not deemed harmful or counter to a socialist education, for instance, "Of course, it is possible to accuse the author of mistakes and shortcomings, but I consider this as counterproductive in view of the masterly achievement of portraying the situation of a part of American and West European adolescents in such a psychologically plausible manner" (Swarthout, *Und sie sind nur Kinder*, 1974, Neues Leben, DR1/3547a).

- Commercial considerations: As already described, this aspect was one which was highlighted to the censor with great regularity. This fact evinces the belief of publishers that books were judged with greater tolerance by the censoring authority, if some kind of financial gain could be attached to them.

3.7 Poetics in Communication

3.7.1 Assessor-Publisher Communication

From what has been said so far, the eminent role of publishers as advocates for books becomes, once again, apparent. As has been mentioned, it was vital in a system like East Germany to make the correct choice of text upfront, in other words, to assess texts according to their suitability and social feasibility in the GDR. As a second step, the text had to be presented to the authorities in a way and in a language (codification) that enabled the authorities to receive it positively and allow it to enter the system. In this process, certain tactics were required, such as those listed previously.

However, it was also pertinent to find appropriate assessors who would act as powerful advocates of a publication. Assessors too wrote their evaluations using the socially accepted codification practices, which is to say that they too looked for analogies in the East German culture to ideological and poetological elements of the English-language texts and, then, used the systematised motifs and the concepts of Socialist Realism.

The files reveal that, in the vast majority of cases, the assessors chosen by the publishers agreed to a production; indeed, they frequently found the publication essential. This goes to show that the publishers had decided not only on an appropriate text but had also nominated the right person to assess it. In many cases the correspondence between the assessor's and publisher's evaluation appears to go as far as the publisher employing the same phraseology, sometimes over a stretch of two to three sentences. This congruence seems to point to two functions of the assessor; firstly, in supplying valid argumentation which the publishers could take up and use for strengthening their case for a publication; secondly, as an endorsement of the publisher's correct decision in making the choice of a book in the first place. An assessor's written agreement absolved the publishers and demonstrated that they had acted with responsibility towards society. There is another fact that appears to give weight to this latter point. Some files, notably the ones dealing with the earlier years, contain evaluations of a second assessor which, it seems, had become necessary as a precaution, in the event of a looming threat to the editor's/publisher's judgment. Such a second opinion assisted in supporting the authority of the first evaluation and in reinforcing the validity of the original choice. A second opinion, however, was also required if the first assessor had come to a negative conclusion about the publication and opposed it.

As much as publishers leant on and echoed positive arguments from assessors, they were required to respond to any negative issues brought up by them. In several of these, they rejected the assessors' observations; in others, they agreed but with reservations. A striking example is Kinderbuchverlag's response to the assessor for Reid's *Die Quarteronin*[6] (1967, Kinderbuchverlag; DR1/2255). In the book, Rutherford, a young Englishman, takes a trip to the Southern states of America, where he becomes involved socially with the possessing classes and their intrigues but also in the question of slavery. He meets a young girl, a quadroon, with whom he falls in love at first sight and, after some turmoil, marries her. Although not entirely disagreeing with a publication, the assessor complained, amongst other issues, that the book did not represent high-brow literature and, in addition, did not sufficiently examine social shortcomings, in particular with reference to slavery. Rather it showed the idle lifestyle of the upper social classes and, thus, would not be educational to the readers. The publisher's reply was extensive and was even given a special heading and numbering. The criticising statements expressed by the assessor "cannot be accepted completely", it started.

> We believe that the standards applied to attitude and behaviour of the characters are not justified. It has to be considered that this book was written in the mid 1800s and, at that time, it was already remarkable that an author had his main protagonist, coming from a high social class, marry a slave . . . When the assessor states that Rutherford does not care about social conditions, then this is true only to a certain degree, namely in so far as the plot depicts exclusively the effects of the social circumstances and not so much the reasons for them in the first place. . . . Nevertheless, the way he [Rutherford] supports the cause of the slaves, the way he treats them—this clearly shows opposition to the prevailing conditions of slavery. It is evident that Mayne Reid does not examine the social causes of slavery, but one ought to consider the period in which this book was written. For this reason, the hero cannot take any other stance than the one he takes.

In words like these, Kinderbuchverlag rejected the assessor's point of view and voiced their own opinion about the main statement of the book. The publisher further argued that the entire text comprised only 100 pages and, given that, they felt that the conditions in the country were reflected adequately. Such conditions, as depicted in the book, included—and here Kinderbuchverlag did not fail to point out that the assessor had also recognised and named these—slave auctions, lynch-law, cruel treatment of slaves and outrageous behaviour of American businessmen. The publisher admitted that the book could not be classed as high-brow literature; however, they emphasised that the literary device of 'love at first sight' (to which the assessor had also objected) was also employed by renowned novelists like Ernest Hemingway and Thomas Mann, thereby deploying the strategy of analogy with socially accepted writers from the canon. Finally, they added that *Die Quarteronin* had been translated into Russian and was used in the Soviet Union as compulsory school literature, calling in the authority of the Soviet standpoint.[7]

Not all publisher's justifications were as lengthy as in this last example; mostly they range from one to several sentences, as was the case in the following example. For a Neues Leben publication of Stevenson's *Die verkehrte Kiste* (1975, Neues Leben), the publisher stated, "The assessor, who wrote an assessment for us for the first time, worked on the assumption that the Kompass-series has as its objective to bring out only adventure literature. He, therefore, concluded that this 'amusing, well-written trivia' was not suitable for this series. Talking with him, however, could overcome these reservations" (DR1/3549a). Or even briefer on another occasion, "we understand the assessor's point when he says that he would have tackled this anthology in a different manner—however, by saying this, he was not demanding a change" (Schneider, *Das schöne Grauen*, 1978, Neues Leben, DR1/3553).

3.7.2 *Paratextual Discourse—Language and Terminology*

When Lefevere refers to "a code which makes ... communication between author and reader possible" (1985b:229), he has in mind primary texts, their writers and readers, but also—and more importantly for this study—everything surrounding primary texts, i.e. all forms of criticism. The production of a primary text takes place within a social context and, therefore, everything in this production environment will affect the text to some degree. Rewriting, notably in an "undifferentiated climate" (Lefevere 1985b:228), does not stop with the boundary of the actual book but has repercussions on all paratextual material. This is particularly the case in totalitarian systems such as the GDR. Under such regimes there are additional constraints and mechanisms involved both in the selection and in the production processes which may, in general, be given the term 'censorship'. Therefore, as has been proposed earlier, the notion of author and reader may be applied to encompass authors and readers of the East German paratextual discourse, who were publishers and assessors, on the one hand, and censors and cultural functionaries, on the other. In the same fashion, Lefevere suggests that a codification of language takes place, whereby writers of books need to speak and use the same language as their audience; again, this holds true for paratextual material, since East German publishers needed to communicate on the same wavelength as the censors.

In studying the files, it becomes evident that publishers and assessors (as the authors of the paratexts) followed the political line and not their own subjective judgement, not only through the kind of argument but also through the kind of language they used. What is more, everyone situated in the cultural establishment (censors, publishers and assessors) appears to have spoken the same language intuitively, as nowhere in the files does one find definitions, clarifications about a term or, indeed, any theoretical background explanation. Frequently, concepts were only mentioned in passing, in order to support an argument; however, no examples or further reasons were provided. This is indicative of a codification being in place, the terms and the meaning of which were generally known and internalised.

Overall, the discourse in the files (used both by the publisher and the assessor) is characterised by black-and-white language laden with a formulaic style, with clichéd terms and stereotypical images, as one would expect to find in propaganda jargon. With its codes, it kept closely to the political rhetoric of the time, using slogans borrowed from ideological agitprop and phrases embellished with emotive adjectives and ritualistic expressions. Repeatedly, use is made of the same language pairs, see for instance Table 3.1.

While throughout the language is bureaucratic, simplistic, even banal in places, it is at the same time unequivocal and determined by the political rhetoric of the day. Occasionally, a term from GDR everyday life has found its way into the criticism of a book, expressing a worldview and a kind of

Table 3.1 Examples of Literary Codification

schonungslos schildern	depict mercilessly
schonungslose Darstellung	merciless portrayal
schonungslose Kritik	merciless criticism
eindeutig parteilicher Standpunkt	clearly partisan standpoint
leidenschaftliche Parteinahme	passionate partisanship
Parteinahme mit Leidenschaft	partisanship with passion
leidenschaftliche Verteidigung	passionate defence
zutiefst humanistische Aussage	deeply humane message
tiefe humanistische Grundhaltung	deep humane position
zutiefst humanistisches Empfinden	deep humane feeling
tiefer Humanismus	deep humanism/humanity
zutiefst humanistische Position	deeply humane position
wahrhaft menschliche Moral	truly human moral
penetrante Frömmelei	pungent and insistent false piety
penetrante Religiosität	pungent and insistent religiousness
mit harter Realität konfrontiert	confronted by a hard reality
tiefverwurzeltes Gerechtigkeitsgefühl	deeply rooted feeling of justice

thinking in a place where one would not expect it and where, therefore, it creates an unusual flavour. For instance, in the file for Charles Dickens' *Christmas Stories*, Toby Veck is described as a man who "has become a victim of capitalist conditioning" and whose "spirit and energy have been shattered by hypocritical *agitation and propaganda* so much so that he himself believes that poverty is a crime" (1970, Kinderbuchverlag; DR1/2261; my emphasis). With these words, the publisher conveys to the censor the Dickensian period as ridden by capitalist indoctrination and with demagogues attempting to brainwash the poor so that, in the end, they are convinced that they have committed a crime, the crime of poverty. It appears that, influenced by daily doses of agitation and propaganda himself, the editor ascribed these very terms to Western society, in order to communicate the concept to the censor. However, 'agitation and propaganda' are words a Western reader might find unusual in this context, as they are (from a Western viewpoint) associated with autocratic propaganda rather than with the criticism of a work by Dickens. Another example is Tolkien's protagonist, Bilbo, in *The Hobbit* (DR1/2314) about whom, in 1989, the editor in Kinderbuchverlag wrote that he, Bilbo, when going out into the world to prove himself, "steps out of his niche", a phrase well implanted into and used in GDR everyday life, in which people retreated from public life to the sanctuary of their own home (or *Datsche*) and led their lives in their 'niches'.

What stands out quite strikingly is the separation of the world into two camps. This distinct expression of the Other, of the opposite political camp, not only manifests itself in the message and interpretation of the book but also in the linguistic material used in the paratexts (primarily 'we' and 'our' and 'us'). This is evident in rather prosaic statements like "*our* ideology is different" (Hans Petersen, *Unser weißer Hirsch*, 1978, Kinderbuchverlag; DR1/2282a; my emphasis) or "*our* children are well-informed" (Crosby, *Winchester wacht auf*, 1973, Kinderbuchverlag; DR1/2268; my emphasis); equally, this notion of 'we, the socialists' versus 'they, the capitalists' is also commonly found in longer, ideological explanations. For example, in his print permit application for the book *Schnappschüsse*, which deals with "racism, racial bias and the battle against the chauvinist, fascist National Front [in Great Britain]", the publisher states, "The topic is of significance particularly for *our* children, who are not familiar with such problems in their own lives", because "racial discrimination is unheard of in *our* land" (Nigel Gray, *Schnappschüsse*, 1982, Kinderbuchverlag; DR1/2292a; my emphasis).

Another interesting observation is that, in the late 1970s and 80s, English terms begin to find their way into the discourse. In the 1960s, there were only rare instances of editors using 'Stories' instead of the German term *Geschichten*; so for instance, "Auch die drei *Stories*, die jetzt in redigierter Fassung vorliegen, können akzeptiert werden" ("also the three stories which have now been edited can be accepted") (Hellendahl, *Ping Pang Poch*, 1967, Kinderbuchverlag; DR1/2255; my emphasis). It seems surprising to find these English terms (some even written without quotation marks around them), given that they all have a German equivalent. This may be a sign that people involved in the publishing arena had access to Western materials and were knowledgeable about what was going on in the world outside the Eastern Bloc. As interviewees reported, all West German children's literature journals were available for experts to analyse and for them to keep up-do-date with developments in the West. Equally, the publishing house Volk & Welt, i.e. the main publisher of translated literature for adults, maintained a well-equipped and well-stocked library of international books (classic and contemporary), which was so comprehensive that even university professors borrowed books from them, because universities were not so fortunate as to be able to get hold of all the copies desired for their institutions (Jähn, personal information, 19 July 2001).

Indeed, from the mid-1970s, the general climate was more accommodating to influence from the West, since East Germany attempted to surround itself with a modern, more enlightened air, in order to be regarded as equal and to be accepted by Western states. Important treaties had been signed for the benefit of the GDR but also in the interest of a united Europe (see Section 1.3.1). One example of this relaxation was that citizens were no longer obstructed when watching West German television and, thus, were exposed to many English-language expressions. However, another observation with respect to these Anglicisms is that they are not used in the afterwords. This would suggest that there was an attempt to keep Anglo-American influence out of the country and/or uphold an intellectual elite, whose upper tier (publishers, assessors, censors) did not want to, or for some other reasons rooted in society, could not pass it on to the second, lower tier, i.e. the ordinary reader. Admittedly, these terms were not used very often, yet frequently enough to detect a trend. What else is noticeable is that the majority of the terms have a connection to social and socio-critical phraseology. The examples shown in Table 3.2 are all found in files from the 1980s (the emphases are all mine):

On the whole, a vocabulary of concrete terms and phrases had been established which emphasised socialist ideals and which was employed widely throughout the discourse in the files. The phrasing is direct and unambiguous; it aims to trigger emotional effects in the censor-readers and, seemingly, distract them from objective analysis of the text. Full use was made of socialist sentiments,

Table 3.2 Examples of English Terms Used in the Files

German	English
"Immerhin gibt es noch Eltern, denen 'Image' and materieller Besitz mehr bedeuten als ein gutes Verhältnis zu ihren Kindern"	After all, there are still parents who think more of image and material possessions than of a good relationship with their children.
(Charles Dickens, *Ferienmärchen*, 1982, Kinderbuchverlag; DR1/2292)	
"Turbulenz und 'action' sind bei diesem, wie überhaupt bei den Wallace-Krimis vorherrschend"	Excitement and action prevail in this as indeed in all crime stories by Edgar Wallace.
(Edgar Wallace, *Der Fälscher*, 1987, Neues Leben; DR1/3559a)	
"Die gute psychologische Motivation der Handlungen von Patsy and Kenny, das Plädoyer für das richtige Verhalten Erwachsener den Kindern gegenüber (weder Vernachlässigung . . . noch overprotection . . .) machen dieses Buch . . . akzeptabel"	What makes this book acceptable is the good psychological motivation of Patsy's and Kenny's actions and the plea for a correct behaviour of adults towards children (neither the neglect nor over-protection).
(Bernard Ashley, *Flucht in die Sonne*, 1985, Kinderbuchverlag; DR1/2301)	
" . . . eine Geschichte, aus der der Leser neben der dargestellten Fabel auch sehr viele Informationen über das alltägliche Leben der bürgerlichen middle-class in den USA erhält"	. . . a story which, apart from the fable, supplies the reader with much information about the everyday life of the bourgeois middle classes in the USA.
(Avery Corman, *Kramer gegen Kramer*, 1982, Neues Leben; DR1/3557)	
"In diesen Sittenkomödien gibt er eine authentische, oft zugleich aber auch ironisierende und karikierende Dastellung der sogenannten High Society"	In these comedies about life and customs he provides an authentic and often also ironic and caricatured portrayal of so-called high society.
(Oscar Wilde, *Das Bildnis des Dorian Gray*, 1987, Neues Leben; DR1/3559a)	
"Die Erfahrung menschlicher Wärme und solidarischen Zusammenhalts geben den hier Lebenden . . . das Gefühl einer Zugehörigkeit, von Community"	Human warmth and solidarity let the people who live here experience a feeling of belonging, of community.
(Buchi Emecheta, *Adah's Story*, 1987, Neues Leben; DR1/3559)	

stereotypes and ringing clichés, with the underlying purpose of conveying to the receiver (censor) agreement and single-mindedness. It is, however, not certain how much of this language was guided from the unconscious of the writers who were exposed to such language day in and day out, or whether it was employed deliberately with the conscious thought of producing officially adopted orthodoxies that the censors were expecting to hear.

3.7.3 Raising the Political Temperature

In their dialogue, or rather monologue, with the censor, the publisher and the assessor at times used somewhat extreme language which followed the political rhetoric of the time. In this, the plot was often overplayed and dramatised, presumably in order to appease the censor. On occasions, blatantly inaccurate remarks were made; forceful anti-Western propaganda and misrepresentations of Western reality were expressed, perhaps in the belief that this would ensure a positive reaction from the censor. These examples of extreme language were rare and were only associated with contemporary texts, where the arguments had to be strong, not only for ideological reasons but also for the ever present economic constraints because higher royalties had to be paid for this kind of literature.

One example which reads "In Britain, the Irish are seen only as second-class citizens and terrorists" is a fairly extreme remark about contemporary attitudes of the English towards the Irish and appears in the publisher's application for Kaufmann's *Irische Reise* (1979, Kinderbuchverlag; originally called in the files *Von Belfast nach Belfast*; DR1/2284a). This comment is followed by an enumeration of instances describing how, in general, England discriminates against Ireland and it concludes with the assessor's thought that "the book illustrates quite clearly that Ireland's freedom and fortune cannot be found abroad", employing the motifs of Active involvement and Optimism and implying that the Irish would achieve more for their country, if they stayed there and fought for a liberated future.

Another example of obvious exaggeration is also concerned with the Irish, stressing the value of true humanist thinking. In *Der Deserteur* (Gray, 1978, Kinderbuchverlag; DR1/2282a), Dave, a soldier stationed in Ireland, has deserted from the British army, because he could no longer cope with the inhumanities there (the file also mentions that he had joined the army not because he enjoyed being a soldier but because unemployment in England was so high that he had had difficulties finding a job). He is escaping to London, Germany, Sweden, in fact anywhere, in order to go into hiding. However, he has hurt his leg and is now dependent on four children, all about ten years old, who hide him from the police and feed him. According to the assessor and the publisher, in so doing, "they all risk their own lives", as it is a criminal act to help deserters from the army; but the fact that they assist a person in danger, even under threat of their lives, demonstrates the extraordinarily humanist action and "helps the soldier to not abandon his hope for a life with more human dignity". Gray published a second book with Kinderbuchverlag which was also described in parts in an overly dramatic fashion. *Schnappschüsse* (1982; DR1/2292a) deals with the problems of black immigrants living in a small English town, namely West Indians who cannot find work anywhere else but in England and, hence, "have left their sunny island in the sea, in order to live in Britain's dirt and cold". However, they are most unwelcome there; coincidentally, in this area, there is also a "group of Fascists involved in their militaristic exercises on a heath land not far from the town". One day, children discover their machinations and report them to the police, because "fortunately the practice of militaristic training of chauvinists who have gone wild is still forbidden in England".

American society appeared to have caused a particular headache, since books originating from the USA or dealing with American topics received especially extreme comments. One target, for instance, was the American Vietnam War, which was condemned outright in the files. Thus, the publisher of *Winchester wacht auf* claimed that "the dissatisfaction about this war amongst the American population—and also the middle classes—is an objective given" (Crosby, 1973, Kinderbuchverlag; DR1/2268). And the assessor informed the censor about a particular section in the book, in which a girl wrote a letter to the president enquiring why American troops were fighting in Vietnam, to which she received a reply from the State Department containing a blatant typo. Laying special weight on this fact, the assessor concluded with a quotation direct from the source text: "A nation of mis-spellers can't win an ideological war."

In the main, it was everyday situations and the American lifestyle which caused disparaging remarks, such as the following: "the majority of [American] children have no parental home"—a statement accompanying the book *Der Planet des Patrick Brown*, which dealt with the issue of homeless and neglected children in American society (Hamilton, 1980, Kinderbuchverlag; DR1/2287). To give another example, the assessor of *Zerrspiegel* (Stone, 1979, Neues Leben; DR1/3554) praised the author for "having depicted with a merciless openness what happens in the USA, reflecting concrete American reality". He contended that it was "an indisputable advantage of this novel that it supplied such an impressive and comprehensive picture" because "our understanding of the full extent [of capitalism] is limited, although daily we hear in the news about the abnormalities and ailments in present American society."

In a similar fashion, the assessor of Swarthout's *Und sie sind nur Kinder* (1974, Neues Leben; DR1/3547a) let the censor know that "the book does not glorify the filth of the [American] system"; or the assessor of *Unser Weißer Hirsch* (Petersen, 1978, Kinderbuchverlag; DR1/2282a) informed the censor of "how difficult it was for white and black Americans to love this America full of contradictions and injustice" and that "not only the black but also the white children were suffering under the meaninglessness, ignorance and intellectual poverty of this sick society."

It was, however, also a main concern to rectify, through the texts, the image of the USA that the East German children had. Thus, *Ich setze auf Danza* was characterised as a book that "does not evoke a transfigured image of America" (Hall, 1983, Neues Leben DR1/5435); or *Der Planet des Patrick Brown* was said to aim at unveiling the fairytale of the free world (Hamilton, 1980, Kinderbuchverlag; DR1/2287). The evaluation on McInerney's *Ein starker Abgang* read, "it is a novel about city life in contemporary America, with all the glitter of the City of New York, with its temptations and enticements". This was, however, an image of a Western society, of the political archenemy, that was not desired and, hence, had to be balanced out, "at the same time, it reveals to the reader that this kind of life asks for its tribute mercilessly of all who abandon themselves to this shimmering and active hustle and bustle, namely utter adaptation and subordination, the foregoing of self-realisation and everything that gives meaning to life" (1989, Neues Leben; DR1/3561a). Equally, Kaufmann's *Das verschwundene Hotel*, a book for novice readers, was given the following description by the publisher Junge Welt (1973; DR1/2665),

> the thinking of younger children is still shaped by their imagination about an America of skyscrapers and cars [cars were a rare luxury in the GDR, it has to be pointed out]; however, they know of the aim of progressive people . . . to change the existing social conditions, they know of the effects of the brutal war in Vietnam. But they do not fully comprehend the whole power mechanism of American imperialism. The author has endeavoured to inform authentically . . . about a world which the child does not know; it facilitates the drawing of conclusions and comparison with the socialist environment; the reader is confronted with hard realities and is forced to think about and digest the events described in the book.

All in all, it was the declared goal of the publications to guide and, if necessary, correct the picture of America held by readers by portraying the Western world, notably the American one, in a negative light and pointing to the deplorable nature of such societies. The evaluations to the censor were directed at highlighting the intellectual and moral degeneration of these systems and their subsequent demise, whereby the censor was indirectly shown that the books informed their audiences that only the socialist society would survive and was heading towards a glorious future.

3.7.4 The Censors

The kind of entries found in the files depended on each censor and on the type of book they had to assess. Most of the books were passed through the system without causing particular difficulties to the censors, in which case the box provided for censorial remarks on the first page of the file (see p 104) was left empty or contained the phrase "manuscript read—no objections". Often censors felt that a book should be given an afterword and, in this case, they would state in the box, "afterword absolutely necessary", or "print permit granted except for the afterword which has to be submitted [or resubmitted]";

sometimes, censors felt that a print permit could not be given unless a correction (in the afterword, for instance) was made, in which case they would only allow for the book to be typeset and the actual print permit followed after rectification of the shortcoming. Other issues which censors deemed necessary to put down in writing were, for example, that the comments made by the evaluator who had been commissioned by the censorship authority had been passed to the publisher and were taken into consideration; that the publisher had acted outside his 'publisher's profile' (see p 96) and was reminded to remain within the limits of his licence; that they, the censors, were worried about one particular feature of the book, who in the publishing house they had contacted about it and what action had been agreed by them and/or the publisher; or on the occasion that they had not read the manuscript personally, a reference would be given to their external evaluator who would have produced a written assessment for them. In the case of a controversial book or of two contradictory evaluations sent in by the publisher, censors would automatically pass the manuscript on for a third opinion under which they could then put their signature.

As the preceding practices demonstrate, the need for self-protection also applied to the censors. This fact is easily understandable when bearing in mind that they also were a product of their culture; in other words, to a certain degree they themselves were subjugated, being subordinate to those higher powers who defined the values and enforced them as the only legitimate interpretation.

From the overall process that has been described, it can be seen that each level within the institutional hierarchy had to justify its actions to the layer above and, at the same time, had to protect its decisions by ensuring that any potential problems were seen to be addressed. Although the discussion with the censors ends here, the actual process continued up to the very top of the hierarchy, namely the Party bureaucracy (as outlined in Section 2.1.1); this was the reason why the censors had to make certain they could demonstrate that they had properly executed their duty, that they had acted responsibly and with due consideration of social circumstances.

3.8 Alterations to the Text

This section will centre on the discourse directly concerned with the actual textual alterations requested by the assessors and commentated on by the editors. However, it should be noted that it is not the aim of this study to perform individual textual comparisons and report on textual changes identified. As stated earlier, it is rather the intention to describe the ideological background which was responsible for these changes and to supply an extensive picture of the existing framework, in order to gain a full impression of the cultural and ideological climate in which East German translation operated. Predictably, the instances in the files that suggested modification are strikingly congruent with the motifs and concepts as outlined in this chapter so far. However, this should not come as a surprise, given the system's codification in alignment with Marxist-Leninist doctrine.

"Rewriters/editors obviously did not wittingly and willingly set out to mutilate the text. They did what they did because they had no other choice" (Lefevere 1992:159). In this quotation, Lefevere refers to the rewriting of Büchner's *Danton's Death*,[8] but he might as well have referred to the situation in East Germany, and there to adult and to children's literature alike. There, too, publishers regarded certain editorial decisions as necessary, in order to bring the texts (books or stories) in line with the dominant ideology and poetics. One of the translators I interviewed conceded, "of course, we had debates and arguments with the editors; some suggestions were reasonable, some were not, but in the end, if you wanted your translation to be published and made available to an audience, you had no other choice than to comply" (Hans Joachim Grimm, personal communication, 8 August 2001).

This necessity of accepting 'a given reality' is reflected in the discourse in the files, notably in the discussions about how to handle certain 'shortcomings' of the texts, that is to say, it deals, on the one hand, with linguistic, literary and aesthetic changes and, on the other, with those motivated through ideology.

3.8.1 'Economic Deletions' and 'Careful Alterations'

In their statement to the censor, publishers strove to give a comprehensive picture of the processes taking place before submitting the manuscript and applying for a print permit (although this was not the case for every assessment). Two areas commented on were the type of problem that occurred during the course of the translation and, also, ultimate translation solutions. For the translation of the book *Peter Simpel*, for instance, Kinderbuchverlag described their having been advised by the assessor not to use an older existing translation and the need for a fresh retranslation (Marryat, 1969, Kinderbuchverlag; DR1/2260). It had been pointed out to them that the translation from the beginning of the nineteenth century lacked vividness and that a revision would not improve the text significantly and, further, would take more time than producing a new translation. Also, during the translation, it had turned out that the help of a nautical expert had become necessary, in order to check the terminology used. In full agreement with the translator, somebody was brought into the team (whose expertise in the nautical field had manifested itself in another project) so that the publisher was now able to report that a correct translation of all seafaring and nautical expressions was available. To give another example, when describing the translation process of a collection of Indian fairytales and short stories, Kinderbuchverlag had to admit to having had problems finding a translator in the first place. Two translators had rejected the commission because of shortcomings in the original which would require the translator "to cover up these shortcomings, [which was] certainly not an easy undertaking" (Anand, *Der König und der Papagei*, 1981, Kinderbuchverlag; DR1/2289). What had happened was that the storyteller, in the original, had joined together the plots of various tales, which resulted in tales that showed logical errors and inconsistencies "that now have to be put right carefully". The advice of an Indologist was sought, which "was of invaluable help to us. The final version of the manuscript, with which all people involved have worked intensively, has turned out to our satisfaction."

As in the preceding case, publishers frequently declared in their assessment that they had taken care to produce a translation which they considered to be of good quality and which could be read and enjoyed by children and adolescents without any problems. So, for instance, Kinderbuchverlag ascertained that the translator of a picture book had worked conscientiously, co-operated personally with the author and that the final text was tailor-made for beginner readers with respect to sentence construction and choice of words. Therefore, "the publication will also attract readers who are less keen to open a book" (Shaw, *Als Robert verschwand*, 1975, Kinderbuchverlag; DR1/2276). Similarly, in the discussion about an anthology of fairytales from England, the publisher wrote, "we have to point out that the English publisher requested a review of the German translation. The present text was classified as good" (Reeves, *Märchen aus England*, 1966, Altberliner Lucie Groszer; DR1/3706).

Tightening and making the language more precise was one of the endeavours of the editors. Circumlocutory passages were frequently cut short, even more so, however, if such passages contained ideologically explosive material. This is illustrated by the assessor's remarks related to the book *Peter Simpel*, where he wrote,

> cuts are necessary in order to tighten the plot, e.g., the description of the party in Barbados . . . can be omitted, [as] in this part a rough brawl takes place. Also, I regard as superfluous the depiction of Methodist worship. On page 420, Marryat describes the symptoms of Peter's father's mental confusion, the details of which can be deleted. The dialogues with Chucks are quite unrealistic and it has to be decided how important they are for the further story. (Marryat, 1969, Kinderbuchverlag, DR1/2260)

3.8.2 Ideologically Motivated Alterations

Due to the poetological codification that determined what was adequate and acceptable, Socialist Realist concepts and key motifs were at work not only in describing the values of a text but also to assist in decision-making for potential text alterations. It is no surprise then that, when it came to actual translation practice or, in more general terms, decisions on what to include or to exclude, a distinct compliance with Marxist-Leninist concepts is discernible. This means that the discourse in the files centred on the Socialist

Realist codes; primarily, however, on Humanism and Realism, i.e. the principal pillars of GDR literature (as described earlier, in Autorenkollektiv unter Leitung von Horst Haase und Hans Jürgen Geerdts, 1976:24), and also on all subordinate positive and negative notions, such as exclusion of violent or discriminatory elements, or stress on aspects of equality and co-operation (see Section 3.5).

Violence, Sexual References:

Arguably, it is not unusual to eliminate such expressions from children's texts; nonetheless, with respect to the poetological parameters specific to the GDR, they violated the motif of Humanism and, therefore, needed to be omitted.

When publisher Holz applied for a print permit to Walter Kaufmann's[9] book *Stefan: Mosaik einer Kindheit* (published in 1966, DR1/2253), he wrote in his assessment to the censor, "Comrade Walter Kaufmann told me several years ago that he would like to write something exceptional, namely memories of his own childhood, stories about the Jewish boy Stefan." Further, Holz had requested an assessor's evaluation of the book, which turned out positive with the exception of one item. After recommending that the readers' age was lowered to ten years, the assessor raised the following point,

> There is one remark that I deem it permissible to make: *Entdeckung* ["Discovery", a story containing erotic allusions] should be deleted from this volume. . . . All other stories deal with themes . . . which are suitable for ten-year-olds, and even more so older readers. Only this one story would require, in my opinion, a raising of the readers' age. . . . *Entdeckung* will not mean much to a ten-year-old child (and one always ought to assume the minimum age) and probably not even to a twelve-year-old. Although our boys and girls are nowadays much more advanced in erotic matters than might have been the case previously, one should not touch on topics which will evoke questions (again prematurely) and which are not appropriate for a ten-year-old child.

Before submitting his paperwork to the censor, Holz made handwritten comments in the place where the assessor had made her remark and described this problem; firstly, he stated that he was in favour of a reader's age of thirteen to fourteen years upwards; secondly, where the deletion of the story was dealt with, he added, "Bitte nein zum Vorschlag der Begutachterin!" [Please, 'no' to the assessor's suggestion]. The censor remained unimpressed by Holz's pleas and, in the box on the form, commented, "Have read manuscript. Fully agree with evaluation. Agreed with Holz that the story *Entdeckung*[10] will be taken out." This instance is indicative of the censor's power over the content of publications. The final decision about the exclusion of the troublesome story was made by the censor despite the plea of the publisher to allow it. There are several reasons that may lie behind the decision. The first, most obvious one is the fact that the story involved references to sexual matters which were regarded as inappropriate for a young audience, especially younger children.[11] Why the assessor decided to advise the lowering of the age to ten cannot be guessed; however, it gave the censor a reason to look more closely at the story and to remove it. Nevertheless, there is also the possibility that the real reason was simply to lower the reading age, as Holz was a publisher for children (aged up to fourteen) and, in accordance with the rigid East German publishers' profiles (see p 96), it was undesirable to have him produce a book more suitable for adolescents and/or adults and, hence, the critical chapter would have been removed regardless of other considerations.

The second aspect discussed in the files was violence. To give an illustration, the assessor of *Binsenkappe* (Krenn, 1975, Kinderbuchverlag; DR1/2274) compared this anthology with a similar compilation of English tales and stories, published in Czechoslovakia, which, on the whole, he held in higher regard. Several of his complaints refer to instances of violence and cruelty:

> No 14, page 73 reads: 'Of course, it is the boy whom you caught yesterday and whom I have cooked for your breakfast this morning.—[in contrast, in the Czech version,] Vladislav skilfully avoids mentioning a further victim: 'Maybe you smell the boy who has carried away the sack of gold'. No 15, page 85: 'Although Tom pulled his sword and fought bravely, he was killed by its poisonous breath. He fell to the floor and the spider sucked all the blood out of his veins'—In Vladislav's version, Tom is victorious and the blood-sucking scene is omitted: 'The spider was a real giant of a spider and Tom Thumb fought from morning till evening, until he defeated it. But when he struck off its head, he sank to the ground next to it and died. The poisonous breath of the spider had killed him.'

This example shows the strategy of using the authority of another approved source (here from another Eastern Bloc country), either to substantiate a point and highlight its legitimacy or, as in the case of *Binsenkappe*, to obtain changes. The publisher responded to these and other remarks in a general way without referring to individual instances (DR1/2274),

> First and foremost, the work with the manuscript entailed creating clear relations and showing the limitations of the bourgeois value system. In her first version, the translator strove to remain close to the source text. However, for ideological and moral reasons, we then decided on a freer rendering, which weakens romantically transfigured and religious attitudes, stresses humour, eliminates violence and avoids circumlocution, monotony and unnecessary repetition. Thus, we have arrived at a version which keeps to the characteristics of the English tales.

Religion, Superstition:

This is an area commented on again and again, a fact which indicates, without a doubt, that there was no place for religion and related issues in the atheist Marxist ideology. On the whole, the files attempted to play down religious passages or expressions; however, if no excuse could be found, the problematic instance had to go.

The abovementioned *Binsenkappe* (Krenn, 1975, Kinderbuchverlag; DR1/2274) also has an example of a passage that the assessor would have preferred to eliminate,

> No 36, pages 180ff: The story of the Magician's Apprentice has an air of religion and superstition which may cause nightmares. On page 181 the Devil Beelzebub screams: 'Give me something to do or I'll strangle you!' But the boy could not speak for fear. There the evil spirit went to him, stretched his hands out to him and touched his throat. His fingers singed the boy's skin.

Similarly, many classic stories contained religious references which were problematic to the publisher. In these cases, the editors made what cuts they thought were required, arguing that these were an unavoidable consequence of the time in which the texts were written and thereby reassuring the censor that everything had been done to adjust and 'modernise' the text in order to be appropriate for a socialist society; so, for instance in the case of the book *Die Waise von Lowood* (i.e. the first part of Brontë's *Jane Eyre*), where the publisher considered it necessary to "cut some passages which were concerned with Helen's religious explanations" (1963, Kinderbuchverlag; DR1/3954a). Equally, in Defoe's story, Robinson is described as

> a creature of his time, representing Colonialism but, on the other hand, he is also a representative of Humanism, a fact that elevates him far above the average business man of his period and his attributes make him a well-suited hero for our young readers (energy, humanist attitude towards the 'savages', criticism of the behaviour of the ruling classes and of the religious narrow-mindedness—notably of militant Catholicism and the Inquisition). However, we don't believe that we can publish this second volume without any cuts . . . certain passages with respect to religion have been removed. (Defoe, *Die späteren Fahrten des Robinson Crusoe zu seiner Insel und rund um die Welt*, 1972, Neues Leben; DR1/3545)

Sentimental, Romantic and Kitschy Expressions:

Frequently, the discourse in the files uses expressions such as "long-winded sentimental expressions" (DR1/3545) or "romantically transfigured traits"

(DR1/2274) and states that these had to go. These are terms associated with the edition of stories to make them more realistic in some way, in order to conform to the motif of Realism, as demanded by Socialist Realism. An example is *Janey und der silberne Tänzer*, a novel about a girl growing up in Britain, missing warmth, care and a loving home (Ashley, 1987, Kinderbuchverlag; DR1/2305). She is exploited by a young boy, exhibiting anti-social characteristics, who forces her to spy into houses, potentially ideal for burglary and, whenever she refuses, he becomes violent and "beat[s] her to within an inch of her life". Again, the editor did not want to destroy such a real-life depiction conveyed in the story by an atmosphere overly mawkish and, thus, Kinderbuchverlag "moderated some sentimental expressions", a procedure about which the West German publisher was in full agreement.

Other Unrealistic Aspects:

Commensurate with the principle of a realistic depiction of life, books had to show, for example, animals in their natural habitat, or American Indians and other indigenous tribes and their ways of living, thinking and feeling without any blemish of beautification or glorification. This endeavour was manifest already in picture books for the youngest. One instance is Adamson's *Der Familienbaum* (1968), a co-production with a Scottish publisher, about which the publisher Altberliner commented in his assessment to the censor,

> this picture book has the aim of making children aware of and watch nature as early as possible. . . . In a factual way, children are told about the life of the animals in the tree. One difficulty, however, has arisen in that the source text gives an incorrect explanation about the way bats hear. We will attempt to look for a better explanation, which is factually correct and corresponds to reality. (DR1/3706)

Another example is Thompson Seton's *Der Wolf von Winnipeg* (1963, Kinderbuchverlag; DR1/5076), a book that, on the whole, was deemed valuable but had the shortcoming of using anthropomorphisms in the animals. Therefore, Kinderbuchverlag maintained, "we have attempted to eradicate the most obtrusive passages through economic deletions". Similarly, *Little Big Man* (Berger, 1977, Neues Leben; DR1/3552) described American Indians "convincingly" and "from a remarkably clear Historical standpoint". They were shown, on the one hand, as "strong, open-minded, responsible for family and tribe, and respectful of personality and achievements of the individual", but on the other hand also "with all their weaknesses such as being unorganised and quarrelsome and the relative inflexibility of their way of life—thus a positive counter-image to the kitschy [Western] notions of the 'noble savages'". In order to maintain this picture, Neues Leben "cut several short passages, in agreement with the Western publisher and the author, where the author evidently had given in to [Western] tastes in the audience and has over-elaborated passages conveying a clichéd Wild West image."

Colonialism, Discriminatory Expressions:

To start with an example, assessor and publisher agreed on the necessity to omit political and ideological instances from the book *Porto Bello Gold* (Smith, 1970, Kinderbuchverlag; DR1/2262a). The assessor recommended that

> these things are easy to even out. Many sentences will simply have to be erased . . .; without any question, the hostility towards Indians by Peter Corlaer, the otherwise good-natured, loyal and strong companion to Robert, has to be removed. He speaks about hunting those Indians as if they were a kind of noble game. Similarly, terms like Blacks, Negroes and Jews have to be considered carefully; nowadays, they have a different tone than in those days.

In a similar fashion, Stevenson's *In der Südsee* was "translated anew by paying attention to a precise and modernised terminology. So, the words 'Insulaner' (islander) and 'Eingeborener' (native) are no longer used . . .; passages, which are counter to the ethnographical thinking of today, were erased" (1972, Neues Leben; DR1/3545a).

Anti-Semitism, Racism:

To exemplify, the assessor of *Peter Simpel* (Marryat, 1969, Kinderbuchverlag; DR1/2260) had several comments on this particular subject; for instance, referring to a remark in the book on page 61, "I say, Peter, you are rich as a Jew". Instead, she proposed to replace the defamatory Jew with usurer, thus using a concept closer to the socialist notion of the evils of capitalism, money and profiteering; or on page 65 another sailor was looking for a Jew who had deceived him, again a sentence that should be modified or, best, taken out; the publisher agreed with the assessor, claiming to have removed these sensitive expressions and extracts, together with all the discriminatory expressions about natives, because both served to create a prejudiced impression "aus heutiger Sicht" [from the standpoint of the present day].

Class system, Social Difference:

There was a fundamental problem with many older fairytales and classic stories in that the main characters were inherently placed within a class system. This was counter to the socialist belief of a classless society. Therefore, social difference was also one of the aspects raised in connection with the necessity of making changes. Thus, the assessor of *Binsenkappe* asked, "Why does the clever saviour from the emergency have to be a courtier of all people?" and continued, "Vladislav [the editor of a Czech version] is more reasonable and uses a neutral horseman" (Krenn, 1975, Kinderbuchverlag; DR1/2274).

In accordance with the socialist maxim of equality of race and nationality, changes in this respect were discussed in the files, so for instance in *Geschichten von Onkel Remus* (Harris, 1964, Kinderbuchverlag; DR1/3993), the publisher's decision was to include the background story only in parts and "only in so far as was absolutely necessary for comprehension of the tales because, in it, patriarchal traits are prevalent in the relationship of Remus, the former slave, to his earlier masters."

In Sherman's *Das Tellereisen* (1971, Neues Leben; DR1/3544a), the publisher stated that all the controversial passages marked out by the assessor had been either deleted or modified, for instance, the episode in which Mali, the gardener and native Indian, spends time with the son of his English colonial master and Mali adapts his behaviour to that expected by servants of his ethnic origin, "He drank in this fashion not only for respect of the feelings of the boy but also out of a deep-rooted sense for all that was right and proper for his race."

Bourgeois Values, Image of America:

Similar to the practice of over- or underplaying socio-critical elements in general, some translations aimed at pointing out the limitations of bourgeois values. In this context, America was identified with the concept of the enemy and some files show that there was an attempt to colour this through translation. For example, in the opinion of the publisher, Swarthout's book *Und sie sind nur Kinder* (1974, Neues Leben; DR1/3547a) represented a text accusatory of the American way of life, with children "helpless and at the mercy of an inhuman environment"; yet, although negative portrayals of such a world were welcome, certain concepts were still deemed unacceptable, such as the following passage, "Cotton dreams of performing heroic deeds in a rice field in Vietnam, of losing a leg and being decorated in the White House. His fear is, amongst others, that the war is over before he has grown into an adult". Although in this text the boys, in places, displayed humanist attributes which added to a legitimisation of the book, those particular passages were considered too inhuman—"America: these are not only the opponents of the Vietnam war but also characters like the murderers of Son My.[12] Describing such circumstances and the education, which bring about such characters, cannot be regarded as trivial and is the objective of realistic literature".

The aforementioned examples confirm the choice of motifs and criteria which were enumerated in Section 3.5, in other words, the codification established for literature that was deemed suitable, necessary, valuable or socially relevant and was, hence, officially sanctioned. Hence, the East German print permit files provide documentary evidence of how a culture selects and adapts literature and, thus, give clear evidence of Lefevere's concept of rewriting at work. Control over all literary output was exercised by those inside and outside the literary system. While the outside forces, i.e. the Party and its representatives, determined the parameters applicable, people on the inside such as publishers, editors or translators had the task of putting these parameters into practice.

Accepting and working under this system of patronage meant that publishers had to choose their programme wisely ensuring that, firstly, it fitted in with the official parameters and, secondly, that for more problematical books an argument could be made that described the book in terms compliant with the poetological and ideological East German norms. This heightened emphasis on ideological matters and 'the right choice' constitutes the primary act of censorship, or in other words self-censorship, the result of working under a totalitarian system. The necessity of East German authors to perform self-censorship has been discussed widely (see e.g. Loest 1984; Wichner and Wiesner 1993; Groth 1994; or Zipser 1995), yet it has rarely been pointed out that publishers had to endure similar restrictions. While translators have frequently been given a voice, this has not often been the case for the publishers; and yet, publishers play a significant role in society. The print permit files demonstrate that, on the one hand, East German publishers were drawn into the business of patronising the populace; yet, on the other, it is apparent that they were operating as puppets of the regime.

Fulfilling their service to the patron dutifully with respect to foreign texts meant that publishers had to rationalise and justify every trace of Otherness that did not match an ideologically satisfactory picture. What therefore was necessary in the evaluations presented to the censor was to anchor these texts in the socialist culture by appropriating them into the receiving culture (socialism). This was performed by skilful employment of motifs and a Socialist Realist vocabulary, whereby the foreign book was given legitimacy. Rewriting English-language texts, thus, meant constructing an often stereotypical image that the censor would recognise as adhering to socialist traditions.

Chapter Four
Case Studies

After the discussion in Chapter 3 on general insights into various aspects around the print permit files, this chapter aims at providing a more detailed analysis of specific files and of how particular genres were dealt with in the files. The objective is first and foremost to demonstrate how an argument was built up throughout a single file and how publisher and assessor co-operated, in order to construct a solid justification that would stand the scrutiny of the censor. What becomes evident is the persistence of publishers and assessors in using Socialist Realist motifs and Marxist-Leninist concepts necessary to hammer home their message to the censor. Again, it becomes apparent that in the description and criticism of books, no difference was made between texts for children and young adults. This approach also suggests that the same treatment was given to children's books and books for adults, a fact corroborated by descriptions, comparisons and examples in the children's book assessments that do not particularly relate to children's literary matters but rather to those of general literary theory. In the foreground was the application of Socialist Realist concepts and motifs to the texts and this was in no way different for books for adults. Print permit applications by publishers of adult literature show the same kind of motifs and paradigms and a similar line of argumentation.

The first three case studies deal with the publication history of individual books, i.e. *Doctor Dolittle*, *The Hobbit* and *The Witches. Doctor Dolittle* and *The Hobbit* have been chosen, because they were each discussed for publication at two different times, thereby enabling the reader to see differences in the argumentation used in the respective periods. Moreover, *Doctor Dolittle* was denied a print permit in 1966 and it is interesting to show where and why matters had gone wrong, and in what way the assessor of the 1980s' publication argued, in order to avoid another fiasco. Roald Dahl presented the East German children's book publishers with many problems due to the 'non-socialist' content of his books. He became publishable as a children's literature author only in the late 1980s, a fact which makes it worthwhile investigating the discourse in the files more closely; thus, Case Study 3 deals with Dahl's only East German publication for children in the GDR, namely *The Witches.* Case study 4 moves the discussion away from the focus on individual books and provides a brief analysis of the topic of anthologies and, with the example of two anthologies (one for younger children and one for young adults), demonstrates the ideological motivation and rationale behind their compilation. The fifth case study is concerned with the genre of crime and detective literature. The introduction of English-language detective stories to the East German children's book market is shown and how, after more than two decades of being frowned upon, they were made acceptable to the system.

4.1 Case Study 1—Hugh Lofting, Doktor Dolittle und seine Tiere

This book is the only book for young people translated from English which, according to the files, did not pass the censor (1966). However, consideration should be given to the fact that, as mentioned earlier (see p 63), the files were cleansed after the collapse of the GDR and, while there might have been other titles that were rejected, the documentation has been lost. *Doktor Dolittle* was eventually published in 1969 (by the then semi-private[1] publishing house Alfred Holz Verlag), but there is no documentation in the files regarding that publication, a fact strongly indicating that the records in the files are not complete. Furthermore, the book was republished in 1980 by Kinderbuchverlag (which by then had entirely taken over Holz). From the history shown in the files, publishing the book in 1980 was considerably different from the earlier attempt by Holz, which in part may be attributed to the fact that Kinderbuchverlag was the main state publisher of children's literature, whilst Holz was, at the time of the first attempt, a tiny semi-private enterprise and, perhaps, also in part to the fact that Kinderbuchverlag had requested a renowned scholar to produce an assessment for their publication.

The following section will analyse both applications, i.e. 1966 (DR1/2253) and 1980 (DR1/2287a). It is believed that the story is well-known and, therefore, the commentary will only be on the discourse in the files. The emphases are not mine, unless otherwise indicated.

Print Permit File: DR1/2253

Publisher Holz applied for a print permit for *Doktor Dolittle* in 1966; his hopes were for a print-run of 18,000 books, with 3,000 of them dedicated for export to a Swiss publisher (Atrium Verlag Zürich und London). With his application, he submitted two assessments, the first of which argued for a publication, the second against. Holz's application for the 15,000 copies for the GDR market was turned down. The purpose of this section is to provide an insight into the argumentation process and to demonstrate the points which were problematic and made the book unsuitable. What should not be forgotten, however, is that 1966 was the year after the so-called *Kahlschlag* (see p 31), a time when East German cultural politics were particularly unforgiving and rigid, and especially so towards private enterprise.

1. Holz, 1966—Assessor: Anne Martens

Anne Martens provided a rather short assessment of the book with a very simplistic argument based on only two basic Socialist Realist principles and a handful of other, minor supportive statements. These were:

Humanism (hinting at colonialism):

Martens began her argumentation with the fact that the book had a clear moral and, hence, was educational. In fact, she stressed, there was not only one moral but several; so, e.g., children were not only taught love for animals, but there was also a lesson about the uselessness of wrongful pride . . ., or the question of the colonies was explained, which was "indeed a highly political issue". However, leaving such a sweeping statement without further clarification might have been a mistake, which not only makes the assessor appear naïve but which may also have cost dearly in terms of a refusal of a print permit.

Collective Spirit:

In an attempt to give collective spirit more weight, Martens stated, "again and again, the entire book speaks about this principal thought: one cannot achieve anything alone"; with an example to support her comment, "this becomes particularly clear on page 119, when the story states that only together were the swallows able to pull the ship and, thereby, to save the passengers from the enemy."

Connection to Accepted Person:

After a short paragraph dealing with stylistic matters, Martens concluded by quoting Maxim Gorki's famous (in the GDR) saying that 'one ought to write for children as one does for adults—but better!' and indeed *Doktor Dolittle* "was written at the beginning of the 1930s and [therefore] it cannot be assumed that Lofting knew Gorki's saying, however, he acted as if he had known it." Citing Gorki, a Russian playwright but also pedagogue and reviewer of children's literature who, in the GDR, was renowned for his love for children and for good children's books, was intended to provide additional symbolic capital in support of the book.

Inappropriate Material:

Martens' last paragraph concerns itself with the illustrations, which she found suitable except for "the picture on page 60, which does not conform with the views and requirements of the present day and which therefore has already been deleted." However, she fails to give a reason or any further explanation as to what exactly she was referring to.

Overall, Martens declared herself in favour of a publication of the book. "One must not forget *when* the book was written and illustrated and, yet, it is (as I have attempted to show and to prove) not only acceptable *in all points* but *very much* to be recommended." Again, Martens' critical discourse lacks depth and familiarity with Marxist doctrine; the mere use of emotive and imprecise expressions without a detailed discussion could not suffice.

Compared with the vast majority of the other assessments in the files, the one by Martens is excessively brief. Martens gives the impression of either having underestimated the severity of having to address a censor and not taking the situation seriously enough, or of being too confident and relying on the fact that Lofting was a household name and, therefore, such a book would not be rejected by the censor. In any case, only making use of two Marxist principles (Humanism, Collective spirit) did not turn out to be sufficient, certainly at a time when the grip of cultural politics had tightened; and, in fact, a comparison with the assessment of 1980 will leave no doubt as to why publisher Holz was not successful.

2 *Holz, 1966—Assessor: Walter Mohrmann*

In contrast to the previous assessment, Walter Mohrmann condemned the production outright, "I really cannot see what the point should be of an edition of this piece". His opinion was based on the following key points:

(Lack of) Optimism:

Mohrmann detected a streak of "resignation. People do not understand Dolittle, they leave him and mock him, because he does good deeds. Whenever Dolittle meets people, they embody all that is hostile to life (with the exception of the citizens of the coastal town in which the fisherman lives who has been saved—page 160)". Commensurate with socialist tradition, Optimism was a trait people should acquire, in order to bring about a societal move forward; hence, it was a positive concept and needed to be found in a text. For the assessor to be able to unearth sentiments in the book adverse to this concept increased the risk of failure for the publication.

Colonialism:

Next, Mohrmann raised the question of the portrayal of the African kingdom. "Although the editor has been at pain to erase words like nigger, half-breeds and all those images that are offensive to an African people, the trend remains to make fun of Africa's populace".

(Lack of) Realism:

Replying to Martens' concept of the love for animals, Mohrmann attacked what he believed to be the missing theme of Realism, "Good animal books for children have a great pedagogical value. This book, however, is not of that kind. Rather, the author mixes several genres into a peculiar fantastic and absurd narration. I doubt whether such a description of nature will resonate in our children, who take an interest in sciences at an early stage in their lives and who, almost daily, come in touch with the most wonderful results of research." It is true that the GDR was proud of all scientific achievements and, also, that animal books for children were published in which emphasis was placed on the description of animals in their natural habitat and on showing the reader where and how these animals lived, rather than equipping them with fantastic or human attributes, since this was deemed uncritical and unrealistic—also in children's books.

Fantasy:

Mentioning the 'fantastic' at a time (1966), when this feature was not yet accepted officially in the canon, also resulted in a strong ideological shortcoming of the book. Therefore, Mohrmann stated that the story would have been acceptable, had it remained in the genre of fairytale, because then at least it would have been explicable why people could learn to speak with animals or why there were animals with two heads.

What the assessor found positive in the book was the fact that the animals helped the doctor in all dangerous situations; "however, in the German Democratic Republic these days, we should be hesitant to adopt the juxtaposition of evil human world and good animal world", playing on the missing premises of Humanism, Realism and Optimism. He then concluded his criticism by succinctly stating, "I am not recommending a publication of the book".

3. Holz, 1966—External Assessor by Censorship Authority: Gerhard Holtz-Baumert

In the event where two contradictory assessments reached the censorship authority, the book was passed on to an external assessor elected by the censor. In this case, it was Gerhard Holtz-Baumert, high-profile literary figure and children's book author and a member of the Writers' Association. He used the first page of his criticism to give a succinct overview of the story and to ponder the question as to whether the book might be part of the children's literary world heritage at all and whether, consequently, there was a necessity to publish it in the GDR. He went on to discuss themes appropriate to Marxist-Leninist discourse.

Lack of Humanism, Social Criticism:

Holtz-Baumert commenced, "Two basic principles indicate that the matter is sensitive. The entire book abounds with instances of turning away from humans: the animals are so much better than the humans!" Admittedly, Holtz-Baumert acknowledged the socio-critical shade in the thought that it is human nature to bring disaster upon itself but, simultaneously, he denied

Dolittle, whom he called "a simple-minded spirit", the ability to take notice of this fact and to see a possibility to change this *status quo*, other than to be resigned to it. It was a vital ingredient of Western books to be able to show a political stance, views of social relevance and commitment to fighting for a goal. The assessor could not detect this. "This book shirks away from social problems and has a middle-class taste to it". He contended that it was

> the animals, and not the humans, who possess humanitarian values, namely being reasonable, clever, honest . . ., supportive and selfless. (However, the author is not consistent here either. He overlooks the fact that on the journey to Africa the Duck Dab-Dab catches herrings in a big way and then everyone on the ship has to eat fish. Well, well, Dr Dolittle, the mighty animal lover, differs between animal-friends and edible animals! What will the poor fish have whispered to him in Herring-speak).

By poking fun at Lofting, Holtz-Baumert hoped to achieve a further decrease in the book's ideological value.

Fatalism, (Lack of) Optimism:

Holtz-Baumert proceeded to speak about the author of the preface, calling him "a representative of the viewpoint of a dark and inexplicable world, whose preface constituted a programme of resignation and passivity", then bringing into play the motif of Fatalism, a motif with strong negative connotations—"but these values are alien to us and we would not want one ounce of them with our children. The world is predictable and can be changed—this is what we want to exclaim."

Racism, (Lack of) Humanism:

Next, he tackled the book's "attitude towards negroes". There, in his view, "the publisher cannot escape by only transforming the word nigger, which is scattered all over the text, to 'African'. One cannot eliminate the meaning in this way." And here, too, the assessor detected a shortcoming in Humanism; indeed, he went even further and stated that, through the episode of the animals taking revenge on the black prince by cheating on him and promising him a white skin, "we will move ourselves into conflict with our clear and unanimous education of friendship among nations . . .; it can come as no surprise that this book was published under the Nazis. Although it did not correspond with their barbaric education in aggression, it fitted exactly their concept of racism." Should the censor by then still have had some doubt about the value of *Doktor Dolittle*, the mention of it being published in the Third Reich would have sealed the book's fate.

All in all, Holtz-Baumert summed up, "Because of the aforementioned reasons, I do not see why we should now publish this book. It has no value in any way, rather it comprises highly dubious ingredients. Is there nothing else to be caught in the ocean of world literature for children?"

These three paratexts demonstrate the need to detect and use Marxist-Leninist values in books, in order to support an argument. Amongst others, the main motifs used were those of Humanism, Realism, Optimism and social criticism. Under the contemporary narrow interpretation of the concept of Socialist Realism, the one assessment arguing in favour of a publication failed to display convincingly imagination, inventiveness and willingness to re-interpret or, to apply Lefevere's theory, rewrite the story, a blatant error which allowed the opponents of the book to gain the upper hand and vote for a ban.

Print Permit File: DR1/2287a

Publisher Kinderbuchverlag applied for a print permit for *Doktor Dolittle* in 1980. This application uses a completely different approach. It radiates optimism and is rich in argumentation with ideologically loaded key-words and motifs. From the outset, both the publisher and the assessor declared full confidence that this book belonged to the world heritage and, therefore, there was no question whether or not to publish it. The publisher contended, "the story of *Doktor Dolittle* is internationally famous and is counted amongst the classic oeuvre of children's literature", and the assessor Ebert commenced on an even more positive note, "actually, every assessment of Hugh Lofting's *Doktor Dolittle* is superfluous. This book belongs to the basic canon of bourgeois humanist children's literature—with all its limits. And therefore, it does not necessitate lavish reflection to vote for a re-edition of this classic title."

1. Kinderbuchverlag, 1980—Assessor: Günter Ebert

Ebert began by referring to aspects of children's literature arriving at the conclusion that *Doktor Dolittle* had all the criteria of a good children's book: simplification, identification, adventure, humour and fantasy. Admittedly, it was easier for him to embed 'fantasy' in a positive argument because, by now, fantastic elements had become an integral part of children's fiction.

Humanism:

Ebert then continued in the same vein, equating the protagonist Dolittle with the concept of 'the child' and, in doing so, pointing to Dolittle's harmlessness and innocence. Ebert called Dolittle "little" and "loveable", both attributes one would also give to a child and both made to create a positive mind-set in the reader of the assessment, i.e. the censor. Simultaneously, by using the word "loveable", he managed to suggest to the reader that this protagonist was somebody who we all loved, and indeed *all* (my emphasis) because, as he had maintained above, this book belonged to the world heritage and was read and loved by everyone.

Ebert then resorted to the motif of Humanism, by linking the notion of kindness to his thought-construct of 'little-ness and likeable-ness'; he finished the sentence by calling Dolittle "weltfremd" (unworldly), thus implying that he was a naïve creature who would do no harm; altogether his attempt was to create a figure who was endearing, warmhearted but perhaps somewhat gullible and eccentric. Hence, Ebert's sentence reads, "because of his kindness and unwordliness (and because of his name), the little loveable doctor is the personified child; which represents the best possible identification figure." And thus, it should be added, it made for an ideal book for children.

Capitalism, Profiteering:

Progressing from his idea of 'Dolittle, the child', Ebert claimed, "the childlike behaviour is also expressed, for instance, in the doctor's helplessness about" (smart move!) "money." Money, as one of the key elements characterising capitalism, manifested everything evil. Telling the reader outright that Dolittle did not know how to handle money, because it meant nothing to him, added another bonus to the description. A few paragraphs further down, Ebert supported this concept of distaste for money by calling on the authority of socialist historical theories, "as a critical reader one recognises, throughout the entire book, the theories of the Fabian Society,[2] social reformism . . . [Accordingly,] our protagonist would so much like to ignore money and all dependency on it. 'Money is an onus', as he says."

Humanism, Positive Attitude, Value of the Book to Society:

Dolittle's love for animals was treated next. "Dr Dolittle loves the animals—creatures, helpless and not understood. He, the doctor for humans, takes care of the creatures so much that he is even able to learn their language, a fact that makes him world famous within the story, and also outside, and assigns him his originality"—thereby again playing on the international fame of the book, suggesting that the GDR could ill afford to leave it off the shelves of its book shops.

Work Ethos, Realism:

Dolittle's "success as a vet is great and striking" (pride in work and success in work was one key socialist concept). "He prescribes green glasses to half-blind horses and the problem is solved. There is method in such facts: the simplification of reality creates humour, which is harmless and unexpected." Ebert's idea to employ the motif of Realism together with humour again added symbolic capital to the text.

Humanism, Money:

The next sentences threw in yet two more concepts, Humanism and the hate of profiteering:

> Dr Dolittle hardly ever thinks of himself; his house and garden turn into an animal asylum. He liberates needy animals from their dependence and captivity. Although he becomes world-famous, he does not become

> rich. And at this point one has to make a tiny remark about the ideology of this book. Dolittle's kindness represents his humanism. . . . [Admittedly,] Hugh Lofting walks on the edge of contempt of human beings, but in no place does he ever cross the border. On the contrary, reading his texts carefully, one finds even more subtle social layers.

This, then, formed the prelude to socio-critical allusions.

Social Criticism:

How Ebert handled and integrated the following explanation about reference to social classes and the way he embedded the book into socio-critical aspects of capitalism is masterly. He argued as follows,

> Already in the first chapter, it literally says: 'I far prefer animals to people of high rank'. We see, he does not reject all humans in general. Similarly, his sister and housekeeper Sarah Dolittle, had said shortly before: 'This is now the fourth person of high standing who has been chased away by your animals'.—With the terms 'people of high rank' and 'of high standing' a very particular social circle is rejected. The last human patient whom he sees is called 'Katzenfuttermann' [cat food man], he is not very rich but loyal and certainly fond of animals. With only a few words a bourgeois author attempts here to embed love for animals and at the same time raise socially relevant problems.

Calling Lofting 'bourgeois' had the aim of ascribing to him a certain political position, from which he, as an author from a capitalist system, could not see nor understand the 'correct' socialist standpoint, as was propagated by Marxist-Leninist doctrine, but doubtlessly he could be granted goodwill and effort in his endeavour to be socially committed and in attempting to point to problems in his society by using the literary device of animals to express them.

Humanism, Superiority of Socialism, Solidarity:

In order to underpin his point, Ebert cited another example from the book, in which a boatman lent Dolittle and his animals a boat which was subsequently shipwrecked. And how did Dolittle react? "He thinks of the boatman, whom he explicitly calls poor, and he tries to find a solution as to how to replace his only boat". Not only did this tie the book more closely to the discourse of Humanism and difference of the social classes; it also prepared the path to incorporate another Marxist premise, as the following sentence went on to say, "Here we realise clearly the core of the book which has ensured that it would never lose its popularity over time: solidarity for ordinary and helpless people. And precisely this offer of readiness to help is something we acquaint our children with", implying that, in the GDR as opposed to Western societies, children were taught the value of humanitarian traits. Harking back to his notion of

Dolittle as the embodiment of 'the child', Ebert concluded his paragraph, "this is the positive factor of this narration: without solidarity Dr Dolittle (that is to say: the child) could not exist."

Reference to an Officially Accepted Person:

Another observation is Ebert's attempt to fit the book in with literature published and, hence, officially acknowledged in the GDR; this was attained by comparing Dolittle's dog with a dog featuring in *Der kleine Zauberer*, an East German children's book written by Uwe Kant, an established author, loyal and high-ranking in the Writers' Association and, thus, a highly acclaimed canonised writer. Ebert explained in more detail, "What I want to say by this is that the book will not trigger loud laughter, but much understanding for minor human (i.e. animal) weaknesses"—thereby again taking the sting out of the potential obstacle of too much emphasis on animals, by aligning them with humans.

Ebert's evaluation is a firework of sharp-witted creativity, making use of Marxist-Leninist concepts and motifs in abundance and uniting them in a hymn to a book which more than a decade previously struggled to pass the censor.

2 *Kinderbuchverlag, 1980—Publisher's Assessment*

As a consequence, publisher Kinderbuchverlag, when writing their assessment, could easily follow, "The author's principal concern is the thought of solidarity and the importance of helpfulness. In the kindness of the doctor lies his humanitarian attitude towards all living beings. . . . For Hugh Lofting, Dr Dolittle personifies both the kind and valuable human being as well as the ethical demands of the author for mankind in general." After this unambiguous reference to Ebert's assessment, Kinderbuchverlag talked about Dolittle's unworldliness and his ignorance of money and its value, adding, "and this in a capitalist society, in which money is the ruling power", thereby stressing the anti-capitalistic stance of the book.

Tackling Shortcomings:

However, the publisher pointed to a criterion that might have become a potential obstacle and that needed to be expressed and toned down. "Dr Dolittle does not want to see problems, he closes his eyes to the facts of life, and yet he is confronted with them continuously"; these were overtones of escapism from reality and something needed to be done about them. Therefore, Kinderbuchverlag contended,

> here we see the limits of the book and of the ideological consciousness of the author. But one ought to add that, on the one hand, social analyses were alien to bourgeois children's books; on the other, the author, living in England, the classic country of capitalism, and thus being biased by its circumstances, was not able to formulate in-depth social thoughts and insights. However, the humanist contents of the book, which demonstrate

> to the reader the importance of solidarity and readiness to help, justifies a re-publication of the book.

Kinderbuchverlag concluded, "there are 12 books about Dr Dolittle, five of which were assessed by the editors. We have decided to select only the first volume because we feel that, here, the author presents his argument most convincingly. All other volumes merely vary the theme of the first volume and offer nothing new and original", words emphasising the selected volume as the one with the best value for East Germany and which, as a result, made it appear worthy of publication.

This example illustrates the strategies that had to be undertaken, in order to make a book appear to comply with the prevalent ideology and poetics and, in so doing, make it publishable. As has been shown, it was vital to pre-empt problematic areas in the text, or with the author, and attempt to defuse them.

Lefevere, in reference to the introduction of Brecht on to the American stage, claims that the playwright would not have had any chances of being performed or published, if he had been translated on his own terms and disregarding the poetics of the receiving system (1982a:14). This is just what had happened to Lofting in 1966 in the first attempt to publish *Doktor Dolittle* in the GDR. By not taking sufficiently seriously the poetics and the sanctioned codification of the East German target system, the book's concepts were left too controversial for it to be received and the critic and censor had no other choice but to reject it. Within ten years of the first attempt, politics and, with it, poetics changed and softened; therefore, together with a line of argument that supported the East German poetological elements and used East German codification, the book no longer presented an insurmountable challenge to the officially propagated paradigms. Taking such mechanisms into consideration seems even more vital in a system of undifferentiated patronage. Contrary to pluralist societies in which there are various forms of patronage and where it may be enough for an author or publisher to find one or two supporters, this is not the case in a totalitarian system. Thus, the East German patron was the guardian of the one-and-only possible orthodoxy and authors needed to be introduced by using the codification and value system sanctioned and implemented by the ruling authority. Failure to be rewritten in these terms meant an exclusion from the canon and a rejection from the system.

4.2 Case study 2—J.R.R. Tolkien, Der kleine Hobbit

For this book, the files show Kinderbuchverlag's plans to publish it twice; there were applications in 1971 and in 1989, respectively; however, for some unknown reason, only the 1971 publication took place. For 1971, the files comprise two evaluations, one by the publisher and one by an assessor appointed by the publisher. For the unrealised 1989 publication, the files contain only the publisher's statement. Although Kinderbuchverlag did not publish *The Hobbit* for a second time, this application will be considered here, in order to compare an application dating from the last year of Ulbricht's leadership with one from the year in which the GDR ceased to exist and to see possible changes in strategy.

Print Permit File DR1/2264a

1. Kinderbuchverlag, 1971—Assessor: Hans Petersen

Petersen commenced by calling to mind the history of the book and underlining the status it had already achieved during the short time of its existence.

Humanism:

Then, Petersen led smoothly to the objective of this publication, calling in the motif of Humanism, while also touching on the book's worldwide fame and its educational value to the child reader.

> John Ronald Reuel Tolkien, whose fairytale novel *Der kleine Hobbit* was published in 1937 for the first time and which, to this date, has already experienced sixteen re-editions, has become a modern classic. . . . In allegoric fashion, the book centres on human virtues and, in an immediate way, achieves its goal—the emotional and ethical education of the young generation.

It may be assumed that Petersen used the term "fairytale novel" intentionally, as by 1971 the concept of 'Fantasy' was not yet entirely integrated in the literary system, although already gaining in awareness and acceptance.

Reputation of the Author:

A few paragraphs further down, Petersen reconfirmed,

> there are classic oeuvres of children's literature, which Kinderbuchverlag should not ignore and Tolkien's *Der kleine Hobbit* is such a work. This book written by the former Oxford professor for Anglo-Saxon (1925–1945) can be recommended for publication. Tolkien has effortlessly used his expert knowledge of Old English literature, to create a children's book . . ., a story to educate both feeling and intellect.

Comparison with Another Canonised Author/Story:

The following passage served to elevate the book to the level of *Alice in Wonderland*, an already acknowledged text in the GDR and, in so doing, to attribute weight and additional value.

> While Lewis Carroll's *Alice im Wunderland* excels in intellectual wit, Tolkien's narrative appears more naïve, richer and less playful. Tolkien does

> not need an introduction using a dream as an allegorical peg [on which to hang his story], he does not use the formula 'Just imagine!', which creates ironic distance, rather he works with the age-old 'Once upon a time' (even if he does not use it literally) . . . This points to differences, which exist in children's literature as much as in literature for adults. Nonetheless, both books are notable and amusing and, at the same time, educational—each in a different way.

The Typical, Bourgeois Characteristics:

Next, Petersen introduced the figure of the Hobbit as a typical example of the species of Hobbits, yet also as somebody outstanding and worth closer inspection. In passing, he also managed to have a side-swipe at the shortcomings of the bourgeoisie.

> Bilbo Baggins . . . is the hero and central character of this story. He is the perfect example of a Hobbit—and yet, he is a very special Hobbit. The author describes the personal growth of this likeable little man who, in his comfortable hole with amenities, food and drink in abundance, cannot develop his personality.

Humanism, Active Involvement:

Having set the scene as an environment hostile to any personal development, Petersen turned to describing how Bilbo Baggins manages to escape and rid himself of his middle-class thinking. He explained that Tolkien invented the wise and powerful wizard Gandalf, who, in his benevolence towards the Hobbit and towards humanity in general, tears Bilbo from his daily monotony and sends him out into the world. There, "a citizen who is friendly, all-around popular and somewhat self-satisfied turns into a circumspect and skilful friend, a personality, who knows how to look after himself in all situations of life." Employing the term 'Persönlichkeit' evoked the image of "sozialistische Persönlichkeit", the ideal ultimate state, for which every East German was to strive.

The Typical, Humanism, Collective Spirit, Positive Attitude:[3]

"This children's book is typical of the attributes of an "*Entwicklungsroman*"[4] . . . and also of an *adventure story*, both of which, however, are subordinate to the pedagogical requirements", thereby expressing the view that children would enjoy the story because of the adventures the heroes encountered, with the main purpose still to educate while reading. This learning process of the readers was in alignment with the Hobbit's exploits, "which are reminiscent of the old *heroic epics*" (a canonised genre in the GDR), where

> the Hobbit deals with trials, in which he has to prove himself or die . . . His growth in personality occurs hand in hand with him *becoming a*

> *human being*, for the simple reason that the reader identifies more and more with the Hobbit and, in the end, even believes in him as a human being and not a Hobbit, a mythical creature—something even the little reader will experience.

Equating the Hobbit with human beings served to weaken the fantastic aspect of the book and to lay stress on the motifs of Humanism and Realism.

Then, Petersen finished his thought by calling on the socialist ideal of Solidarity and the Collective spirit, linking the book to Marxist virtues, "Finally, he recognises that he is a little cog in a complicated whole to which he, like innumerable others, belongs. Without him and the others, the machine will stop." But Bilbo is not without fault,

> we all know that he is incapable of doing the impossible, but he achieves his best, and this is what makes him so likeable. And when the dying Thorin says in the end, 'there is more in you of good than you know—courage and wisdom, blended in measure. If our peoples valued food, cheer and song more, it would be a merrier world',[5] he states something that the little readers have already found out themselves, because the little Hobbit has demonstrated this to them in the course of his dangerous adventures.

Using quotations from the book is a strategy frequently performed in assessments, in order to give weight to the way the book has been interpreted, and this is just what Petersen tried to attain, namely putting special emphasis on Bilbo's achievements and stressing that, as long as a human being strives and does not give up in his efforts, his personality will shine and he will be a valuable member to his society.

Realism, Humanism:

Since *The Hobbit* is a fantastic book, there was the danger that it was rejected on grounds of lack of reality. Although by 1971 (or in fact 1968, the date shown on Petersen's evaluation) the fantastic element had slowly begun to find its way into literature (see pp 32 and 45), it was not yet anchored firmly in the canon and, as a corollary, the evaluator had to take precautions and put this aspect into the correct light (hence also the classification of the story as a fairy-tale novel, as discussed earlier). He called the book enigmatic and beautiful,

> because it grips children where it is easiest to get hold of them: with their emotions. In doing so, Tolkien shows us a realistic story, despite all its fantasy; this fact is, without doubt, an achievement, similar to his foregoing of sentimentalities and mawkishness, which is a definite bonus of this book.

Further to the realistic streak in the book, Petersen exemplified,

> Tolkien succeeds in displaying the polarity of good and evil, however without simplifying. He makes transparent the various shades, in the main with the dwarves (see e.g. Thorin's avarice) and the elves, also with Beorn, the rough, shape shifting bear, and what's more, he has an upright man (Bard) replace the old, sly 'master' of Laketown, a move, with which he puts in place the ideal leader to a (bourgeois) ideal state.

Bourgeois Society:

Petersen also found references in the book to "the bourgeois world" in the shape of ironic comments, such as "the auction at the end of the story, the raid of greedy relatives, the allusion to Hobbit's memoirs"; these comments, he believed, constituted an effective final chord and were in correspondence with the funny and ironic notions of the entire book.

Quality of Translation:

In his final passage, Petersen dealt with the translation (which had been performed by a West German translator and was used for the East German edition), demanding urgent checks and editorial proofreading, because the translator "had not taken his profession seriously enough. There are countless translation errors, generalisations, omissions, ugly word-for-word translations and unnecessary additions."

2. *Kinderbuchverlag, 1971—Publisher's Assessment*

With such a favourable and clearly expressed assessment in their hands, the publisher did not have much to do other than to follow Petersen's line of argument. Indeed, the first motifs made use of are:

Humanism, Personal Growth:

In a few sentences, Kinderbuchverlag summarised the storyline, finishing with, "it all requires such huge effort, and so much courage and wit are necessary to destroy the evil in the shape of the dragon. When the little Hobbit makes for home, it turns out that, from a being who lived an idle life, there has evolved a brave little chap who has a better understanding of the world and his place in it."

Bourgeois Society:

There is a direct reference to the assessor's evaluation, with the purpose of demonstrating agreement between Kinderbuchverlag and Petersen's interpretation. Kinderbuchverlag wrote, "As the evaluator states quite rightly, this book is an 'enigmatic book'," because "it shows us a replica of the bourgeois world with its predilection for idleness, regardless of what is happening in the world around, with its unscrupulous pursuit of riches and with its avarice that does not even stop between friends. The entire book abounds in allusions to the bourgeois England of our time."

Collective Spirit, Battle Against Bourgeois, Materialistic Thinking, Active Involvement:

Kinderbuchverlag took as their vantage point the idle capitalist world, then claiming,

> diametrically opposed to this world is the struggle of all forces which fight this [bourgeois] sickness. They have to put in all their effort and come together in a common front, in order to be victorious. Simultaneously, the author outlines that these fronts are not always clear-cut, as e.g. the dwarves are not all good and, also, they are not always good. This means that one has to be cautious and observant and must never lose sight of the main questions of battle.

Here, the assessment uses the propaganda term 'die Hauptfragen des Kampfes nicht aus den Augen verlieren' (never lose sight of the main questions of battle), perhaps to give the story a stronger badge of legitimacy.

The penultimate passage was a summary of the key motifs to demonstrate compliance with the state ideology; in summary, the ideological weight lies in the message that it does not suffice to live a happy, isolated life by oneself. Rather, one must participate in life in general and fight for a better world. Collecting riches is not the main virtue in life; it is work and peaceful coexistence of everyone. This alone will bring happiness and satisfaction.

Similar to Petersen's assessment, the last paragraph dealt with the quality of the (West German) translation, agreeing with the assessor on all weak points of the translation and maintaining that the editor had had to put in serious work, in order to improve it. The reworked version had been, as Kinderbuchverlag put it, shown to the original translator and, overall, he had agreed with the improvements.

Print Permit File DR1/2314

This file does not show an evaluation by an assessor but only consists of the publisher's statement. This is not to say that the publisher had not asked an assessor to write a critical statement of the book; it might have been lost in the turmoil of the last days of the regime; for instance, it might also have been shredded, together with some other documents. However, it is just as conceivable that Kinderbuchverlag had decided to apply for a publication only submitting their own assessment for two reasons; firstly, it was a publication which had already been given a print permit two decades earlier and, therefore, one could expect the censor to be more benevolent towards the project; secondly, it was the year in which censorship dramatically relaxed and in which there was discussion about abolishing the entire application procedure and putting more responsibility on each publisher as to how to handle their projects. This is also in accordance with the observation that the files become thinner in the 1980s since, for several (mostly classic) books, only a publisher's evaluation was submitted which, in addition, was frequently kept quite brief.

Kinderbuchverlag 1989—Publisher's Assessment

Briefly and in passing, the publisher began by mentioning the fact that *Der kleine Hobbit* belonged to the classics of children's literature and that the book was read not only in England but all over the world. Drawing on Petersen's assessment from two decades ago, the publisher classified the story as a mixture of fairytale, adventure story, *Entwicklungsroman* and old English heroic epic; in short, a story full of suspense and fun. Kinderbuchverlag proceeded to claim that, unfortunately, the translation did not live up to the witty and light narrative of the original; this despite a fair amount of reworking in 1971, in order to eliminate inconsistencies, mistakes and inaccuracies.

Bourgeois Society, Affluence:

Like Petersen in 1971, Kinderbuchverlag detected overtones of the Bourgeois. Introducing Bilbo Baggins, the publisher explained that he

> lives an idle and quiet life in his luxurious hole. After his forefathers have made a fortune and have earned a good reputation, Baggins now enjoys a secluded life, with good food and drink, smoking his pipe in front of the fireplace and having a friendly conversation every now and then. In their surroundings, the Bagginses are viewed as respectable—because they are wealthy, because they have never been involved in adventures and have never done anything unexpected.

Personality and Personal Growth:

According to Kinderbuchverlag,

> the actual miracle of this story is . . .: the idle, friendly and portly, stoic hero who was only concerned with his own well-being, the unwilling hero who always longs to return to his cosy hole indeed turns into a real hero, into a clever, brave and responsible friend, who not only frees himself from life-threatening situations with resourcefulness, wit and courage, but who also engages himself with the dwarves and gains their respect. . . . So, in the end, Thorin can assure Bilbo Baggins . . . that 'there is more in you of good than you know—courage and wisdom, blended in measure.'

After quoting Thorin, similar to twenty years before, Kinderbuchverlag concluded that the story was also a *Menschengeschichte*, a human story, the story of somebody who is encouraged to step out of his niche, to prove himself in life and contribute to improving the *status quo* and a better and fairer world. And in fact, "he does not care at all that he is no longer considered as respectable by those who remained Hobbits, because he knows that he has participated with all his energy in putting into practice the old prophecies of a happy life in the countries around the 'Lonely Mountain'."

Although the key motifs of Personal growth, of Bourgeois and materialistic thinking, of Humanism and of being Active were still employed in the 1989 application, there are some differences. One lies in the concluding sentence of Kinderbuchverlag for their later edition, which put much more weight on Individuality (a concept that had become acceptable during the 1970s), so much so that the publisher even wrote that the Hobbit did not care any longer whether he was considered respectable by his fellow-people. Also, there is no longer an extra-emphasis on Collective actions. The publisher merely re-tells the story as an adventure, in which Bilbo has been persuaded by Gandalf to recapture the dwarves' treasure and he does so with a group of other dwarves. On the contrary, rather than emphasising equality, Kinderbuchverlag stated that Gandalf made Hobbit the "master thief", thus attributing to him more status than his fellows. The motif of "the Typical" is no longer used, again an indication of a society that embraced individuality and was not fixated on notions of 'sameness' and characteristic stereotypes. Lastly, the motif of Realism is missing from this discourse, a sign that the Fantastic had been fully incorporated into East German poetics and there was no longer any need to write a passage in its defence. On the whole, these (together with the fact that publisher Kinderbuchverlag submitted their evaluation without the 'aid' of the secondary opinion of an assessor) are all indications of a society that had grown in self-confidence, had realised its own worth and was no longer afraid of expressing this. Little wonder then that the people had become ready to stand up for their rights so much that they overthrew the political leadership.

4.3 Case study 3—Roald Dahl, Hexen hexen

Dahl, although not unpublished in the GDR,[6] did not have any of his children's stories published until 1988. It may be assumed that, apart from copyright issues and ensuing foreign currency problems, the main reason for the lengthy rejection of Dahl's children's oeuvre can be put down to the lack of realistic plots, an exuberance of nonsense and fantastic elements, 'bad' language and violence, all of which were contrary to the publishing policies of the GDR. Nevertheless, Kinderbuchverlag decided in the late eighties that the time was ripe for a publication. This fact evidences a move towards a more open system of publication, topped by fervent calls for the abolition of censorship being voiced in 1987 (see p 41). With the publication of Dahl's *The Witches* (*Hexen hexen*) in 1988, it can be deduced that the hostility towards light-hearted, entertaining reading for children and the emphasis on didactic literature had changed significantly. Despite changes taking place, there still appears to have been a legacy of the earlier restrictions to overcome; hence, Kinderbuchverlag regarded it necessary to ask a person of high standing to produce the assessment, namely Günter Ebert.

Print Permit File DR1/2307a

1 Kinderbuchverlag, 1988—Assessor Günter Ebert

One of the foremost tasks for the assessor was to demonstrate to the censor that *Hexen hexen* conformed to East German standards and did not represent an inappropriate choice of book.

Appropriating Author and Content of Book:

Hence, Ebert's first move was to embed Dahl in the literary system by comparing the author with writers approved in the GDR and by highlighting that Dahl was an author who had already been published in the GDR and, hence, was not new to the canon.

> We know him from collections for adults, such as *Lammkeule* and *Kuschelmuschel* and we are fascinated by the astonishing and horrific turning points of his stories. Although nasty and wicked in character, they are amusing at the same time. Dahl reminds us of Edgar Allan Poe and Ambrose Bierce; however, I detect greater humour in his stories, which makes bearable many a macabre situation. But above all, Dahl's children's stories are reminiscent of Lewis Carroll and his *Alice in Wonderland*. Indeed, I would not even consider it out of the question to compare Dahl's stories with Saint-Exupéry's *The Little Prince*.

Ebert's next step was to assure the censor of the harmlessness of *Hexen hexen* and to stress the ease with which children could cope with such writing.

> Those who place too much emphasis on the shocking descriptions and on certain violent events, do not understand the essence of the narration. . . . The decisive question here is the discrepancy between the relaxed tone of the stories and the terrible details told, and between the apparent seriousness, with which the narrator treats the content, and the fantastic nonsense which lies at the heart of the story.

Next, Ebert introduced the notion of "Risikotraining" and his interpretation of it, by which he referred to the fact that "children, too, want and have to learn to deal with fears, problems, dangerous ideas and dubious fantasies." Therefore, horror effects and exaggerated nasty descriptions, Ebert claimed, constituted a useful instrument to help children overcome their preconceptions and accept horror. From the line of argument given, it can be seen that Ebert was reinterpreting the literary rules, in order to accommodate the new, broader understanding of what was acceptable for children's literature. To a lesser or greater degree, this type of reinterpretation took place in every assessment and depended on the assessor skilfully assessing the political climate of the time and pitching the assessment in such a way that the censor could accept the new interpretation.

The Fantastic, the Typical:

After mentioning that the protagonist's grandmother, from Norway, was a witch and that she had explained to the boy about the existence of witches and how to identify them, Ebert pointed to the roots of the story which, he claimed, lay in the Norwegian tradition; Norway, being a country "in which trolls and other fantastic figures have a recognised place in everyday life ('in Norway . . . we are used to such events')", thereby reconciling the Fantastic with the Typical and rendering witches (quite evil and malicious creatures in German literature) as harmless or, at least, nothing to be afraid of.

Reality, Link to Real Life:

Describing the "extermination programme" of the witches and the chief witch's order to "eliminate from this world all the children", the assessor detected a streak of inhumanity, which "immediately made me think of Fascism, although such parallels might not have occurred to the author". By that, Ebert attempted to express that *Hexen hexen* was by no means fantasy but depicted a very realistic scenario, one that had taken place in history. An indicator of how much the climate had changed within literary criticism is the fact that the assessor was able to mention incidents in the text as reminiscent of Fascism. Twenty years earlier, such associations would have caused a censor to ban the book from publication (see Section 4.1, Case Study 1, Hugh Lofting, *Doktor Dolittle und seine Tiere*). Ebert proceeded to state that all witches had to operate undercover and had to appear to conform to society, so that they would not be found out, "whereby the fantastic plot becomes reality, as it were." Ironically, when reading the assessor's statement, one wonders whether he was aware of the correlation to East German reality and, if so, whether he had wanted to make this point deliberately.

Humanism, Active Involvement, Individuality:

The assessor began by describing the relationship between the boy and his grandmother as establishing slowly but firmly a stronghold against the evil in the story. Therefore, later in his assessment, Ebert was able to interpret the boy's transformation into a mouse entirely positively, in that

> it is a key moment in the story. Firstly, the new shape assists the boy to operate effectively against the witches and their evil intentions; secondly, after a brief struggle, the boy is not disturbed by his new shape, because he can still communicate with his grandmother and she accepts him also as a mouse and assures him that he has not lost his identity; thirdly, as a result, the boy arrives at the recognition that 'it does not matter who you are and how you look, as long as there is someone

> who loves you', a recognition which gives the entire book a distinctly humanist dimension.

Also, at the end of the story, boy and grandmother return to Norway, having saved all the English children. However, as Ebert emphasised, they do not want to retire but they have plans to carry on fighting the witches.

Pre-emption of Potential Problems with the Censor:

"Up to this point, there is no doubt that everybody can accept this modern fairytale"—by calling *Hexen hexen* a fairytale, the assessor helped fit it into a genre which had been socially and culturally acknowledged. However,

> one may expect objections against a few cruelties, or scenes that have been portrayed in too much detail, or depiction of nasty incidents. Admittedly, occasionally some of these exceed the extent of what has been tolerated here in this country. But what needs to be taken into account is, firstly, the English fairytale tradition and the specific English sense of humour; secondly, our fairytales are certainly not harmless either . . . , although they do not depict details in such a shocking manner; thirdly, through television, children are accustomed to even worse images; and after all, words do represent a kind of distancing barrier between reader and story. What is more, Dahl uses dialogue to describe several of these cruelties.

Concluding his thought, Ebert diverted from the points that might have caused an obstacle with the censor and stated, "if I have found anything irritating, it was the strange and distorted dialect of the chief witch; its unimaginativeness got on my nerves."

Humanism, Optimism, Active Involvement:

Coming to a conclusion, Ebert declared himself in favour of a publication and gave the following reasons:

> To put it simply, I am for a publication of *Hexen hexen* here in East Germany; it is an original and, above all, amusing fairytale with a humanitarian tenor (which can even be found in minor details—see page 35, the remark about slugs that have been crushed underfoot completely pointlessly). All repulsive descriptions or evil plans are counterbalanced by the action of the first person narrator, because he is not deterred from his positive actions in spite of the dangerousness of his enemies,

thus stressing that the boy made an exemplary socialist personality and a model for readers to emulate.

2. *Kinderbuchverlag, 1988—Publisher's Assessment*

Kinderbuchverlag was very much aware that this project was controversial and required careful argumentation. With a positive assessment by Ebert in their hands and based on his powerful arguments, all the publisher was required to do was to recapitulate the assessor's main points. Therefore, they began with a reference to *Lammkeule* and *Kuschelmuschel*, speaking of English black humour in its epitome and posing the question of whether it was possible and justifiable to publish this kind of literature for child readers; in fact, as Kinderbuchverlag conceded, strong reservations had been expressed amongst several editors regarding such a project because of its "disgusting details [and because] horror effects might shock sensitive readers, might create fear in them or, vice versa, contribute to making the readers get used to horror and cruelties."

Appeasing the Censor:

However, Kinderbuchverlag informed the censor that reservations of this kind were groundless for two reasons; firstly, the editors had read *Hexen hexen* themselves and, secondly, the children test reading the book had wholeheartedly taken to it, because "children are more skilled in dealing with the fantastic than the adult reader, they understand immediately [the discrepancy between an apparently serious situation and the actual fantastic nonsense of the story]." Making mention of Ebert's *Risikotraining*, Kinderbuchverlag argued that *Hexen hexen* enabled readers to deal with their fears and dubious fantasies in a calm and happy manner, in that horror was exaggerated to the absurd extreme and triggered liberated laughter.

Next, Kinderbuchverlag referred to a second factor that, as they hoped, would aid in dispersing all doubts about the book, which was the humanitarian aspect. The "very deep, warm-hearted, loving relationship between the seven-year-old and his grandmother", which makes the boy feel secure and accepted. His grandmother comforts him, encourages him and gives him loving care, all of which "make this book a genuine children's book."

Thirdly, the publisher touched on the subject of witches, in order to counter a possible complaint about magic creatures which might frighten readers. Calling in Ebert's authority, the publisher highlighted the fact that other cultures had fantastic creatures, which were commonly used in their tales and were typical of their heritage. Thus, Kinderbuchverlag wrote, "we find his [Ebert's] reference to the Norwegian folklore of importance. Here, Astrid Lindgren's *Ronja Robber's Daughter* has already prepared the ground for the reception of alien and, hence, unfamiliar fantasy with its grey gnomes and other subterranean creatures." Then, Kinderbuchverlag legitimised the alien fantastic elements by pointing out that *Ronja Robber's Daughter* had already been shown as a film in the GDR and that a book production was planned for 1988, i.e. the same year as *Hexen hexen* was coming out. The publisher finished, "and Dahl's witches are really not any nastier than our own time-honoured, well-known, indigenous witches—they are just different."

Agreement with the Assessor's Evaluation:

Kinderbuchverlag pointed out that they were in agreement with Ebert's arguments and opinion, although they added that "literary parallels—Carroll and Saint-Exupéry—and political parallels—Fascism—appear too farfetched." Kinderbuchverlag also shared Ebert's opinion about the chief witch's dialect. However, they finished their evaluation with the remark that they had entered a licence agreement with the West German publisher and they did not see sufficient reason to re-enter negotiations with the Western publishing house as, on the whole, the translation was good, read fluently and was humorous.

4.4 Case study 4—Anthologies

The practice of compiling anthologies, too, constitutes a form of rewriting and, in fact, Lefevere confirms, "anthologies are shaped by ideological and poetological constraints" and "the putting together of anthologies tends to reflect 'the judgements of literary history' where it really matters: in shaping the taste of a wider audience and, most importantly, in education" (1985b:234). This need to educate and to form the discernment of readers through anthologies becomes more than evident in the GDR. The files reveal that the selection mechanism was motivated by an explicit desire to promote ideological values, as will be shown.

"When the children in the GDR read a book by a foreign writer, they ought to hear something about life in other countries. Things that differ from the immediate sphere of experience of the children in our country will be the most interesting for them"; these words can be found in the assessor's comments for the book *Janey und der silberne Tänzer* by Bernard Ashley (DR1/2305). Although it was argued that young readers would benefit from such content, at the same time, they were not allowed a complete picture but rather a carefully selected view of reality. This attitude in the country is also reflected in the compilation of anthologies. Similarly, the assessor for a fairytale publication commented,

> not all tales can be supportive of the new order in the same way and be sanctioned without change. In some, violence and deceitfulness remain victorious, in some there is not much else besides dead corpses, and in most a good cause only succeeds through involvement of a higher supernatural power. This is not the view of a world we want to offer to children for them to take with them into their lives. (Krenn, *Binsenkappe*, 1975, Kinderbuchverlag; DR1/2274)

It was precisely for this reason that themes and ideas were carefully sifted. The discourse in the files for collections of fairytales and anthologies shows unmistakeably that a selection process took place in the publishing houses and many tales or short stories never reached the translation stage because of their alleged unsuitability. In his search for suitable stories for an anthology of American short stories, editor Petersen (DR1/2282a) turned to Francelia Butler, Professor at the University of Connecticut, for advice. She maintained that "so much American children's literature is propagandistic in nature—single idea books—that it is difficult to make recommendations, though I edit a journal of children's literature". Hence, Petersen, in his criticism, proceeded to define what he understood by 'propagandistic', stating that "American children's literature evades problems of everyday life, that it celebrates the American reality as the home of the proud and free people . . . and consciously intends to divert young readers from conflicts under capitalist conditions." Because of this "light-weightedness", Petersen felt he had to select carefully the stories suitable for translation from those on offer.

Kinderbuchverlag, publisher of the book *Binsenkappe*, a collection of translated English fairytales mentioned previously, struck a similar chord, pointing out that the fairytales in the anthology had been written at a time when magic had lost its significance for the genre of British fairytales and when daily routine had found entrance into the narrative, thus opening the door to notions tainted by capitalist thinking;

> the appearance of Mayors and merchants, the descriptions of magnificent courts and beautiful clothes reveal [certain] social structures; capitalism was the prevalent form of society, and bourgeois values and norms appeared in fairytales. Riches and luxury were desirable and money granted social status and power. Through our selection, we have ensured that those tales displaying such contents do not become predominant. In accordance with the assessor's remarks and those of the editorial office, several contributions, ideologically and morally unjustifiable, have been omitted from the collection. These are texts which do not have a progressive tendency, which teach superstition, or which are weak in their message and their content. (DR1/2274)

A few lines further down, the assessor declared outspokenly, "contents that we could not salvage were taken out" (DR1/2274).

Contrary to complete books which had to be either accepted or rejected in their entirety, anthologies could be remoulded by incorporating or omitting that which matched the official rationale of the particular time. "With this title, Kinderbuchverlag publishes a representative collection of American short stories for children . . .; it is the aim to give readers an insight into the life of American children"—publisher Kinderbuchverlag announced in their evaluation of Petersen's *Unser weißer Hirsch* (DR1/2282a). Yet, what Kinderbuchverlag called 'representative' has to be understood from the standpoint of a socialist rewriter; it was neither an objective nor a typical compilation of American life. Although it may have allowed East German children an insight into the life of

American children, it was a limited view of American life and certainly not the full picture. Therefore, when East German children read an anthology of, for instance, Australian or American short stories, to them this represented the epitome of Australian or American culture, because they were not in a position to find out about the gaps in the picture and to realise what had been omitted. What took place in East German reality is exactly what Lefevere was referring to when discussing the accessibility of the original to target readers and the limitations of experiencing only the translation—in this instance, the rewritten and adapted source text. All of which leads to a situation in which "the refraction, in other words, [becomes] the original to the great majority of people" (Lefevere 1982a:16). Thus, anthologies helped create a picture in the East German audience that was hiding the 'real' reality, because it was a literature that had been carefully selected before being passed on to readers.

The East German production of anthologies was a reflection of the wider process of text selection; they demonstrate, on a smaller scale, what was happening on a larger scale with entire books. In order to exemplify this, in what follows the selection process for a book of fairytales and a book of short stories for adolescents will be described, providing an example of an East German publication of each anthology. As would be expected, the selection criteria were in both cases those of the adapted poetics and codification and were no different from any other literary discourse. As has been said before, the same codes were used for both adult and children's literature, since the codification was based on the dominant ideology rather than the literary sphere.

4.1.1 Fairytales

Ernst Adler, *Die Legende vom Bumerang. Australische Märchen*

Verlag Alfred Holz, 1966

The selection of fairytales on the whole took place by applying the same positive and negative motifs as selection criteria, whereby stories with positive motifs were considered suitable for an inclusion in the publication, and stories exhibiting too many negative concepts were rejected. For example, for the collection of fairytales from England (Reeves, *Märchen aus England*; DR1/3706) the following selection criteria for the publication were mentioned: peace, justice, optimism, smartness, clever reasoning, trust in one's own skills and bravery, energy, humanity, friendliness and kindness, usefulness of acquired knowledge, autonomous thinking, absence of violence and of elements of fear and horror. Accordingly, the story *Tim Tot Tot* was deemed inappropriate due to its questionable moral, since a girl becomes queen on grounds of a fraud and not through her own achievements, nor through her kindness or other qualities. This suggests that the assessor had not found sufficient motifs in this story with a positive connotation, in order to justify an inclusion in the collection. Instead, the story championed reward as a consequence of a criminal action, which was clearly viewed as being undesirable behaviour on which children should not model their own behaviour. As the story's theme hinged on this motif, it was also something that could not easily be weakened by a skilful translation; hence, the evaluator recommended omission. The compilation of *Märchen aus England* is exemplary of all other cases where individual fairytales were put together and published in one book, as is also the case with Adler's *Die Legende vom Bumerang*, an anthology for younger children published by Holz.

Print Permit DR1/2252

Three years before the publication took place, publisher Holz had asked Lieselotte Remané, translator from English and Russian, to assess nine books of Australian fairytales with respect to a possible future translation and publication. After Remané's pre-selection from these books, Holz decided on the final choice and, subsequently, applied for a print permit.

1. Verlag Alfred Holz, 1964—Assessor: Lieselotte Remané

After reading the nine books, Remané instantaneously discarded three books with the argument that they encompassed only anecdotes of white Australian settlers or narrations which did not really constitute fairytales but only used fairytale-like motifs. In a second selection round, two more books were rejected; the first one because the stories appeared to be retellings with the view to a European reader and, therefore, contained elements untypical of Australian tribes, such as excessive wallowing in emotions and long-winded narrative. The second displayed, amongst others, overloading of the stories with meaningless place names, absence of true-to-life descriptions, no motivation for plots and "shocking brutality (e.g. women and children are continuously torn to pieces, murdered and eaten up, etc.) [and] an openness in the depiction of sexual activities which, to our moral standards, appears pornographic." The remaining four books were described by Remané as authentic and original, reflecting atmosphere and life of those tribes, whilst abstaining from primitive brutalities. From the 156 fairytales of these four books, Remané chose 60, naming her criteria: they had to show as much variety as possible, they should not Europeanise the content, and fairytales should not contain any violent or sexual episodes. Otherwise she suggested their omission.

Remané concluded her assessment by expressing her concern about the fact that she had heard that the translator "had the intention to 'filter' the contents" and she suggested rather to "translate and publish only those tales that conform directly with our taste and don't have to be altered".

2. Verlag Alfred Holz, 1966—Assessor: Magda Liepe

Projects by private publishers were assessed by an external assessor commissioned by the censorship authority, in this case Magda Liepe. She commenced her assessment by stating that the collection was neither entertaining nor instructive, but that it had been an ordeal having to read through all 53 stories (the original 60 as suggested by Remané apparently having been further refined in the intervening years). Liepe found it essential for the publisher to produce a preface, explaining about Aborigines in more detail, mentioning the fact that these were tribes who either lived in reservations or, as day labourers, worked on capitalist plantations without any right of citizenship. The reader ought also to be told, Liepe suggested, that these fairy stories took their origin at a time when the Aboriginal tribes were still at a very low evolutionary stage in which the people still believed, for instance, that animals had once been humans, or that life on the Earth was possible without sun; in other words, providing knowledge without which the stories would be meaningless to the children. Hence, "an introduction should say something about the geography, the people and the characteristics of the literature of these people."

Liepe continued to enlist groupings of criteria for the selection process, which show the similarity to the officially accepted motifs. Those were:

Stories against envy
Stories against stupidity
Stories that show that war does not have an advantage
Stories against self-satisfaction
Stories against greed for possession and miserliness
Stories against bragging
Stories dealing with reward for loyalty and courage
Stories demonstrating the importance of being clever and of learning from experience

Although Liepe's evaluation finished with this enumeration along with her signature and although she failed to declare herself in favour or against a publication, the censor granted a print permit with the reservation that an introduction to the book be written, stating "something about the geography, the people and the characteristics of the literature of these people". This detail of the censor using the exact wording of his commissioned assessor is striking and points to the safe-guarding role of the assessors for the censors. It is also interesting that the censor did not, in his remark, insist on Liepe's other comments about the abuse and mistreatment of the Aborigines. A brief glance into the book, however, confirms that these suggestions indeed have been incorporated, which indicates that the content of the assessment must have been made accessible in some form to the editor of the book.

4.1.2 Short Stories

David Craig, *Rapunzel, laß dein Haar herunter. Erzählungen aus Großbritannien*
Verlag Neues Leben, 1984

Print Permit File DR1/5438

This collection of short stories was published by Neues Leben for young adolescents in 1984 and therefore constitutes an example of an anthology for young adults and it is evident that, again, the same criteria are at work. Its contributors were British authors and the declared objective of the publication was to illustrate the typical life of young people in contemporary Great Britain. The file comprises one evaluation by an assessor; a second evaluation by the same assessor, after some alterations had become necessary to the proposed stories; and thirdly, the publisher's assessment with reference to both evaluations.

1. Verlag Neues Leben—Assessor: Karl-Heinz Magister

Defence of publication, Author's Status:

Although Magister detected a few shortcomings in this publication, he called attention to the fact that it was the first publication of its kind, containing stories dealing with youth problems in Britain, which therefore ought not to be jeopardised, despite these shortcomings. Another main reason was that the reputation of the editor, David Craig, resulted in the expectation of publishing good quality stories which provided a realistic picture, since he was "a famous author and editor of many literary critical publications produced from a distinct Marxist standpoint."

Reality, Social Criticism:

As a word of caution, Magister warned against having too high hopes of "contemporary English literature", because of the question "how far the literature of the present day can live up to the unprecedented crisis in British society." Magister stated that one would, for instance, expect to find a reflection of the "horrendously high youth unemployment" in a literature centring on the life of the young generation; but unfortunately

> we wait in vain for a direct, critical and Historically objective expression of the contemporary economic, political and ideological crises in Great Britain. Rather, reality is depicted only indirectly and shows much political indifference. Plots do not take place against the backdrop of social conflicts, but on the basis of the thinking, feeling and acting of individual characters. One has to take into consideration that, increasingly, the arts are also subjected to capitalist conditions and that, consequently, they are oriented more and more towards clichés and the mediocre standards of a bourgeois mass culture.

Sexual Depictions, L'art pour l'art, Reality:

Next, Magister dealt with an area that was highly taboo in East German society and could seriously endanger any publication, even more so with literature for young people, namely sexual behaviour. His device was to link these instances with the depravity and deficiency of capitalism, thus using it to point to the degree of perversion and corruption in the West.

> One criterion, amongst many, of these second-rate standards is the exaggerated description of abnormal sexual behaviour, which serves not so much to characterise the protagonists but to devalue and decry them—at least in extreme cases. Here we have the difficult decision to make whether such a convention is entirely without any aesthetic function or whether it does show some significant moments, after all, of an inwardly torn and uprooted individual personality in late-capitalist society.

What had to be avoided, at all costs, was the approach of a literature that had no function in society but referred to itself alone, a literature that was immoral, decadent and degenerate. In the 1950s and 60s, such literature had been called 'formalistic' and was frowned upon (see p 17); from Magister's carefully worded explanations it would appear that such a standpoint had still not fully been overcome, at least not in the area of children's literature. Therefore, Magister vindicated the choice of stories by declaring, "a momentous characteristic of these narrations is their frequently deep and psychological analysis of human behavioural patterns, which therefore show part of reality. Thus, these stories contain elements of a wider social context." With this, the motif of Realism had come to the rescue and the anthology was made to fit the paradigms.

As a next step, Magister set out to give brief descriptions of every individual contribution, providing a short summary with the inclusion of motifs relevant for a justification of the story. Those were in the main: emptiness of a life in capitalism, alienation of interpersonal relationships, pessimism, social inequality and injustice, attitudes of protest against capitalist life, moralistic corruption of the bourgeoisie, passivity due to overdependence on religion, hypocrisy and moral depravity of church representatives, intellectual dullness.

In his final paragraph, the assessor expressed a positive opinion with respect to a publication, stating that, despite the limitations pointed out, important elements and strata of society were depicted. He regarded it as unfortunate that the aspect of work was not touched upon in any of the stories but "this may be accounted for by the ideological suppression and the fragmentation of the working classes in Great Britain, in accordance with which the intellectual and moral profile of the worker was painted unsatisfactorily"; but Magister was quick in mentioning that this very much corresponded with reality and actual conditions, whereby he played down the unsatisfactory and potentially objectionable picture portrayed of the working classes in Britain.

2. *Verlag Neues Leben—Assessor: Karl-Heinz Magister*

After having submitted his assessment to Neues Leben, changes must have been made by the publisher in terms of the final selection of the stories, because this second assessment referred to alterations of which Magister had clearly been informed and had been asked to comment on. The second assessment was also dated only four months before the publisher Neues Leben completed and dated their own evaluation, ready to be sent to the censor, which suggests some last-minute changes in the content of the anthology.

In this second assessment, Magister wrote, "I can only agree to the suggested re-organisation of this collection of short stories". He then named four stories which had been removed by the publisher, whereby the fourth one had been blacked out and the title obscured. Interestingly, he defended the decision by Neues Leben to eliminate these four stories by claiming, "the glorification of violence, obscenities, human fallibility and the portrayal of anti-social behaviour that does not serve to criticise capitalism did not correspond with our ethical didactic values from the very beginning." This sentence appears paradoxical, given that, in his first evaluation, Magister had not opposed a publication of the stories; rather, he had written in their defence, having found only shortcomings that, in the end, appeared acceptable and did not stand in the way of a publication.

Magister found only praise for the revised version.

> It is a successful attempt at revealing the momentous tendencies of a literature in present-day Great Britain that displays a positive attitude toward the working classes and to social change. Each of the stories in this edition succeeds in depicting real human conflicts and individual attempts at their solution within the contemporary class society, even if this may only mean powerlessness of the individual vis-à-vis the oppressive apparatus.

Next, Magister described and characterised all four new stories, again using Marxist-Leninist concepts, after which he briefly and tersely concluded in one single sentence, "all four additional stories integrate well into the anthology".

2. *Verlag Neues Leben—Publisher's Assessment: Edda Fensch*

Justification and Objectives for the anthology:
Neues Leben commenced by pointing to their series of books in which each volume dealt with the life of young people in a particular country; with this anthology, it was the intention to inform readers about life in Great Britain. However, Fensch claimed, "there are not many British novels available which discuss social problems in a critical and politically engaged fashion", thereby indicating that it had been difficult to find suitable short stories to be incorporated in the anthology. Fensch continued,

> It is a known fact that general instances of crises in the capitalist countries have taken on crass proportions. On the other hand, literature (at least this literature which is launched officially) does not take any note of this. Even if authors dedicate themselves to these themes, they have hardly any opportunity to publish their works with renowned publishing houses; in this respect, there are more opportunities to publish short stories, because they can be published in magazines and journals.

The objective for a production of this kind, Fensch contended, was "to introduce various problematic issues of Great Britain which will be of relevance and meaningful for the young readers. A wide spectrum is to be shown of present-day life and of concrete examples of the conditions with which young people of different social strata have to cope." However, when putting together this anthology, "the main emphasis lay on a depressing and oppressing portrayal of the situation of youth, as without any doubt it corresponds with reality."

Justifying the Author:

"We have contacted David Craig, who, through his literary, critical and publishing activities, had good opportunities to put together an anthology for us. In 1968, David Craig also published a similar anthology for Aufbau Verlag". With these words, the author was introduced and legitimised as an accepted and published author and, also, as an author who had sufficient authority and experience to enable him to successfully compile the 'right kind' of stories. Also, mentioning Aufbau Verlag as the prestigious publisher of contemporary socialist literature provided an additional badge of legitimacy.

Changing the Selection Criterion:

Next, Fensch gave an explanation why some stories had been substituted for others.

> Our wish was to include more stories in which young people play a more active role and fight against their circumstances. Equally, the sphere of work, which had not been touched upon, should be given more attention. Therefore, we have taken out four stories.

This explanation appears imperfect and not exhaustive, because no mention is made of the main reasons why the stories had not been deemed sufficiently suitable, i.e. the explicit description of various kinds of sexual behaviour, including lesbianism, combined with an over-emphasis on obscenities and perverted practices. This contradicted the approach of the assessor, who clearly specified "violence, obscenities and human abnormal behaviour as well as the portrayal of a kind of anti-socialism" as principal motifs antagonistic to Marxist principles.

The publisher's itemisation of the newly included stories causes another discrepancy. While indeed three contributions match the assessor's list, the fourth was not one of the newly considered stories, since it had been previously discussed by Magister in his first assessment. It is unclear why Neues Leben included this story here and no reason can be found other than perhaps an error on the publisher's side.

Fensch then proceeded to describe the main concepts of each story of the compilation in one or two sentences, with the main motifs matching those of the assessor. What is noticeable in Fensch's descriptions is the overuse of effusive vocabulary; so, for instance, "the stories prove convincingly"; "alarming is the chasm between urban and rural regions"; "unemployment is arguably the most dramatic problem of youth at present"; or "the reader senses distinctly the helplessness and fear of youth".

Final Justification:

Fensch began on a positive note, "I think that it has become obvious that these stories of the 1970s reveal significant problems of British young people at the time", whereupon she tackled the limitations of the anthology of which Neues Leben was well aware.

> Of course, it cannot be expected that these stories provide a social analysis. Dr Magister is right in saying that many of the literary figures do not show active, only unambiguous political involvement. But I do not believe that, at present, one can expect this from English literature; there is no progressive and rebellious literature such as that of the angry young men in the 1950s. I feel we have achieved much by presenting an anthology to our young readers which demonstrates in many respects the difficulties young people have in Great Britain and the conditions under which they live; how individuals attempt to find solutions and alternatives; how they fight but also how helpless and bitter they are; and how in any case they are dissatisfied with what society has to offer them.

Then, Fensch went on to describe the aim of the publication, namely correcting the picture of the West for the East German readers:

> Our young readers are familiar with the present-day situation in Great Britain through our media. However, in many respects, an idealised picture is conveyed to them, especially through the rock music from Great Britain—even more so, as mostly the lyrics are not understood. This anthology will inform readers about new issues and also give them a different outlook on issues with which they are familiar, issues that make one reflect and become filled with consternation.

Afterword:

Finally, Fensch remarked on the question of the afterword that was to be published in the volume. Originally, the publisher's idea had been to include an afterword by the British editor David Craig, illustrating the situation and conditions in Britain in more detail; it had been hoped that Craig, as an author resident in the country itself and with the extra bonus of exhibiting sympathy with the socialist cause, would provide sharp criticism of British society. Although in the end incorporated in the finalised book, Craig's afterword, in fact, turned out to be too tame and insufficiently scathing for the publisher's taste and, therefore, the audience was provided with another, second afterword, produced by Magister, in which the 'real Britain with its authentic shortcomings' found closer attention. However, the censor needed to be informed of the fact that a second afterword was to be included in the volume; hence, Fensch stated, "In the beginning, our plan was to have an afterword only by the editor of the book, which was to inform on the political and social background. Since D. Craig has, however, given only a brief explanation of this topic, we have decided to incorporate Dr Magister's afterword in addition."

The discourse in this file about this anthology was characteristic of all anthology publications, that is, every individual contribution needed to be discussed and analysed commensurate with the recognised paradigms prevalent at the time. In this particular anthology (*Rapunzel, laß dein Haar herunter*, published in 1984), it becomes evident that stories with what were regarded as negative motifs (violence, religious attitudes, sexual and lesbian/homoerotic activities, pessimism, escapism, resignation) still appeared in the final publication. There are several possible explanations. *Rapunzel, laß dein Haar herunter* was published in the 1980s, a time in which censoring processes had relaxed and the incidence of one or two negative concepts no longer presented an insurmountable obstacle for publication. However, all stories with negative motifs, eventually integrated in the volume, also had counterbalancing positive motifs, especially the harsh social criticism of Western society, which made the decision in favour of inclusion easier; and indeed, stories with too much emphasis on negative concepts and none or little on positive aspects were eliminated. It is also not inconceivable that the actual 'publishing practice' of anthologies (which was to take advantage of introducing unorthodox authors or concepts since such stories could be hidden more easily in the bulk of the other contributions) played a role in the eventual incorporation of these slightly more sensitive stories.

Nevertheless, whatever may have been the case, there is a distinct tendency discernible in the stories of *Rapunzel, laß dein Haar herunter* and, in fact, all GDR anthologies. They all express the norms and values of East German society and, moreover, constitute a re-assertion of the codification system in place, namely Marxist-Leninist dogma. Therefore, in agreement with Lefevere's contention of anthologies being part of the rewriting process, there is a clear indication that East German anthologies were indeed used to rewrite the country's literature, and it was performed in such a way as to converge with the officially accepted and sanctioned paradigms. When the publisher Neues Leben wrote that their "main emphasis lay on a depressing and oppressing portrayal of the situation of youth, as without any doubt it corresponds with reality", this is to be understood as an attempt to shape the perceptions of the readers of the literature; emphasis was placed on only one particular section of reality, yet overall this practice was justified as corresponding with the real-life situation, when in fact it is not. This process is evidence of, firstly, the endeavour of the literary system to uphold its *status quo* and, secondly, the requirement to make the book fit the prevalent poetics by obeying the conventions; otherwise "the publication . . . would not have taken place" (Lefevere 1992:159).

One thought, however, may be added. The majority of the contributions to *Rapunzel, laß dein Haar herunter* would never have been considered for a volume published twenty or even only ten years earlier (the record shows that this was the first publication of British short stories addressed to young adults published in the GDR). This suggests that both the political and ideological situation as well as the poetics of a society are subject to change. A literary system is in a state of continuous flux, and authors and texts that would not be acceptable at one given time may become adequate candidates (with more or less adaptation) in another, as captured by Lefevere when he maintains, "the natural language and the politics of the receiving system keep changing: the spectrum through which refractions are made changes in the course of time" (1982a:14). Rooted in this permanent development of poetics is the following phenomenon: a change in poetological structures allows new poetological devices to find entrance into a society. This can lead to more or less significant changes and may even allow whole genres to be established, which was precisely what happened in the GDR. The following section demonstrates that, through a change in standards, the reputation of a whole genre was rewritten allowing foreign, translated crime and detective literature for children to be introduced into the literary system.

4.5 Case study 5—Introducing a Genre. Crime and Detective Literature

Forerunners of crime and detective stories, such as Poe, Collins or Conrad, had been accepted into the canon and published with the argument that they belonged to the classic literary heritage. Authors of more contemporary crime stories had, from the constitution of the GDR, a difficult standing because of the genre's reputation as low-brow literature and, secondly, because of its integral themes of crime and violence, both constituting negative motifs.[7] Only during the thaw at the beginning of the 1970s did children's book publishers embark on regular publications of translated detective stories. It was the time when the GDR craved international reputation and endeavoured to prove to the world that the fact that they belonged to the Eastern Bloc did not necessarily mean they were lagging behind. During this period, the orthodox concept of Socialist Realism began to crumble. The ideal of the 'Positive hero' had begun to be questioned and, with it, more individuality had begun to enter literary works (see Section 1.3.3). Slowly, room was made for a new notion of literature, fantastic elements had become acceptable and the canon of the cultural heritage had experienced a widening. It is certainly no coincidence that, in 1972, thus one year after Honecker's rise to power and his oft-quoted remark suggesting a relaxation in taboo subjects, science fiction became a recognised genre, with a new section established in the Writers' Association and with the first science fiction publications also for children.

Publication programmes of translated children's book publishers reflect this new mood and demonstrate a clear turn-around in their production with an increasing number of translated crime and detective stories. However, these stories had still to be made fully acceptable. They needed to be rewritten, i.e. re-interpreted and equipped with cleverly worded criticism as a justification. Overall, adapting these stories to the East German system aimed—and this was even more visible in their afterwords—at portraying the difference between the socialist and the capitalist societies. It was claimed that the capitalist system with its class system and subsequently derived social problems brought about corruption and criminality, while socialism, as a society subscribing to equal status and equal opportunities, had managed to do away with all illegal acts. Hence, the assessor for a Conan Doyle publication in 1982 argued that "with works of this genre, which derive from earlier times [i.e. times before socialism], the reader has an amicable ironic feeling of superiority, which is reinforced for readers in socialist societies" (DR1/3557).

There was, not surprisingly, an economic factor involved—crime and detective stories sold well. From the 1970s, publishers were put under more pressure to make profits which, on the whole, resulted in the publication of more literature that was both easy to read and provided suspense and excitement. Crime stories constituted just such literature; these were stories that many young people, but also adults, consumed after a long, tiring day. Thus, the assessor mentioned earlier declared himself in favour of the Conan Doyle publication, because this production promised a sure financial success; he did, however, not fail to mention in the same sentence that this contribution "will not have any disadvantageous effect on our objective of shaping all-round socialist personalities" (DR1/3557). Additionally, crime and detective literature was also popular in the West, which meant potential co-productions with West Germany or the opportunity to sell rights or entire books to the West. However, it was expensive to produce Western detective literature because Western foreign currency was scarce in the GDR. This is one reason why, in the 1980s, Arthur Conan Doyle and, albeit, to a lesser degree, Edgar Wallace appeared in a fair number of publications. They had died in 1930 and 1932, respectively, and, according to GDR law (which stipulated that a period of 50 years elapse after an author's death), had gone out of copyright in the 1980s. This is further corroborated by considering Agatha Christie, who died in 1976, and again it can be assumed that for cost reasons, no publisher for young people produced her books, and adult book publishers only produced a total of six first editions (Das Neue Berlin, Verlag Volk & Welt, Henschelverlag, Aufbau Verlag).

Something else that becomes discernible, particularly in the case of publications by Arthur Conan Doyle, is the practice of introducing more controversial authors into the literary system by using their less controversial works or by using a short story, either in an anthology or on its own, until more of their oeuvre became acceptable. Once one work had been officially accepted by the system, it was easier to introduce another, maybe more critical, by alluding to the legitimacy of that already published. Thus, Arthur Conan Doyle was first published with one of his most famous stories, *The Hound of the Baskervilles* (1954, publisher Das Neue Berlin; 1966, publisher Aufbau Verlag), and soon after with *The Lost World* (1956 and 1961, publisher Das Neue Berlin). Both works belong to the genre of adventure literature, which was an officially recognised genre. Only in later years, after having introduced Conan Doyle as 'acceptable' and after a widening of the canon, did it become possible to publish more of his works which, as detective stories, were more problematical to the system.

Crime and detective authors, published by Kinderbuchverlag and Neues Leben, were G.K. Chesterton, Arthur Conan Doyle, and Edgar Wallace; in addition, Neues Leben put out two anthologies on this genre. When analysing the publication dates, it is immediately evident that, indeed, the year 1972 marked a watershed and all translated crime and detective stories for young people were brought out after this date. With this noticeably late recognition of a whole genre, what arguments did publishers Kinderbuchverlag and Neues Leben put forward to make their productions appear socially relevant? The following section gives a brief assessment of the content of the print permit files for each of the main crime and detective authors. Each description is organised according to the main ideological criteria used to justify the publication.

Arthur Conan Doyle

Fünf Fälle des Sherlock Holmes, Kinderbuchverlag, 1987, DR1/2305
Sherlock Holmes—17 Detektivgeschichten, Neues Leben, 1982, DR1/3557

World Literature, Political Acceptability (DR1/2305; DR1/3557):

The files show that it was deemed important to stress the fact that Sherlock Holmes belonged to world literature and that readers would not be harmed by reading this kind of literature, so, for example, Kinderbuchverlag stated, "now, classic detective stories also count as world literature and contribute to entertaining and developing logical thinking and skills of deduction"; similarly, the assessor for a Neues Leben publication commented that he thought that the book was "culturally and politically acceptable . . ." and it "demonstrates our openness to the world", thereby reflecting the official political rhetoric of the time.

Comparison with Another, Officially Acknowledged Genre (DR1/2305):

In order to illustrate the genre's harmlessness, the assessor of *Fünf Fälle des Sherlock Holmes* attempted to align this genre to another genre that was incorporated in the canon, namely fairytales. She stated,

> Crime literature is akin to fairytales because of its obligatory happy ending (i.e. discovery of the criminals and their bringing to a just punishment). Like the fairytale, the detective story differentiates very clearly between good and evil. The evil is brought to justice, the wrong is paid for, justice and humanity are helped to victory. . . . The classic detective story should not be understood as dealing with social conditions. One surrenders in order to enjoy, similar to the fairytale.

Mentioning that classic detective stories did not revolve around social conditions was telling the censor not to expect any socio-critical remarks in Conan Doyle's stories, because these stories were written not to point out issues worthy of criticism in British society but for the mere reason of giving pleasure and relaxation to the reader.

Presence in the Media (DR1/2305):

Next, she continued to play down any damaging effect which it may have been claimed regarding crime stories, by arguing that television and cinema showed films of that kind, and children were already exposed to this genre, pointing to a certain appropriation that had already taken place in the country, "children have an interest in gripping literature, to which cinema and television have already reacted. Now, literature follows suit with this proposed series"; and the publisher echoed, "we believe that we have made a good choice to begin this series with the legendary Sherlock Holmes and his friend Dr Watson, for a long time well-known to our children familiar with the characters from cinema and television."

Violence, Fatalism, Humanism (DR1/2305):

One of the principal points was to reject a potential accusation that the stories were too violent and, secondly, that the solution of the crime was based on an irrational, deus-ex-machina explanation rather than on the detective's brain power and deductive skill, both notions contradicting the Marxist-Leninist concepts of Humanism and Realism. Therefore, the publisher wrote,

> Sherlock Holmes does not solve his cases through strength or violence, nor through a stroke of fortune. His success is based on solid knowledge and on a logical and creative thinking process. This is precisely why we

> like these stories. They stand out pleasantly from a large part of contemporary Western crime stories. The author neither uses violence and horror, nor does he stage dramatic chases for criminals; and the classic detective is no shining superman but a taciturn, withdrawn and sensitive gentleman with a dry sense of humour and sharp wit.

These words of the publishers were in alignment with the assessor, who was of the opinion that "the present stories are an expression of the successful struggle of human beings for justice in an unjust world"—and, of course, it was an extra bonus that that unjust world was British and thus belonged to the capitalist camp.

No Anti-Bourgeois Criticism (DR1/2305):

However, should there be someone who was "looking for criticism of power and the people in power, e.g. regarding their failure in the social domain or remarks about the class character of the bourgeois system, they will look in vain. Doyle does not reflect on class constellations", which did not necessarily mean a disadvantage because "never is a character of a worker or a farmer depicted in a negative light".

Omission of Drugs (DR1/3557):

Holmes' habit of using drugs caused a problem, because children were not to be made aware of the existence and effects of drugs; therefore, the assessor appeased the censor by writing, "The editor of the volume was absolutely right in not having included those stories, in which Doyle explains Sherlock Holmes' success on the grounds of the use of drugs or in which Holmes justifies his habit to Watson. . . . Even Doyle himself [in later years] has viewed this ploy as superfluous and has given it up."

Commercial Considerations (DR1/2305; DR1/3557):

In the light of the shortage of foreign currency, publisher Kinderbuchverlag emphasised that mainly those texts would be used which had gone out of copyright, thus hoping to put the censor in a more favourable mood. In a similar fashion, the assessor for Neues Leben stressed the opportunity of making a profit with this publication.

Gilbert Keith Chesterton

Der geflügelte Dolch, Kinderbuchverlag, 1988, DR1/2307

Chesterton had already been introduced to the system in earlier publications by Neues Leben and St Benno and therefore in 1988, when planning their production, Kinderbuchverlag did not have to act as a forerunner. Nevertheless, as Father Brown stories belonged to detective literature and, additionally, were associated with religion and church, the discourse in the application process had to refer to those key aspects carrying negative connotations, i.e. Religion and Violence, and aim at balancing these concepts with positive connotations and a proof that the stories would not be harmful to the young audience.

Link to an Officially Acknowledged Author and Sanctioned Literature:

The assessor Schmidt began with a comparison of Chesterton with Conan Doyle, by pointing to their similar fate. Both had not taken their detective stories "too seriously" and had hoped to become known for their belletristic literature but "ironically, both had achieved world fame with exactly those stories." Indeed, the success Arthur Conan Doyle had with Sherlock Holmes was so legendary that he became known worldwide and evoked enduring interest for detective literature in audiences, thus making Father Brown Chesterton's counterpart to Sherlock Holmes.

Humanism:

Remaining with similarities between the two famous detectives, Schmidt stated that, like Holmes, Father Brown "dedicates himself to the pastime of solving crimes and [like Holmes] has the style of the successful loner." However, they had nothing else in common. While Holmes was unapproachable, eccentric and extravagant, Brown was friendly, philanthropic, inconspicuous and modest. While Holmes was a master of logic and facts, Brown was a master of human reasoning. While Holmes' success was grounded in a vast scientific specialist knowledge, Brown's resulted from an extraordinary knowledge of human nature. While both had the same aim, they had different priorities and had to follow different paths to reach it.

> Father Brown is not happy merely to solve a riddle; for him, it is not about revenge or punishment, rather—if possible—about bettering the culprit . . . A passionate interest for sin and sinner blazes in the little man . . . He knows about the limitations of human reasoning, about the imperfections of people and their institutions . . . Father Brown represents the endearing moralist and teacher-philosopher, the propagandist of human reason.

Social Criticism, Religion:

Evidence needed to be given about the stories' social relevance, especially in the case of the negative motif of Religion; thus, Schmidt contended that she saw plenty of instances where Father Brown criticised his society, for instance, "the parasitic English aristocracy, the bourgeoisie which behaved [superficially] progressively, Puritanism, religious sects, the German Emperor, the French Foreign Legion or the wrong glorification of British colonial heroes. These, more or less unambiguous side-swipes provide fun for the reader of today. Despite this", and here Schmidt had to make a concession,

> one must not judge too hastily and claim that the author has an incorrect political view of the world. He, for instance, lumps together socialism with anarchism; another example is his attempt to convert the world to Catholicism, by painting a picture romantically transfigured, almost medieval. As often as he criticises social circumstances and conditions, he misinterprets them.

The following sentence then had the purpose to weaken this flaw: "But none of these six stories puts too much weight on this aspect". The publisher followed suit, commentating on and toning down Chesterton's view of the world and of religion, "explaining the crime and the motive for the crime, spiced up with his views about this life and the next world. From our standpoint, of course, this cannot be taken seriously and should be taken with a pinch of salt but, for sure, it makes entertaining reading."

Commercial Considerations:

Four of the six stories were taken from a 1927 volume, thus fallen out of copyright, "which were edited slightly and the orthography of which was modernised". For two stories, as the publisher pointed out to the censor, royalties had to be paid for the use of the translation.

Edgar Wallace

Der Fälscher. Der feuerrote Kreis, Neues Leben, 1987, DR1/3559a
Geschichten vom Hexer, 1988, Kinderbuchverlag, DR1/2309

Popularity, Suitability for Children:

The assessment of both books began with a brief biography of the author. Then Schmidt, as the assessor of the edition for younger children, tackled the fact that the young age of the audience might pose a problem with the censor. She wrote, "Today still more than a million Wallace books are sold. Even the films from the 1960s experience undiminished popularity, with one difference however: nowadays, parents enjoy suspense and turmoil and shudder together with their children"; and Kinderbuchverlag echoed, "There can be no doubt that children have a huge interest in suspenseful and entertaining literature (and not only children); especially the twelve to fourteen year olds are constantly looking for new 'fodder'."

Violence:

Whereas the motif of violence was not mentioned in the file referring to the edition for young adults, it was still a key concept for younger readers. Therefore, Kinderbuchverlag's assessor stated, "from Wallace's extensive oeuvre only those stories were selected in which violence and brutality are not in the foreground". Kinderbuchverlag followed by remarking that the editor of the book "has chosen thirteen texts and edited them for children" and, in any case, "one cannot take these stories overly seriously today, but they make for good entertainment and gripping literature."

Action, Social Criticism:

Schmidt entered a philosophical debate about the difference between Arthur Conan Doyle and Agatha Christie, on the one hand, and Edgar Wallace, on the other. The two former placed, as Schmidt maintained, all emphasis on the intellectual achievement of their detectives, leaving aside more or less the circumstances of the crime. Wallace's detective, however, knew the criminals already and, hence, the main stress was on action, on chasing and punishing them. The fact that there was more action and violence in Wallace's stories might have been an obstacle for a print permit; hence, Schmidt was required to find an argument as to why violence was necessitated. This argument she found in the fact that society had been changing since Holmes' times. She explained that this difference had to be seen as rooted in a different kind of society. Holmes had always been the detective and never the judge and jury; he had had faith that when the evidence was given to the authorities, they would punish the criminals appropriately for their crime. "The culprit is found out, and Holmes can confidently leave judgement and punishment in the hands of the state authorities." However, Wallace's detective, thirty years later, "can no longer have faith in bourgeois justice; it proves to be either corrupt . . . or incapable. . . . Therefore, he is compelled to punish the criminal himself."

Another of Schmidt's observations lay in the different depictions of the figure of the police inspector. While Conan Doyle gave him a dumb appearance, Wallace's inspector was quite capable but "is hindered by a corrupt system which is contemptuous of human life. It is a capitalist society, in which law and order are purchasable." Schmidt therefore concluded, "this means to say that crime in such a world is no longer the exception" and, because of this, it could and should be the subject of books, as it reflected reality.

The publisher's assessment written by Neues Leben struck a similar chord,

> Wallace, in his work as a reporter in a criminal court, experienced the questionable machinations of people who possess the most money. He has seen the apparatus which recklessly and thoughtlessly wears out and destroys the 'little people'. Corresponding to this is his attitude towards the dubious or reprehensible representatives of the higher social strata, as he describes them in his stories. The temptation to attain power and reputation through money is huge for anybody who comes close to this universal remedy and, simultaneously, it is the best breeding-ground for crime, a fact that Wallace clearly shows.

Commercial Considerations:

Kinderbuchverlag wrote, "The author's rights are free. The stories are available in the German language in West Germany. However, as the translation is still under copyright protection, we have retranslated, from the English original." Neues

Leben did not mention any economic detail regarding their production, but it may be expected that, with their two stories, they would have experienced similar problems and would have acted in a similar fashion and, indeed, the colophon in the book does not show any licence agreement with a Western publisher.

Slow-Moving Publishing Machinery:

The production of Wallace's *Geschichten vom Hexer* presents a fine example of how ponderous East German publishing could be. According to the information in the file, the publisher's contract was concluded in November 1984 and the contract with the translator in February 1985. It was planned to have the manuscript back from the translator in February 1986, granting her a year to translate the thirteen stories. In parallel, the assessor was producing her assessment of the book (showing the date of July 1985). Submission for the application took place in summer 1986, ready for a publication in 1987. The manuscript remained in the censorship authority for only six days. However, although it does not appear that there were any problems with the text as such (as the censor did not make any remarks in the box reserved for comments), there is a second date shown in the file, indicating a second submission to the censor (dated May 1987). It is not quite clear what had occurred to delay the printing; however, the book was incorporated only into the production plan for 1988, the year when the actual production took place.

Chapter Five
If in Doubt, Spell It Out

5.1 Afterwords for the Benefit of the Reader

It was the purpose of the previous two chapters to analyse how the process of rewriting operated and how reader-reception was steered (this was achieved by identifying those categories, according to which texts were selected) and to explore how these categories were employed by publishers in their quest to make books acceptable for publication. It has been found that, commensurate with the codification of the East German poetics, positive and negative motifs were in use which had the function of classifying (children's) books as suitable or not. These classifications have been elaborated based on the discourse in the documents applying for a print permit, where the publishers' argumentation was crucial for swaying the censor in favour of a publication. The concepts and motifs established have been shown to play a significant role in the decision-making process. It has also been discussed that the inclusion of afterwords was a key factor for the publication of certain books, i.e. books in which the censor found minor shortcomings that needed to be clarified for the reader. Indeed, the record shows that there was explicit direction on the use of prefaces/afterwords by the authorities. By inference, it can be assumed that the same poetics also took a central role in the production of these afterwords that accompanied books for young people.

This chapter has the objective to revisit the classifications defined in Chapter 3, in order to affirm their validity and illustrate their importance for society, in general, and for the publishing process in particular. While, however, the previous chapter was concerned with textual material dedicated solely for the eyes of the censor and, thus, not published together with the primary text, the text type under investigation here, namely the afterword,[1] appeared in the actual book and was therefore addressed to the public.

It was back in 1953, a time when the construction of the socialist society had been announced and everything in the country was directed at societal change and progress, that a circular was sent out to all publishers from the censorship authority[2] (DR1/1896); in it, the importance of commentaries in books was addressed and publishers were urged to take these commentaries more seriously. Referring particularly to classics (which in those days represented the main source of translated literature, in particular for children's literature), it was contended that, under the new social conditions, classic works required a new interpretation and that they, therefore, needed to be lifted above their traditional interpretation. As a consequence, prefaces—to which the circular referred—had to reveal the new outlook on life.

> Often, in applications for a print permit, classic works are submitted together with the old prefaces which, however, no longer suffice for a forward-looking interpretation. Sometimes they have been revised in such a manner that the outdated concepts have been omitted and passages inappropriate for our time have been removed. For obvious reasons, such a truncated foreword can not suffice to provide the correct interpretation of a classic work of literature. What is more, forewords that have been written afresh frequently discuss only minor issues and focus only on aesthetic matters rather than dealing with the true interpretation of the work and its socio-critical content. (DR1/1896)

In those cases, where the authors of such commentaries were still uncertain about subject matter and material to be put into forewords, it was suggested that they team up with people who had had some training in Marxism-Leninism or, at least, that they should have "a thorough, clarifying discussion . . ., which will open editors' minds to the new viewpoints in the works and the time of their origin." This example reveals that, even in the early stages, conscious attempts were undertaken at rewriting literature to make it fit the prescribed didactic purposes. Literature was, after all, used as a pedagogical device for putting emphasis on patriotic aspects and, in order to ensure the creation of a model socialist state, it was deemed necessary to shape the taste of a wider audience; and young readers, as the future citizens, were a prime target. What, however, seems astonishing is that, apart from rare exceptions, most commentaries appear not as a foreword but as an afterword behind the main story. In this context, it is striking that the Ministry's circular referred specifically to forewords and not to afterwords, a circumstance that suggests that at some stage the commentary section must have been moved to the end of a book, despite the higher probability of readers ignoring it. Therefore, one might even assume that the people responsible for the publications deliberately moved this section back, in order to spare the reader from reading it.

On the whole, afterwords had to affirm literary political paradigms and were never to call into question the maxims of the Party. In other words, they had to deliver evidence that texts (for adults and children alike) were concerned with cultural political issues and that they were convergent with the political line. Afterwords to children's books from a non-socialist country had to show that, despite the text being bourgeois, it would not stand in the way of a socialist education and, hence, would not pose a threat to Historical progress. Similar to the discourse in the print permit files, a clear Marxist interpretation had to stress the forward-looking aspects and to tie the foreign book in with the socialist canon. Afterwords accompanying contemporary, socio-critical Western literature had to uncover ideological weaknesses and limits of those societies and to demonstrate that only socialism was in possession of the one-and-only truth. Similar to the evaluations for the print permit, afterwords divided the world into two camps—the capitalist and the socialist. The message to child readers was made clear: communist ethos is superior to capitalism. Regardless of the historical period in which a book was set, afterwords communicated that capitalist, imperialist and bourgeois societies epitomised all the world's evils, while socialism and communism represented all that was noble and caring for a common good in the world. It is perhaps not surprising that the finger was pointed predominantly at Great Britain and the United States—the former for its leading role in the Industrial Revolution and its desire to rule the globe politically and economically, the latter for its status as the contemporary world power with imperialistic claims.

Just like the actual book itself, the text of the afterword was also vetted for its suitability for readers. This took place in the application process for a print permit for a book, either together with the evaluation of the primary text or in a separate assessment dedicated only to the afterword. In the application procedure, the main text and its afterword were regarded and treated as one entity, and only the resulting merged text was to convey the correct insights. This is to say that, in the case of ideological shortcomings of the main text, the afterword had to balance out these weaknesses and instruct the readers as to the correct interpretation of the book. Therefore, only the totality of main text and peritext[3] was deemed to describe the ideological content of a book in the right light. This amalgamation of the two text types becomes evident in the frequent demand of censors to add or improve an afterword; a fact suggesting that a clear, partisan afterword in the right spirit increased the chances of publication.

It lay close to the hearts of publishers to make accessible to their audience international books and, as pointed out, one way of achieving this goal was the production of an effective afterword. Commensurate with this objective, publishers were at pains to find the most suitable writer for their afterwords, who would provide a thorough, critical and, most importantly, socially correct interpretation. Particularly books that carried alien concepts—as was the case with translated books from the West—needed to be presented in a way in which officials in the censorship authority could recognise and accept these concepts as socialist traits. The aim was to find a convincing argument of the viewpoint of the source text author as identical to that of the East German regime and its cultural politics, or at least acceptable enough for the censors to grant a print permit; an aim that is clearly in accord with Genette's assertion that paratext[4] does not have the function "to look nice around the [primary] text" (1997:407) but "to present and comment on the text itself" (1997:345).

This leads to the question of who was responsible for the peritextual commentaries in children's books. East German afterwords to translated children's books were hardly ever written by the foreign authors themselves, nor by the publishers. Neither were they a forum where translators could voice their opinion about the text in question or point to translation problems and strategies to solve them. Producers of afterwords were, in the majority of the cases, editors of anthologies, or linguists and specialists of Anglo-American culture, or social historians. Given this kind of writer, there is no doubt that afterwords had the sole function of interpreting the source text in a socialist light. Another of Genette's views maintains that paratext ought "to ensure for the [primary] text a destiny consistent with the author's purpose" (1997:407). However, with respect to translated texts for children and adolescents in the GDR, it was not so much the view of the author of the original which was to be conveyed but that of the author of the afterword, being an authorised third party who understood the source text author correctly and could explain to the readers what he or she had wanted to express through the book. Hence, writers of afterwords "help[ed] the reader pass . . . from one world to the other" (Genette 1997:408); in other words, the East German afterword facilitated the transition from bourgeois capitalist values to the socialist society.

In most instances, authors of afterwords did not remain anonymous but put their names under their work, as is evident in children's books. Since they were reputable authorities in their respective fields, their signatures attributed a great deal of legitimacy to their interpretation of the main text, a fact that weighed heavily in favour of a print permit. Furthermore, as these authors were mostly East German, their afterwords constituted original home-grown writing, and this writing process had one distinct advantage: it could be controlled. This is to say that, whereas the main text could only be altered to a certain degree during the translation process, the production of an afterword could be guided and influenced, and publishers could request an afterword to be rewritten so that it matched the poetological requirements. An example is Sigrid Wirzberger's afterword to the publication of two Dickens stories (*Weihnachtsgeschichten*, 1970, Kinderbuchverlag), which she was requested to rewrite twice (DR1/2261). Equally important, however, afterword authors, as East German citizens, were familiar with the literary, cultural and political environment. They knew what was demanded of them and what facets and angles their text was required to exhibit. As expected, they employed in their writing the poetological codification in use for literary critical discourse, which was constituted by precisely those principles and concepts made use of in the publishers' evaluations. This meant that, frequently, the same arguments were used, particularly when the writer of the afterword had also been the assessor of the book in the print permit application.

Translated books could be given two kinds of afterwords. Firstly, there were those that aimed at smoothing out things which may have disturbed the reading experience by making references to manners, customs and folklore. These experiences were different from those of an East German child, since many source texts originated from periods long gone or had their origin in cultures inaccessible to the young readers and were thus very different from the East German culture. For this reason, glossaries or explanatory lists made the foreignness less of an obstacle by providing clarification about currency, customs, titles, measures and objects of everyday life. The provision of such explanatory sections explaining these foreign terms to the children indicates that East German children's literary translation practice followed Klingberg's recommendation of keeping cultural context adaptation to a minimum, in order to enable children to experience the foreign elements in the text (1986:18). The second category of afterword—and by far the largest part—were afterwords of an ideological nature, attempting to guide the readers' understanding of the book in the 'right' direction. These provided text interpretation with a clear ideological bias. The fact that home-grown East German books for children were hardly ever given any explanatory sections, yet a great many of the foreign translated ones were, demonstrates how seriously authorities took this task of political ideological mediation. Information and critical comments were provided on the socio-historical background of the story, on the biography of the source text authors and on the motivations for actions of the protagonists. These ideological afterwords were what Lefevere called "theory-cum-criticism" (1991:135) or "criticism cum interpretation" (1985b:234), which means that they were to explain the foreign source text in agreement with socialist ideology and place it in line with the Marxist-Leninist belief system. These afterwords, therefore, represent examples of rewriting in action, because they too, like the discourse in the print permit files, were designed to influence the way in which readers received the stories.

There is no doubt that afterwords had to fulfil a didactic purpose. They were a device of socialisation, supplying young readers with the 'real meaning' of a story. They make visible the regime's desire to take care of reader response; accordingly, it seems it was not only considered necessary to publish the right kind of literature but also to make sure that readers understood why this was a valuable book they were reading. It becomes apparent that independent thinking of children was not called for. There was no room to accommodate subjective views. Ambiguities were interpreted for children and, on the whole, an attempt was made to condition them into interpreting stories in the officially acceptable way.

One ought, however, to consider that every text published not only had its obvious target reader, the child, but that there was another, covert reader, the censor, who resided between the stages of production and dissemination of the book. Publishers not only published with an eye to their child reader, but also to the censor. Their aim was twofold: to give enjoyment to their young audience and also satisfy the censor. The previous two chapters have demonstrated that it was of prime importance to signal to the censor that the right choice of book had been made. Acting as the representatives of the state, censors had the ultimate say in whether or not a book fulfilled the social requirements and was allowed on the bookshelves. As mentioned earlier, publishers were conscious of this fact and used afterwords as an instrument to safeguard books. Aware that the message was all-important, they (or rather their commissioned writers) moulded the afterword's content to conform to the regime's discourse. Hence, discursive techniques in afterwords employed criteria from Marxism-Leninism and from Socialist Realism throughout; for instance, condemnation of violence, of materialism, of passivity, of religion and superstition, or praise of an honest work ethos, an optimistic stance, and collective spirit. The two principal criteria, however, used for interpretation, which spanned the discourse as umbrella postulates, were the two Socialist Realist concepts of Realism and Humanism, precisely as they were in the discourse in the print permit files. This should not come as a surprise, since these were the two key principles on which the East German literary system rested and by which books were measured (see Autorenkollektiv unter Leitung von Horst Haase und Hans Jürgen Geerdts, 1976:24). Indeed, every single afterword made use of them, in order to highlight the ideological position of the primary text and the viewpoint of the source text author. To provide an illustration of how afterwords employed relevant concepts, three areas will be explored on which every afterword commented: historical and socio-cultural context, authors, and protagonists.

5.1.1 Historical and Socio-Cultural Context

The majority of translated publications in the sector of children's books and books for young adults revolved around themes from history and around social problems of the societies from which the books originated. It was precisely in these two areas that authors of afterwords deemed it necessary to provide their readers with a 'full' picture of the circumstances in those societies; and certainly it was a picture produced from the perspective of Marxist-Leninist ideology. Thus, the afterword to Scott's *Ivanhoe* (1965, Neues Leben), written by Ilberg, stated,

> Scott commenced *Ivanhoe* with a short portrayal of the social conditions 'around the finish of the reign of King Richard I', which doubtlessly has the purpose to facilitate the readers' comprehension. Today, nearly one and a half centuries later, this may no longer be sufficient, especially for German readers. An explanation of the historical background will increase their enjoyment of the book. (1965:541)

What then followed was a description of events in the eleventh and twelfth centuries which—albeit true to history—was told in the spirit of socialist ideals. The Normans were described as "behaving like all feudalist—and later capitalist—conquerors towards their subjects", namely "arrogantly"; there is an emphasis on the growing importance of money which "had to be, of course, squeezed out of the populace" and which created "hatred in the people against its oppressors"; the Saxons who had been "fighting for national liberation" were finally accepted as equals by King Richard, a noble deed which "already reflected the thoughts of the American War of Liberation and of the French Revolution about the equality of all humans". Ilberg stressed the closeness of Scott's novel to reality, for instance, through the battle for freedom or the struggle for a humanist life. Equally, according to Ilberg, even though Scott used figures from legend like Robin Hood or Friar Tuck, his narrative reflected the true conditions of that time and, in order to exemplify this, he had the example of Tuck, whose figure clearly revealed the difference between the high and the low clergy of the time,

> On the one hand, there is the simple, yet crafty honesty without any hypocrisy, on the other, there is only hypocrisy without any honesty. Prince-bishops committed one crime after the other, always trusting to confession and absolution. In Scott's words, 'the closer to the church, the further away from God', by which he wants to say: the further away from the true rights of the people. (Ilberg 1965:542–545)

The historical era of the Industrial Revolution is described in Dickens' *Ferienmärchen* (1982, Kinderbuchverlag), a text for younger readers,

> It is the time of the powerful. The country is the most powerful in the world. The masters over factories and palaces rule over this country and also over large parts of the world. They have the first trains run, in order to serve their purposes. They turn the wonderful steam engine to their service . . . And they make laws so that their order prevails in this most powerful country. (Kant, in Dickens *Ferienmärchen* 1982:6)

In the commentary on *Weihnachtsgeschichten* (Wirzberger 1970:214, 215, in: Dickens, Kinderbuchverlag), Dickensian times were portrayed in detail. The children learned about "proletarian children who were objects of exploitation by factory owners from their early childhood"; they learned how Dickens as a shorthand secretary in parliament "came to hear about resolutions which were made for hypocritical reasons and served only to rob people of all their rights"; they learned about "legislation through which people lost their freedom because they were not able to pay their debts". However, they also learned about some principles by Engels and Malthus which appear advanced given the readers' age. This leads to the conclusion that, either such teachings were incorporated in school curricula and were, therefore, familiar to children; or that the general view was that children did not need to understand everything completely; or more likely, that the commentary was intended for an adult reader, for instance, the censor or parent.

Many books concerned with socio-political problems—contemporary and historical—were given an afterword, in particular books dealing with ethnic minorities that were suppressed and exploited. Needless to say, slavery and the Afro-American question were discussed comprehensively in afterwords. So, for instance, Beecher-Stowe's *Uncle Tom's Cabin* appeared in multiple editions, the last of which (sixteenth edition) with Neues Leben in 1981, which had an afterword of over 30 pages. Lessons were provided even for the youngest amongst readers; hence, a short story by E.A. Poe (*Der Goldkäfer*, 1962, Knabe) was accompanied by a commentary which told children about

> the old negro Jupiter whose droll gibberish you will surely have found funny. One hundred years ago, such childlike, obsequious [black] servants really existed. Slavery sat still in their bones through and through; and the author whose ancestors resided in the Southern States [of America], which held slaves, had not seen it as a problem to portray Jupiter in such a way. Although he lived at the time of the arising slave liberation, he did not care much about this burning issue and could not imagine the tenacious patience with which future negro generations would fight for freedom and equality. (The publisher 1962:6)

Similar to other countries, German children enjoy playing 'Cowboys and Indians'; however, it is a particular German tradition to supply German children with literature about native Americans. The genre *Indianerliteratur* has been thriving in Germany since the nineteenth century (amongst which the *Leather Stocking Tales* and *Karl May Tales* are the most popular). In the same fashion, the GDR published several books on this topic.[5] One may assume that one motivation for this was to inform children about the injustice done to native peoples. In order to interpret events in the right light, most of the books were published with a commentary. What they all had in common were accounts of the North American natives' "heroic and bitter defence against the merciless advance of the white conquerors" (Petersen 1977:191, 192, in: Arnold, *Der Geist von Cochise*, Kinderbuchverlag). In another afterword the young audience read, "The few Indians [left] eke out their existence in the America of the present day in so-called reservations, regions allocated to them, remote, infertile and miserable" and "bear witness to the injustice that has been committed in past times" (Gerull-Kardas 1963:182, in: Cooper, *Die Ansiedler*, Kinderbuchverlag). In *Der letzte Mohikaner* (Cooper, 1966, Kinderbuchverlag), the afterword stated, "the few remaining tribes are now kept alive in reservations by the Americans as propaganda, and they are presented in newspapers and broadcasts like fairground attractions and as peculiar remainders of a great past" (Gerull-Kardas 1966:210). The last paragraph of the afterword to Arnold's *Der Geist von Cochise* even had explicit propaganda, "The foundation of the permanent 'Committee for the liberation of Indians' and also the various means of support granted to the just demands of the American natives are evidence of how much the Communist Party in America values the importance of the Indian liberation battle" (Petersen 1977:194, Kinderbuchverlag).

As much as readers were instructed about black people and their historical background, critical commentaries also pointed out their contemporary situation. So, for example, when Neues Leben brought out *Die Farbe Lila* (Walker, 1987, Neues Leben), the afterword informed the readership about "the tough reality of racial problems in the USA", about Afro-Americans "being kept away from education, linked with an orientation to a belief in the inevitability of their fate" and "the belief in God as their only support" (Skotnicki in Walker *Die Farbe Lila* 1987:226). Similarly, afterwords to books concerned with the present-day situation of Africans in Africa discussed the repression, discrimination and injustice done by invaders who seized economic and political control in the respective African countries (e.g. Benson, *Im Augenblick der Stille*, 1974, Neues Leben; or Ngugi, *Der Fluss dazwischen*, 1970, Neues Leben).

Since most of the books translated from English stemmed from capitalist systems, the afterwords given to these books saw it as their task to confront these systems with their shortcomings. They made them responsible for inhumanity, endless suffering and victimisation of people evoked by the desire for power of a minority of people. *Zerrspiegel* (Stone, 1979, Neues Leben) is just one such book. Ihde, writer of the afterword, criticised capitalism, not failing to mention that the American anti-social and criminal reality was alien to socialist countries and must appear unreal to the citizens there. He reasoned that

> that world is depressing with its terrible hopelessness. Traditional concepts such as duty, honour and human dignity prove to be nothing but empty phrases. In that society where everything is purchasable—love as much as conscience—the satisfaction of the senses plays a big role; and the portrayal of the depressions and hallucinations caused by alcohol and drugs is abominable and ugly to such a degree that it makes us shudder. (1979:426)

Suffice to say that the main attacks were launched at the class enemies America and Great Britain, with the majority of criticism aimed at America. A remarkable example in this respect is the book *Das verschwundene Hotel* (Kaufmann, 1973, Junge Welt), a book consisting of 29 pages for novice readers. Instead of an afterword as such, one finds a fact list at the end of the story, entitled *Wußtest du schon* (Did you know). Although only half a page long and comprising seven sentences, this list provides clear propaganda directed against the USA. Three sentences may suffice as an example:

- Did you know that there are 10,000 children in the American town of Washington who do not have any shoes and that, in many families, several children share a single shirt and a single pair of trousers?

- Did you know that, in 1971, 73,000 children in New York could not attend their first school day because they did not have any clothes?
- Did you know that, out of 1,000 newly born babies in the poorest area of New York, 45 will die before they are one year old, and that 14,000 babies are gnawed at by rats?

As surreal as this information may sound, it can be assumed that it would have made an impression on the mind of many a child.

5.1.2 Authors

When writing the afterword for London's *Der Seewolf* (1968, Neues Leben), Wirzberger cited a reviewer of a progressive American literary journal: "A true proletarian author not only writes about the working classes, he must also be read by them. A true proletarian author not only uses the life of the proletariat as the material [for his novels], but what he writes must be imbued with a spirit of indignation" (1968:394). How better to incite such indignation than by going through tough experiences personally? In fact, from the study of the afterwords, several of the source text authors had experienced hardships in their own childhood. Mark Twain, for example, left school and worked as an "apprentice in a printer's shop" and it was at that time that "the hardships of the survival struggle began for him under conditions of capitalist exploitation" (Poschmann 1965:156, 157, in: Twain, *Tom Sawyer im Ausland*, Neues Leben); or Jack London, who, at the age of ten, had to "carry out physical work under the most inhuman conditions of capitalism" (Ihde 1973:309, in: London, *Südseeabenteuer*, Neues Leben) and, early in his life, "had the same bitter experiences as the children of proletarians . . ., suffering from the same humiliation and from the same dirt, through which the disinherited of the welfare society also had to go" (Wirzberger 1968:394, in: London, *Der Seewolf*, Neues Leben).

Without doubt, such childhood experiences will have had an effect on the authors' personalities and may have caused them to rebel by writing literature that did not conform with the values and beliefs of a conservative establishment. However, it is also quite likely that these instances were mentioned in afterwords for children, so they could identify with the suffering of these authors as children like themselves; but perhaps also, in order to demonstrate to them model behaviour and to show them the kind of work ethos desired in a socialist society. This assumption seems reasonable because diligence and industriousness were also mentioned in connection with other authors who did not necessarily have to go through such tough childhood experiences. One of them is Edgar Wallace, of whom the writer of the afterword claimed that he had been capable of finishing a novel within 14 days, due to his "immense enthusiasm for work" (Chowanetz 1988:173, in: Wallace, *Geschichten vom Hexer*, Kinderbuchverlag). Another one is Walter Scott, of whom Ilberg informed his readers that he "had a share in the business of his publisher, and when this man went into bankruptcy, Scott faced high debts, which he managed to pay back entirely through tireless literary work" (1965:545, in: Scott, *Ivanhoe*, Neues Leben).

Two authors were presented to children as examples showing that ill-health and physical handicap did not have to stand in the way of achievement. The first was Robert Louis Stevenson, whose weak lungs had forced him to give up his career. "Disappointed and bitter, he had to come to terms with the fact of not being able to perform physical work. However, his active intellect rebelled" (Malberg 1965:88, in: Stevenson, *Der Pavillon auf den Dünen*, Knabe), and he became an author, which "was a way for him to participate in life and to achieve something of value for society" (Malberg 1967:60, in: Stevenson: *Das Flaschenteufelchen*, Knabe). The second author was the Australian Alan Marshall, who, as Schnierer reported in her afterword, had caught polio as a six-year-old; "but this has not had any influence on his adventurous life. He has overcome his disability with steadfast energy, and rides horses, drives a car and travels around in the country frequently" (Schnierer 1969:no page, in: Marshall, *Ich bin dabei*, Kinderbuchverlag).

Another noticeable characteristic exhibited by some authors and, on many occasions, highlighted in afterwords was the realisation of the uselessness of money and possessions. So, Gerull-Kardas described Stevenson's distinct social sense, stating that "he refused to accept an inheritance, and he also contended that it was not right to use money which one had not earned oneself. Indeed, he even went as far as to view money given to him by his well-off father, in order to restore his health . . . , as money only lent to him which he strove to pay back" (1969:246, in: Stevenson, *Entführt*, 2nd edition, Neues Leben). Likewise, Walter Scott, although a landowner with a title, did not lead an ostentatious and flamboyant lifestyle, but was characterised as having been "fond of the people who lived on his land", as "never displaying the condescension of a lord of the manor" and as being "hospitable not only to friends but also to farmers, shepherds and manual workers" (Krenn 1964:468, in: Scott, *Quentin Durward*, Neues Leben).

From the print permit files, as described in Section 3.6.1, it has become noticeable that the main criteria for selecting authors were either their convergence with the socialist cause, or the potential for rewriting their biographies and making them fit the profile of a socialist author. As becomes evident from the afterwords, authors' lives—wherever possible—were used in the commentaries to point out exemplary behaviour or personal characteristics desired of a socialist personality, such as discipline, will-power, toughness, pulling oneself together or disregard of materialistic and financial thinking. However, the trait most mentioned and praised in every single afterword is Humanity, a fact which was to be expected, since one of the Socialist Realist principles was the demand for Humanity in literary works. Indeed, all authors were reported to have done their share with respect to showing love for people from the lower social classes and for the exploited and disadvantaged. Frequently, the author's compassion found expression in a positive phrase. Thus, Daniel Defoe was called "the courageous champion of the rights of the poor" who was therefore 'celebrated by the poor' and, because of his actions, ended up in the pillory three times (Biester 1963:328, in: Defoe, *Robinson Crusoe*, Kinderbuchverlag). Similarly, the "amateur detective and advocate of victims of injustice" Arthur Conan Doyle committed noble deeds, such as "acquitting a life convict from his imprisonment by proving a verdict of not-guilty for the prisoner" (Hillich 1982:371, in: Doyle, *Sherlock Holmes. 17 Detektivgeschichten*, Neues Leben). In the case of *Peter Simpel*, the afterword commented on the author Marryat, namely that "in his private life, Marryat showed sympathy [to coloured people] by bringing home with him a negro boy and providing him with a good education" (Wirzberger 1969:262, in: Marryat, Neues Leben).

5.1.3 Protagonists

The description of the protagonists of the books makes very visible the attempt to guide children towards a certain, correct way of behaving. Clearly, from the outset, particular books were selected by publishers, books in which characters demonstrated the socially desired way of thinking and behaviour. However, it was the afterword that completed the education. This is to say, whereas the process of reading will have triggered an identification process with the heroes of the stories and a subconscious incorporation of behavioural patterns, the afterword subsequently spelt it out, thereby affirming and re-enforcing what had been read and experienced before. Thus, children were instructed that Alice (from Carroll's *Alice in Wonderland*) "has all the best traits of the simple people in England, tenacity, common sense and courage"; also that she was gentle and polite to everybody, no matter whether she spoke to a king or to a caterpillar; and "this is very important: to her, all the creatures are equal . . .; also she is curious, has an incredible thirst for knowledge and is filled by deep love of life" (Washdajew 1976:200, 201, in: Carroll, *Alice im Spiegelland*, Edition Holz im Kinderbuchverlag).

What most protagonists had in common was the active stance of a fighter, a healthy portion of wit, courage and sympathy for the weak, the suffering and the oppressed. Therefore, an innumerable proportion of heroes have either already realised or came to realise throughout the story that active involvement, rather than hesitation or passivity, was the way forward. Thus, in *Zerrspiegel*, Ihde (1979:427, 428, in: Stone, Neues Leben) described the social worker Rainey

> as having the highest level of social consciousness [of any character in the book]. He fights for the ideals of humanity. In contrast to the other characters in the novel who subordinate themselves to the feeling of loneliness and isolation or who have abandoned their search for a meaning in life, he has the desire to participate actively in social battles in the name of humanity . . ., it is he who finds the courage to challenge the prosecution attorney of New Orleans, a reactionary and racist. Increasingly gaining insights into the

> practices of the exploiters, he loses his doubting insecurity and turns into an active fighter against the inhumanity of the imperialistic society.

Repeatedly, afterwords emphasise that the isolated individual battle does not achieve maximum effect. In order to succeed entirely, people have to unite and fight together. Will Fern, the protagonist of Dickens' short story *The Chimes*, has come to precisely this realisation and, hence, the afterword stated,

> Will Fern who is chased by the rich noblemen like a deer, demonstrates the resistance which lives, in spite of all the humiliation, in the exploited. He rebels against his oppressors in his way: 'Again and again I have noticed: this is how slavery begins, this is how it continues and this is how it ends, and never is there a change. When I see this, I say to these noblemen: leave me alone! . . . We have nothing in common!' It was people like Will Fern who became conscious that only a unified battle of all exploited people will change social conditions. (Wirzberger 1970:217, in: *Weihnachtsgeschichten*, Kinderbuchverlag)

Not only were the traits of human protagonists examined; so also were those of animal heroes, as happened, for instance, in the case of Brer Rabbit in *Geschichten von Onkel Remus*. Rabbit, as the afterword pointed out, was simple and physically weak, yet smart and full of a will for freedom, but he was surrounded by powerful enemies. It was only through his wit and desire to live that he escaped them. As such, the afterword stated, he resembled black people who also had to fight for their freedom (Petersen 1984:148, in: Harris, Kinderbuchverlag). In 1962, publisher Holz brought out another version of the *Brer Rabbit Tales* which entered the GDR via a Soviet source text (Chwostenko, *Geschichten vom Bruder Rabbit*, Holz). The Russian editor who had translated the tales from English sources had also produced an afterword which was now used for the GDR edition. In it, the Russian followed the same line of argument as the 1984 GDR version, coming to the conclusion that

> the main thought of the tales is Rabbit's ongoing and persistent battle for the right to live in peace with his neighbours, for the right to work in peace and for the right to befriend those who do not want to cause harm. . . . In the face of powerful and evil enemies, Brer Rabbit has to develop smartness, skilfulness and resourcefulness, traits which replace strength and force. (Chwostenko 1962:9)

5.2 Afterwords for the Benefit of the Producer

So far, it has been shown that afterwords were, firstly, a tool to educate young readers, with the objective of promoting socialist culture and, secondly, a means to appease the censor, with the objective of obtaining a print permit for the book. Yet another fact has to be taken into consideration. Afterwords not only served to protect the main text and ease it past the censorship authority; they also had the function of safeguarding the people and institutions who were responsible for the production of a book (see. e.g. Links 1997:244, 245, 246; similarly Petersen 2005:176). As has been mentioned on p 99, publishers were to regard themselves as "political functionaries" (DR1/1234) and, as such, had to represent the Party line. This meant accepting personal responsibility for the suitability of every book. The commissioning and subsequent authorisation provided by afterwords was one of several strategies adopted by the publishers to legitimise the decision to publish a book.

Additionally, while afterwords were used by publishers to appease censors, the censors themselves used them as a tool of self-protection, since they were accountable for their decisions to the Central Committee of the Party. Hence, censors would look for sensibilities and whether they were counterbalanced or weakened by the right interpretation, because this validated their decision to allow a book to pass to the printer's. In this non-pluralist society, in which all decisions were based on the judgement of a handful of functionaries, protection strategies of the publishing and state sector were of vital significance. Dieter Schlenstedt (GDR literature specialist) confirmed this need to make secure and protect one's own position. In his view, afterwords acted as "a pre-defence mechanism against complaints by the orthodox literary establishment" (as quoted in Mix 1993:228). While Schlenstedt referred specifically to literature for adults, several of my interviewees held the same opinion about books for children and adolescents, claiming that efforts to produce an afterword were undertaken solely to please the censor and not so much to instruct or inform young readers, because they were of the opinion that hardly any of them would have cared to read it anyway. Remarks like these are substantiated by the observation that nearly all commentaries appear as an afterword and not as a foreword, a fact indicating silent agreement between all parties concerned when allowing the explanatory sections to appear behind the story, despite the high probability that children (or readers, in general) would close the book and put it aside at the end of the story. In this light, a remark by Petersen, chief editor with publisher Volk & Welt, has to be seen which, although somewhat amusing, makes the point. Petersen suggested moving the most important contents of the afterword to the blurb or, even better, to perforate the pages of the afterword so that readers could tear them out immediately after purchasing the book (2005:176). As humorous as this suggestion may be, it highlights once again the fact that "the afterwords addressed censorship authority and Central Committee" and that "on the whole, editors did not fool themselves with the illusion that readers paid much attention to the 'reading aids' supplied by publishers" (Petersen 2005:176).

Two features of afterwords indicate this necessity of having to address the next-highest level in the hierarchy and defend one's own position in deciding on the choice of book (the editor's, the publisher's and the censor's); firstly, anticipation of ideological political objections and toning them down and, secondly, intertextual references to sanctioned aspects, both of which will be dealt with in the following two sections.

5.2.1 *Anticipation and Weakening of Ideological Political Objections*

So far, it has been shown that the afterwords provide a similar picture to that found in the discourse between publisher and censor. This does not come as a surprise, when bearing in mind the far-reaching cultural policies implanted by the regime. Similar to the print permit files, sensitive areas in the books which might evoke objections from censors (or from the Party level located higher up) needed to be identified, pointed to and toned down or invalidated. It might be thought that, compared with publications for adults (translated and indigenous), foreign children's books were not regarded as causing any difficulties, in other words that the establishment might have believed that the content of these books was less sophisticated and unlikely to contain controversial ideas. However, a study of afterwords reveals that publishers did indeed make provision for anticipated objections and, as a matter of fact, publishers' defence strategies focus on the same issues.

Two key problems given regular attention by publishers were religion and superstition. Thus, Herzfelde, writer of the afterword to *Onkel Toms Hütte*, stated that, quite often in the story, religious references turned into preaching; in so doing, Beecher-Stowe may have impressed her contemporaries, "but today these parts of the book appear as a weakness. . . . It is obvious how sickly sweet and meaningless they are, especially the scenes, in which little Evangeline dies and in which Tom has a vision briefly before his death".[6] Herzfelde finished this section by claiming that "undeniably the Bible was a powerful and almost the only intellectual weapon of slavery; and that the best and most activist of the slaves interpreted the Bible in a different way to the author, namely in a revolutionary way". By telling the children/censors that the Bible had, in fact, been used as a weapon, Herzfelde appropriated the notion of religion to the socialist society (1968:396–398, in: Beecher-Stowe, Neues Leben).

Similarly, superstitious beliefs were considered problematical. Hence, for instance, the afterword to Dillon's *Die Insel des großen John* (Walch 1968:231; in: Dillon, Neues Leben) instructed the child/censor that, to that day, in the whole of Ireland, much superstition and magical stories remained and the belief in elves, who were considered the masters over illness and death, was still widespread. Nonetheless, the Irish increasingly began to view them "with a cool distance, as was also done by Roddy and Pat in our story." The afterword also pointed out that life in Ireland had not changed considerably for the simple people since those times when such beliefs and cults came into being, which was the reason for their continued existence in the Irish society of the present day. Consequently, the existence of superstition was explained away to the readers as a characteristic of a society still backward in Historical development; in contrast, the GDR, as a developed progressive society, had overcome this period and had no reason to feel threatened by it any longer.

Another aspect in need of a defence strategy was violence. Thus, Petersen was given the task to comment on E.A. Poe's predilection for cruel descriptions (1979:266, in: Poe, *Der Goldkäfer*, Kinderbuchverlag, an anthology of some of Poe's short stories). Petersen reasoned that "Poe attached immense importance to the principles of probability and absolute credibility. He used poetic detail with great care. This is why cruel, eerie and horrendous events and facts are sometimes described with more explicitness than appears necessary." The genre of crime and detective literature is closely linked with violence. As mentioned in Section 4.5, this genre did not find much support by the authorities due to the violation of the Humanity principle of socialist society and the narration of events that did not correspond with the socialist notion of Reality. Hence, similar to the discourse in the censorship files, afterwords put emphasis on the fact that it was not the description of the criminal act *per se* which was of significance, but the finding of the solution to the crime; also that the stories resembled the reality of the capitalist society, and that the good was always victorious over the evil (see e.g. Hillich 1982:367, in: Doyle, *Sherlock Holmes. 17 Detektivgeschichten*, Neues Leben; or Chowanetz 1988:153, in: Chesterton, *Der geflügelte Dolch*, Kinderbuchverlag).

Literature needed to be realistic, down-to-earth, purposeful and comprehensible to the reader. Therefore, fiction following the artistic principle 'art for art's sake' (*l'art pour l'art*) was deemed opposed to Marxist-Leninist dogma and useless for society. Oscar Wilde was an author with the flaw of propagating art as valuable in itself and arguing that it did not have to serve a didactic purpose; thus, the afterword had to come to his rescue,

> In his oeuvre, Wilde subscribed to quite contradictory views. On the one hand, he believed that art had no use for society and, therefore, knew no purpose and moral. Art only ought to be beautiful and the ugly facts of life must not appear in it. On the other hand, he himself rarely kept to this principle in his work. Especially his fairytales are not only beautiful but show the injustice and the wrong prevalent in the world. They cause indignation in the readers and the desire to overcome such bad conditions. (Anonymous 1959:192, in: Wilde, *Der glückliche Prinz*, Kinderbuchverlag)

As might be expected, fantasy was another awkward concept. This is exemplified by *Alice's Adventures in Wonderland*, a story abounding in fantastic and nonsensical elements. Explaining these to the reader, the afterword clarified what the author had 'really' wanted to show,

> . . . but this jungle of nonsense is nothing else but the everyday life of the educated English society under the legendary reign of Queen Victoria. Elegant life in those days was surrounded by the troubled waters of bitter

> poverty. The Industrial Revolution blew through England in a whirlwind of smoke and steam, consuming people whose working days were endlessly long and miserably paid, deepening the abyss which separated the owners from the workers. (Washdajew 1976:200, in: Carroll, *Alice im Spiegelland*, Holz im Kinderbuchverlag)

Similarly, Edgar Allan Poe was criticised for withdrawing from reality by escaping into a fantastic narrative. However, the afterword author defended him because of his handicap of having to live and create in a capitalist society; the afterword read, "the excessively fantastic narrative helped him to survive all the humiliation and deprivation and constituted his way of fleeing the narrow-mindedness and hostility to the arts of American society. . . . The more fantastic his descriptions, the more obvious his existential fear and his difficulties to adapt to the pressure of an achievement-oriented society" (Petersen 1979:264, in: Poe, *Der Goldkäfer*, Kinderbuchverlag).

It was not only the contents of the book that had to be neutralised; equally, some authors' biographies needed to be toned down. It has been demonstrated previously that the value and belief system of an author was presented to children as a motivation to be emulated. Some authors, however, exhibited shortcomings which needed to be counterbalanced. This was true mostly for classic authors, as most contemporary literature selected for publication revolved around socio-critical aspects and was written by authors with a leaning to the left who did not require much further defence. So, for instance, Stevenson was reported (Berger 1969:247–249; Stevenson, *Der schwarze Pfeil*, Neues Leben) to be the descendent of a well-to-do family, having had the particular misfortune to be raised by an over-religious nanny who turned him into a sanctimonious child; because of this, he had to find a great deal of painful energy later in his life, in order to liberate himself from this mysticism and superstition; also, the afterword hastened to say that he did not know any class differences but loved the simple, hard-working people; and proceeding in Stevenson's defence, "but there was not as yet a revolutionary Marxist workers' party, which would have been, through class struggle, the only force capable of bringing about heroes of a kind worth creating and who would have incited and gripped poets and authors alike".

This notion of authors not yet being sufficiently conscious about social circumstances is found time and again in afterwords, followed by an understanding remark, an excuse or by the statement that people in the GDR had gained more developed Historical knowledge and, therefore, were in the position to interpret correctly what the author had attempted, yet failed to express. One example out of numerous others is the afterword to *Zerrspiegel*, which stated about author Robert Stone, "he does not provide any analysis about the conditions he has noticed; he does not recognise the actual reasons for social defects and he cannot offer any real ways of improving the situation, however, the portrayal of the authentic American reality is expressed with such a vigour that his novel turns into a condemnation and a distressing contemporary document" (Ihde 1979:429, in: Stone, Neues Leben). By the same token, Krenn maintained, "in many a point we disagree with Charlotte Brontë. We regret that she did not recognise the significance of the bourgeois revolutions in Europe and of the powerful Chartist movement in England. Nevertheless, we hold her books in high esteem, as she has portrayed lively and permanently the sufferings of those disadvantaged by society"[7] (1963:164, in: Brontë, *Die Waise von Lowood*, Kinderbuchverlag).

5.2.2 *Intertextual References*

Intertextual elements served to stress the significance of the text or the author. With respect to the text, the attempt was either to demonstrate its deserved place within the world heritage or its importance as a tool for education. Regarding the author, it was sought to prove that he or she had rightfully earned a place among the socially acknowledged authors. The function of such references was to point out that distinguished people had also recognised the value of work or author and that the book, therefore, would be worth a publication. Although citations from many renowned personalities were used, those from left-wing writers and ideologists attributed more weight to the reference. For instance, "Fjodor Dostojewski, one of the most important representatives of critical realism in Russian literature in the nineteenth century" was quoted as stating about Edgar Allan Poe that "he differs from all other authors by his imagination and the capability to describe emotional conditions and occurrences in a detailed and astute manner" (Petersen 1979:266, in: Poe, *Der Goldkäfer*, Kinderbuchverlag).

To give an example referring to the works themselves, Hillich equalled Dickens' oeuvre with that of several other socio-critical writers, amongst them Kingsley, Disraeli and Gaskell, all of whom had "worked on the picture of the [Victorian] era with its depressing situation for the workers, its sixteen-hour days and minimal wages, children's work in the factories, the slums and the medieval conditions in the judiciary and penal system" (1979:568, in: Dickens, *Große Erwartungen*, Neues Leben).

The aforementioned discussion reveals that concepts and tactics used in the discourse were identical to those used in the print permit files. The observation may also be made that some explanations seem somewhat theoretical, dry and sophisticated. Given that the overt reader was the child or adolescent, they appear to be very reader unfriendly. This may be an indication that, although the declared intention was to instruct the primary reader, the ultimate addressee was more mature and ideologically literate.

5.3 Analysis of Afterwords in Book Production

A study of the occurrences of afterwords in books for young people shows no obvious patterns and it appears that there was no visible policy about the inclusion of afterwords. Hence, for example, there were four first editions for Carroll's *Alice's Adventures in Wonderland* (1967 Holz, 1976 Kinderbuchverlag, 1985 Altberliner, 1987 Altberliner); however, only one of them (1976) appeared with an explanatory section in it; or the book *Doctor Dolittle*, which had caused severe problems for the publisher at his first attempt at publishing it and was even denied a print permit, was nevertheless not given an afterword in either of the two following productions (1969 Holz, 1980 Kinderbuchverlag). Some editions of a book were published with an afterword and, several editions later, the afterword was dropped, and in some cases, the first editions had no afterword and one was added later. This has been corroborated in the statements of several interviewees who confirmed that it depended on a number of factors whether an afterword was published; for example, because a book had a controversial message that needed to be toned down. Some editors (or censors) were particularly cautious and commissioned an afterword to a book for self-protection; in some cases, it provided an opportunity for scholars to publish an academic article; some scholars even approached the publishers actively when they had finished an article and asked whether there was room for its publication. What this section attempts to determine is whether the publication of afterwords happened solely on an arbitrary basis, or whether it is possible, after all, to identify developments and trends by studying patterns in the publication history.

The total production of books translated from English sources between 1961 and 1989 amounts to 405 books of which 325 are significant for the analysis of afterwords. These 325 books exclude:

1. Picture books (12) As a rule, picture books were never given afterwords.
2. Books from the *Das neue Abenteuer* series and *Poesiealbum* series by Neues Leben (49 in total) These were small paperback books of around 30 pages, containing short adventure stories or poetry, respectively. They were preselected by the publisher, deemed to be non-controversial and were never published with an afterword (although they still had to pass the censor).
3. Books by indigenous authors and by foreign authors resident in the GDR[8] (19), including five books that were not translations as such but retellings; yet excluding anthologies, since these used to have an afterword as a rule. These authors were considered as part of the establishment and consequently were rarely regarded as requiring an afterword.

What remains represents the majority of the books for which ideological afterwords were considered by publisher and censorship authority. Bearing in mind the total of 325 books, this means that, on average, ten translated books per year were considered for publication. Of these ten, only four or five on average were eventually published with afterwords, as illustrated next (Figure 5.1):

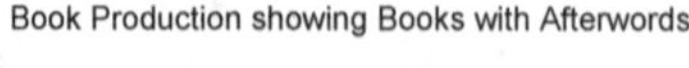

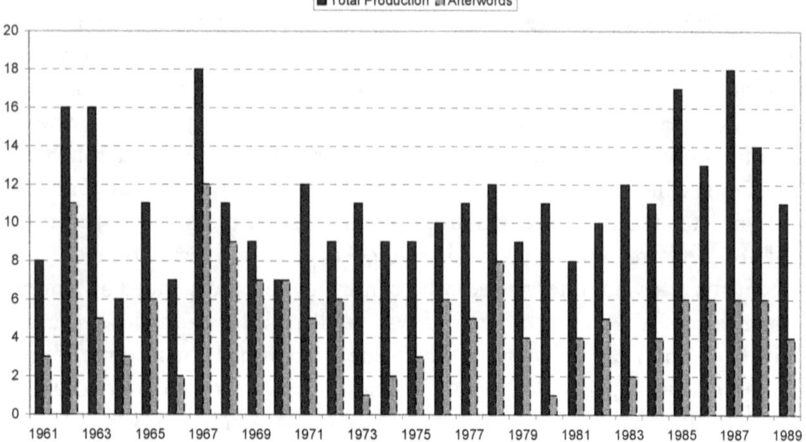

Figure 5.1 Book production showing books with afterwords.

Figure 5.1 shows a fairly constant book production throughout the period investigated, albeit never higher than eighteen books per year. Nevertheless, the number of books produced with an afterword varied considerably from year to year. From this figure, it is difficult to detect any clear trends; however, if an analysis is performed on the figures to determine the percentage of afterwords produced in each year, a definite trend is detectable, showing a significant decline towards the end of the period examined, as is illustrated in Figure 5.2. The two lines at the bottom of Figure 5.2 represent the entire production of books and afterwords of the period, respectively. From these values the other three lines have been calculated as an analysis of the percentage of books with afterwords, the linear trend and the moving average.

The proportion of afterwords produced (Afterword %) varies greatly from year to year: nevertheless, the amplitude of the variation appears to decrease over the years, which can be verified by observing the linear trend line (Linear [Afterword %]). To obtain an indication of local variances over the period, a moving average can be calculated (3 per. Mov. Avg. [Afterword %]), which shows the mathematical average change over the period as a graph; in other words, the variances have been averaged out, smoothing the graph of the percentage of afterwords, in order to show the trend on a year-by-year basis. Comparing this trend to the linear trend, it can be seen that there are two periods which show a distinct upwards trend in the production of afterwords. These took place between 1967 and 1970 and between 1976 and 1978. The first period corresponds with the aftermath of the Eleventh Plenary session of the Central Committee in December 1965 (also known as the 'Axing Plenary session', see p 31), which introduced to the society a more rigid approach towards the arts. The second increase corresponds to the so-called Biermann

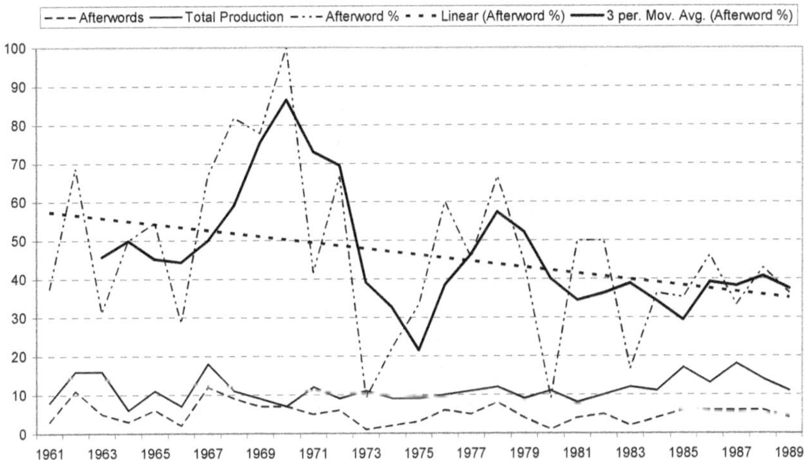

Figure 5.2 Percentage of afterwords by year.

Legend

————	Total production of children's books
– – – – – –	Actual production of books with afterwords
–··–··–···	Percentage of books from the total production that have afterwords
··············	Linear trend. This shows the linear approximation of the percentage of afterwords over the entire period, i.e. it gives an indication of whether the percentage of afterwords was increasing or decreasing over the entire period.
————	3 % moving average. This shows a graph which averages out the fluctuations in the percentage of afterwords by calculating the average from year to year, i.e. it gives an indication of how the percentage of afterwords changed on a shorter time scale by averaging out any annual anomalies.

incident (see pp 40 and 41), which again resulted in a more controlling atmosphere with respect to arts and literature. The significant decline in afterwords between these two peaks corresponds with the change of leadership in 1971, after which there was considerable relaxation in the cultural political climate, which manifested in the production of fewer afterwords until the events of 1976. The graphs also show that there was a steady decline in the average number of afterwords from 1979 to the end of the GDR. This is in accord with the development marking a general relaxation of the political and cultural political situation over this period. The slight increase from 1985 coincides with Gorbachev taking presidency of the USSR and introducing his policies of Glasnost and Perestroika, policies to which the GDR regime objected and, instead, continued to steer a hard course. Hence, the slightly larger production of afterwords of this period is suggestive of greater tension in the political climate in East Germany. What these data appear to indicate is that there was a relationship between political events in the GDR and the production of afterwords in books for children and adolescents, and it can be assumed that afterwords as an ideological safeguard reflected the tensions in the political situation. What is more, yet again evidence is provided that the production of books for young people was not marginalised but was included in and affected by political and cultural political developments.

The aforementioned investigation provides an overview of the situation, taking into account the entire book production. However, additional, more detailed insights are provided by breaking down the data further, based on classification of the data by publishing house (Kinderbuchverlag and Neues Leben as the two main publishers for children and young adults, respectively) and type of literature (classic and contemporary).

An analysis of the data (Figure 5.3) sorted by publishing house demonstrates that Neues Leben was the more significant of the two state publishing houses; firstly, since data are supplied for every production year and, secondly, its production figures lie significantly higher than those of Kinderbuchverlag (the mathematical average shows that Neues Leben produced twice as many translated books as Kinderbuchverlag). On the other hand, Kinderbuchverlag published several picture books and/or books written by foreigners resident in the GDR, which have been excluded from the count and, therefore, show Kinderbuchverlag's production as zero in three instances (1972, 1974 and 1986). Nonetheless, the general trend can still be detected in the literary production of Kinderbuchverlag.

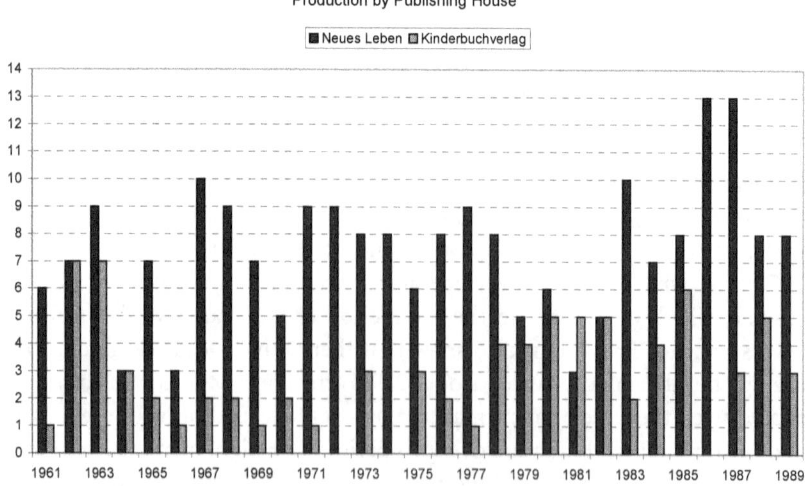

Figure 5.3 Production by publishing house.

Figure 5.4 and Figure 5.5 show an analysis of the production of afterwords as a percentage of the books published, sorted for each publisher. As expected, the linear and moving average trends over the period are similar to those of the overall production figures. This means that the general decline in the production of afterwords becomes noticeable. As might also be expected, Neues Leben shows a closer correlation with the overall production figures because of its larger data set.

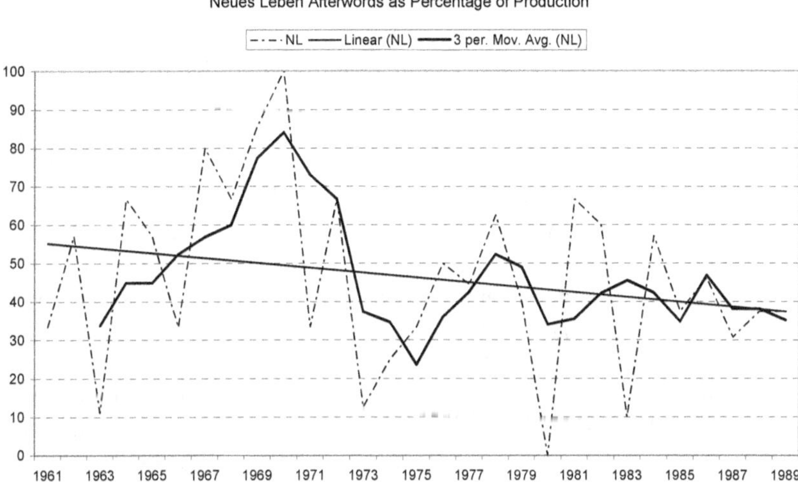

Figure 5.4 Neues Leben afterwords as percentage of production.

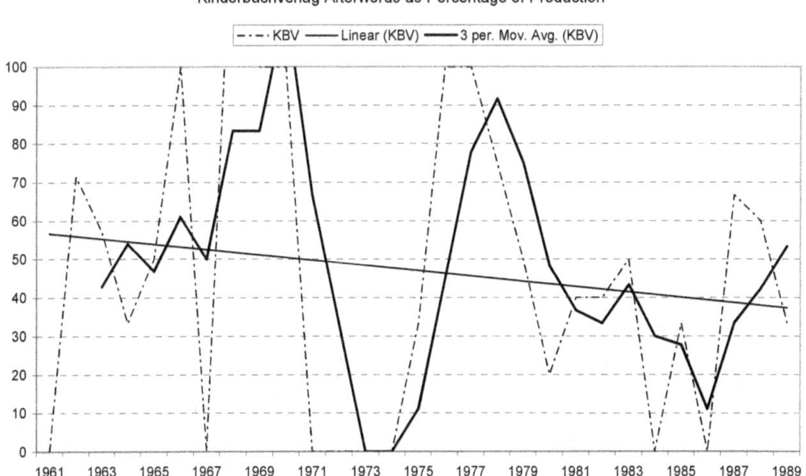

Figure 5.5 Kinderbuchverlag afterwords as percentage of production.

The legend used is the same as for the overall production figures given earlier, i.e. the linear trend line shows a general average of the entire time examined; the moving average trend makes visible significant peaks and troughs during the period. With respect to the production of afterwords for the younger readers versus those for adolescents, the figures reveal a very similar picture. Bearing in mind that the actual book production of Neues Leben and Kinderbuchverlag displayed a ratio of 2:1, the number of afterwords demonstrates the same relation, which means, in other words, 46% of the books produced by both publishers contained an afterword. Hence, the linear trend lines, both averaging just below 50%, indicate that there was no significant distinction made between younger and older readers. The second noticeable aspect is that both lines decline at the same rate over the period, being within 1% of each other.[9]

This observation is remarkable in two ways; firstly, because it shows that the generally lower production of afterwords by Kinderbuchverlag did not affect the statistical trend, since it followed closely the production ratio of Neues Leben; secondly, as the two lines run absolutely parallel, they reveal the same practices performed by the two publishers throughout. Another indication of the same policies being followed is the fact that the moving average lines experience highs and lows at the same time. What this suggests is an attempt by both publishers Neues Leben and Kinderbuchverlag to publish approximately half their books with afterwords. Additionally, it is indicative that both of them produced more afterwords in times of political tension, while relaxing the production of afterwords in times when the political pressure was easing off.

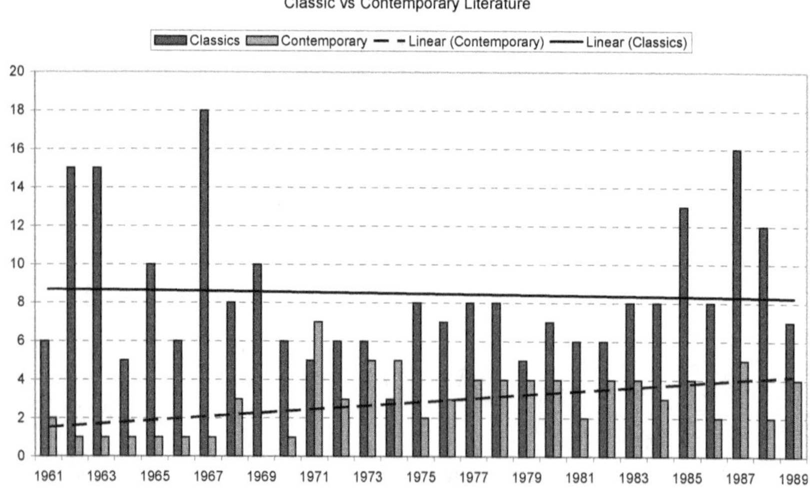

Figure 5.6 Classic vs contemporary literature.

Continuing to analyse the data, it was decided to divide the publications into two types of literature, classic and contemporary.[10] For this purpose, the following definition in accord with the GDR measure was adopted, in the hope of arriving at meaningful information that is specific to the situation of the GDR; classics entail those books that, in the GDR, were regarded as classic heritage and out of copyright. The remainder of the literature can be considered as contemporary foreign texts, still within their copyright period.

Figure 5.6 shows the overall production of classic and contemporary literature from 1961 to 1989. Immediately, the linear trend for contemporary and classic literature becomes visible. The production of classic literature remains virtually constant throughout the period, while the production of contemporary literature shows a significant increase. This may be explained by the situation and atmosphere in the country. Prior to 1970, literary politics propagated a more rigid line, more closely oriented at Socialist Realism and its paradigms. Not much contemporary literature was allowed into the country. However, it also ought not to be forgotten that, during these earlier decades, children's literature in foreign countries was still of a more conservative nature, displaying social values that were opposed to the socialist worldview and, hence, made it more difficult, if not impossible, to import this kind of literature for the GDR. Of course, there is the issue with the shortage of foreign currency; yet this shortage also held true for the later years when contemporary fiction was translated, a fact that seems to indicate that the financial aspect did not play a decisive role in this development. What with absolute certainty played a major role in the later two decades was the fact that the climate within the country had changed. Because of international treaties, the country opened itself towards other countries and, to a certain degree and in a very controlled environment, foreign influences were allowed to enter. Tied in with this development, the GDR displayed a more lenient approach towards contemporary literature. Literary life had become more lively and Socialist Realism was interpreted less narrowly (see Section 1.3). This opened doors to contemporary (socio-critical) books, a circumstance demonstrated by these statistics.

Further analysis of the data on classic and contemporary literature reveals that together on average 50% were published with an afterword, thus every second publication. However, the proportion of afterwords in contemporary literature was a mere 7.7%, thus approximately every thirteenth book; in other words, contemporary literature had significantly fewer afterwords than classic literature. This may be attributed to one of two factors; firstly, contemporary literature was specifically chosen out of the worldwide production to avoid any controversy; and secondly, a considerable proportion of contemporary texts was produced in co-production with a West German or Swiss publisher and, therefore, afterwords were not appropriate. In contrast, classic literature generally came from a period in history alien to socialism and, hence, it was deemed necessary to explain the context in a socialist light.

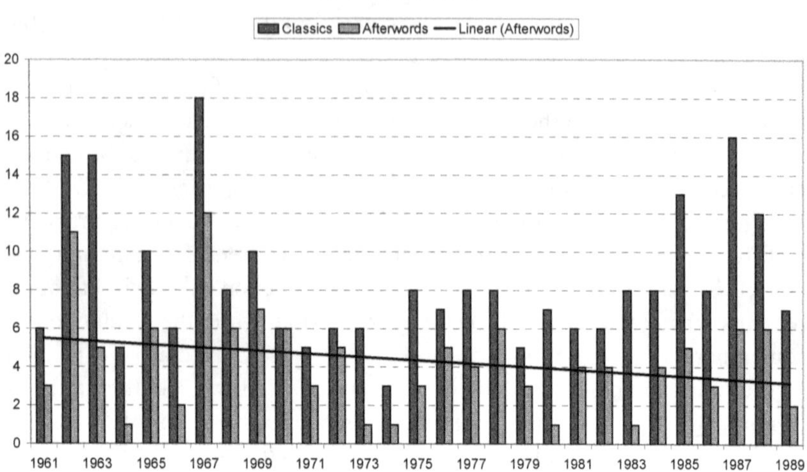

Figure 5.7 Classics with afterwords.

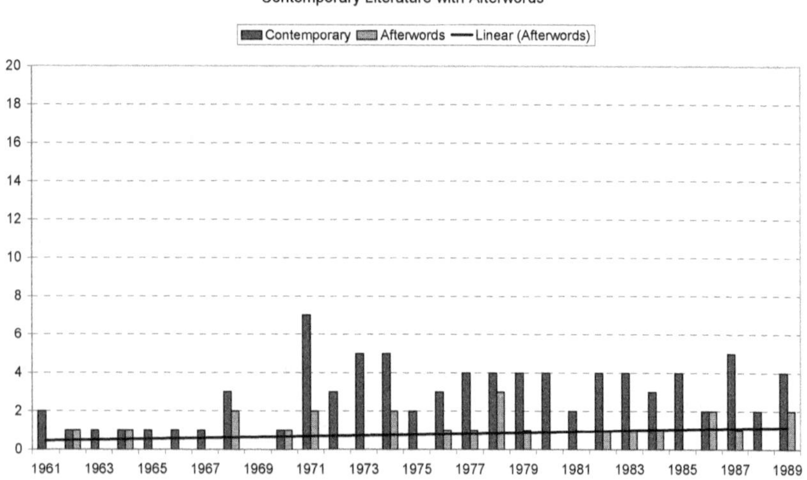

Figure 5.8 Contemporary literature with afterwords.

Figures 5.7 and 5.8 show the proportion of classic literature with afterwords and the corresponding graph for contemporary literature. As can be seen, the graphs show trends moving in opposite directions; however, the decline in the proportion of classics with afterwords is significantly steeper compared to the rise in contemporary literature with afterwords. Again, however, this may be due to the smaller production figures.

According to Figures 5.7 and 5.8, a significant increase becomes apparent in the production of contemporary fiction from 1971. However, it may be assumed that this development set in as early as 1970 because it has to be taken into account that this decision must have been made prior to this date, in order to obtain the print permits for the year 1971. Yet no significant political or cultural political events took place in 1970 that might explain this change in policy. As there was a change in political leadership in May 1971, this increase may be indicative of a mood swing in the country, foreshadowing a time in which the limits of tolerance were widened. Another thought, however, may be that there had been a noticeable decline in the production in classics during the previous three years, and it may be that the publishing houses decided to submit a larger number of contemporary texts in that year to compensate, resulting in the spike in the production for 1971; and having succeeded in publishing more contemporary literature, publishers then continued to submit more texts of this kind in all of the following years, a strategy supported by the more tolerant attitude prevalent in the country.

The previous discussion has unearthed some information that was expected, but some that is surprising. There is little doubt that afterwords were used as one strategy to rewrite the literature that was imported into the country. The information supplied to readers focuses first and foremost on text explanation, interpreting the books through Marxist-Leninist concepts and in alignment with the poetological requirements of literary politics, thereby asserting the books' suitability as reading for socialist children. However, analysing the data providing facts about numbers and publication dates of afterwords has also brought to the fore some surprising findings. It would appear that afterwords not only functioned as contextual background for the children to understand alien concepts but were used rather as a means in publishers' (and censors') strategies to defend the book chosen for translation and, ultimately with it, to defend their position. This becomes visible when discovering their correspondence to the political and social conditions in the country. A distinct difference was made between ideological and non-ideological afterwords, providing evidence of the need for some books to give additional, ideologically reasoned comments. Also, contrary to literature for adults where both translated and indigenous fiction could appear in print with an explanatory section, it was in the main translated books for children and adolescents that had such sections. The majority of afterwords were printed after the main text, and they were monotonous and tiresome, if not too sophisticated, and on the whole not reader-friendly, all suggesting that children and young adults were not the intended readers. Furthermore, the high correlation between the timing of the publication of afterwords and political events makes their real purpose more than evident; this even more so, as both the main state publishers, Neues Leben and Kinderbuchverlag, demonstrate the same trends: they tended to include more afterwords in politically difficult times, a procedure which, in the course of time, eased off; equally, the amount of afterwords decreased for both publishers over the period, as the general political climate relaxed more and more. Finally, the data also confirm the principal finding of Chapter 1, which identified the astonishing parallels between literature for adults and that of young people. Children's literature was very much part of the East German society and was taken seriously. The fact that books for children and adolescents oriented themselves to the general political and ideological atmosphere and were not marginalised as unimportant trivialities seems to substantiate this.

Chapter Six
Conclusion

To say that literature reflects the values and beliefs of the socio-cultural environment in which it is produced is a truism; in other words, ideology is inseparable from literature. These two are inextricably linked and what remains to be determined is the nature of that connection. Back in 1983, literary critic Terry Eagleton alluded to literature as a "notably unstable affair" (1983, here 1996:12). He based this notion on the fact that literary writing hinges on value-judgements which, in turn, are temporary as they depend on whatever is valued by certain people in specific situations. Eagleton therefore concluded that the "so-called 'literary canon' . . . has to be recognized as a *construct*, fashioned by particular people for particular reasons at a certain time" (1996:11, emphasis in original). Indeed, the findings of this study are consistent with Eagleton's claim. Setting out to explore the extent to which ideology and politics dominated cultural issues, and in particular the translation of books, this study has identified a definite connection between the literary output in East Germany and the doctrine maintained by the small group of people holding the power at that time.

As the first three chapters have demonstrated, Party ideology was omnipresent and permeated the publishing industry at all levels. Indeed, one of the key findings of Chapter 2 has been that all decision-making was controlled by SED party officials who considered themselves, alone, as being capable of leading the populace toward a new communist future. Although only small in number, they represented what could be called the official society, constructing a colossal state bureaucracy to ensure the smooth running of their ideal society. Within this scenario, the generally accepted notion of 'the state' as the controlling and guiding force is not an accurate description. Rather, as has been demonstrated, it was the Party that claimed hegemonic rule and the state was used as an instrument for Party machinations. One indication of this is seen in the fact that all state offices were overlain by Party offices which issued comprehensive sets of directives regarding the government of the country and which wielded tight control over the operation of the state apparatus. The East German literary establishment was absorbed into this structure. It did not only comprise a handful of publishers and booksellers but was perceived as a "social system, encompassing the Party, the Ministry of Culture, publishers, booksellers and all other institutions which bring about communication between authors and their readers" (Hermann Kant, member of the Central Committee of the SED and president of the East German Writers' Association, as quoted in Darnton 1990:9).

A shared ideological and moral framework was installed which was to form the basis of all thinking and behaviour. Accordingly, there was only one ideological view acceptable to the regime, namely Marxism-Leninism and its cultural manifestation, Socialist Realism. In alignment with this worldview, literary writing was regarded as a political articulation, with the result that the political orientation of a text determined its value (or lack of value) to East German society. The notion of literature acceptable to society was that ideas in books be convergent with the Party ideology and provide what was considered useful education for young readers. The prevalent codification of what was acceptable or unacceptable provides evidence of a didactic literature and points to the regime's desire to become directly involved in the education of the next generation. Within this framework, literature for young readers was not so much about entertaining children, but more for their education, in that it needed to instruct them in the socially appropriate values and beliefs. Given the mission of building a socialist nation, literature was attributed transformational powers and, as such, was required to be 'useful' and, according to the dominant ideology, not damaging to the intellectual and moral development of young readers and the evolution of the new society.

From foreign-language literature, the majority of English-language books for young people available in the global market for translation originated from capitalist societies and, thus, represented concepts not welcome in the GDR. Translated books, including English-language books, had the task of supplying readers with the appropriate 'correct' insights. It is therefore hardly surprising that the regime reacted to Otherness by applying a filter and carefully categorised thought concepts into those which were to be neglected, overlooked or removed, and those to be embraced and allowed in. Given that literature produced in capitalist societies contained much that was unacceptable to the development of citizens in a socialist state, much of it was rejected out of hand and books that were accepted were 'reinterpreted' for the socialist reader. When East German children's book publisher Holz stated that "a book can only be called good, if the young audience finds in it elements that they know, and if they can also find in it very much more that they have not known of, yet that they ought to learn about" (as quoted in Holland 2000:98), this appears to describe a situation which was the antithesis of East German society, in that unknown and unacceptable concepts were deliberately excluded, allowing children only a limited view of the West. Clear evidence of rationalisation and justification for all traces of Otherness not in line with the ideologically accepted picture of the world has been provided in Chapters 3, 4 and 5, which are concerned with the publishers' discourse in the print permit files and the content of afterwords found in the children's books published.

Drawing on Lefevere's theory of rewriting and patronage, rewriting in the East German context manifested itself most strongly in the selection of ideologically suitable texts leading to the creation of a socialist literary canon; an indication of this practice is, for example, given by the careful choice of contributions for anthologies. The most visible form of rewriting took the form of text modifications, which were performed on the manuscripts during the translation process; hence, for example, in their evaluations, publishers voiced the need to eliminate certain concepts from the chosen texts, such as religious or violent references. Also, more subtle forms of rewriting took place whereby texts were re-interpreted by attributing new, socialist meaning to a given foreign source text. This practice was identified both in the discourse of the print permit files and, also, in the afterwords which were included in a large number of translated children's and juvenile books. All these forms of rewriting served to adapt foreign literature to the East German dominant literary system. However, as has also been revealed, rewriting (and here, in particular, the practice of interpreting texts through the use of Marxist-Leninist concepts in both the print permit files and the afterwords) had another function to fulfil, namely self-protection. Indeed, one ought to bear in mind that publisher and censor, with their signature on the application for a print permit or, respectively, on the print permit itself, were made accountable in person for the 'quality' of a text and, in the case of an ideologically 'incorrect' choice of book, could be reprimanded. Hence, these re-interpretations also served as a safeguard to those people who were responsible for the selection and production of a book.

Given the findings of this study, the claim by East German officials that they took children really seriously and treated them as adults is at best a misrepresentation. In fact, the findings in the analysis of publishers' discourse and the afterwords to translated texts give evidence of a situation in which children were not entrusted with the whole truth but had to make do with a segment of the world that the state allowed them to experience. One may, however, come to the conclusion that children were, in a way, treated like adults, however, in a sense different from the officially conveyed statement; that is, they were disenfranchised in a similar way to adults. Adult and children's literature alike had the purpose of socialising readers and integrating them into a model socialist state. In this endeavour, readers, grown-up or growing up, were patronised by what was passed on to them. The fact that all literature had a purpose to fulfil has been shown by the comparison of developments in adult and children's literature, which brought to light remarkable similarities between these two literary systems, revealing attempts by the establishment to influence and direct both systems and, indeed by aligning them with the official Party politics, turning them into a vehicle of nation-building. This explains why indigenous children's books took centre stage and why translated English-language books existed rather at the fringes of the literary system. It also accounts for the unusually high status of literature for children and adolescents in the GDR in general, a status unheard of in modern Western societies. The pedagogical importance in children's fiction is also shown by the fact that a considerable quantity of translated children's and juvenile fiction was given an afterword. This is a further indicator of the lengths taken to tell readers directly how to read and interpret the contents of a book.

This vision of a literature with a mission, located within a dogmatic, autocratic society, points to a situation where institutions associated with literary production were not free in their decision-making. Close investigation of archival documentation and interviews with *Zeitzeugen* (contemporaries) from the East German publishing industry have unearthed the constraints imposed on publishing houses, regardless of whether a publisher was concerned with the production of literature for adults or, indeed, for children and adolescents. Not only did publishers have to deal with a censoring authority, placed above them by the regime, which vetted all the potential book projects for their ideological and moral suitability for young readers; they also had to cope with mechanisms of 'indirect' censorship in the guise of daily struggles with resources, such as paper and print facilities, and, even more important for translated literature, foreign currency. Authorities like the *Büro für Urheberrechte* observed and guided every action and decided on a 'suitable' distribution of the available resources. These procedures have provided remarkable insights into the power relations prevailing in the East German publishing industry. Hence, publishers hoping to bring out a translation from English frequently had frustrating battles on both the ideological and on the economic fronts. The findings described earlier and fully discussed in Chapter 2 substantiate the main element of this study, i.e. the tangible effects of ideology on the production of children's literature.

The special role of East German publishers as mediators in book production is apparent. Situated between the state (as the representative of the Party) and the readers, it was publishers who had to decide on particular books and on 'marketing' them to the censor. In this process, the print permit files have shown the publishers' responsibility as advocates for their chosen projects. In an examination of the various strategies adopted by publishers to promote their chosen books, their endeavour to publish English-language literature has come to light. This can be seen, for instance, in their careful choice of assessors who would expediently express support for the production of a title; it is, however, also visible in the carefully selected words and phrases used in the publishers' and assessors' submissions to the censors, which was demonstrated to be firmly rooted in the socially accepted ideology. Here, a clear tendency to appropriate texts for East German culture has been revealed. In their role as critics, as it were, publishers reviewed foreign texts from a socialist standpoint. Any analogies between indigenous literature and poetological elements in the foreign texts served as a mechanism to assimilate the Otherness such that it became acceptable. The moral qualities and/or political stances of foreign authors aided in aligning them with authors of the indigenous canon. Notably with translations, this mediating position was vital. Unlike indigenous literature written by East German authors who, if required, had to defend the ideological content of their works in person and, on some occasions, were even called before the censor to be persuaded to make changes to their texts, English-language texts had generally been written abroad and publishers alone were responsible for their choice and their presentation to the censor. In the same way that authors would self-censor their writing in order to get it past the censor, publishers weighed all aspects, both favourable and unfavourable, before making a decision for or against a translation.

The fact that publishers exercised self-censorship is clearly demonstrated by various factors; for example, the discourse in the print permit files indicates that publications with a socialist concept were favoured, and typically 'bourgeois' titles that one might find in middle-class, Western households were frowned upon and not published, books such as *Little Women*, *Little Lord Fauntleroy*, *Mary Poppins*, *Peter Pan*, *The Famous Five* or *Charlie and the Chocolate Factory*; similarly, the print permit files provide evidence that only one book was denied a print permit, which supports the argument that a thoughtful and shrewd choice of books had taken place. From this it can be seen that, despite their efforts and best intentions, publishers were a product of their environment. Society had conferred on them a duty, a *gesellschaftlicher Auftrag* (social mission), by assigning them the role of educators and ideologues who were to make it their task to influence the formation of a socialist consciousness in their readers and, thereby, transform them into worthy members of a future communist society. In this sense, the Party can be viewed as the benefactors and the publishers as the agents of the Party.

This leads on to the notion of patronage. Lefevere directs attention to the forces behind literary power in societies and he distinguishes control over literary output as wielded by those inside and outside the literary system, where the common Western viewpoint is that publishers are on the outside. With respect to the situation in the GDR, however, publishers and editors have been identified as acting from within the literary system, putting into practice the directives issued from a higher authority, i.e. the Party and its representatives. Because of this framework, a re-assignment of the forces has been suggested in this study whereby publishers have been located on the inside having to accept and work under the system of patronage provided by the Party. Acting as agents of a far-reaching process of selection and adaptation, yet under the strictures of the East German social and literary system, publishers have been defined as 'rewriters of literature'. As such, they were in a place of influencing the literary canon by selecting and rejecting certain themes and certain books. In contrast, those people performing the direct work with the individual manuscripts, i.e. the translators, have been defined as 'rewriters of texts', which means that the process of rewriting entailed two phases, both, however, in alignment with the socially prescribed parameters.

On the whole, the East German set-up has implications for the roles attributed to all players in East German children's literature. Whereas in modern pluralist societies it is, normally, the publishers who have exclusive power over their publishing decisions and, more often than not, it is adults in an authoritative position such as parents or teachers who decide which books to pass on to children, it would appear that roles in the GDR were assigned in a different way. It seems safe to maintain that it was the Party and its functionaries who exercised power over ideological and political matters and that their policies led to specific measures being adopted by the publishers to work within this environment. Publishers, although in a position to make choices albeit within strict boundaries, were made to comply with the paradigms dictated by the Party. This demonstrates clearly a shift in power from the individual enterprise to the central authority. Moreover, while in Western societies, in general, adults tend to be in a position to make empowered decisions, this was lost in the GDR. Teachers and parents found themselves in a place of powerlessness, a place where only restricted decisions were possible in the selection of literature for children. After the regime had pronounced the kind of texts it wished to see in the country, after publishers had searched the market for texts that would be deemed appropriate, and after the censoring authority had overseen the text and validated it by granting a print permit—only then were approved books allowed on the shelves of the bookshops. There, however, it was again inequality that came to the fore, since books that were in great demand (such as translations from Western countries) were not sold over the counter but as *Bückware*, under the counter, ending up in the shopping baskets of privileged customers.

What has been demonstrated is that there is corroborating evidence of an extensive censorship system in place in the entire East German book production. This was, however, a kind of censorship that was multi-faceted and by no means limited to only textual changes. Rather, censorship consisted of a string of manipulative measures resulting in the effective rewriting of foreign literature and which, in short, may be broken down into three steps. Firstly, thematically suitable and economically affordable texts were selected; secondly, if necessary, reductions on the linguistic, stylistic and semantic level were applied; and thirdly, an attempt was made to exert further influence on the readers by instructing them, in an afterword, how to read and understand the story. Of these measures, it has been shown that the selection of books was the principal criterion, and the publishers' willingness to pre-censor and choose suitable books represented an integral part of the process. Because of its closeness to political matters, all literary output for children and adolescents was affected by Party politics and state ideology. Further, since the

Party did not trust publishers sufficiently to conform to the principles postulated, institutions were established to ensure close convergence, all of which put severe pressure on publishing houses, leading them to adopt careful and orthodox behaviour in their production of children's texts.

Looking beyond the results of this study, the previous discussion raises the question of whether the study's findings can only be applied to the situation in East Germany and, thus, remain restricted to a unique historical situation, or whether they have wider implications and may assist future studies that dedicate themselves to investigations of censorship, control and suppression of opinions. Without doubt, this research sheds light on wilful acts of power by the East German regime. However, attention ought to be drawn to the fact that the processes exposed by this study are not necessarily limited to socialist East Germany or other totalitarian states, but may be extrapolated to all societies (see Thomson-Wohlgemuth 2005). Given that all societies wish to uphold and pass on their values and standards to young readers, protective mechanisms have been installed to implement corresponding measures under different guises ever since the creation of a literature specially written for and addressed to children. Claiming that it is done 'for the best', publishers have always—to varying degrees—censored their manuscripts and parents have always considered their choice of books for their children. For example, concepts such as violence or depiction of scenes of a sexual nature caused problems a hundred years ago as much as they do today. Thus, even in contemporary 'enlightened' cultures there are rules governing what may and may not be published and not every source text finds itself readily accepted in the target culture. This then raises questions about the meaning of censorship in this context. Can one, for instance, call it censorship, when certain concepts in modern pluralist societies are omitted due to an over-emphasis on political correctness? Or is it censorship when the GDR, in an endeavour to raise educational levels, would not let 'trash' literature into the country? What forms does censorship take, and is there a moral border between acceptable omissions and unacceptable ones? And who is to judge, ultimately, what is acceptable? Undeniably, the basic structures in book production are similar, regardless of East, West or other modern societal forms. Where they differ, however, is in their underlying motivation. Pluralist societies operate on the principle of self-determination within a free market structure. According to the principles of this economic structure, the prime motive of an enterprise is, in most cases, profit. For publishing houses, this implies the need to sell as many books as possible to achieve maximum revenue. This often leads to the production of any kind of literature, as long as it sells, with the necessity of having to appeal to the masses with its corresponding drawbacks. What took place under centralised control in East Germany could, at its best, be described as over-interference and over-protection by the state, driven by the intention to raise standards and transform children into better citizens; a policy that brought about elevated importance of the children's literary system and the high visibility and status of literary translators in East German society.

In other words, Western (or contemporary) publishers tend to base their selection on what creates sales, either by choosing literature that appeals to adults (by omission of controversial concepts) or to children (who may choose low-brow literature). Apart from the financial motivation, their judgement is governed by the norms for, or the ideologies of, the society in which they operate. However, as opposed to the GDR's autocratic society, in Western societies there is freedom to interpret these norms as needed within each publishing house. As a consequence, each publisher's interpretation is hinged only on what they personally deem 'socially acceptable to the wider society' as subject matter for children's books, bearing in mind the conventions of the time when the translation is carried out or the book is produced; thus, their judgements are 'society-driven' with the general population constituting the society. On the other hand, the *status quo* in the GDR was directed by a central power. Choice of books occurred in alignment with Party ideology and no other subjective view was permitted. Thus, publishers' decisions were rooted in what they believed was 'socially acceptable to the Party', since the Party represented the society. Consequently, it can be said that a level of freedom to make choices was completely removed in East Germany, a fact further underlined by the existence of an official censoring body implanted in society whose task it was to monitor and control. It may therefore be argued that, while all societies censor information, censorship is manifested in varying degrees, ranging from loose instances made on a personal subjective level to those being rigidly performed by a central authority in conformance with political prescriptions laid upon it. Whichever stance is taken on the meaning of censorship, it has been shown that the wider social context has a direct effect on the literary production of a society. This research points to ideology and socio-cultural norms as key factors in the determination of what and how literature is produced. The policy-makers, the patrons of literature, whether it is governments or publishers, determine the ideology that shapes the literature available at any given period in history. It is with the patrons that important decisions are made about knowledge and information that is (allowed to be) passed on in texts for young people and, in a wider sense, about educational values and norms governing a society.

Notes

Introduction

1. German language has the term *Kinder- und Jugendliteratur*, which makes it possible to differentiate between literature for younger readers and for older ones, adolescents. Although American English has coined the term 'juvenile literature', or more recently young adult literature, on the whole, it tends not to make a difference between books for children and adolescents and simply uses 'children's literature' to cover both sectors. This study follows the English tradition, employing 'children's literature' to cover all books for a younger audience, unless specifically stated otherwise.
2. History with a capital 'H' is taken to refer here to the Marxist definition of a Historical timeline, according to which all societies—each at their own pace—develop and progress and end up as a communist community.
3. All quotes from German source material have been translated by me here and throughout the study in order to allow for more fluent reading.

Chapter 1

1. The concept of Positive heroes was taken very seriously (see e.g. Branstner 1959:226, 227). Vexed questions were, for instance, whether a Positive hero was allowed to have shortcomings at all, and if so, what was the right mixture and amount? While the ideal Positive hero without any shortcomings was dismissed by some, as this created flat, boring books without any conflicts, others again contended that conflicts were a sign of weakness which created the wrong image of a hero and of a socialist personality. In their opinion, Positive heroes had to be ideal in all cases. Because of the danger, however, of creating the same type

of personality without any shortcomings again and again and, therefore, to bore the readers, their solution was to create ideal heroes who distinguished themselves from each other by their virtues. Another issue, vehemently debated, was the question of what, at some stage, authors would write about, once their readership had identified with the Positive heroes and had called into life the ideal socialist society without any conflicts.

2. The article *Kann man eigentlich über alles schreiben?* (Is one actually allowed to write about any topic?) by Christa Wolf, then a conformist author, reveals how partisanship distorted the concepts of reality and truth. In her position as the editor of the journal *Neue deutsche Literatur*, Wolf received many articles about truthful, yet pessimistic portrayals of everyday life; however, Wolf categorically denied the truth in what these people wrote about, claiming "They only believe it is the truth." On this basis, she stated that such articles could not be published, "because it is dangerous to disseminate half truths or even lies", and the only solution she saw was that the authors of such texts needed to be "helped" to understand their misconception (1958:3–16).
3. The official definition of Formalism was that the decisive significance lies in the 'form' and not in the content and the idea of the piece of art. "In all instances where form prevails over content, art loses its humanist and democratic character" (Zentralkomitee der SED, 1951, in Schubbe 1972:179). It becomes apparent that such art was in the way of, or even contradicted, the principle of realistic and true-to-life description which could be easily understood by the readers as part of their daily lives.
4. As opposed to construction literature, in which the decision of the protagonist for socialism happened automatically without much portrayal of the protagonist's convictions, novels of arrival no longer portrayed the choice of socialism as an automatic process, but as one with conflicts and diversions. Novels of arrival, however, no longer require manifest literary explanations of socialism, as its moral superiority over other social systems has already become self-evident.
5. Arkadij Gajdar, author of the cult book *Timur und sein Trupp* (*Timur and His Troop*), which was absorbed into the GDR culture as a model of socialist behaviour, celebrating the idea of patriotic battle. The boy Timur became the prototype for socially active and brave heroes. The name Timur was used by the GDR Young Pioneer movement in the *Timurhilfe* (young children who volunteered for social work).
6. This tale served to prove that anti-Semitism functioned as an outlet for the Germans; hatred, anger and indignation felt against the ruling classes dared not be expressed against them because they were merciless and well protected; however, Jews acted as the scapegoats for feelings

of revenge which were, in fact, engendered by the ruling classes (Zweig 1948:59).

7. Volkseigener Betrieb—nationally owned factory.
8. Originally called NÖS (New Economic System), it was later re-named to ÖSS (Economic System of Socialism), hinting at greater closeness to the state ideology.
9. *Das Hölzerne Pferd*, 1968, Franz Fühmann, Neues Leben.
10. *Prometheus—die Titanenschlacht*, 1974, Franz Fühmann, Kinderbuchverlag.
11. *Nibelungenlied*, 1971, Franz Fühmann, Neues Leben.
12. Erich Honecker had been involved in youth matters since the 1940s; he had, for instance, been the co-founder of the state publishing house for adolescents Neues Leben in 1946. Honecker's wife Margot had played a role in East German politics since 1963, when she became Minister for Education.
13. According to Emmerich, shortly before the country's demise, productivity lay at 30–40% of the productivity of its Western counterpart (1996:245).
14. Wolf Biermann: lyric poet and songwriter, one of the country's most vocal critics of internal policy; because of his frequent criticism of the system, in 1965, he was banned from performing and publishing his songs; isolation and Stasi observation followed in order to silence him; in 1976, he was expatriated after a concert tour in West Germany, although he had been guaranteed re-entry to the GDR (Groth 1994:280).
15. Although officially abolished, censorship indirectly remained in that publishers were declared to be responsible from now on for their output, which led either to confusion amongst publishers or to feelings of uncertainty or discomfort, because they now bore the sole responsibility for their decisions and could no longer fall back on the censor's approval.
16. For instance, in earlier years, a picture book parrot, sitting in his cage, had been forbidden to say "Let me out"—the allusion to the GDR as a cage with a locked door had apparently been too obvious and too dangerous for the censors. In 1978, however, a children's poem with a similar topic did pass the censor:

    A cage/water bowl/feed bowl

    A better cage/water bowl/feed bowl/swing

    The best cage/an open door (Peltsch 1990a:14).

17. This is a way of writing which uses language rich in innuendo and allusion, in order to conceal the real meaning; hence, outsiders would read what seems to be a harmless, innocuous text, which, however, holds a covert meaning to informed members of society.

18. This definition has been taken from the *Oxford Companion to Children's Literature*, which states that adventure stories descend directly from Robinson Crusoe, a book that has been imitated by authors like Captain Marryat (Carpenter and Prichard 1999:6–8).

Chapter 2

1. Hans Modrow was chosen as prime minister of the GDR on 13 November 1989.
2. *Hauptverwaltung Verlage und Buchhandel*, which was the main institution in the Culture Ministry responsible for matters of book publishing and book censorship.
3. An exception to this rule was three publishers who did not make profits; these were Akademieverlag (publications by various scientific institutions in the GDR), VEB Domowina-Verlag Bautzen (publishing house for the Sorbian minority, living in Saxony and Brandenburg) and VEB Fotokinoverlag Leipzig (literature in the fields of photography and film) (Karlheinz Selle, personal communication, 1 November 2004).
4. *Vereinigung organisationseigener Betriebe*; merger of enterprises owned by a mass organisation.
5. VOB Zentrag, in fact, had not only the function to administer all printing but in general all Party-owned enterprises. Amongst these were also several publishing houses; e.g. Kinderbuchverlag, Neues Leben and, from 1979, Altberliner Verlag (Walther 1999:45). It is this complicated interconnection between enterprises owned by a mass organisation (i.e. VOB) and the Party that sometimes causes confusion as to the ownership of Kinderbuchverlag and Neues Leben.
6. Literature differs about the exact administration of the thematic plans. Some have it that they were submitted to the HV in June/July at the latest (e.g. Löffler 2002:30); others speak of trickles of proposals for projects planned which all were registered and stored in the HV on index cards, with relevant information about the general nature of the book and, once a year's worth of dossiers and index cards had accumulated, the office itself began to prepare the plan according to the publishers' project applications (Darnton 1990:7).
7. It was up to the publishers to agree with printers on date and details of printing, as long as they remained within the framework stipulated by their plans authorised by the HV. Also, as all printers were under direct control of the SED (Zentrag), there was no danger of publishers going astray.
8. According to Barck et al., literary advisory boards were founded as early as 1954 but renamed in 1958 (1998:43).

9. *Welturheberrechtsabkommen*; 24 July 1971 revised agreement, i.e. *Pariser Verbandsübereinkunft* (Paris Agreement).
10. WIPO, aka OMPI (*Organisation Mondiale pour la Propriété Intellectuelle*), aka *Weltorganisation für geistiges Eigentum*.
11. Disregarding the period of the Third Reich, the GDR took the stand that they were the legal successor to the copyright agreements signed by Germany in the 1920s, concerning the part of Germany under their sovereignty. This viewpoint was confirmed by the Council of Ministers of the GDR on 16 April 1959. Heinz Püschel, GDR professor for copyright law at the Berlin Humboldt-University, explained that this announcement had only had declarative character and that these multilateral agreements, as a matter of fact, had never been out of force (1982:34; and an opinion which he also confirmed to me in an interview in July 2002). Similarly, one year earlier in 1958, Anselm Glücksmann, director of the BfU, argued that "the Berne Convention had applied without interruption and the governmental declaration only symbolised its willingness to participate, which had been interrupted through war and capitulation" (1958:313). To what extent East Germany lived up to its obligation to acknowledge foreign copyright before these two declarations cannot be judged here. However, after 1955, and certainly after 1959, it can be assumed that rights were traded according to these multilateral agreements. Therefore, it can be further presumed that after 1961, the date of the erection of the Berlin Wall, protection of domestic and also foreign authors was most certainly recognised. (While recognising author's copyright on the one hand, the GDR frequently attempted, with success, to avoid paying the full royalties and save money in book publishing, by signing licence contracts for a certain number of copies of books but then printing many more copies than stipulated contractually. Although neither Kinderbuchverlag nor Neues Leben so far have been found to follow such a strategy, several prestigious publishing houses for mainstream literature were involved in what is called "Plusauflagen" [see e.g. Faber 1991 or 1995]).
12. The Berne Convention was revised and updated three times during the existence of the GDR: 26 June 1948 Brussels version; 14 July 1967 Stockholm version; 24 July 1971 Paris version.
13. In 1982, the Berne Convention covered the whole of Europe (with the exception of Albania) and several states in Africa, Asia and South and Middle America; but more importantly for this study also Australia, New Zealand, Canada and India (Püschel 1982:44, 45), thus the main territory of the old British Empire. It should be noted that the USA were not a member to the Berne Convention but were only linked to copyright law by their membership to the World Convention for the Protection of Copyright (Kaemmel 1956:126–132; Glücksmann et al. 1966:58; Püschel 1975:99, 317; Püschel 1982:33).

14. As the administrator of the state's foreign currency plan, the BfU held the amount of *Ostwährung* and *Westwährung* that had been granted and allocated to every publisher. Simultaneously, a foreign currency plan (*Valutaplan*) was drawn up annually by the accountancy department in the HV with respect to the foreign currency expected to come in and go out. Subsequently, this plan was co-ordinated with the Finance Ministry/Sector Culture, since it was incumbent on the Finance Ministry to organise the national budget and to administer income and expenditure of foreign currency (the actual banknotes, however, were kept in the *Deutsche Notenbank*). Finally, this plan was synchronised with the BfU, which had been made responsible for the administration of the foreign currency plan, acting as the control authority over the foreign currency allocation in all publishing deals.
15. *Winnie-the-Pooh* did get a print permit and was published in 1960.
16. Three supplements to this *Index librorum prohibitorum* were issued: on 1 January 1947, on 1 September 1948 and on 1 April 1952. With 35,000 items, this represented the most comprehensive blacklist in Germany (Mix 1999:118, 119).
17. Amongst the six publishers for children and adolescents he lists: Altberliner Verlag Lucie Groszer, Alfred Holz Verlag, Kinderbuchverlag, Gebrüder Knabe Verlag, Prisma Verlag, Verlag Neues Leben (what has to be pointed out is that, by this time, the publishing house 'Alfred Holz Verlag' no longer existed as a publisher in his own right but had been fully taken under the wing of Kinderbuchverlag, following Holz's death on 28 September 1974; also, it is not clear in how far Prisma published children's books as, in the 1985 publication by Börsenverein der Deutschen Buchhändler *Die Verlage der Deutschen Demokratischen Republik* (1985:51), this publisher was classified as producing popular science literature in the fields of archaeology, cultural history and art).
18. Amongst the seven other children's book publishers, Doderer has: Rudolf Arnold Verlag, Helingsche Verlagsanstalt, Postreiter Verlag, Dr. Herbert Schulze Buch- und Kunstverlag, Verlag Abel & Müller, Verlag Rudolf Forkel, Verlag Karl Nitzsche, the majority of which experienced closure of their businesses in the ensuing years.
19. All production of licenced publishers needed a print permit by the HV. However, all print products by state institutions, regional Party authorities, mass organisations or for personal need, e.g. catalogues, forms, entrance tickets, diaries, calendars, paper for letters or notes, etc. required a print permit by a regional authority; this print permit only depended on paper and print capacity available (Gesetzblatt der Deutschen Demokratischen Republik 1959/1988:73, 74).
20. Cadres were people in a position in which they were responsible for a collective. They were to stand out through high technical knowledge

in their field, through loyalty to the working class, through consistent fulfilment of Party resolutions and exemplary behaviour in conducting their lives (Jegensdorf 1980:25).

21. Variations of these proportions were found, 30% at contract conclusion and 70% at acceptance; or 35–65%; or 40–60%; or even 50–50%.
22. One rather curious incident may be accounted for by the immense demand for Western and especially American literature in the East German society: in the late 1980s, two native authors (Hans Bräunlich and Hans-Ulrich Lüdemann) thought up the idea of using parts of their names to create an English pseudonym, John U. Brownman, and to write Western-style crime stories located in various American cities. As Hans-Ulrich Lüdemann described (personal communication, 8 September 2001), this idea had been motivated purely by economic reasons and it had been supported by Kinderbuchverlag, the publishing house of this series. The fall of the Wall and the subsequent re-organisation of the East German publishing industry had put an end to this project, yet the chosen name had proven so successful that John U. Brownman was still mistaken for a genuine English author and received post by fans.
23. The word *Bückware* explains the fact that those goods in great demand were normally hidden away, out of sight of the other customers, under the counter and the shop owner had to bend down (i.e. *bücken*) to pick them up.

Chapter 3

1. Lefevere defines the codification of literature in a system as 'poetics' which, he claims, consists of two components: one is an inventory of literary devices, genres, motifs, symbols, prototypical characters and situations; the other is a concept of what the role of literature is, or should be, in society at large. Also, according to Lefevere, a pluralistic society has various strands of poetics, which are in competition with each other (1985b:229).
2. In two of his earlier articles, Lefevere referred to this concept as refraction (see 1982a, 1982b) and in a paper written in 1991 as repackaging (see 1991); the underlying idea, however, is the same, namely that literature is adapted to fit certain ideological and poetological constraints.
3. Attention is drawn to the fact that publishers and editors are used in this chapter synonymously. This is done for the reason that editors acted on behalf of the publishers. They frequently suggested possible projects; they worked with the translators to produce the final version; they wrote the assessments to be submitted to the censors and, hence, were responsible for acceptance or rejection of a book, and they signed their assessments

with their names on the application form; at the same time, publishers countersigned the applications and, thus, guaranteed with their name the correctness and quality of contents.

4. It seemed practical not to include in this figure those motifs which have a negative counterpart, as they represent the antonym and can be found there. So, e.g. 'antifascism', a motif with clearly positive connotations, stands vis-à-vis its antonym 'fascism', which can be found in the list of negative motifs.
5. Another category of authors who were taboo for publication were those who had gone into the West (*Republikflüchtige*). Admittedly, this is not of so much interest for English-language literature; it is mentioned here only as it concerned translated literature in the shape of translators and illustrators. Thus, in 1967, the re-edition of *Der Brahmane, der Tiger und der Schakal* was completely retranslated by a new translator, since the translator of the first edition had "illegally left our Republic" and her name could no longer appear in the colophon (DR1/2254); equally, for the re-edition of *Mora* for the year 1963, the publisher had to commission new illustrations, as the illustrator of the first edition had left the country in 1961 (DR1/3940).
6. "A quadroon commonly refers to a person with three European or white grandparents and one African grandparent. This term is now considered obsolete and is no longer in general use . . .; it was part of a race classification used primarily in the Southern United States in the 19th century" (<http://en.wikipedia.org/wiki/Quadroon> visited 27 March 2006).
7. To complete the publishing history of this publication, the file shows that the manuscript arrived at the censorship authority on 25 August 1966 (Kinderbuchverlag's evaluation in which the publisher responded to several areas of criticism was dated 9 September 1964). In order to safeguard his position, the censor commissioned an assessor to give his opinion on the book; this evaluation, dated 16 September 1966, argued for a publication on grounds of authentic and human descriptions in the book and contemporariness and connection with present-day America. After receiving this assessment, a print permit was granted on 26 September 1966, and the book was published in 1967.
8. Lefevere describes the rewriting of Büchner's play as performed by two rewriters at two different points in time, leading to publications in 1835 and 1916, respectively. While the earlier resorted to deletions and alterations, in order to make the work palatable to the political powers of his day, the latter one had the intention of making the play stageable, driven by the belief that, otherwise, the concepts and historical references of Büchner's original would no longer have been understood by the audience of the early twentieth century. Despite the two different underlying motivations, both rewriters acted in the endeavour to adapt

Büchner's manuscript to the contemporary requirements, achieving a change not only of the superficial wording but of the principal meaning (1992:150–160).

9. Born in Berlin, emigrated to Australia in 1939 but returned to Germany and settled in the GDR. He wrote some of his books in English, thus producing works that needed to be translated.
10. Interestingly, the story was published sixteen years later, in 1982, in another compilation of short stories by Walter Kaufmann, *Kauf mir doch ein Krokodil*, Edition Holz im Kinderbuchverlag. However, that was a time when attitudes had changed considerably; not only in the GDR but Germany-wide the atmosphere had relaxed regarding values in child-rearing; and, equally importantly, East German censorship was not as rigid.
11. The story describes an incident where a girl joins a group of twelve-year-old boys and has to pass a simple initiation test where she has to go into a dark cupboard for five minutes. She asks one of the boys to come with her. In the cupboard she kisses the boy and the others hear a noise and open the cupboard, spoiling the initiation for the girl.
12. "In the Vietnam War, a massacre of Vietnamese civilians by U.S. soldiers. On Mar. 16, 1968, a unit of the U.S. army Americal division, led by Lt. William L. Calley, invaded the South Vietnamese hamlet of My Lai (more correctly, Son My), an alleged Viet Cong stronghold. In the course of combat operations, unarmed civilians, including women and children, were shot to death (the final army estimate for the number killed was 347)" (<http://www.infoplease.com/ce6/history/A0834642.html> visited 5 November 2006).

Chapter 4

1. As Holland (2000:79–83, 105–112) points out, since 1956, the GDR had been trying to nationalise Alfred Holz Verlag, in order to attain economic, legal and ideological influence over the private publisher. In November 1962, a contract was signed which came into effect on 1 January 1963, whereby Holz was partially incorporated into Kinderbuchverlag, by setting up the *Produktionsgruppe Alfred Holz*. It was established that all financial questions were dealt with by Kinderbuchverlag, while Alfred Holz would keep independence in thematic and aesthetic matters, in editing, producing and the export of his books. Only after Holz's death, on 28 September 1974, did Kinderbuchverlag fully take over the small publishing house. The print permit files confirm this arrangement as, until 1974, all applications for a print permit were registered by the publisher under the name 'Alfred Holz Verlag', demonstrating Holz's autonomy in selecting and requesting the publication of his books.

2. "Founded in 1884, the Fabian Society was an intellectual movement concerned with the research, discussion, and publication of socialist ideas" (<http://www.lse.ac.uk/resources/LSEHistory/fabian.htm> visited 3 March 2006).
3. Emphases in the source text.
4. Novel showing the development of a protagonist in a book.
5. What is interesting here is that the original says, "if more of us valued food and cheer and song above hoarded gold, it would be a merrier world" (Tolkien 1981, 4th ed: 270, 271), and one would have expected the East German assessor to take up this opportunity of portraying the bourgeois world as a society of materialistic thinking, yet Petersen lets the opportunity pass. One explanation for this may be that he has produced his assessment from the West German translation (which was in fact underlying the version published in the GDR), and the West German translator had originally omitted this phrase about striving for gold and riches. This suspicion is substantiated at a later stage, when Petersen discusses the doubtful quality of the West German translation.
6. Dahl was first published in 1977 with a publication for adults, i.e. *Lammkeule und andere Geschichten* ("Lamb to the Slaughter and Other Stories" by publisher Volk und Welt; re-issued in 1978, 1983, 1988 and 1989); four more collections of his stories appeared in 1979, 1986 and 1988 (all produced by publisher Volk und Welt and intended for adults).
7. It was not the case that crime novels did not at all exist in the GDR, particularly in indigenous adult literature. Although frowned upon due to its low aesthetic quality, this genre generated large sales. Therefore, because of the profit that could be expected for each production, indigenous crime stories were published, however, with the proviso that they be educational and convergent with the orthodox rhetoric. This discrepancy between ideology and reality was mitigated by one of Marxist-Leninist premises which held that, due to the high moral standard of socialist society, crime was dying out and, in communism, the genre of crime literature would therefore no longer exist (see Hillich 2005).

Chapter 5

1. Occasionally a foreword was produced. These rare forewords are treated in the same manner as afterwords throughout this discussion, as they represent an equivalent paratextual item.
2. In 1953, this was the *Amt für Literatur und Verlagswesen* (Office of Literature and Publishing), i.e. the institution preceding the long-term censoring authority HV, which was in place from 1963 (see Chapter 2).

3. All the elements found inside the confines of a bound volume (Genette 1997:xviii); or to put it differently, the presentational material "that is the direct and principal . . . responsibility of the publisher" (Genette 1997:16).
4. Peritexts, to which afterwords belong, are a subcategory of paratexts; put in Genette's formula, Paratext = Peritext + Epitext (1997:xviii).
5. It may be added that Karl May made it to the bookshelves in the GDR only in the 1980s; the two main reasons for which are problems with copyright and also the desire to do away with "hypocritical Wild West romanticism" (advertisement for a book by Julius Lips in the back of *Der Geist von Cochise*, 1977, Kinderbuchverlag) and to remain factual and realistic.
6. A footnote informed the reader here that these scenes and similar passages had been omitted, constituting one of the rare instances in which translation strategies were mentioned in an afterword.
7. "The 'People's Charter,' drafted in 1838 by William Lovett, was at the heart of a radical campaign for parliamentary reform of the inequities remaining after the Reform Act of 1832" (<http://www.victorianweb.org/history/hist3.html> visited 2 December 2006).
8. This includes English native speakers who married an East German, people who had returned from exile, and people who stayed in the GDR through political belief.
9. Even if the entire production, inclusive of the excluded books, is taken into consideration, the data do not change significantly.
10. From the analysis of the files, it seems clear that a distinction was made between classic and modern literature, hence the choice of these categories to test the theory.

Bibliography

Primary Literature Cited

Adamson Jean and Gareth (1968) *Der Familienbaum* [*Family Tree*] Berlin: Altberliner Lucie Groszer

Adler Ernst (ed) (1966) *Die Legende vom Bumerang. Australische Märchen* Berlin: Holz

Aldridge James (1975) *Der letzte Zoll* Berlin: Neues Leben

Anand Mulk Raj (1960) *Mora* [*Mora. Autobiography of a Little Elephant*] Berlin: Holz

Anand Mulk Raj (1964) *Mora* [*Mora. Autobiography of a Little Elephant*] 2nd edition Berlin: Holz

Anand Mulk Raj (1967) *Der Brahmane, der Tiger und der Schakal* [*from: Indian Fairy Tales and More Indian Fairy Tales*] Berlin: Holz

Anand Mulk Raj (1981) *Der König und der Papagei: Märchen und Volkserzählungen aus dem Pandschab* [*Folk Tales of Punjab*] Berlin: Kinderbuchverlag

Anderson Edith (1962) *Der verlorene Schuh* Berlin: Kinderbuchverlag

Anderson Edith (1978) *Der Klappwald* Berlin: Kinderbuchverlag

Arnold Elliott (1977) *Der Geist von Cochise* [*The Spirit of Cochise*] Berlin: Kinderbuchverlag

Ashley Bernard (1984) *Terry in der Klemme* [*Terry on the Fence*] Berlin: Kinderbuchverlag

Ashley Bernard (1985) *Flucht in die Sonne* [*Break in the Sun*] Berlin: Kinderbuchverlag

Ashley Bernard (1987) *Janey und der Silberne Tänzer* [*Janey*] Berlin: Kinderbuchverlag

Beecher-Stowe Harriet (1968) *Onkel Toms Hütte* (Uncle Tom's Cabin) 12th edition Berlin: Neues Leben

Beecher-Stowe Harriet (1981) *Onkel Toms Hütte* [*Uncle Tom's Cabin*] 16th edition Berlin: Neues Leben

Benson Mary (1974) *Im Augenblick der Stille* [*At the Still Point*] Berlin: Neues Leben

Berger Thomas (1977) *Little Big Man* [*Little Big Man*] Berlin: Neues Leben

Beseler Horst (1970) 'Der Baum'. In Edith George (ed) *Der Baum* Berlin: Kinderbuchverlag, pp 143–196

Brecht Bertolt (1949) *Der verwundete Sokrates* Berlin: Kinderbuchverlag

Brontë Charlotte (1963) *Die Waise von Lowood* [First part of *Jane Eyre*] Berlin: Kinderbuchverlag

Caldwell Erskine (1968) *Molly Baumwollschwänzchen* [*Molly Cottontail*] Berlin: Kinderbuchverlag

Carroll Lewis (1967) *Alice im Wunderland* [*Alice's Adventures in Wonderland*] Berlin: Holz

Carroll Lewis (1976) *Alice im Spiegelland* [*Through the Looking-Glass*] Berlin: Edition Holz im Kinderbuchverlag

Carroll Lewis (1985) *Alice im Wunderland* [*Alice's Adventures in Wonderland. Through the Looking Glass*] Berlin: Altberliner Lucie Groszer

Carroll Lewis (1987) *Alice im Wunderland und im Spiegelland* [*Alice's Adventures in Wonderland. Through the Looking Glass*] Berlin: Altberliner Lucie Groszer

Chesterton G.K. (1988) *Der geflügelte Dolch. Detektivgeschichten* [*The Dagger with Wings. Detective Stories*] Berlin: Kinderbuchverlag

Chwostenko Lew (1962) *Geschichten vom Bruder Rabbit. Volksmärchen nordamerikanischer Neger* [*from: Brother Rabbit, his Friends and Enemies*] Berlin: Holz

Cooper James Fenimore (1963) *Die Ansiedler* [*The Pioneers, or the Sources of the Susquehanna*] 3rd edition Berlin: Kinderbuchverlag

Cooper James Fenimore (1963) *Die Ansiedler* [*The Pioneers*] Berlin: Neues Leben
Cooper James Fenimore (1966) *Der letzte Mohikaner* [*The Last of the Mohicans*] 4th edition Berlin: Kinderbuchverlag
Corman Avery (1982) *Kramer gegen Kramer* [*Kramer versus Kramer*] Berlin: Neues Leben
Craig David (ed) (1984) *Rapunzel, lass dein Haar herunter. Erzählungen aus Großbritannien* [*Rapunzel Let Down Your Hair. Tales from Great Britain*] Berlin: Neues Leben
Crosby Alexander (1973) *Winchester wacht auf* [*One Day for Peace*] Berlin: Kinderbuchverlag
Dahl Roald (1988) *Hexen hexen* [*The Witches*] Berlin: Kinderbuchverlag
Defoe Daniel (1963) *Robinson Crusoe* [*The Life and Strange Surprising Adventures of Robinson Crusoe*] Berlin: Kinderbuchverlag
Defoe Daniel (1972) *Die späteren Fahrten des Robinson Crusoe zu seiner Insel und rund um die Welt* [*The Farther Adventures of Robinson Crusoe Being the Second and Last Part of His Life, Written by Himself*] Berlin: Neues Leben
Dickens Charles (1970) *Weihnachtsgeschichten* [*The Chimes, A Christmas Carol*] Berlin: Kinderbuchverlag
Dickens Charles (1979) *Große Erwartungen* [*Great Expectations*] 2nd edition Berlin: Neues Leben
Dickens Charles (1982) *Ferienmärchen* [*Holiday Romance*] Berlin: Kinderbuchverlag
Dillon Eilis (1968) *Die Insel des großen John* [*The Coriander*] Berlin: Neues Leben
Dillon Eilis (1977) *Das Haus an der Küste* [*The House on the Shore*] Berlin: Neues Leben
Doyle Arthur Conan (1954) *Der Hund von Baskerville* [*The Hound of the Baskervilles*] Berlin: Das Neue Berlin
Doyle Arthur Conan (1956) *Die verlorene Welt. Abenteuerroman* [*The Lost World*] Berlin: Das Neue Berlin
Doyle Arthur Conan (1982) *Sherlock Holmes—17 Detektivgeschichten* Berlin: Neues Leben
Doyle Arthur Conan (1987) *Fünf Fälle des Sherlock Holmes* Berlin: Kinderbuchverlag
Durian Sibylle (1985) *Der Tag, an dem die Schule verschwand* Berlin: Kinderbuchverlag
Emecheta Buchi (1987) *Adah's Story* [*Second Class Citizen. In the Ditch*] Berlin: Neues Leben
Franck Dorothea (1966) *Die Geschichte vom musikalischen Kater Tobias* [*The Cat Who Loved Bach*] Berlin: Holz
Friskey Margaret (1961) *Der kleine Zweifuß und sein Pferd* [*Indian Two Feet and His Horse*] Berlin: Altberliner Lucie Groszer
Fühmann Franz (1964) *Reineke Fuchs* Berlin: Kinderbuchverlag
Fühmann Franz (1968) Das hölzerne *Pferd*: Die Sage vom Untergang Trojas und von den Irrfahrten des Odysseus Berlin: Neues Leben
Fühmann Franz (1968) *Shakespeare-Märchen, für Kinder erzählt* Berlin: Kinderbuchverlag
Fühmann Franz (1971) *Das Nibelungenlied* Berlin: Neues Leben
Fühmann Franz (1972) *Ein Sommernachtstraum* Berlin: Kinderbuchverlag
Fühmann Franz (1974) *Prometheus: die Titanenschlacht* Berlin: Kinderbuchverlag
Gajdar Arkadij (1950) *Timur und sein Trupp* Berlin: Neues Leben
Gray Nigel (1978) *Der Deserteur* [*The Deserter*] Berlin: Kinderbuchverlag
Gray Nigel (1982) *Schnappschüsse* [*Shots*] Berlin: Kinderbuchverlag
Hacks Peter (1962) *Der Frieden* Berlin: Henschelverlag
Hacks Peter (1975) *Meta Morfoß und Ein Märchen für Claudia Puppe* Berlin: Kinderbuchverlag
Hall Lynn (1983) *Ich setze auf Danza* [*Danza*] Berlin: Neues Leben
Hamilton Virginia (1980) *Der Planet des Patrick Brown* [*The Planet of Patrick Brown*] Berlin: Kinderbuchverlag
Harris Joel Chandler (1964) *Geschichten von Onkel Remus* [*Hours with Uncle Remus*] Berlin: Kinderbuchverlag
Harris Joel Chandler (1984) *Geschichten von Onkel Remus* [*Hours with Uncle Remus*] Berlin: Kinderbuchverlag
Harte Bret (1962) *Allein in der Prärie* [*A Waif of the Plains*] Berlin: Kinderbuchverlag
Hellendahl Margaret (ed) (1967) *Ping Pang Poch* Berlin: Kinderbuchverlag
Hellstrom-Kennedy Marika (1961) *Johnny geht zur Schule* Berlin: Neues Leben
Jerome K. Jerome (1967) *Drei Mann in einem Boot, vom Hunde ganz zu schweigen* [*Three Men in a Boat, to Say Nothing of the Dog*] Berlin: Neues Leben
Kant Uwe (1974) *Der kleine Zauberer und die grosse Fünf* Berlin: Kinderbuchverlag
Kaufmann Walter (1966) *Stefan: Mosaik einer Kindheit* [*Beyond the Green World of Childhood*] Berlin: Holz
Kaufmann Walter (1973) *Das veschwundene Hotel* Berlin: Verlag Junge Welt
Kaufmann Walter (1979) *Irische Reise* Berlin: Kinderbuchverlag

Kaufmann Walter (1982) *Kauf mir doch ein Krokodil. Geschichten* Berlin: Edition Holz im Kinderbuchverlag
Kožik Christa (1980) *Moritz in der Litfaßsäule* Berlin: Kinderbuchverlag
Kožik Christa (1983/1989) *Der Engel mit dem goldenen Schnurrbart* 4th edition, Berlin: Kinderbuchverlag
Kožik Christa (1990) *Kicki und der König* Berlin: Kinderbuchverlag
Krenn Ruth (ed) (1975) *Binsenkappe und andere Märchen und Schwänke aus Großbritannien* Berlin: Kinderbuchverlag
Lewis Reba (1971) *Der Brahmane und das Mädchen* [*The Brahman and the Belle*] Berlin: Neues Leben
Lindgren Astrid (1988) *Ronja, Räubertochter* [*Ronja Robber's Daughter*] Berlin: Kinderbuchverlag
Lofting Hugh (1969) *Doktor Dolittle und seine Tiere* [*The Story of Doctor Dolittle*] Berlin: Holz
Lofting Hugh (1980) *Doktor Dolittle und seine Tiere* [*The Story of Doctor Dolittle*] Berlin: Kinderbuchverlag
London Jack (1968) *Der Seewolf* [*The Sea-Wolf*] Berlin: Neues Leben
London Jack (1973) *Südseeabenteuer* [*Tales from the South Seas*] Berlin: Neues Leben
Marryat Frederick (1969) *Peter Simpel* Vol. 1; Vol. 2; and Vol. 3 [*Peter Simple*] Berlin: Kinderbuchverlag
Marshall Alan (1969) *Ich bin dabei* [*I can jump Puddles*] 3rd edition Berlin: Kinderbuchverlag
Marshall Alan (1973) *Windgeflüster* [*Whispering in the Wind*] Berlin: Kinderbuchverlag
McInerney Jay (1989) *Ein starker Abgang* [*Bright Lights, Big City*] Berlin: Neues Leben
Miller Arthur (1969) *Jannis Deckchen* [*Jane's Blanket*] Berlin: Kinderbuchverlag
Milne A. A. (1960) *Pu der Bär* [*Winnie-the-Pooh*] Berlin: Holz
Moody Anne (1971) *Erwachen in Mississippi* [*Coming of Age in Mississippi*] Berlin: Neues Leben
Ngugi James (1970) *Der Fluß dazwischen* [*The River Between*] Berlin: Neues Leben
Ostrovskij Nikolaj (1947) *Wie der Stahl gehärtet wurde* Berlin: Neues Leben
Petersen Hans (ed) (1978) *Unser weißer Hirsch: Kurzgeschichten aus den USA* Berlin: Kinderbuchverlag
Poe Edgar Allan (1962) *Der Goldkäfer. Eine phantastische Erzählung* [*The Gold Bug*] Weimar: Knabe
Poe Edgar Allan (1979) *Der Goldkäfer und andere phantastische Geschichten* [*The Gold Bug and Other Fantastic Stories*[Berlin: Kinderbuchverlag
Reeves John (ed) (1966) *Märchen aus England* [*English Fables and Fairy Stories*] Berlin: Altberliner Lucie Groszer
Reid Mayne (1967) *Die Quarteronin* [*The Quadroon*] Berlin: Kinderbuchverlag
Reimann Brigitte (1961) *Ankunft im Alltag* Berlin: Neues Leben
Renn Ludwig (1954) *Trini: die Geschichte eines Indianerjungen* Berlin: Kinderbuchverlag
Saalmann Günter (1987) *Umberto* Berlin: Kinderbuchverlag
Satyanarayan Sinha (1966) *Munna und Munni* [*My Playmate-Baby Elephant*] Berlin: Holz
Schmoll Werner (1962) *Mit siebzehn ist man noch kein Held* Halle/Saale: Mitteldeutscher Verlag
Schneider Gerhard (ed) (1962) *Englische Erzähler des 19. Jahrhunderts* Berlin: Neues Leben
Schneider Rolf (ed) (1978) *Das schöne Grauen* Berlin: Neues Leben
Scott Walter (1964) *Quentin Durward* [*Quentin Durward*] Berlin: Neues Leben
Scott Walter (1965) *Ivanhoe* [*Ivanhoe*] Berlin: Neues Leben
Seton Ernest Thompson (1963) *Der Wolf von Winnipeg und andere Tiergeschichten [Animal Heroes]* Berlin: Kinderbuchverlag
Shaw Elizabeth (1975) *Als Robert verschwand* Berlin: Kinderbuchverlag
Sherman Ronald (1971) *Das Tellereisen* [*Old Mali and the Boy*] Berlin: Neues Leben
Singer Isaac Bashevis (1971) *Zlateh die Geiß und andere Geschichten [Zlateh, the Goat and Other Stories*] Berlin: Altberliner Lucie Groszer
Smith Arthur Douglas Howden (1970) *Porto Bello Gold* [*Porto Bello Gold*] Berlin: Kinderbuchverlag
Smollett Tobias (1978) *Die Abenteuer Roderich Randoms* [*The Adventures of Roderick Random*] Berlin: Neues Leben
Spillner Wolf (1984) *Wasseramsel: die Geschichte von Ulla und Winfried* Berlin: Kinderbuchverlag
Spillner Wolf (1987) *Taube Klara* Berlin: Kinderbuchverlag
Stevenson Robert Louis (1965) *Der Pavillon auf den Dünen* [*The Pavilion on the Links*] Weimar: Knabe
Stevenson Robert Louis (1967) *Das Flaschenteufelchen* [*The Bottle Imp*] Weimar: Knabe
Stevenson Robert Louis (1969) *Der schwarze Pfeil: Erzählung aus der Zeit der Rosenkriege in England* [*The Black Arrow—a Tale of the Two Roses*] Berlin: Neues Leben

Stevenson Robert Louis (1969) *Entführt [Kidnapped]* 2nd edition Berlin: Neues Leben
Stevenson Robert Louis (1972) *In der Südsee [from: The Beach of Falesa, The Bottle Imp, The Isle of the Voices, In the South Seas]* Berlin: Neues Leben
Stevenson Robert Louis (1975) *Die verkehrte Kiste [The Wrong Box]* Berlin: Neues Leben
Stone Robert (1979) *Zerrspiegel [A Hall of Mirrors]* Berlin: Neues Leben
Strittmatter Erwin (1954) *Tinko* Berlin: Aufbau-Verlag
Strittmatter Erwin (1954) *Tinko* Berlin: Kinderbuchverlag
Suhl Yuri (1983) *Die Purimziege [The Purim Goat]* Berlin: Kinderbuchverlag
Swarthout Glendon (1974) *Und sie sind nur Kinder [Bless the Beasts and Children]* Berlin: Neues Leben
Tolkien John Ronald R. (1971) *Der kleine Hobbit [The Hobbit or There and Back Again]* Berlin: Kinderbuchverlag
Tolkien, J.R.R. (1981) *The Hobbit or There and Back Again* 4th reprinted edition London: Unwin Paperbacks
Twain Mark (1965) *Tom Sawyer im Ausland [Tom Sawyer Abroad]* Berlin: Neues Leben
Walker Alice (1987) *Die Farbe Lila [The Color Purple]* Berlin: Neues Leben
Wallace Edgar (1987) *Der Fälscher. Der feuerrote Kreis [The Forger. The Crimson Circle]* Berlin: Neues Leben
Wallace Edgar (1988) *Geschichten vom Hexer [Again the Ringer]* Berlin: Kinderbuchverlag
Welskopf-Henrich Liselotte (1951) *Die Söhne der großen Bärin* Berlin: Altberliner Verlag
Wilde Oscar (1959) *Der glückliche Prinz. Märchen [The Happy Prince]* Berlin: Kinderbuchverlag
Wilde Oscar (1987) *Das Bildnis des Dorian Gray [The Picture of Dorian Gray]* Berlin: Neues Leben
Winnington Alan (1969) *Silberhuf [Silver Hooves]* Berlin: Kinderbuchverlag
Winnington Alan (1972) *Silberhuf zieht in den Krieg [Silver Hooves Goes to War]* Berlin: Kinderbuchverlag

Critical Works

Abraham Peter (1990) 'Bücherschreiben unter der Zensur', *Kinder-Bücher-Medien, Perspektiven BRD-DDR-BRDDR. Was bleibt? Was wird?* Vol. 35/36, pp 6–7
Abusch Alexander (1950a) 'Aktuelle Fragen unserer Kulturpolitik'. In Elimar Schubbe (ed) *Dokumente zur Kunst-, Literatur- und Kulturpolitik der SED* Stuttgart: Seewald, pp 140–144
Abusch Alexander (1950b) 'Die Diskussion in der Sowjetliteratur und bei uns'. In Elimar Schubbe (ed) *Dokumente zur Kunst-, Literatur- und Kulturpolitik der SED* Stuttgart: Seewald, pp 144–148
Ackermann Joachim (2000) 'Der SED-Parteiapparat und die Bildende Kunst'. In Hannelore Offner and Klaus Schroeder (eds) *Eingegrenzt-ausgegrenzt: Bildende Kunst und Parteiherrschaft in der DDR 1961–1989* Berlin: Akademie Verlag, pp 15–88
Aijmer Karin and Cecilia Alvstad (eds) (2005) *New Tendencies in Translation Studies*, Selected Papers from a Workshop 12 December 2003, Göteborg University
Alcandre Jean-Jacques (1991) *BRDDR: Von der Wende in der DDR zur Vereinigung Deutschlands* Strasbourg: Presses Universitaires de Strasbourg
Altner Manfred (1972) *Das sozialistische Menschenbild in der Kinder- und Jugendliteratur der Deutschen Demokratischen Republik* Berlin: Kinderbuchverlag
Altner Manfred (ed) (1988) *Das proletarische Kinderbuch. Dokumente zur Geschichte der sozialistischen deutschen Kinder- und Jugendliteratur* Dresden: VEB Verlag der Kunst
Autorenkollektiv (1970) *Weltall Erde Mensch. Ein Sammelwerk zur Entwicklungsgeschichte von Natur und Gesellschaft* Berlin: Neues Leben
Autorenkollektiv unter Leitung von Heinz Püschel (1969) *Urheberrecht der Deutschen Demokratischen Republik* Berlin: Staatsverlag der Deutschen Demokratischen Republik
Autorenkolletiv unter Leitung von Horst Haase und Hans Jürgen Geerdts (1976) *Geschichte der Literatur der Deutschen Demokratischen Republik* Berlin: Volk und Wissen VEB
Bähring Helmut (1962) *Die Absatzabteilung im sozialistischen Verlag* Reihe Verlagsökonomik, Lehrbriefe für das Fachschulfernstudium Leipzig: Fachschule für Buchhändler
Barck Simone and Martina Langermann and Siegfried Lokatis (1998) *Jedes Buch ein Abenteuer: Zensur-System und literarische Öffentlichkeiten in der DDR bis Ende der sechziger Jahre* 2nd edition, Berlin: Akademie Verlag

Barck Simone and Siegfried Lokatis (eds) (2003) *Fenster zur Welt: eine Geschichte des DDR-Verlages Volk & Welt* 1st edition, Berlin: Links

Barck Simone and Siegfried Lokatis (eds) (2005) *Fenster zur Welt: eine Geschichte des DDR-Verlages Volk & Welt* 2nd edition, Berlin: Links

Bassnett Susan and André Lefevere (1990) *Translation, History and Culture* London: Pinter

Bassnett Susan and André Lefevere (1998) *Constructing Cultures. Essays on Literary Translation* Clevedon, Philadelphia: Multilingual Matters

Baumgärtner Alfred (ed) (1993) *Robinson in roten Socken. Kinder- und Jugendbücher in der ehemaligen DDR* Deutsche Akademie für Kinder- und Jugendliteratur

Becher Johannes R. (1953) 'Unsere Kulturpolitik'. In Elimar Schubbe (ed) *Dokumente zur Kunst-, Literatur- und Kulturpolitik der SED* Stuttgart: Seewald, pp 316–320

Becher Johannes R. (1956) 'Von der Größe unserer Literatur'. In Altner M (ed) (1988) *Das proletarische Kinderbuch. Dokumente zur Geschichte der sozialistischen deutschen Kinder- und Jugendliteratur* Dresden: VEB Verlag der Kunst, pp 154–155

Becker Fritz (1962) *Der Absatz im Inland* Reihe Verlagsökonomik, Lehrbriefe für das Fachschulfernstudium Leipzig: Fachschule für Buchhändler

Böhm Ursula (1980) *Der junge Held in der zeitgenössischen erzählenden Kinder- und Jugendliteratur der UdSSR und der DDR* Unpublished doctoral thesis at Pädagogische Hochschule Dresden

Borde Inge (1967) 'Mädchenbücher . . . oder Bücher für Mädchen?', *Neue Deutsche Literatur* Vol. 12, pp 173–180

Börsenverein der Deutschen Buchhändler zu Leipzig (1985) *Die Verlage der Deutschen Demokratischen Republik* Leipzig

Börsenverein der Deutschen Buchhändler zu Leipzig 'Perspektiv-Programm', *Börsenblatt für den Deutschen Buchhandel (Ost)*, Vol. 5, 2. Februar 1965, pp 93–104

Bourdieu, Pierre (1993) *Sociology in Question* London: Sage Publications

Branstner Gerhard (1959) 'Der positive Held und seine Widersacher. Vom Wert einer richtigen Theorie', *Neue Deutsche Literatur* Vol. 9/10, pp 223–227

Brecht Bertolt (1956) 'Der neue Held'. In Klaus Jarmatz (ed) (1970) *Kritik in der Zeit. Der Sozialismus-seine Literatur-ihre Entwicklung* Halle/Saale: Mitteldeutscher Verlag, pp 385–386

Bruyn Günter de (1988) 'Rede zum X. Schriftstellerkongreß der DDR', in *X. Schriftstellerkongreß der DDR, 24.–26. Nov. 1987* Berlin, Weimar: Aufbau-Verlag, pp 128–131

Carpenter Humphrey and Mari Prichard (1999) *The Oxford Companion to Children's Literature* Oxford, New York: OUP

Charbon, Remy (1998) "Auferstanden aus Ruinen und der Zukunft zugewandt. Literatur der sowjetischen Besatzungszone und der Deutschen Demokratischen Republik (1945–1990)". In Walter Lenschen (ed) *Literatur übersetzen in der DDR*, Bern: Lang, pp 163–178

Clauss Roland (1978) *Held oder kollektives Subjekt* Unpublished doctoral thesis at Georg-August-Universität Göttingen

Creutziger Werner (1998) 'Die Zukunft und der Staat. Literaturübersetzer in der DDR'. In Walter Lenschen (ed) *Literatur übersetzen in der DDR* Bern: Lang, pp 13–38

Dahne Gerhard (1991) 'Draußen vor der Tür—nicht von Borchert. Gedanken eines ostdeutschen Verlegers', *Börsenblatt für den Deutschen Buchhandel* Vol. 33, 26. April 1991, pp 1591–1593

Dahrendorf Malte (1995) *Kinder- und Jugendliteratur: Material* Berlin: Volk und Wissen

Darnton Robert (1990) 'Aus der Sicht des Zensors', *Lettre International* Vol. 3(10), pp 6–9

Darnton Robert (1991) *Berlin Journal 1989–1990* New York, London: W.W. Norton & Company

Dietrich Gerd (1983) *Um die Erneuerung der deutschen Kultur. Dokumente zur Kulturpolitik 1945–1949: Dokumente zur Kulturpolitik 1945–1949* Berlin: Dietz

Dimitru, Rodica (2006) 'From Robinson Crusoe to Robinson in Wallachia: The Intricacies of the Reception Process'. In Anthony Pym, Miriam Shlesinger and Zuzana Jettmarová (eds) *Sociocultural Aspects of Translating and Interpreting* Amsterdam, Philadelphia: John Benjamins, pp 73–82

Doderer Klaus (1975) *Lexikon der Kinder- und Jugendliteratur* Weinheim: Beltz/Verlag Dokumentation

Doderer Klaus (1993) *Jugendliteratur zwischen Trümmern und Wohlstand. 1945–1960* Weinheim, Basel: Beltz

Dolle-Weinkauff Bernd and Hans-Heino Ewers (eds) (1996) *Theorien der Jugendlektüre: Beiträge zur Kinder- und Jugendliteraturkritik seit Heinrich Wolgast* Weinheim, München: Juventa

Drewes Uwe (1985) 'Die Jugendpolitik der SED bei der Gestaltung der entwickelten sozialistischen Gesellschaft in der DDR (1961–1981)'. In Stiftung Archiv der Parteien und

Massenorganisationen der DDR im Bundesarchiv, Bibliothek (1985) *Zur Geschichte der Jugendpolitik der SED*, pp 1–85
Eagleton Terry (1996) *Literary Theory. An Introduction* 2nd edition, Oxford & Cambridge: Blackwell
Ebert Günter (1976) *Ansichten zur Entwicklung der epischen Kinder- und Jugendliteratur in der DDR von 1945 bis 1975* Berlin: Kinderbuchverlag
Emmerich Wolfgang (1996) *Kleine Literaturgeschichte der DDR* Erweiterte Neuausgabe. Leipzig: Kiepenheuer
Emmrich Christian (1979) *Literatur für Kinder und Jugendliche in der DDR* Berlin: Kinderbuchverlag
Emmrich Christian (1987) *Literatur und Medienkünste für junge Leute* Berlin: Kinderbuchverlag
Emmrich Christian and Manfred Altner and Heinz Arnold (1971) 'Grundpositionen sozialistischer Kinder- und Jugendliteratur', *Weimarer Beiträge* Vol. 6, pp 72–93
Ewers Hans-Heino (2000) *Literatur für Kinder und Jugendliche. Eine Einführung in grundlegende Aspekte des Handlungs- und Symbolsystems Kinder- und Jugendliteratur* München: Wilhelm Fink
Ewers Hans-Heino and Emer O'Sullivan (eds) (1994) *Kinderliteratur im interkulturellen Prozeß—Studium zur Allgemeinen und Vergleichenden Kinderliteraturwissenschaft* Weimar: Metzler
Faber Elmar (1991) 'Plus minus Extra=DDR?', *Börsenblatt für den Deutschen Buchhandel*, Vol. 83, 18. Oktober 1991, pp 3623–3624
Faber Elmar (1995) 'Zur Geschichte der Plusauflagen: Freibeuterei . . . ist keine Lebensform', *Börsenblatt für den Deutschen Buchhandel*, Vol. 11, 7. Februar 1995, pp 21–25
Feustel Günther (1967) 'Worin sehen Sie den Einfluß der sowjetischen Kinderliteratur auf die Kinderliteratur der DDR?', *Beiträge zur Kinder- und Jugendliteratur* Vol. 10, pp 16–17
Franke Konrad (1993) '"Deine Darstellung ist uns wesensfremd". Romane der 60er Jahre in den Mühlen der DDR-Zensur'. In Ernest Wichner and Herbert Wiesner (eds) *"Literaturentwicklungsprozesse". Die Zensur der Literatur in der DDR* Frankfurt am Main: Suhrkamp, pp 101–128
Fühmann Franz (1983) *Essays, Gespräche, Aufsätze 1964–1981* Rostock: VEB Hirnsdorff Verlag
Genette Gérard (1997) *Paratexts. Thresholds of Interpretation*, Cambridge: University Press
Gersch Christel (1998) 'Französische Klassiker in der DDR übersetzen'. In Walter Lenschen (ed) (1998) *Literatur übersetzen in der DDR* Bern: Lang, pp 85–96
Gesamtdeutsches Institut, Bonn (without year) *13. August 1961* Seminarmaterial zur deutschen Frage. Die Fluchtbewegung aus der DDR und Ostberlin 1949 bis 1961, p 22
Gesetzblatt der Deutschen Demokratischen Republik, *Anordnung über das Genehmigungsverfahren für die Herstellung von Druck- und Vervielfältigungserzeugnissen vom 20. Juli 1959.* In Gesamtdeutsches Institut Bonn (1988), Arbeitsunterlagen, pp 73–76
Gesetzblatt der Deutschen Demokratischen Republik, *Anordnung über die Honorierung von Sprachmittlungsleistungen-Honorarordnung für Dolmetscher und Übersetzer vom 19. Mai 1971*, Sonderdruck Nr. 707, Berlin, 5. Juli 1971, pp 3–8
Gesetzblatt der Deutschen Demokratischen Republik, *Anordnung über die Honorierung von Sprachmittlungsleistungen-Honorarordnung für Dolmetscher und Übersetzer vom 5. April 1974*, Sonderdruck Nr. 772, Berlin, 30. Mai 1974, pp 3–10
Gesetzblatt der Deutschen Demokratischen Republik, *Anordnung über die Honorierung von Sprachmittlungsleistungen-Honorarordnung für Dolmetscher und Übersetzer vom 19. Dezember 1979*, Sonderdruck Nr. 1031, Berlin, 15. Februar 1980, pp 1–8
Giovanopoulos Anna-Christina (2000) *Die amerikanische Literatur in der DDR: Die Institutionalisierung von Sinn zwischen Affirmation und Subversion* Essen: Verlag Die Blaue Eule
Glücksmann Anselm (1958) 'Die Deutsche Demokratische Republik und die Berner Übereinkunft', *Börsenblatt für den Deutschen Buchhandel (Ost)* Vol. 20, 17. Mai 1958, pp 313–318
Glücksmann Anselm (1960) 'Der nächste Schritt-Musterverträge', *Börsenblatt für den Deutschen Buchhandel (Ost)* Vol. 52/53, pp 832–836
Glücksmann Anselm (1962) *Das Urheber-, Verlags- und Presserecht der Deutschen Demokratischen Republik* Lehrbrief 1, Fernstudium der Journalistik, Leipzig: Karl Marx Universität
Glücksmann Anselm (1964) 'Zur Gestaltung der vertraglichen Beziehungen im Urheber- und Verlagsrecht', *Neue Justiz.Zeitschrift für Recht und Rechtswissenschaft* Vol. 7 (18), pp 207–211
Glücksmann Anselm (1975) *Gesetze, Verordnungen, Abkommen und sonstige Dokumente zum Urheber-, Verlags- und Presserecht der Deutschen Demokratischen Republik* Leipzig: Karl-Marx-Universität
Glücksmann Anselm and Herbert Rieger and Rudolf Walther (1966) *Das Urheberrecht und die wissenschaftlich-technische Information und Dokumentation* 2nd edition, Leipzig: VEB Bibliographisches Institut

Good Colin (1991) *Language and Totalitarianism. The Case of East Germany* Unpublished Inaugural Lecture, Guildford: University of Surrey

Göritz Stephan (1986) 'Katschelap alias Rumpelstilzchen oder die Verwandlungen eines Märchens'. In *Schauplatz. Aufsätze zur Kinder- und Jugendliteratur und anderen Medienkünsten* Berlin: Kinderbuchverlag, pp 155–164

Groth Joachim-Rüdiger (1994) *Widersprüche. Literatur und Politik in der DDR 1949–1989* Frankfurt/Main: Peter Lang

Haendcke-Hoppe Maria (1982) *Privatwirtschaft in der DDR: Geschichte–Struktur—Bedeutung* Berlin: Forschungsstelle für Gesamtdeutsche Wirtschaftliche und Soziale Fragen

Hager Kurt (1972) *Zu Fragen der Kulturpolitik der SED; 6. Tagung des Zentralkomitees, 6./7. Juli 1972* Berlin: Dietz

Haid Bruno (1963) 'Unsere Bücher müssen auf den wissenschaftlich-technischen Höchststand orientieren', *Börsenblatt für den Deutschen Buchhandel (Ost)* Vol. 23, 4. *Juni 1963*, pp 390–399

Hamberger Eva (1996) *Was heißt moralisch und welchen Platz hat Moral in der Politik?—Mit einer Analyse am Beispiel der deutschen Wiedervereinigung* Linz: Universitätsverlag Rudolf Trauner

Hanke Irma (1987) *Alltag und Politik: zur politischen Kultur einer unpolitischen Gesellschaft; eine Untersuchung zur erzählenden Gegenwartsliteratur der DDR in den Siebzigerjahren* Opladen: Westdeutscher Verlag

Hänsel Regina (1969) 'Märchen heute', *Beiträge zur Kinder- und Jugendliteratur* Vol 13, pp 90–93

Haraszti Miklos (1987) *The Velvet Prison* New York: Basic Books

Harik Sabine (1999) 'Staatliche DDR-Akten als historische Quellen zum Bibliothekswesen der DDR'. In Peter Vodosek and Konrad Marwinski (eds) *Geschichte des Bibliothekswesens in der DDR* Wiesbaden: Harrassowitz, pp 11–37

Havekost Hermann (1993) 'Einleitung'. In Hermann Havekost and Sandra Langenhahn and Anne Wicklein (eds) *Helden nach Plan? Kinder- und Jugendliteratur der DDR zwischen Wagnis und Zensur* Oldenburg: Bibliotheks- und Informationssystem der Universität Oldenburg, pp 11–31

Helwig Gisela (1986) 'Einleitung'. In Gisela Helwig (ed) *Die DDR-Gesellschaft im Spiegel ihrer Literatur* Köln: Verlag Wissenschaft und Politik, pp 7–20

Hermans Theo (ed) (1985) *The Manipulation of Literature. Studies in Literary Translation* London, Sydney: Croom Helm

Hillich Reinhard (2005) 'Krimi in der DDR—DDR im Krimi'. In Franz Huberth (ed) *Die DDR im Spiegel ihrer Literatur: Beiträge zu einer historischen Betrachtung der DDR-Literatur* Berlin: Duncker und Humblot, pp 105–116

Holland Brit (2000) *Die privaten Kinder- und Jugendbuchverlage 'Altberliner Verlag Lucie Groszer' und 'Alfred Holz Verlag'* Unpublished MA dissertation, Universität Leipzig

Honecker Erich (1965) 'Bericht des Politbüros an das 11. Plenum des ZK der SED, 16. bis 18. Dezember 1965'. In Elimar Schubbe (ed) *Dokumente zur Kunst-Literatur- und Kulturpolitik der SED* Stuttgart: Seewald, pp 1076–1081

Huberth Franz (ed) (2005) *Die DDR im Spiegel ihrer Literatur: Beiträge zu einer historischen Betrachtung der DDR-Literatur* Berlin: Duncker und Humblot

Institut für Bibliothekswissenschaft und wissenschaftliche Information (1974) *Verlagswesen und Buchhandel der Deutschen Demokratischen Republik* Berlin: Humboldt Universität

Institut für Marxismus-Leninismus beim ZK der SED (ed) (1958) *Liebknecht, Karl: Gesammelte Reden und Schriften*, Vol. 8, Berlin: Dietz

Jäger Manfred (1982) *Kultur und Politik in der DDR. Ein historischer Abriß* 1st edition, Köln: Edition Deutschland Archiv im Verlag Wissenschaft und Politik

Jäger Manfred (1993) 'Das Wechselspiel von Selbstzensur und Literaturlenkung in der DDR'. In Ernest Wichner, Herbert Wiesner (eds) *"Literaturentwicklungsprozesse". Die Zensur der Literatur in der DDR* Frankfurt am Main: Suhrkamp, pp 18–50

Jäger Manfred (1994) *Kultur und Politik in der DDR. Ein historischer Abriß* 2nd edition, Köln: Edition Deutschland Archiv im Verlag Wissenschaft und Politik

Jarmatz Klaus (1970) 'Vorwort' in Klaus Jarmatz (ed) *Kritik in der Zeit. Der Sozialismus—seine Literatur—ihre Entwicklung* Halle/Saale: Mitteldeutscher Verlag, pp 5–84

Jegensdorf Lothar (1980) 'Kulturpolitik und literarische Zensur in der DDR', *Aus Politik und Zeitgeschichte. Beilage zur Wochenzeitung Das Parlament*, Vol. 46, pp 21–36

Jones Derek (ed) (2001) *Censorship. A World Encyclopedia* London, Chicago: Fitzroy Dearborn Publishers

Kaemmel Ernst (1956) *Das geltende Urheber- und Verlagsrecht der Deutschen Demokratischen Republik* Leipzig: VEB Verlag für Buch- und Bibliothekswesen

Kahlo Gerhard (1954) *Die Wahrheit des Märchens* Halle/S: VEB Max Niemeyer

Kalhöfer Karl-Heinz and Helmut Rötzsch (eds) (1972) *Beiträge zur Geschichte des Buchwesens* Vol.5, Leipzig: VEB Fachbuchverlag

Kay Thomas (2001) *Der Verlag 'Neues Leben' Berlin im Zeitraum seiner Gründung im Jahre 1946 bis zur Errichtung der Berliner Mauer im Jahre 1961* Unpublished MA dissertation, Universität Leipzig

Kielmeyer Otto (1947) 'Der Kulturelle Beirat und das Verlagswesen', *Börsenblatt für den Deutschen Buchhandel (Ost)* Vol. 34, 29. November 1947, pp 329–336

Klingberg Göte (1986) *Children's Fiction in the Hands of the Translators* Studia Psychologica et Paedagogica. Series altera LXXXII. Lund: Bloms Boktryckeri Ab.

Köhler Heinz (1962) *Der sozialistische Verlag* Reihe Verlagsökonomik, Lehrbriefe für das Fachschulfernstudium Leipzig: Fachschule für Buchhändler

Köhler Ursula (1988) 'Lesekultur in beiden deutschen Staaten. 40 Jahre—ein Vergleich'. In Horst Machill (ed) (1991) *Archiv für Soziologie und Wirtschaftsfragen des Buchhandels LXIV*, Beilage zum Börsenblatt für den Deutschen Buchhandel (West), pp 2369–2462

Könner Alfred (1957) 'Vom Aschenputtel zum Lieblingskind. Das Mädchenbuch, Enfant terrible der Jugendliteratur', *Neue Deutsche Literatur* Vol. 2, pp 101–109

Korn Ilse (1952) 'Zum deutschen Volksmärchen. Eine Anregung zur Diskussion', *Der Bibliothekar* Vol. 7/8, pp 437–451

Kožik Christa (1992) 'Was sieht "das dritte Auge" heute?', *Die Grundschule, Sonderteil, Beiträge zur Kinder- und Jugendliteratur* Vol. 4, pp 1–2

Kretzschmar Sylvia (1999) *Der Kinderbuchverlag Berlin* Unpublished seminar paper, Universität Leipzig, Institut für Kommunikations- und Medienwissenschaft

Kruschwitz Hans and Johannes Gnad (1962) *Die Bedeutung des Außenhandels der DDR und die Aufgaben der Verlag* Reihe Verlagsökonomik, Lehrbriefe für das Fachschulfernstudium Leipzig: Fachschule für Buchhändler

Küchenmeister Wera (1967) 'Worin sehen Sie den Einfluß der sowjetischen Kinderliteratur auf die Kinderliteratur der DDR?', *Beiträge zur Kinder- und Jugendliteratur* Vol. 10, pp 6–7

Kuhnert Heinz (1991) 'Kinderliteratur der DDR. Was bleibt?', *JuLit* Vol. 2, pp 33–53

Lange Günter (1993) 'Zusammenfassung der Arbeitsgruppenergebnisse'. In Günter Lange and Wilhelm Steffens (eds) *Literarische und didaktische Aspekte der phantastischen Kinder- und Jugendliteratur* Würzburg: Königshausen & Neumann, pp 149–150

Lange Günter and Wilhelm Steffens (eds) (1993) *Literarische und didaktische Aspekte der phantastischen Kinder- und Jugendliteratur* Würzburg: Königshausen & Neumann

Lange Günter and Wilhelm Steffens (eds) (1995) *Moderne Formen des Erzählens in der Kinder- und Jugendliteratur der Gegenwart unter literarischen und didaktischen Aspekten* Würzburg: Königshausen & Neumann

Langewellpott Christel (1973) *Erziehungswissenschaft und pädagogische Praxis in der DDR. Zwei wissenschaftstheoretische Modelle (1945–1952)* Düsseldorf: Pädagogischer Verlag Schwann

Lathey Gillian (ed) (2006) *The Translation of Children's Literature: A Reader* Clevedon: Multilingual Matters

Lauter Hans (1951) *Der Kampf gegen den Formalismus in Kunst und Literatur, für eine fortschrittliche deutsche Kultur. Referat, Diskussion und Entschließung von der 5. Tagung des Zentralkomitees der Sozialistischen Einheitspartei Deutschlands vom 15.-17. März 1951* Berlin: Dietz

Lefevere André (1982a) 'Mother Courage's Cucumbers: Text, System and Refraction in a Theory of Literature', *Modern Language Studies*, Vol. 12 (4), pp 3–20

Lefevere André (1982b) 'Literary Theory and Translated Literature', *Dispositio*, Vol. 7 (19–20), pp 3–22

Lefevere André (1985a) 'Systems in Evolution. Historical Relativism and the Study of Genre', *Poetics Today*, Vol. 6 (4), pp 665–679

Lefevere André (1985b) 'Why Waste Our Time on Rewrites? The Trouble with Interpretation and the Role of Rewriting in an Alternative Paradigm'. In Theo Hermans (ed) *The Manipulation of Literature. Studies in Literary Translation* London, Sydney: Croom Helm, pp 215–243

Lefevere André (1986) 'Why the real Heine Can't Stand Up in/to Translation: Rewriting as the Way to Literary Influence', *New Comparison* Vol. 1, pp 83–92

Lefevere André (1991) 'Translation and Comparative Literature: The Search for the Center', *TTR*, Vol. 4 (1), pp 129–144

Lefevere André (1992) *Translation, Rewriting and the Manipulation of Literary Fame* London, New York: Routledge

Lehmstedt Mark and Siegfried Lokatis (eds) (1997) *Das Loch in der Mauer. Der innerdeutsche Literaturaustausch* Wiesbaden: Harrassowitz

Leitung der Sektion Lektoren (1960) 'Wem soll die Berufsbezeichnung Lektor (Buchredakteur) zuerkannt werden?', *Börsenblatt für den Deutschen Buchhandel (Ost)* Vol. 6, 6. Februar 1960, pp 92–93

Lenschen Walter (ed) (1998) *Literatur übersetzen in der DDR*, Bern: Lang

Lewerenz Walter (1969) 'Jugend und Literatur heute. Fragen und Bemerkungen', *Beiträge zur Kinder- und Jugendliteratur* Vol. 12, pp 37–54

Liebknecht, Karl (1958) 'Der Antimilitarismus in Deutschland und die deutsche Sozialdemokratie'. In Institut für Marxismus-Leninismus beim ZK der SED (ed) *Liebknecht, Karl: Gesammelte Reden und Schriften*, Vol. 8, Berlin: Dietz

Links, Roland (1997) 'Was war die ‚Mauer', was war das 'Loch'? Ein Versuch'. In Mark Lehmstedt and Siegfried Lokatis (eds) *Das Loch in der Mauer. Der innerdeutsche Literaturaustausch* Wiesbaden: Harrassowitz, pp 236–247

Loest Erich (1984) *Der vierte Zensor. Vom Entstehen und Sterben eines Romans in der DDR* Köln: Edition Deutschland-Archiv im Verlag Wissenschaft und Politik

Löffler Dietrich (2002) *Literaturplanung. Verlagsarbeit im Aufbau-Verlag nach der 6. Tagung des ZK der SED 1972* Medien- und Kommunikationswissenschaft, Halle-Wittenberg: Martin-Luther-Universität

Lüdtke Alf and Peter Becker (eds) (1997) *Akten, Eingaben, Schaufenster: Die DDR und ihre Texte. Erkundungen zu Herrschaft und Alltag* Berlin: Akademie Verlag

Ludwig Nadeshda (1958) 'Parteilichkeit und sozialer Auftrag im dichterischen Schaffen', *Beiträge zur Gegenwartsliteratur* Deutscher Schriftstellerverband, Vol. 14, pp 3–54

Ludwig Nadeshda (1964) 'Zu einigen Fragen unserer Jugendliteratur', *Der Bibliothekar* Vol. 8, pp 875–878

Ludz Peter Christian (1977) *Die DDR zwischen Ost und West: Politische Analysen* München: C.H. Beck'sche Verlagsbuchhandlung

Machill Horst (ed) (1991) *Archiv für Soziologie und Wirtschaftsfragen des Buchhandels LXIV*, Beilage zum Börsenblatt für den Deutschen Buchhandel (West)

Mathäs Alexander (1992) *Der Kalte Krieg in der deutschen Literaturkritik—der Fall Martin Walser* New York: Lang

Mazi-Leskovar Darja (2003) 'Domestication and Foreignization in Translating American Prose for Slovenian Children', *META* Vol. 48/1–2, pp 250–265

Mazi-Leskovar Darja (2006) 'Bridging the Gap between Cultures: Slovenian Translations of American Children's Literature'. In Pat Pinsent (ed) *No Child is an Island: The Case for Children's Literature in Translation* Lichfield: Pied Piper Publishing, pp 155–169

Meier Bernhard (1987) ' ". . . den Puls der Zeit spüren . . .". Zum Kinder- und Jugendbuch der DDR', *Buch und Bibliothek* Vol. 6, pp 576–589

Meinck Willi (1967) 'Worin sehen Sie den Einfluß der sowjetischen Kinderliteratur auf die Kinderliteratur der DDR?', *Beiträge zur Kinder- und Jugendliteratur* Vol. 10, p 5

Meyer Gerd (1991) *Die DDR Machtelite in der Ära Honecker* Tübingen: Francke

Ministerrat der Deutschen Demokratischen Republik, Ministerium fur Hoch- und Fachschulwesen (1974) *Studienplan für die Grundstudienrichtung Sprachmittler* (Nomenklatur-Nr. 73701–76701)

Mix York-Gothart (1993) 'Gespräch mit Dieter Schlenstedt'. In York-Gothart Mix (ed) *Ein Oberkunze darf nicht vorkommen, Materialien zur Publikationsgeschichte und Zensur des Hinze-Kunze-Romans von Volker Braun* Wiesbaden: Harrassowitz, pp 223–230

Mix York-Gothart (1995) ' "Verstehn Sie's?" "Nein. Nichts . . ." Varianten literarischer Camouflage in U. Plenzdorfs "Die neuen Leiden des jungen W.", S. Dörings "weilen" und R. Kunzes "Sensible Wege" ', *Zeitschrift für Germanistik*, Neue Folge 5, Vol. 1, pp 48–59

Mix York-Gothart (1998) 'DDR-Literatur und Zensur in der Honecker-Ära (1971–1989). Teil I', *Internationales Archiv für Sozialgeschichte der Deutschen Literatur* Vol. 23 (2), pp 156–198

Mix York-Gothart (1999) 'Das richtige Buch für den richtigen Leser und die falschen Bücher von Leo Perutz, Armin T. Wegner und Karl Kautsky'. In Peter Vodosek and Konrad Marwinski (eds) *Geschichte des Bibliothekswesens in der DDR* Wiesbaden: Harrassowitz, pp 117–133

Müller-Römer Dietrich (1968) *Ulbrichts Grundgesetz. Die Sozialistische Verfassung der DDR* 3rd edition, Köln: Verlag Wissenschaft und Politik

Münzer Georg (1963) *Kulturrecht. Eine Sammlung kulturrechtlicher Bestimmungen für Kulturfunktionäre und Kulturschaffende* Berlin: Staatsverlag der Deutschen Demokratischen Republik

Münz-Koenen Ingeborg (ed) (1979) *Literarisches Leben in der DDR 1945–1960 Literaturkonzepte und Leseprogramme* Berlin: Akademie-Verlag

Neubert Reiner (1995) 'Komisches in der Kinder- und Jugendliteratur der DDR'. In Malte Dahrendorf (1995) *Kinder- und Jugendliteratur: Material* Berlin: Volk und Wissen, pp 179–185

O'Sullivan Emer (2000) *Kinderliterarische Komparatistik* Heidelberg: Winter

Offner Hannelore and Klaus Schroeder (eds) (2000) *Eingegrenzt-ausgegrenzt: Bildende Kunst und Parteiherrschaft in der DDR 1961–1989* Berlin: Akademie Verlag

Oittinen Riitta (1993) *I am Me—I am Other: on the Dialogics of Translating for Children* Tampere: University of Tampere

Oittinen Riitta (2000) *Translating for Children* New York: Garland Publishing

Orlow N (1951) 'Wege und Irrwege der modernen Kunst'. In Elimar Schubbe (ed) *Dokumente zur Kunst-, Literatur- und Kulturpolitik der SED* Stuttgart: Seewald, pp 159–170

Otto Ulla (1968) *Die literarische Zensur als Problem der Soziologie der Politik* Stuttgart: Ferdinand Enke Verlag

Oy Marianne (1993) 'Aufbruch zu neuen Klischees? Die Entwicklung der Mädchenliteratur in beiden Teilen Deutschlands', *Buch und Bibliothek* Vol. 6/7, pp 580–584

Pätzold Jörg (1992) 'Zwischen Indirektheit und Sprachlosigkeit—der Umgang der Presse in der DDR zwischen dem Stern-Interview Hagers und Oktober 89 mit der Wirklichkeit des real Existierenden'. In Klaus Welke and Wolfgang Sauer and Helmut Glück (eds) *Die deutsche Sprache nach der Wende* Hildesheim, Zürich, New York: Georg Olms, pp 93–110

Peltsch Steffen (1990a) 'DDR Kinderliteratur. Zwischen Herkommen und Zukunft', *JuLit* Vol. 2, pp 8–23

Peltsch Steffen (1990b) 'Den aufrechten Gang schon früh trainiert. Bemerkungen zur Kinderliteratur der DDR', *Kinder-Bücher-Medien* Vol. 34, pp 16–18

Petersen Hans (2005) ‚Über Faulkner und die Erschließung der amerikanischen Literatur'. In Simone Barck and Siegfried Lokatis (eds) *Fenster zur Welt. Eine Geschichte des DDR Verlages Volk & Welt* 2nd edition, Berlin: Ch. Links Verlag, pp 175–178

Pezold Klaus (1998) 'Die DDR und fremde Literaturen: die der deutschsprachigen Schweiz zum Beispiel'. In Walter Lenschen (ed) (1998) *Literatur übersetzen in der DDR* Bern: Lang, pp 97–118

Picaper Jean-Paul (1982) *DDR-Bild im Wandel* Berlin: Colloquium Verlag Otto H. Hess

Picken Catriona (ed) (1989) *The Translator's Handbook* 2nd edition, London: Aslib, The Association for Information Management

Pieper Katrin (1979) 'Getragen vom Bewußtsein editorischer Verantwortung', *Börsenblatt für den deutschen Buchhandel (Ost)* Vol. 3, p 46

Pieper Katrin (1987) 'Einige Überlegungen zur Gegenwartsprosa für Kinder', *Kinderliteratur-Report* Vol. 1, pp 27–37

Pieper Katrin (1988a) 'Jugendbuchverlage und Jugendliteratur in der DDR. Umschau', *1000 und 1 Buch* Vol. 4, pp 13–19

Pieper Katrin (1988b) 'Einladung zur Emanzipation. Über Themen und Tendenzen in der Gegenwartsprosa für Kinder', *1000 und 1 Buch* Vol. 5, pp 1–11

Pinsent Pat (ed) (2006) *No Child Is an Island: The Case for Children's Literature in Translation* Lichfield: Pied Piper Publishing

Poiger Uta (1997) 'Amerikanischer Jazz und (ost)deutsche Respektabilität'. In Alf Lüdtke and Peter Becker (eds) *Akten, Eingaben, Schaufenster: Die DDR und ihre Texte. Erkundungen zu Herrschaft und Alltag* Berlin: Akademie Verlag, pp 119–136

Püschel Heinz (1975) *Urheberrecht* Leipzig: VEB Bibliographisches Institut

Püschel Heinz (1982) *Internationales Urheberrecht* 1st edition, Berlin: Staatsverlag der Deutschen Demokratischen Republik

Pym Anthony and Miriam Shlesinger and Zuzana Jettmarová (eds) (2006) *Sociocultural Aspects of Translating and Interpreting* Amsterdam, Philadelphia: John Benjamins

Raecke Renate and Ute Baumann (eds) (1995) *Zwischen Bullerbü und Schewenborn. Auf Spurensuche in 40 Jahren deutschsprachiger Kinder- und Jugendliteratur* München:Arbeitskreis für Jugendliteratur e.V.

Reid James Henderson (1990) *Writing without Taboos: the New East German Literature* Oxford, Müchen:Berg

Richter Götz R. (1954) 'Abenteuerliteratur dringend gesucht', *Neue Deutsche Literatur* Vol. 6, pp 162–165

Richter Karin (1987) *Wirklichkeitsmodellierung und Adressatenbezug. Wirkungsästhetische Analysen zur zeitgenössischen Kinder- und Jugendliteratur der DDR (1970–1985)* Unpublished doctoral thesis at Universität Halle/S., Germany

Richter Karin (1988) 'Der junge Held zwischen Traum und Wirklichkeit. Märchenhaft-phantastische Elemente in der zeitgenössischen Kinder- und Jugendliteratur der DDR'. In *Schauplatz. Aufsätze zur Kinder- und Jugendliteratur und zu anderen Medienkünsten* Berlin: Kinderbuchverlag, pp 22–33

Richter Karin (1990) 'Kinderliteratur und Kinderliteraturkritik in der DDR', *Informationen, Jugendliteratur und Medien* Vol. 3, pp 111–117

Richter Karin (1995a) 'Vom "Hasenjungen Dreiläufer" zum "Engel mit dem goldenen Schnurrbart". Gedanken zum Zusammenhang von Modernität und kritischem Gestus in der kinderliterarischen Prosa der DDR'. In Günter Lange and Wilhelm Steffens (eds) *Moderne Formen des Erzählens in der Kinder- und Jugendliteratur der Gegenwart unter literarischen und didaktischen Aspekten* Würzburg: Königshausen & Neumann, pp 83–98

Richter Karin (1995b) 'Entwicklungslinien in der Kinder- und Jugendliteratur der DDR. Vorüberlegungen für eine neue literaturhistorische Betrachtung des kinderliterarischen Schaffens von 1945–1989', *Zeitschrift für Germanistik*, Neue Folge 5, Vol. 2, pp 290–300

Richter Karin (1995c) 'Die andere Kinderwelt. Ein Blick ins Kinder-und Jugendbuch der DDR'. In Renate Raecke and Ute Baumann (eds) *Zwischen Bullerbü und Schewenborn. Auf Spurensuche in 40 Jahren deutschsprachiger Kinder- und Jugendliteratur* München: Arbeitskreis für Jugendliteratur e.V., pp 29–46

Richter Karin (1996) 'Kinderliteratur und Kinderliteraturforschung in der DDR'. In Bernd Dolle-Weinkauff and Hans-Heino Ewers (eds) *Theorien der Jugendlektüre: Beiträge zur Kinder- und Jugendliteraturkritik seit Heinrich Wolgast* Weinheim, München: Juventa, pp 191–209

Rouvel Claudia (1993) 'Das wichtige Kind. Unvollständiges über die Kinderliteratur der DDR'. In Alfred Baumgärtner (ed) *Robinson in roten Socken. Kinder- und Jugendbücher in der ehemaligen DDR* Deutsche Akademie für Kinder- und Jugendliteratur, pp 8–14

Rouvel Claudia (1995) 'Macht nichts, Leute, was wir erlebt haben, kann uns keiner nehmen. . .'. In Renate Raecke and Ute Baumann (eds) *Zwischen Bullerbü und Schewenborn. Auf Spurensuche in 40 Jahren deutschsprachiger Kinder- und Jugendliteratur* München: Arbeitskreis für Jugendliteratur e.V., 177–186

Rumland Marie-Kristin (1993) *Veränderungen in Verlagswesen und Buchhandel der ehemaligen DDR 1989–1991* Wiesbaden: Harrassowitz

Sauerstein Hans-Joachim (1981) 'Die verlagsrechtliche Lizenz im neuen Urheberrecht der DDR'. In Büro für Urheberrechte (ed) *Aus der Arbeit/Büro für Urheberrechte Berlin: 1956–1981* Berlin: Büro für Urheberrechte

Schlenker Wolfram (1977) *Das 'kulturelle Erbe' in der DDR: gesellschaftliche Entwicklung und Kulturpolitik 1945–1965* Stuttgart: Metzler

Schmitz Manfred (1989) 'The Translation Scene in the GDR', in Catriona Picken (ed) *The Translator's Handbook* 2nd edition, London: Aslib, The Association for Information Management, pp 126–129

Schoeller Reinhild (ed) (1981) *Blaue Kinderschaukel—ein Lesebuch zur Geschichte der Kinderliteratur in der DDR* Berlin: Kinderbuchverlag

Schubbe Elimar (ed) (1972) *Dokumente zur Kunst-, Literatur- und Kulturpolitik der SED* Stuttgart: Seewald

Schulz Gudrun (1993) 'Phantastische Kinder- und Jugendliteratur in der ehemaligen DDR'. In Günter Lange and Wilhelm Steffens (eds) *Literarische und didaktische Aspekte der phantastischen Kinder- und Jugendliteratur* Würzburg: Königshausen & Neumann, pp 135–148

Schütz Hanns Lothar (ed) (1990) 'Verlage in der DDR: ein Service vom Börsenblatt für den deutschen Buchhandel', *Börsenblatt für den deutschen Buchhandel, Frankfurter Ausgabe* Frankfurt am Main: Verlag der Buchhändler Vereinigung GmbH, pp 1–55

Schwenger Hannes (2000) 'Sozialistische Künstlerorganisation. Akademie und Künstlerverband im Herrschaftssystem der DDR'. In Hannelore Offner and Klaus Schroeder (eds) *Eingegrenzt-ausgegrenzt: Bildende Kunst und Parteiherrschaft in der DDR 1961–1989* Berlin: Akademie Verlag, pp 89–162

Sekretariat des Zentralvorstandes der LDPD (1979) *Zur antikommunistischen Politik und Ideologie des Imperialismus* Politische Bildungszirkel, 22. Zirkeljahr, Vol. 8

Selle Karlheinz (1972) Zur Geschichte des Verlagswesens der Deutschen Demokratischen Republik. Ein Abriß der Entwicklung des Buchverlagswesens 1945–1970. In Karl-Heinz Kalhöfer and Helmut Rötzsch (eds) *Beiträge zur Geschichte des Buchwesens* Vol. 5, Leipzig: VEB Fachbuchverlag, pp 16–72

Shavit Zohar (1986) *Poetics of Children's Literature* Athens and London: The University of Georgia Press

Shavit Zohar (1994) 'Beyond the Restrictive Frameworks of the Past: Semiotics of Children's Literature—A New Perspective for the Study of the Field'. In Hans-Heino Ewers and Emer O'Sullivan (eds) *Kinderliteratur im interkulturellen Prozeß—Studium zur Allgemeinen und Vergleichenden Kinderliteraturwissenschaft* Weimar: Metzler, pp 3–15

Shaw Elizabeth (1990) *Irish Berlin. Wie ich nach Berlin kam* Berlin: Aufbau-Verlag

Siegel Eva-Maria (1985) 'Eine Flaschenpost ins Meer geworfen. . . . Gespräch mit Christa Kožik', *Beiträge zur Kinder- und Jugendliteratur* Vol. 75, pp 46–52

Sontheimer Kurt (1990) *Deutschlands politische Kultur* München: Piper

Spiewok Wolfgang (1974) 'Zur Erbediskussion aus der Sicht der Mittelalterforschung', *Weimarer Beiträge* Vol. 1, pp 87–100

Staritz Dietrich (1985) *Geschichte der DDR (1949–1985)* Frankfurt am Main: Suhrkamp

Streul Irene Charlotte (1988) *Westdeutsche Literatur in der DDR. Böll, Grass, Walser und andere in der offiziellen Rezeption 1949–1985* Stuttgart: Metzler

Tarrend Ave (2005) 'Translations of Children's Literature in the Clutches of Ideology: the Case of Estonia'. In Jean Webb and Mare Müürsepp (eds) *Sunny Side of Darkness. Children's Literature in Totalitarian and Post-Totalitarian Eastern Europe* Tallinn: TLÜ Kirjastus, pp 66–96

Thomaneck Jürgen and James Mellis (eds) (1989) *Politics, Society and Government in the German Democratic Republic: Basic Documents* Oxford, München: Berg Publishers Ltd

Thomson-Wohlgemuth Gaby (2004) 'A Socialist Approach to Translation: A Way Forward?', *META*, Vol. 49/3, pp 498–510

Thomson-Wohlgemuth Gaby (2005) 'Eastside story–Westside story. What is Happening in the Market of Translated Children's Books?'. In Karin Aijmer and Cecilia Alvstad (eds) *New Tendencies in Translation Studies*, Selected Papers from a Workshop, 12 December 2003, Göteborg University, pp 83–92

Tiede Hans-Otto (1971) 'Einiges über Bilderbücher', *Beiträge zur Kinder- und Jugendliteratur* Vol. 18, pp 23–40

Ulbricht Walter (1953) 'Die Partei neuen Typus'. In Walter Ulbricht (1953) *Zur Geschichte der deutschen Arbeiterbewegung. Aus Reden und Aufsätzen (1946–1950)*, Vol. 3, Berlin: Dietz, pp 290–311

Verfügungen und Mitteilungen des Ministeriums für Kultur, *Anordnung zur Änderung der Honorarordnung Verlagswesen*, Berlin, 31. Mai 1988, pp 1–4

Verfügungen und Mitteilungen des Ministeriums für Kultur, *Einige Fragen der Planung der kulturellen Entwicklung im Bereich Kultur und die Aufgaben der Jahre 1958 und 1959*, Sonderdruck, Berlin, Februar 1958, pp 1–3

Verner Paul (1965) 'Diskussionsbeitrag auf dem 11. Plenum des ZK der SED, 16. bis 18. Dezember 1965: Der Künstler soll Mitgestalter unserer Gesellschaftsordnung sein'. In Elimar Schubbe (ed) *Dokumente zur Kunst-, Literatur- und Kulturpolitik der SED* Stuttgart: Seewald, pp 1111–1113

Vodosek Peter and Konrad Marwinski (eds) (1999) *Geschichte des Bibliothekswesens in der DDR* Wiesbaden: Harrassowitz

Walther Joachim (1999) *Sicherungsbereich Literatur. Schriftsteller und Staatssicherheit in der Deutschen Demokratischen Republik* (1st edition 1996 Chr. Links Verlag) Berlin: Ullstein

Wardetzky Kristin (1991) *Märchen-Lesarten von Kindern. Eine empirische Studie zum Verhältnis 6 bis 10 Jähriger zum Märchen* Unpublished doctoral thesis at Humboldt Universität Berlin

Webb Jean and Mare Müürsepp (eds) (2005) *Sunny Side of Darkness. Children's Literature in Totalitarian and Post-Totalitarian Eastern Europe* Tallinn: TLÜ Kirjastus

Wedding Alex (1954) 'Der Schrei nach dem Mädchenbuch', *Neue Deutsche Literatur* Vol. 2, pp 164–167

Welke Klaus and Wolfgang Sauer and Helmut Glück (eds) (1992) *Die deutsche Sprache nach der Wende* Hildesheim, Zürich, New York: Georg Olms

Wendt Dieter (1961) 'Vor einem neuen Mustervertrag', *Börsenblatt für den Deutschen Buchhandel (Ost)* Vol. 11, 18. März 1961, pp 169–172

Wendt Dieter (1967) *Die Beendigung des Verlagsvertrages im neuen Urheberrecht der Deutschen Demokratischen Republik* Unpublished doctoral thesis, Humboldt Universität Berlin

Wendt Erich (1963) 'Der Verleger ist voll verantwortlich auf seinem Gebiet', *Börsenblatt für den Deutschen Buchhandel (Ost)* Vol. 23, 4 June 1963, pp 384–390

Wichner Ernest (1993) ' "Und unverständlich wird mein ganzer Text". Anmerkungen zu einer zensurgesteuerten Nationalliteratur'. In Ernest Wichner and Herbert Wiesner (eds) *"Literaturentwicklungsprozesse". Die Zensur der Literatur in der DDR* Frankfurt am Main: Suhrkamp, pp 199–217

Wichner Ernest and Herbert Wiesner (eds) (1991) *Zensiert—gefördert—verhindert. Zensur in der DDR: Geschichte, Praxis und „Ästhetik" der Behinderung von Literatur* Texte aus dem Literaturhaus Berlin, Vol. 8

Wichner Ernest and Herbert Wiesner (eds) (1993) *"Literaturentwicklungsprozesse". Die Zensur der Literatur in der DDR* Frankfurt am Main: Suhrkamp

Wild Reiner (ed) (1990) *Geschichte der deutschen Kinder- und Jugendliteratur* Stuttgart: J.B. Metzlersche Verlagsbuchhandlung

Wolf Christa (1958) 'Kann man eigentlich über alles schreiben?', *Neue Deutsche Literatur* Vol. 6, pp 3–16

Zentralkomitee der SED (1951) 'Der Kampf gegen den Formalismus in Kunst und Literatur, für eine fortschrittliche deutsche Kultur, 15. bis 17. März 1951'. In Elimar Schubbe (ed) *Dokumente zur Kunst-, Literatur- und Kulturpolitik der SED* Stuttgart: Seewald, pp 178–186

Zipser Richard (ed) (1995) *Fragebogen: Zensur—zur Literatur vor und nach dem Ende der DDR* Leipzig: Reclam

Zweig Arnold (1948) 'Der Jude im Dorn', *Ost und West* Vol. 11, pp 58–65

Unpublished Sources

Files from *Bundesarchiv Berlin, Akte Ministerium für Kultur* (Files of GDR Ministry of Culture)

DR1/1073
DR1/1157
DR1/1234
DR1/1287
DR1/1337
DR1/1827
DR1/1896
DR1/2252
DR1/2253
DR1/2253a
DR1/2254
DR1/2255
DR1/2257
DR1/2260
DR1/2261
DR1/2262a
DR1/2264a
DR1/2268
DR1/2269
DR1/2274
DR1/2276
DR1/2282a
DR1/2284a
DR1/2287
DR1/2287a
DR1/2289
DR1/2292
DR1/2292a
DR1/2298
DR1/2301
DR1/2305
DR1/2307
DR1/2307a
DR1/2308
DR1/2309
DR1/2312
DR1/2314
DR1/2665
DR1/3539
DR1/3541
DR1/3544
DR1/3544a
DR1/3545
DR1/3545a
DR1/3547
DR1/3547a
DR1/3549a
DR1/3552
DR1/3553
DR1/3554
DR1/3554a
DR1/3557
DR1/3558
DR1/3559
DR1/3559a
DR1/3560a
DR1/3561a
DR1/3706
DR1/3707
DR1/3940
DR1/3954a
DR1/3993
DR1/5039a
DR1/5076
DR1/5117
DR1/5435
DR1/5437
DR1/5438
DR1/7751

Files from *Stiftung Archiv der Akademie der Künste*, Berlin
Archiv des Schriftstellerverbandes der DDR (Files of GDR Writers' Association)

DV 1321/2 (alt)
DV 332 (neu)
SV 1118 (alt)
SV 609 (neu)
SV 777 (neu, Mappe 1988)
SV 758 (neu)
VS 257 (neu)

Index

For Product Safety Concerns and Information please contact our EU representative GPSR@taylorandfrancis.com
Taylor & Francis Verlag GmbH, Kaufingerstraße 24, 80331 München, Germany

www.ingramcontent.com/pod-product-compliance
Lightning Source LLC
Chambersburg PA
CBHW071502110726
47908CB00003B/700

* 9 7 8 1 1 3 8 8 2 8 3 9 1 *